11-19-82

THE WORKS OF JONATHAN EDWARDS

VOLUME 6

John E. Smith, General Editor

"That which is most astonishing is that very often there appears at the end of these webs, spiders sailing in the air with them, doubtless with an abundance of pleasure, though not so much as I have beheld them and shewed them to others. And since I have seen these things I have been very conversant with spiders." (From Edwards' letter of October 31, 1723. Courtesy of The New-York Historical Society, New York City.)

JONATHAN EDWARDS

Scientific and Philosophical Writings

THE "SPIDER" PAPERS

"NATURAL PHILOSOPHY"

"THE MIND"

SHORT SCIENTIFIC AND PHILOSOPHICAL PAPERS

EDITED BY WALLACE E. ANDERSON

ASSOCIATE PROFESSOR OF PHILOSOPHY

OHIO STATE UNIVERSITY

New Haven and London

YALE UNIVERSITY PRESS, 1980

Copyright © 1980 by Yale University.
All rights reserved. This book may not be
reproduced, in whole or in part, in any form
(beyond that copying permitted by Sections 107
and 108 of the U.S. Copyright Law and except by
reviewers for the public press), without written
permission from the publishers.

Designed by John O. C. McCrillis
and set in Baskerville type.
Printed in the United States of America by
The Vail-Ballou Press, Inc., Binghamton, New York.

Published in Great Britain, Europe, Africa, and
Asia (except Japan) by Yale University Press,
Ltd., London. Distributed in Australia and
New Zealand by Book & Film Services, Artarmon,
N.S.W., Australia; and in Japan by Harper & Row,
Publishers, Tokyo Office.

Library of Congress Cataloging in Publication Data

Edwards, Jonathan, 1703–1758.
    Scientific and philosophical writings.

    (The works of Jonathan Edwards; v. 6)
    Includes index
    CONTENTS : The spider papers.—Natural philosophy.—
The mind.—Short scientific and philosophical papers.
    1. Philosophy—Collected works.   2. Science—Collected
works.   I. Anderson, Wallace Earl, 1931–
BX7117.E3 1957 Vol. 6 [B870.A5] 285'.8s [191]
ISBN 0–300–02282–4   78–26663

CONTENTS

T HIS volume of Edwards' scientific and philosophical papers brings together a large number of different manuscript writings from virtually every period of his life. Many of these have been previously published, some of them in several editions. "Natural Philosophy" and "The Mind" were first published in 1829 by Sereno Dwight[1] and have since been reedited and published again, as a whole or in part, by others.[2] Dwight also first published "The Soul" (which he mistakenly took to be Edwards' work),[3] and the draft of his "Spider" letter.[4] In 1890 Egbert C. Smyth added Edwards' "Of Insects" to the list of his published manuscripts[5] and followed with "Of the Rainbow" in 1895.[6] William P. Upham transcribed and published the shorthand notes in "Natural Philosophy" in 1902.[7] Finally, in 1948, Perry Miller included the short essay "Beauty of the World" in his edition of Edwards' "Images of Divine Things."[8] All these are presented complete

1. Sereno E. Dwight, ed., *The Works of President Edwards with a Memoir of His Life* (10 vols., New York, 1829–30), *1*, pp. 664–702 ("The Mind"), pp. 702–61 ("Natural Philosophy"). Dwight titled the latter "Notes on Natural Science." Hereafter cited as Dwight.

2. Harvey Townsend, ed., *The Philosophy of Jonathan Edwards from his Private Notebooks* (Eugene, Oregon, 1955) includes "The Mind" and "Of Atoms," "Of the Prejudices of Imagination," and "Of Being" from JE's "Natural Philosophy." Hereafter cited as Townsend. Leon Howard, ed., *"The Mind" of Jonathan Edwards: a Reconstructed Text* (Berkeley and Los Angeles, 1963) includes "The Mind" and the essays "Of Being" and "Of the Prejudices of Imagination." Hereafter cited as *"The Mind" of JE*.

3. Dwight, *1*, pp. 20–21. For a discussion of the authenticity of "The Soul," see below, pp. 401–04.

4. Dwight, *1*, pp. 23–28.

5. "The Flying Spider—Observations by Jonathan Edwards when a Boy," *Andover Review*, *13*, pp. 5–13. Smyth also includes in his paper a new edition of the draft of JE's "Spider" letter.

6. "Some Early Writings of Jonathan Edwards," *Proceedings of the American Antiquarian Society, 10* (1895), pp. 238–41. Hereafter cited as "Early Writings of JE." Smyth also includes new editions of "The Soul," the essay "Of Being," and an article titled "Colors" from "Natural Philosophy" in this paper.

7. "An Account of the Shorthand Writings of Jonathan Edwards," *Proceedings of the Massachusetts Historical Society*, 2nd series, *15* (1902), pp. 514–21.

8. *Images or Shadows of Divine Things* (New Haven, 1948), pp. 135–37.

in this volume, including in some cases passages or sections that were omitted in earlier editions.

In addition to these well-known writings, the reader will find several here which have not been previously published. Perhaps the most notable of these is the "Spider" letter itself, which Edwards actually sent and which is now presented with the permission of the New York Historical Society, where the manuscript is located. Also, an untitled fragment which is here given the title "Of Light Rays" is a significant addition to the published works resulting from Edwards' early scientific interests.[9] The other shorter and hitherto unpublished papers include "Wisdom in the Contrivance of the World,"[1] an outline for a treatise that Edwards planned to title "A Rational Account of the Main Doctrines of the Christian Religion,"[2] and another late fragment of various philosophical notes which has here been titled "Notes on Knowledge and Existence."[3]

1.   *Biographical Background*

Although the manuscript writings in this volume span nearly the whole of Edwards' career, the larger part of them were written by the time he settled as assistant to his grandfather in the pastorate at Northampton, Massachusetts, at the age of twenty-three. From a biographical point of view this is perhaps the most obscure and problematic part of his life. Family and public records are far from complete and, except for some personal letters and a private diary kept for a few years which he devoted primarily to reflections upon his inner moral and spiritual life, Edwards' own extant writings of the time are almost devoid of autobiographical comment. Most important, he neglected to date any of the manuscripts connected with his private studies, so that all questions of the times and order of their composition have been left to the judgment of later scholars.

Unfortunately, the dates that have been traditionally accepted for most of Edwards' early writings are quite mistaken. These dates were originally proposed by Sereno Dwight and Egbert Smyth, the earliest editors of Edwards' papers on science and philosophy. Subsequent accounts of Edwards' early life that are based upon the mistaken dates have consequently projected a distorted picture of his intellectual development, and they have unwittingly ignored some of the most

9. MS in the Andover coll.
1. MS in the Yale coll.
2. MS in the Yale coll.
3. MS in the Yale coll.

significant features of the papers themselves. Such recently debated questions as the sources of Edwards' thought, the relations between his scientific and philosophical interests and his theology, and the modernity of his thought, are all affected by assumptions concerning the order and dating of his private manuscripts. In treating the biographical background of his scientific and philosophical papers, therefore, it will be necessary to correct some of the misrepresentations that have prevailed for well over a century, since Dwight and Smyth published their conclusions.

Recent techniques in manuscript investigation, together with the discovery of some important new material bearing upon Edwards' early life, have yielded a much more accurate and detailed dating for his undated papers than has been possible hitherto.[4] Several important points remain open to question, but the main body of conclusions so far reached is sufficiently complete and well established to form a coherent picture of the course and background of his scientific and philosophical writings. Full discussions of the problems of dating the manuscripts may be found in the introductory notes that precede the texts of each work or group of related works below. In treating their biographical backgrounds in the present chapter it will suffice only to summarize the conclusions reached in those discussions, and to point out their variances from the dates that have traditionally been assumed.

For our present purpose, Edwards' early life is most conveniently divided into three periods: his childhood from 1703 until the fall of 1716 when he matriculated at the Collegiate School (Yale College), his six years of undergraduate and graduate study from 1716 to 1722, and the period from 1722 to 1726 which included his New York pastorate, a year of study and preaching in Connecticut in 1723–24, and the two years of his Yale tutorship. This chapter will conclude with a summary of the relevant background of the scientific and philosophical writings dating from his settlement in Northampton in 1726 until his death in 1758.

PRECOLLEGIATE PERIOD: 1703–16

Jonathan Edwards was born on October 5, 1703, in East Windsor,

---

4. Thomas Schafer has conducted an intensive and exhaustive study of the dates of all Edwards' early manuscripts. Most of the information concerning dating in this volume was disclosed by his investigations, and corroborated wherever possible by the editor. Schafer's own full account of the dating of Edwards' early writings will be presented in the introduction to his edition of JE's "Miscellanies," in this Yale edition of Edwards' works.

Connecticut, where he lived until he matriculated in September 1716. His father, the Reverend Timothy Edwards, was pastor of East Windsor. His mother was Esther Stoddard Edwards, daughter of the Reverend Solomon Stoddard of Northampton, Massachusetts. Jonathan was the fifth of the Edwards' eleven children and their only son.

Timothy Edwards had received his B.A. and M.A. from Harvard at the same commencement in 1694, just before he was called to East Windsor. Most of his preparation for the degrees, however, was made under the tuition of the Reverend Peletiah Glover of Springfield; he seems to have spent only his first year of college in residence in Cambridge.[5] Except for the military campaign to Canada in which he served as chaplain in 1711, and occasional visits to Harvard at commencement time to renew friendships with his former classmates,[6] Timothy spent his career quietly in East Windsor. His main published writing is the Election Sermon he delivered in Hartford in 1732. But he also made some other contributions to the literature of his time, and was publicly acknowledged by two prominent New England writers. His fellow townsman, Maj. Roger Wolcott, who was later governor of the Colony, published his volume, *Poetical Meditations*, in 1725. He added a lengthy dedication to "the Reverend Timothy Edwards of Windsor," in which he praised some verses of Edwards which have since been lost.[7] Timothy Edwards was also acquainted with Judge Paul Dudley, a justice of the Superior Court of Massachusetts and a member of the Royal Society of London. In a paper published in the *Philosophical Transactions of the Royal Society* in 1724 Dudley acknowledged Edwards' contribution of some of the observations he reported.[8] This circumstance is directly related to Jonathan's composition of his "Spider" letter, as will be discussed later.

Timothy Edwards conducted the grammer school for the parish, and

5. *Sibley's Harvard Graduates*, ed. C. K. Shipton (17 vols., Cambridge, Mass., 1933), 6, pp. 93–94.

6. John Stoughton, *Windsor Farmes: A Glimpse of an Old Parish* (Hartford, 1883), pp. 105–106.

7. Roger Wolcott, *Poetical Meditations, Being the Improvement of some Vacant Hours,* with a preface by the Reverend Mr. Bulkely of Colchester (New London, 1725), pp. i–ii. The third and fourth stanzas read: "Yet when you Censure, Sir, don't make the Verse / You pin'd to Glover's venerable Hearse / The standard for their Trial: nor Enact / you never will acquit, what's less Exact.

"Sir, that will never do; Rules so severe / would ever Leave Apollo's Alters bare / His Priests no service: All must starve together / and fair Parnassus verdant tops must wither." Wolcott's dedication is dated Windsor, January 4, 1722–23.

8. See below, pp. 151–52.

so supervised Jonathan's earliest education. Candidates for the Collegiate School (it was renamed after Elihu Yale in 1718) were required to be "duly prepared and expert in Latin and Greek Authors both Poetick and oratorical As also ready in making Good Latin."[9] Jonathan was well along in his study of the classical languages before he reached his eighth birthday. In a letter dated August 7, 1711, Timothy instructed his wife concerning the children's schoolwork while he was away on the military campaign. The letter indicates that Jonathan had already mastered the Latin "Accidence" and was memorizing a piece called *propria Quae moribus*. His mother was advised to have him review by reciting to his sisters, and he was also to help them progress as far as he himself had gone. Timothy added a last instruction: "And [I] would have both him and them keep their writing, and therefore write much oftener than they did when I was at home."[1]

Languages and elementary arithmetic were the principal content of grammar school instruction throughout colonial New England, and except for Timothy's emphasis upon writing, there is no evidence that Jonathan's earliest education included more than this. Logic and natural science, in particular, were subjects reserved for the collegiate curriculum. Nevertheless, Sereno Dwight and Egbert Smyth infer from Edwards' earliest writings a considerable acquaintance with both subjects before he entered college. Dwight judged that two of the papers presented in this volume, "The Soul" and Edwards' draft of his "Spider" letter, were written before he matriculated.[2] Smyth later assigned two others, the essays "Of Insects" and "Of the Rainbow," to this same early period.[3] Subsequent biographers have accordingly supposed that Edwards exhibited an astonishing genius for scientific investigation and philosophical argumentation even at that early age. The resulting picture of his life and activities in East Windsor proves to be unwarranted, however, for none of the four pieces can reasonably be assigned to this period. Indeed, the only precollegiate writing among Edwards' extant manuscripts is a letter to his sister Mary, which he dated May 10, 1716, only a few months before he matriculated.

Of these four pieces, "The Soul" has proved to be undoubtedly

9. Franklin Dexter, *A Documentary History of Yale University, 1701–1745* (New Haven, 1916), p. 30.

1. The letter is in the Andover coll. It has been printed in full in Ola Winslow, *Jonathan Edwards: 1703–1758* (New York, 1940), pp. 40–41.

2. Dwight, *1*, pp. 20, 22–28.

3. "Flying Spider," pp. 3–4; "Early Writings of JE," pp. 224–25.

spurious. The manuscript itself contains evidence that it was actually composed much later than Dwight supposed, probably in 1725.[4] By this time Edwards was a tutor at Yale College and can hardly be counted the author of so juvenile a production. The writer of "The Soul" was evidently some member of the Edwards household in East Windsor, but his or her identity is at present still in doubt.

The other three manuscripts in this group are unquestionably in Edwards' hand, but "Of Insects" and "Of the Rainbow" were evidently written while he was a student in New Haven. The draft of the "Spider" letter was composed even later. Its date is conclusively fixed by that found on the "Spider" letter itself, which has only recently been located. The letter is dated October 31, 1723, a few months after his return to Connecticut from his New York pastorate, more than seven years after the time Dwight supposed.

The revisions in the dating of these pieces must lead to some significant reassessment of Edwards' early intellectual development. Although "The Soul" was probably not Edwards' own work, it might fairly be considered a reflection of intellectual life in the East Windsor parsonage. But the scientific papers are now to be associated with Edwards' later interests and educational experiences. Some of the mysteries which have hitherto been connected with these papers—for example, how Edwards could have learned of Isaac Newton's optical works at so early a time and in such a remote village—may now be dismissed altogether. Nor is there any longer much basis for supposing that even as a child he had an interest in and highly developed skill for minutely observing the phenomena of nature. His reputation as a scientific observer has been based almost entirely upon the essay "Of Insects." One passage in this essay refers specifically to his boyhood observations of flying insects during the late summer: "I remember that, when I was a boy, I have at the same time of year lien on the ground upon my back and beheld an abundance of them, all flying southeast, which I then thought were going to a warm country." But the systematically conducted observations of the manner in which spiders do their spinning were most probably made at a later time, not long before the essay itself was composed. In any case, Edwards' scientific efforts were never much directed to experimental inquiry; the observations reported in "Of Insects" are almost unique in his scientific writings in this respect.

4. See further in App. A below, pp. 403–04.

It appears, in fact, that during his childhood Edwards roamed the woods and fields around East Windsor as much to commune with God as to satisfy curiosity. In the "Personal Narrative" which he wrote in later years,[5] he describes the intense religious affections he experienced during one of the frequent seasons of revival in his father's church. He and his companions built a secret prayer booth in a swamp, and he kept other secret places in the woods besides where he would retreat for private prayer and meditation. In the same narrative he explains how his experience of conversion, at a later time, brought a new sense of the presence of God in nature: "God's excellency, his wisdom, his purity and love, seemed to appear in everything; in the sun, moon, and stars; in the clouds and blue sky; in the grass, flowers, trees; in the water and all nature; which used greatly to fix my mind."[6] These and many other passages throughout his writings show that Edwards' enduring admiration of the harmonious order, beauty, and economy of the created world arose from his own first-hand experiences of nature, whereas his scientific interests seem to have been primarily a product of reading and study. It may reasonably be argued that his treatment of natural phenomena in such later writings as "Beauty of the World" and "Images of Divine Things" is more directly and profoundly related to his childhood experiences than that in "Of Insects" and "Natural Philosophy."

COLLEGIATE AND GRADUATE STUDIES: 1716–22

The course of Edwards' education after his matriculation in the fall of 1716 was directly affected by a controversy over the choice of a permanent site for the Collegiate School. The Trustees had only recently voted to remove the college from Saybrook to New Haven, where a new hall was to be built that would accommodate the students and faculty, and provide a suitable library for the large collection of books that had been sent from England by the colonial agent, Jeremiah Dummer. But the two dissenting trustees from Hartford, who were determined to secure the college for their own town, appealed to the Assembly to overturn the majority decisions. Throughout the ensuing controversy the scholars themselves were divided into two main groups. One met in New Haven in accordance with the directives of the Trus-

---

5. The "Personal Narrative" was written by JE some time after January 1739. It was first published by Samuel Hopkins, *Life and Character of the Late Reverend Mr. Jonathan Edwards* (Boston, 1765). The MS is lost.

6. Hopkins, *Life*, p. 27.

tees, while the other gathered under their own tutors in the town of Wethersfield, in open defiance of the Trustees.

Edwards belonged to the latter group. He came at first to New Haven where he matriculated, but within a month he and nine other freshmen from Connecticut River towns joined the contingent that had already formed at Wethersfield. The dissident party remained there throughout his freshman and sophomore years. In the meantime the Trustees' arrangements went forward in New Haven; the new hall was finished by the fall of 1718, and at the commencement that year the college was renamed after Governor Yale. Dummer's gift of books, which had remained in their crates in Saybrook, was brought over despite the opposition of some Saybrook partisans. And at about the same time, in December of that year, the Wethersfield scholars returned to New Haven in a short-lived attempt at reunion. But within six weeks Edwards and all but one of the others had gone back to Wethersfield, declaring their dissatisfaction with the New Haven tutor, Samuel Johnson. The affair was brought before the Governor's Council where the Trustees defended Johnson, but the students won their suit. On March 26, 1719, Edwards wrote to his sister Mary from Wethersfield, "The council and trustees having lately had a meeting at New-Haven concerning it, have removed that which was the cause of our coming away, viz., Mr. Johnson from the place of a tutor, and have put in Mr. Cutler, Pastor of Canterbury, President."[7] Cutler was already in residence when a permanent reunion was achieved in June 1719. Edwards thus had his senior year in New Haven. He gave the valedictory oration at the commencement in 1720 when he received his B.A. degree. He then remained in New Haven for two more years of graduate study in divinity until August 1722, when he went to New York for his first pastorate.[8]

It was during these last three years of study at Yale in New Haven that Edwards wrote his earliest scientific and philosophical papers. "Of Insects" was evidently done first, probably during his senior year in 1719–20.[9] The first parts of "Natural Philosophy" followed, probably during the first year of graduate study. The chronological order of this manuscript is particularly complicated, since it does not correspond to

7. Dwight, *1*, pp. 29–30. The letter is in the Andover coll.

8. Richard Warch has treated this part of the history of Yale College fully in chs. 3 and 4 of *School of Prophets: Yale College, 1701–1733* (New Haven, 1973).

9. See below, pp. 147–51.

the sequence of articles on its pages.[1] Edwards began it with the series of propositions and corollaries we have entitled "Of Atoms," and with the first few entries in what is here called the long series (LS) of "Things to be Considered and Written fully about." These were followed by the beginning paragraphs in "Of Being" and "Of the Prejudices of Imagination"; the later parts of both essays were added after his New York pastorate. At about the time he wrote the twenty-seventh entry in the long series of "Things to be Considered," Edwards started a second series of notes, which we here call the short series (SS). He added new entries to both series concurrently throughout his second graduate year; by the time he left for New York he had written No. 44 in the long series and No. 21b in the short. Later articles in both were added after his return to Connecticut in the spring of 1723.

Two other papers, both concerned with topics in optics, were also written during the second year of graduate study. "Of the Rainbow," which Smyth judged to be a precollegiate writing, is probably the earlier. The other, the surviving portion of an essay we have titled "Of Light Rays," is nearly contemporary with the entry No. 37 in the long series in "Natural Philosophy."[2]

Sereno Dwight judged that Edwards began "The Mind" at an even earlier time, during his sophomore year while he was still in Wethersfield;[3] but in fact he did not write the first entry in "The Mind" until after his New York pastorate. Dwight also mistakenly supposed that two other major series of notes, the "Miscellanies" and "Notes on Scriptures," were begun during Edwards' collegiate period.[4] Evidence shows he started "Miscellanies" during his New York sojourn, and "Notes on Scriptures" during the year following it.[5]

Having surveyed the course of Edwards' writing during this period, we may now examine in greater detail the nature and content of his educational experience. Once again, contemporary records are incomplete; public documents are largely concerned with political controversies surrounding the college, and personal records—for example, the autobiography of Samuel Johnson—are of doubtful value in some

1. See below, pp. 176–81.
2. See below, pp. 296–97.
3. Dwight, *1*, pp. 39–40.
4. Ibid. p. 34.
5. Thomas Schafer has furnished these conclusions from his investigations of the dating of of JE's manuscripts. Hereafter the former series is cited as "Miscellanies" and its individual entries as Miscell. no.

important details. Nevertheless, indirect evidence allows us to construct a fairly reliable picture of Edwards' course of studies, and his own writings give indications of the particular works that stimulated and shaped his earliest thought.

Despite its irregular status, the collegiate operation at Wethersfield could hardly be judged inferior to the officially sanctioned school in New Haven. On the contrary, the schism brought a serious problem in retaining adequate faculty in New Haven, while at Wethersfield there was a full contingent of tutors who were held in high regard by all parties in the controversies. Elisha Williams, who headed the Wethersfield group, was already becoming a popular and influential figure in the Colony—"a man of splendor," Ezra Stiles later called him.[6] He had taken his B.A. in 1711 and his M.A. in 1714 at Harvard, where he was said to excel in classical learning, logic, and geography. In 1717, in the midst of the schism, the Trustees invited him to fill the vacant post of senior tutor in New Haven.[7] In a later period he was to serve as rector of Yale College from 1726 until 1739.

Samuel Smith, the senior tutor at Wethersfield, had been appointed senior tutor for New Haven in 1716, just before the schism developed. Despite his defection to Wethersfield, the Trustees tried to gain him for New Haven again the next year.[8] Smith had received his B.A. from the Collegiate School in 1713 and his M.A. in 1716. Samuel Hall, the junior tutor, had taken his B.A. at the Collegiate School in 1716. According to records of tuition payments in Timothy Edwards' account book for these years, Jonathan received most of his instruction in Wethersfield from Smith and Hall.[9]

By comparison, the New Haven institution was badly understaffed. The Trustees sought to appoint two tutors in addition to a resident rector before classes convened in the fall of 1716, but with Smith's refusal to occupy the senior tutorship, the only regular tutor in residence through that year and the following one was Samuel Johnson.[1] He had received his B.A. from the Collegiate School in 1714, and

6. Sibley, p. 591. See also the "Memoirs" in James Lockwood, *Man Mortal: God Everlasting* (New Haven, 1756), p. i.

7. Dexter, *Documentary History*, pp. 143, 145.

8. Ibid., pp. 77, 144.

9. The account book, located in the Yale library, records payments for Jonathan's instruction to Smith on the dates Jan. 7, 1717, June 18, 1717, and Feb. 24, 1718; to both Smith and Hall on Sept. 10, 1718; and a final payment for both Hall and Williams on Apr. 23, 1719.

1. Johnson was appointed junior tutor in the fall of 1716. Dexter, *Documentary History*, pp. 74, 76.

had been teaching in Guilford, Connecticut, during the two previous years. The Reverend Joseph Noyes, who had formerly been a tutor and was now minister of New Haven, agreed to take the senior class until a senior tutor could be found. The college was still without a resident rector, and remained so until Cutler was appointed in 1719.

These faculty arrangements were not improved until the fall of 1718, when Johnson's friend and classmate Daniel Browne accepted the junior tutorship.[2] Johnson himself was then presumably given the senior post, and would have been in charge of Edwards' studies when the Wethersfield scholars returned briefly that winter, during his junior year. It was Johnson, in fact, whom the students cited as the cause of their quick return to Wethersfield.[3] Johnson departed to take the pulpit in nearby West Haven at the end of the term in 1719, and for the following three years of Edwards' residence as a student the Yale faculty consisted of Daniel Browne and Timothy Cutler. From a letter of Edwards to his father shortly after his arrival in New Haven in June 1719, it appears that Cutler supervised his studies during the senior year.[4] Edwards continued to live at the college during the two years of graduate work afterward, where he apparently made good use of the library for further studies in philosophy and natural science, as well as theology.

There are no extant records of the curriculum at Wethersfield, and accounts of the program in New Haven during this time are incomplete. Apparently the content of instruction in the latter underwent a major transformation in 1717 or 1718, when the modern scientific works in the new library were introduced. In both places the general curriculum was probably similar to that of Harvard at about the same time, though there were apparently some differences in the textbooks used.

The Harvard program was described by one of the tutors in 1723.[5] According to this account, students began the freshman year with a review of Latin and Greek grammar, and studied rhetoric from William Dugard's *Rhetorica Elementa* or Thomas Farnaby's *Index Rhetoricus et Oratorius*.[6] Later in the year they took up Hebrew and logic. Sophomore

2. Ibid., p. 173.
3. Ibid., pp. 189ff. In the same volume Johnson's own detailed account is included in his "Some Historical Remarks Concerning the Collegiate School of Connecticut," pp. 159–163.
4. The letter is in the Andover coll. See Dwight, *1*, pp. 29–30.
5. Samuel Eliot Morison, *Harvard College in the Seventeenth Century* (2 vols., Cambridge, Mass., 1936–37), *1*, pp. 146–47. Hereafter cited as Morison.
6. Both were standard texts in rhetoric in the seventeenth century. A seventh edition of

students continued the languages, but their principal study was logic. They began with the system of Peter Ramus, then advanced to Franco Burgersdijck's *Institutio Logicae*[7] and a manuscript logic, *The New Logic, extracted from LeGrand and 'Ars Cogitandi'*, by tutor William Brattle.[8] Brattle's textbook reflected the most recent developments in logic, based upon the Cartesian methods of inquiry. Later in the year sophomores began natural philosophy with Adrian Hereboord's *Meletemata Philosophica*.[9]

Natural philosophy formed the principal study of the third year. Besides Hereboord's work, a manuscript manual by tutor Charles Morton, *Compendium Physicae*, was a standard textbook for Harvard students.[1] Juniors also studied ethics from Henry More's *Enchiridion Ethicum*,[2] and learned "a system of geography" and "a system of metaphysics." In the senior year students were taught arithmetic and geometry, and studied astronomy from Pierre Gassendi's *Institutio Astronomica*.[3] Later in the year seniors reviewed the whole program of the arts and sciences. The upper three classes had weekly disputations upon their principal subjects, and each Saturday they read divinity from Wollebius' *The Abridgment of Christian Divinity* and William Ames' *Medulla Theologicae*, both stable authorities for New England orthodoxy.[4]

Dugard's *Rhetorica Elementa* was published in London in 1673, and Farnaby's *Index* appeared in a "new" edition in 1652.

7. First published in 1626, Burgersdijck's *Institutio Logicae* remained a standard textbook in Aristotelian, as opposed to Ramist, logic. Its use at Harvard, together with the Ramist textbooks in logic, is discussed in Morison, *1*, pp. 187–93.

8. Brattle, who was a Harvard tutor from 1686–97, introduced his MS logic into the curriculum there in about 1686; it was used thereafter until late in the eighteenth century. At first it was circulated in student copies; but finally it was printed in Boston under the title *Compendium Logicae* in 1735, and again in 1758. In the published versions there are many footnotes discussing John Locke's and others' views on substance and other related topics.

9. This was first published in 1654; it remained in use at Harvard as late as 1740 (Morison, *1*, p. 234). Hereboord was himself an early admirer of Descartes, who attempted to synthesize the Aristotelian and Cartesian approaches in his systematization of natural philosophy.

1. Morton wrote his textbook in England, and brought it to Harvard when he came over to assume a tutorship in 1686. Because it incorporated many recent discoveries, the work was an important contribution to the understanding of the new science in the colonies. *Compendium Physicae* has been edited by Theodore Hornberger and published in *Collections of the Historical Society of Massachusetts, 33* (1942). A good summary of the work is in Morison, *1*. pp. 236–49.

2. *Enchiridion Ethicum* (London, 1666).

3. *Institutio Astronomica* (London, 1653) was used by JE in his senior year at Yale (see below, p. 21).

4. For a discussion of the use of these works at Harvard in the seventeenth century, see Perry Miller, *The New England Mind: The Seventeenth Century* (Cambridge, Mass., 1939), pp. 95–96.

From these textbooks it appears that Harvard students were not instructed according to a single rigid intellectual scheme, but were exposed to the variety of competing views current in the late seventeenth century. In logic both the Aristotelian system of Burgersdijck and the anti-Aristotelian system of Ramus were taught, and in addition students were given some exposure to the method of Descartes and the logic of Port Royal in Brattle's work. Gassendi's *Institutio Astronomica* presented the elements of astronomy and summarized the three main systems of the heavens as understood in the early seventeenth century, the Ptolemaic, the Tychonic,[5] and the Copernican. Hereboord's *Meletemata* offered both the Aristotelian and the Cartesian systems of rational physics, and Morton's *Compendium Physicae* emphasized the experimental science that was promoted by the Royal Society of London. Although Morton organized his presentation according to standard scholastic distinctions, he devoted the contents of his chapters to explaining the discoveries of Galileo, Harvey, Boyle, Hooke, and other contributors to the modern era.

By comparison, the intellectual diet that Edwards' tutors had received at the Collegiate School was apparently much more limited. Benjamin Lord, a classmate of tutors Smith and Johnson, later recalled studying Tully and Virgil, the Greek Testament and the Psalms in Hebrew, the logics of Ramus, Burgersdijck, and Hereboord, the rudiments of mathematics, and natural philosophy from a manuscript textbook by Abraham Pierson, the first rector of the college.[6] Pierson wrote this manual while he was a student at Harvard in the class of 1668, when Aristotelian science was still supreme there. Samuel Johnson scornfully described the same course of studies as "nothing but the scholastic cobwebs of a few little English and Dutch systems that would hardly now be taken up in the street, some of Ramus and Alsted's works was considered the highest attainments. They heard indeed in 1714 when [I] took [my] Bachelor's Degree of a new philosophy that of late was all in vogue and of such names as Descartes, Boyle, Locke and Newton, but they were cautioned against thinking anything of them because the new philosophy it was said would soon bring in a new divinity and corrupt the pure religion of the country." Johnson's

5. As formulated by the Danish astronomer Tycho Brahe. He held that all the planets except Earth revolve about the sun, but the sun itself and the entire solar system revolve around the stationary earth.

6. Franklin Dexter, *Biographical Sketches of the Graduates of Yale College, with Annals of the College History* (6 vols., New York, 1885–1912), *1*, p. 115.

writing of a "technologia" was his main scholastic achievement. He
later described this work as "a little system of all parts of learning
then known in nothing else but a curious cobweb of distributions
and definitions which only served to blow [me] up with a great conceit
that [I] was now an adept."[7] Ramus' logic and such Ramist works as
John Alsted's *Encyclopedia Scientiarum Omnium* gave the basis for these
student technologiae.

Although Johnson disavowed scholasticism when he read Bacon's
Advancement of Learning, the substance of his knowledge still was that
of the technologia; at first he probably had little more than that to
offer his own students. The changes that he was partly instrumental
in effecting were not begun until 1717 or 1718, and even then they
could hardly have amounted to an instantaneous revolution in the
curriculum. The instruction that Edwards received in Wethersfield
during his first three years was probably superior in some respects.
Elisha Williams, who presided there, would have promoted a program
in conformity to his own Harvard training. Evidence that he did so
is found in two volumes of hand-copied textbooks in logic and natural
philosophy that Edwards received from his father, apparently for studies
during his sophomore and junior years.[8]

These volumes had been prepared by a Harvard student, William
Partridge, between 1686 and 1688. The first, which Edwards signed
and dated 1718, contains a synopsis of the Ramist logic of George
Downame[9] and a copy of William Brattle's *Compendium of Logic* (the
New Logic). Edwards' notes at the back of the book show he used the
Brattle logic again while teaching the subject during his tutorship.
The second volume, which he signed and dated 1719, includes William
Ames' unpublished Ramist synopsis of physics[1] and a collection of
theses taken from Henry Gutberleth's scholastic *Physicae, hoc est, Na-
turalis Philosophiae*.[2] This volume also contained an untitled copy of

7. *Samuel Johnson, President of King's College: His Career and Writings*, ed. Carol Schneider
and Herbert Schneider (4 vols., New York, 1929), *1*, pp. 6–7.

8. The volumes are now in the Beinecke Rare Book and Manuscript Library at Yale
University, the first catalogued as MS Downame, and the second as MS Partridge. JE still
had them in his own library as late as 1751, when he again signed and dated them.

9. Under the title *Expositionis Georgii Dounami, in Petri Rami Dialecticam Catechismus*.

1. Morison, *1*, p. 225. In his *Technometria*, Ames defines physics as "the art of doing the
work of nature well." For an account of *Technometria* and its place in colonial education,
see Lee Gibbs, "William Ames' Technometry," *Journal of the History of Ideas*, 33 (1972), pp.
615–24.

2. Published in *Herbornae Nassoviorum*, 1613.

Charles Morton's manuscript *Compendium Logicae*[3] and a copy of his *Compendium Physicae*.

When Edwards and his Wethersfield classmates appeared in New Haven for the brief reunion of the college in December 1718, the program there was being modernized to an even greater extent. Samuel Johnson reports that he and Daniel Browne introduced the teaching of Locke and Newton using the resources in Jeremiah Dummer's fine collection of books in the new library:

> They joined their utmost endeavors to improve the education of their pupils by the help of the new lights they had gained. They introduced the study of Mr. Locke and Sir Isaac Newton as fast as they could and in order to this the study of mathematics. The Ptolemaic system was hitherto as much believed as the Scriptures, but they soon cleared up and established the Copernican by help of Whiston's Lectures, Derham, etc. Some opposition would probably have been made to these innovations if it had not been for the public quarrels about the college, and it was hoped these new and better instructions would promote the credit of it. Mr. Johnson greatly desired to study Sir Isaac himself but wanted mathematics, a study he was averse to; but finding it necessary to that purpose, he was resolved to overcome that aversion, and by laborious application he gained the mastery of Euclid, Algebra, and the Conic sections, so as to read Sir Isaac with understanding and his aversion turned into a great pleasure.[4]

Up to this time neither Locke nor Newton had been taught in any American college. The innovations at Yale were a major step forward into the intellectual life of the eighteenth century—if we credit Johnson, a single step from Ptolemy to Newton! He suggests that they were begun in 1717, but since Browne was not appointed until the following year this date might well be in error.[5] It is more likely that the changes

3. This MS logic has apparently never been published. Perry Miller gives a general description of it in *New England Mind*, pp. 122–23.

4. Schneider and Schneider, *Johnson: Career and Writings*, pp. 8–9.

5. Dates in Johnson's "Autobiography" differ from those in public records at certain points. At the same time, the published theses for the Yale commencement in 1718 suggest that some post-Copernican science had been taught during the previous year. *Ut sol est Centrum hujus Systematis, sic stellae fixae aliorum*, states the plurality of worlds hypothesis expounded by William Derham in his *Astro-theology* (London. 1714). *Cometae sunt massae indigestae, Orbe parabolico circa Solem revolvestes*, suggests a study of Whiston's *Astronomical Lectures;* and *Mundus non est infinitum, sed indefinite extensus*, states the thesis of Descartes which Henry More par-

were only begun about the time the Wethersfield students came down in December 1718; and since this coincided with the opening of the new library, the promise of such improved instruction could have been the main attraction. If so, they must certainly have been disappointed, for with Johnson's own confessed inability to read Newton with understanding the initial attempt was likely to have had mixed success. In fact, this might have been one of the causes of the Wethersfield scholars' drifting back "two and two at once" within six weeks. Political antagonism and the friction of personalities no doubt also had a part in the renewed defection.[6]

According to the report of Edwards' early life given by Samuel Hopkins, his friend in later life and his first biographer, Edwards had already studied Locke's *Essay Concerning Human Understanding*[7] by this time:

ticularly disputed in their correspondence of 1648–49 (published by More in 1662). (Dexter, *Biographical Sketches,* p. 179.)

6. According to the Connecticut public records, at a meeting with the Council in March, 1719, "the trustees present did declare, that Mr. Johnson, against whose learning it has been reputed that the deserting scholars had objected, had been for some years improved as a tutor in the said college, and was well known to be a gentleman of sufficient learning; and that they cannot but look upon it as a very unworthy part in them, if any of those that have deserted the college have endeavored to scandalize a gentleman in such a manner, whom much more competent judges esteem as a man of good learning, and in that respect very well accomplished for the charge he is in." (Dexter, *Documentary History,* pp. 189–90.) Samuel Johnson, in his own narrative, charges the students with covert connivance against the college (ibid., pp. 157–63).

7. John Locke (1632–1704) has been known since the mid-eighteenth century as the founder of modern British empiricism, who set in motion a course of thought that led to George Berkeley's phenomenalistic idealism and then to David Hume's philosophical scepticism. Locke is often considered the single most important philosopher in the development of eighteenth century American thought (see e. g., Morton White, *Science and Sentiment in America,* [New York, 1972] ch. 1). The nature and extent of Locke's influence upon JE's philosophical views has long been the subject of investigation, particularly since the publication of Perry Miller's *Jonathan Edwards* (see especially pp. 54–61).

In his most important philosophical work, *An Essay Concerning Human Understanding* (London, 1690), Locke undertakes to investigate the origins, certainty, and extent of human knowledge, and the grounds and degrees of opinion. His inquiry begins with a full-scale attack on the theory of innate ideas, a theory which he considered not only to be mistaken in fact, but one which could seriously impede rational inquiry and could become an excuse for the imposition of authority in matters of belief and practice. He maintained, on the contrary, that every person's knowledge originates from and depends upon his own conscious experiences, and that it reaches no further than can be discovered from the ideas presented in experience. The main part of the *Essay* is thus devoted to explaining how such knowledge as we have is derived, how various complex ideas of substances, modes, and relations are formed from the simple ideas presented in sensation and reflection, how signs and discourse about ideas are possible, how knowledge of general and particular truths concerning objects is attained, and what limits such knowledge is subject to.

In his second Year at College, and the thirteenth of his Age, he read Locke on the human Understanding, with great delight and profit. His Uncommon Genius, by which he was, as it were by Nature, form'd for closeness of Thought and deep Penetration, now began to exercise and discover itself. Taking that Book into his Hand, upon some Occasion, not long before his Death, he said to some of his select Friends, who were then with him, That he was beyond Expression entertain'd and Pleas'd with it, when he read it in his Youth at College; that he was as much engaged, and had more Satisfaction and Pleasure in studying it, than the most greedy Miser in gathering up handsful of Silver and Gold from some new discover'd Treasure.[8]

It should be noted that Edwards is here quoted as saying only that he read Locke "in his Youth at College"; that the exact time was during his second year could have been Hopkins' own inference. Every other discoverable fact about the introduction of Locke's work into New England stands as evidence to the contrary. The only copy of the *Essay* that I have discovered there as early as 1717 is that in the first edition of 1690 which was included in Jeremiah Dummer's gift of books for the Collegiate School.[9] This copy would have been inaccessible to any of the students or tutors in Wethersfield, and might not have been available even in New Haven until the collection was brought over from Saybrook in the winter of 1718.[1] A catalogue of the Harvard College library published in 1723 mentions none of Locke's works, though a 1725 supplement lists the three-volume edition of 1722.[2] Nor is the *Essay* mentioned in the inventories of any of the private libraries advertised for sale during this period.[3] By 1726 Cotton Mather,

A standard work on Locke's life and philosophical views is R. I. Aaron, *John Locke* (2nd ed., Oxford, 1955).

8. Hopkins, *Life*, p. 3.

9. The complete inventory of the Dummer collection, as prepared by Louise May Bryant and Mary Patterson, is printed in *Papers in Honor of Andrew Keogh* (New Haven, 1938), pp. 432–92; cited hereafter as *Keogh*. Locke's *Essay* is listed on p. 435.

1. The question of the availability of Locke's work was raised by Perry Miller, in *Jonathan Edwards* (New York, 1949), p. 57. It is possible that Johnson had gone through the collection before, and removed such volumes as he had an immediate interest in and use for.

2. *Catalogus Librorum Bibliothecae Collegii Harvardini* (Boston, 1723), and *Continuatio Supplementi Catalogi* (Boston, 1725).

3. Ebenezer Pemberton's library was the most imposing of these. It contained Locke's *Reasonableness of Christianity, with a Vindication* and his *Second Vindication,* together with two volumes of his letters to the Bishop of Worcester, Nicolas Malebranche's *Search After Truth,* various works of Descartes, Antoine LeGrand, and Gassendi, Bayle's *Critical and Historical*

the most articulate popularizer of the "new philosophy" in America at the time, could speak of the *Essay* as a work that was then "much in vogue,"[4] but in his *Christian Philosopher*, which he published in 1721, there is no mention of Locke or his writings.

Much the same report can be given of Newton's works in New England. The *Philosophiae Naturalis Principia Mathematica* was published in 1687 and the *Optics* in 1704. Dummer's collection brought to Yale a second-edition copy of the *Principia*, which also contained Newton's *System of the World*, and a first edition of Samuel Clarke's Latin translation of the *Optics*, which appeared in 1706.[5] The Harvard library cata-

---

Dictionary, Harris' *Lexicon Technicum* and Sprat's *History of the Royal Society* together with works of Ray, Derham and Woodward, and various volumes of Addison's and Steele's *The Spectator* and *The Tatler.* In view of the immediate popularity of Locke's *Essay* in England and elsewhere, it is almost surprising that Pemberton's library did not include it in 1717, when it was advertised for auction. See *A Catalogue of Curious and Valuable Books Belonging to . . . Mr. Ebenezer Pemberton . . . to be sold by Auction* (Boston, 1717).

4. *Manaductio ad Ministerium* (Boston, 1726), p. 36.

5. The second edition of the *Principia* was published in Cambridge, England in 1713. Newton himself donated the copy of it, and that of the first Latin edition of *Optics* (London, 1706), which Dummer sent to the college (*Keogh*, p. 464). Isaac Newton received early recognition at Cambridge for his ability in the mathematical sciences. He was elected Lucasian professor of mathematics before his twenty-seventh birthday in 1669, after Isaac Barrow resigned the chair. When the Royal Society of London elected him a Fellow in 1672, Newton directly presented the body first with an account of a reflecting telescope he had newly invented, and then with the first of his several important papers on the composition of light.

His researches in mathematics and problems of motion led to his discovery that the planetary orbits, as calculated by Kepler, could be explained by a force extending outward from the sun and varying in inverse ratio to the square of the distance from it. He further calculated that the same force explained the observed paths of comets (especially the comet of 1680), and that, when attributed to the earth, it accounted for the lunar orbit and the regular accelerations of bodies moving freely near the earth's surface. These results, he argued, were sufficient inductive grounds for pronouncing the gravitational force of attraction to be a universal principle that obtains for all the bodies in the universe. This revolutionary theoretical achievement, with his mathematical demonstrations of it, was presented to the world in the first edition of the *Principia* in 1687.

In his General Scholium in the *Principia,* Newton declined to speculate openly about the cause of gravitational attraction among bodies. But in the Queries at the end of the first edition of his *Optics* (1704) he proposed a number of basic ideas concerning the nature of matter and the "non-mechanical" attractive and repulsive forces that act upon bodies. These discussions were significantly enlarged in the 1706 Latin edition of the work, and were rearranged and developed further in later editions. JE was stimulated most by these theoretical passages in Newton's works, and they will be cited frequently hereafter. References to *Principia* will cite by Newton's internal subdivisions only, e.g., Bk. I, prop. X; where relevant, the page of the 1713 ed. which JE presumably used will also be cited. Unless otherwise noted, quotations in English from *Principia* are taken from the translation of Andrew Motte, revised by Florian Cajori (2 vols., Berkeley, 1966). References to *Optics* will also cite by Newton's internal subdivisions: e.g., Bk. III, Q. 8, according to the text of the 4th ed. of 1730; where

logue of 1723 lists only a first edition copy of the *Optics*. It must be added that Newton's contributions were well known, at least in Boston and at Harvard, well before this time. Thomas Brattle, brother of William, had communicated his observations of the comet of 1680 to the Royal Observatory, and they were used by Newton to confirm his theory of the comet's orbit.[6] Cotton Mather had read the *Optics* by 1712, when he pronounced Newton "the *Perpetual Dictator* of the Learned World in the Principles of Natural Philosophy."[7] His knowledge of Newton did not go far, however; in *The Christian Philosopher* he discusses at length Newton's optical theories, but in writing on gravity he credits Newton only once, for calculating the difference between the earth's polar and equatorial diameters.[8]

Besides the scarce volumes of Locke and Newton, Dummer's gift brought to Yale a collection of other recent works that made its library unrivaled in the colonies. There were included the major scientific works of Robert Boyle, the posthumous papers of Robert Hooke, John Harris' scientific encyclopedia *Lexicon Technicum*,[9] various publications of the Royal Society,[1] and Jacques Rohault's *Physica*, a widely used textbook in the Cartesian physics to which Samuel Clarke had added footnotes explaining Newton's corrections of and improvements upon Descartes' theories.[2] Whiston's *Astronomical Lectures* and William Derham's *Astro-theology* and *Physico-theology* are the works Johnson refers to as being used to "clear up and establish" the Copernican system at Yale.[3]

---

relevant the 1706 Latin ed. which JE presumably used will also be cited. Unless otherwise noted, quotations are taken from the 4th ed. as published in *Opticks* (New York, 1952).

6. The observations are in Newton's *Principia*, Bk. III, prop. 41, prob. 21, ex.

7. *Thoughts for the Day of Rain* (Boston, 1712) p. iii.

8. *The Christian Philosopher* (London, 1721), p. 82.

9. John Harris' *Lexicon Technicum* (2 vols., London, 1704–10) was an important collection of short articles upon recent scientific discoveries and contributions. It was almost unique among the scientific works at Yale in that it made no attempt to organize the topics under any formal system, but arranged them alphabetically instead.

1. According to Dummer, in 1719 Elihu Yale also promised to donate "another parcel of books, part of which he has promised me shall be the Royal transactions in seventeen Volumes" (Dexter, *Documentary History*, p. 193). But Bryant and Patterson list none of the *Philosophical Transactions of the Royal Society* in *Keogh*. Yale did contribute a copy of *Museum Regalis societatis* (London, 1681), however, as well as the library's copy of Locke's *Essay*. And the collection also included the Royal Society's *Miscellanea Curiosa* (London, 1708). See *Keogh*, pp. 435, 443.

2. Rohault's *Physica* (London, 1697) with Clarke's annotations, was an important instrument in the dissemination of Newton's scientific method and physical theories in the late seventeenth and early eighteenth centuries; it clearly exhibited the conflict between the Newtonian and the Cartesian approaches to physical science. The Yale library's copy was of the third edition, 1710.

3. Whiston's *Astronomical Lectures read in the Public Schools at Cambridge* (London, 1715)

Dummer's gift also included Galileo's *Systemata Cosmicum*,[4] Christian Huygens' *Celestial Worlds Discover'd*,[5] and David Gregory's *Elements of Astronomy*.[6] Besides Derham's works, modern physico-theology was represented by John Ray's *The Wisdom of God Manifested in the Works of Creation*[7] and Whiston's *New Theory of the Earth*.[8]

Philosophical works of the modern period had been almost as scarce as those in science in the Colonies. The Yale library now possessed not only Locke's *Essay*, but the works of Bacon and Descartes, Gassendi's *Disquisitio metaphysica anti-Cartesianas*,[9] Jean LeClerc's *Opera Philosophica*,[1] Nicolas Malebranche's *Search after Truth*,[2] and major works of

---

provided a quite thorough and systematic introduction to astronomy, including Newton's celestial mechanics. Derham's *Astro-theology* and his *Physico-theology* (1713; London, 1715) attempted to demonstrate "the being and attributes of God from his works of creation," as the subtitle of the latter declares. Because of the footnotes into which he compressed vast amounts of current scientific information and opinion, Derham's books were an important and popular vehicle for disseminating the new science in the early eighteenth century.

4. Published in *Augustae Treboc* in 1635.

5. Whether the remote stars might have systems of planets like that of our sun, which might be inhabited by rational creatures like ourselves, was a subject of much popular scientific speculation in the late seventeenth century. Huygens' contribution was published in an English translation in London in 1698.

6. Gregory was a close associate of Newton, who recommended him for the Savilian professorship of astronomy at Oxford. His two-volume *Elements of Astronomy* was published in London in 1715.

7. Ray, a noted seventeenth-century biologist and Fellow of the Royal Society of London, published this popular work in natural theology in London in 1691. The Yale library's copy was of the sixth edition of 1714.

8. Whiston, Newton's successor as Lucasian professor of mathematics at Cambridge, published this work in 1696 as a scientifically updated version of the Biblical account of world history, from the creation through the deluge, and even to the final conflagration. In 1710 Whiston was charged with Arianism and expelled from the University. The Yale library received a second edition of his *Theory of the Earth* (1708); an eighth edition was published as late as 1755.

9. Gassendi attacked the Cartesian system and its philosophical foundations, first in his objections to Descartes' *Meditations* (published with the *Meditations* itself in 1641 as the fifth of the seven sets of Objections with Descartes' Replies), and then in this extended critique which appeared in Amsterdam in 1644.

1. Jean LeClerc was a prominent figure among the Remonstrants in Amsterdam in the late seventeenth century, and a friend and correspondent of John Locke. His *Opera Philosophica* (3rd ed., Amsterdam, 1704) includes his writings on logic, ontology, and pneumatology.

2. The first volume (Books I-III) of Malebranche's *Recherche de la Verité* was published in Paris in 1674, and appeared in an English translation by Thomas Taylor in London in 1694 as *Father Malebranche's Treatise concerning the Search after Truth*. His detailed examination of sensation and imagination were important contributions to the current literature on the mind. His occasionalist metaphysics, and his doctrine that we see all things in God, were topics of critical philosophical discussion by Locke, Arnauld, Leibniz, Berkeley, and others.

the later seventeenth-century English Platonists, especially the philosophical and theological works of Henry More, which were to have an early and lasting influence upon Edwards' thought.

Seventeenth-century rational theology was further represented in works by Stephen Charnock, Edward Stillingfleet, and others. In addition to many older works in ethics, the eleven volumes of *The Tatler* and *The Spectator*,[3] and Shaftesbury's *Characteristicks of Men, Manners, Opinions, Times*,[4] afforded views of the direction of moral thought and sensibility in the early eighteenth century.

Such matter offered Edwards a much wider and richer field of literature to explore than any of his predecessors at Yale had found. Indeed there is every appearance that his studies during his last three years in the college stimulated a major intellectual awakening. From his writings of this period it is clear that he enthusiastically devoted himself to the scientific works.

It is doubtful, however, that his earlier studies had prepared him to go far in this field on his own. In a letter to his father written shortly after he arrived in New Haven for his senior year, Edwards lists the books and supplies Cutler had advised him to acquire for his studies: "Alsted's Geometry and Gassendus' Astronomy; with which I would entreat you to get a pair of dividers, or mathematician's compasses, and a scale, which are absolutely necessary in order to learning mathematics; and also, the Art of Thinking, which, I am persuaded, would be no less profitable, than the other necessary to me."[5] Although he

---

Probably the most important of Malebranche's disciples was the English idealist John Norris, whose *Essay towards the Theory of the Ideal or Intelligible World* (2 vols., London, 1701–04) was also included in the Dummer collection.

3. Sir Richard Steele presented copies of *The Tatler* (4 vols., London, 1710, 1711) and *The Spectator* (7 vols., London 1712, 1713) which were included in the Dummer collection.

4. Anthony Ashley Cooper, third Earl of Shaftesbury, *Characteristicks* (3 vols., 1711; London, 1714). The work is a collection of various discourses he had written during the previous several years. Its popularity can be measured by the fact that it appeared in its eleventh edition in 1790. The Yale library received a copy of the second edition of 1714; unless otherwise noted, this edition is used here throughout. JE refers to the work in one of his later notes on the cover of "Natural Philosophy" (see below, p. 194).

5. Dwight, *1*, pp. 31–32. The original letter is in the Andover coll. The Yale library contains a copy of Antoine Arnauld, *The Art of Thinking*, ed. John Ozell (London, 1717), that bears JE's signature; it is undoubtedly the one he received from his father on this occasion. Arnauld first published the famous *Ars Cogitandi*, together with Pierre Nicole, in 1662. He had already made his philosophical mark by his astute objections to Descartes' *Meditations* (published with it as the fourth set of the Objections, with Descartes' Replies), and would later be an important critic of Malebranche (*Traité des Vraies et Fausses Idées* [Paris, 1683]) and of Leibniz (*The Leibniz-Arnauld Correspondence*, ed. H. T. Mason and G. H. R. Parkinson

had probably studied Morton's textbook in physics, his lack of mathematics would seriously hinder any systematic reading of Newton's *Principia*. In fact, it appears that Edwards never acquired much skill in mathematics, and his reading of Newton was largely confined to the more general and philosophical discussions. Again, the request for Gassendi's *Institutio Astronomica* shows that he had not yet begun astronomy by that time. The writings of his first graduate year indicate that he was only then reading Whiston's *Astronomical Lectures*.

The succession of Edwards' own writings through the following three years gives some evidence of the course of his scientific studies and interests. He does not appear to have been interested in biology; even "Of Insects" is primarily concerned with the physical explanation of the spider's flight. When Edwards wrote this paper during his senior year he had read something of Newton's theory of the "incurvation" of light, but evidently had not yet studied the copy of *Optice* in the college library.[6] The paper shows his early interest in optical questions, which might have been stimulated in part by his study of astronomy. "Of the Rainbow," which he probably wrote near the start of the next year, indicates his actual reading in Newton's work; but it, like "Of Insects," also suggests a study of Descartes' *Dioptrics* or some Cartesian treatment of optics based upon it. The fragment "Of Light Rays" draws from Huygens' conjectures concerning the plurality of worlds, which Edwards might have known about from reading Huygens' own *Celestial Worlds Discover'd* or Derham's *Astro-theology*. The scientific notes in "Natural Philosophy" indicate that during his two graduate years he also studied Whiston's *Astronomical Lectures* and perhaps his *Sir Isaac Newton's Mathematick Philosophy more easily Demonstrated*,[7] Derham's *Physico-theology*, and most especially Newton's *Optice*.

[Manchester and New York, 1967]). Despite these critical challenges to major figures in the developing stream of continental rationalism, the logic of Arnauld and Nicole is in many respects a classic in the modern rationalist tradition. It incorporated much from Descartes' *Regulae* and *Discours*, and from Pascal's *De l'Esprit Geometrique*. Following the general spirit of the rationalist movement, *The Art of Thinking* is aimed primarily at the training of the judgment so that error and uncertainty may be avoided in reasoning. Accordingly, the forms of syllogistic reasoning are not insisted upon, but presented as a useful aid to accurate reasoning. The "topics" of the Ramist logic are treated even more slightly, as being relatively less useful. On the other hand, the Cartesian distinctions between sensation, imagination, and conception, the methods of analysis and synthesis, and the notions of clarity and distinctness as marks of intelligibility and certitude, are emphasized.

For further discussion, see introduction to the recently published translation of *The Art of Thinking* by James Dickoff and Patricia James (Indianapolis, 1964).

6. The term Newton uses for light diffraction in *Optice* is *"inflexio"* (in the English editions, "inflection").

7. Although this work is not listed in the inventory of the Dummer collection, there is

Edwards was particularly stimulated by the Queries that Newton added at the end of the *Optice*. He was interested in the variety of unusual and experimentally discovered phenomena that Newton mentioned there, and jotted notes upon several of them with his own proposals about their correct explanation. His hypotheses reflect his excitement over one of Newton's main suggestions in the Queries, that many phenomena cannot be explained by mere mechanical collisions among particles of matter, but must arise from attractive and repulsive forces by which the particles act upon each other without surface contact. It is clear that Edwards never mastered the mathematics of Newton's theory, any more than most of his contemporaries who soon championed it. But he seems from the outset to have had a unique appreciation of the theory's revolutionary implications for the fundamental framework of concepts that had traditionally been used to interpret the intelligible order of the world.

In some respects the intellectual stage had already been set for Edwards' ready response to Newtonian physics. Not long before, probably during his senior collegiate year or early in the first year of graduate study, he had read some of the metaphysical works of the Cambridge Platonist Henry More.[8] The earliest portions of "Natural

---

some evidence in his writings that JE might have used it. The work, which appeared in London in 1716, is one of the earliest expositions of the Newtonian physics to follow upon the publication of the *Principia*.

8. Henry More (1614–87) was one of the leaders of the Cambridge Platonists, a group of scholars and divines that included Ralph Cudworth, John Smith, and Benjamin Whichcote. By his own account, he rejected Calvinism in his early youth, and after a bout with scepticism during his student years in Cambridge, he found both philosophical and spiritual direction from the works of Platonic writers, Plotinus, Hermes Trismegistus, Marsilius Ficinus, and from the mystical *Theologia Germanica* (author unknown). In about 1646 More read Descartes' *Principles of Philosophy* (Amsterdam, 1644), and for a time was the most enthusiastic champion of Cartesianism in England. In 1648 More was persuaded to enter upon a philosophical correspondence with Descartes, which ended only with the latter's death in 1650. After Clerselier published Descartes' letters in 1657 and 1659, More published his own to Descartes in *A Collection of Several Philosophical Writings* (London, 1662). The same volume included second editions of his earlier works, notably, *An Antidote against Atheisme*, *Enthusiasmus Triumphatus*, and *The Immortality of the Soul*. A copy of this volume was included in the Dummer collection for the Yale library, and might have been the edition of More that JE studied. It is used as the edition of reference here.

By 1668 More came to believe that Cartesianism was encouraging to freethinking and atheism; in *Divine Dialogues* (2 vols., London, 1668) he turned his former respectful disagreements into a forthright attack upon Cartesian doctrines, and thenceforward became a bitter opponent of the system. In contrast to Descartes, More argued that space is immaterial, necessary, infinite, and immutable, that both bodies and spirits are extended, and that they differ essentially in that bodies are entirely passive and divisible while minds are active, self-moving, and indivisible. Newton is known to have studied More's works in his youth, and it has been argued that Newton's later conceptions of absolute space, inert matter, and force

Philosophy" show how More influenced Edwards' thought concerning
the general problem of the refutation of metaphysical materialism.
Edwards' arguments in "Of Atoms" and the opening paragraphs of
"Of Being" incorporate conceptions of matter, space, and time that are
urged by More in his *An Antidote against Atheisme* and *The Immortality
of the Soul,* and Edwards' line of demonstration is quite similar to that
of More. Newton too, at an early stage of his career, had been much
influenced by More's ideas concerning matter and space,[9] and the
Newtonian concept of force quite readily lent itself to Platonistic and
spiritualistic interpretations during the late seventeenth and early
eighteenth centuries.

There remains the major question whether Edwards might have read
Locke's *Essay* during these final three years while he was a student in
New Haven. Certainly, none of the writings we have discovered to belong to this period bear any obvious and outward marks of a receptive
exposure to the *Essay.* The essay "Of the Prejudices of Imagination,"
where such marks might be expected to appear, reflects none of the
characteristic ideas or vocabulary of Locke. On the contrary, this paper
is thoroughly rationalistic in tone and emphasis; Edwards was much
more likely to have been inspired to it by reading the discussion of
clarity and distinctness, and the obscurity and confusion of ideas, in
Arnauld's *Art of Thinking.*[1] Indeed, we find Edwards' earliest dateable
reference to Locke's *Essay* appears in his "Catalogue," or list of books
he was interested in studying or acquiring. He began this list about the
time he left New Haven for his New York pastorate,[2] but he did not
include Locke's *Essay* until later, probably in the early part of 1724
after returning from New York.[3] There is nothing in this to indicate

---

were significantly influenced by More's views in these particulars. See John Tullock, *Rational
Theology and Christian Philosophy in England in the Seventeenth Century* (2nd ed., 2 vols., London,
1874), Vol. II, ch. 5; John Tull Baker, *An Historical and Critical Examination of English Space
and Time Theories from Henry More to Bishop Berkeley* (Bronxville, N.Y., 1930), chs. 2, 4; E.A.
Burtt, *The Metaphysical Foundations of Modern Science* (rev. ed., New York, 1951), pp. 127–44.

9. In one of his early MS notebooks (1661) Newton wrote, "Yt Matter may be so small as
to be indiscerpible the excellent Dr More in his booke of ye Soules immortality hath proved
beyond all controversie" (Portsmouth Colls., Cambridge, Add. MSS 3996, no. 8).

1. See Pt. I, ch. 9, "The clearness and distinctness of ideas and their obscurity and confusion."

2. Thomas Schafer has provided this approximate dating for the beginning of JE's "Catalogue." The MS is in the Yale coll.

3. The fifteenth entry on the first side of a letter-sheet which JE inserted into the "Catalogue" is "Lock [sic] of Human understanding." It is immediately followed by the entry
"Art of Thinking." These entries were evidently made early in 1724. JE's reference to Locke
in "The Mind," No. 11, might date from about the same time. It is interesting, too, that JE

that he seriously studied the work during any part of the period of his undergraduate and graduate study.

There is nevertheless some significant evidence that Edwards was exposed to the *Essay* during his student years. He could hardly have resided at the college during those three years as a student without being aware that a rare copy of Locke's work was at hand; and in view of his apparent excitement with works that represented the new science, it would be astonishing to learn that he had had no interest in Locke's work at that time. There are also some possible signs of his reading it in "Of Atoms": the concept of solidity treated there might have been derived partly from Locke's discussion of that property and our idea of it;[4] and there seems to have been no other work actually available to Edwards from which he could more readily have formed the notion of "the certain unknown substance which philosophers used to say subsisted by itself," the notion he so explicitly and finally rejects in this early piece.[5]

Subsequent writings also indicate that Edwards might have read Locke's *Essay* earlier, during these student years. In Miscell. no. aa, which he wrote in New York, he discusses faith as a unique mode of apprehension of the "complex idea" of God; the expression itself might point to his earlier reading of Locke's account of how we form that idea.[6] More important, when we at last find clear and unmistakable evidence of the influence of Locke, in early articles in "The Mind," it appears that Edwards might not have been reading Locke for the first time when those articles were written. From the sequence of passages that show his attention to Locke's views, it seems that he was at least not reading through the work systematically, as one would expect for the first reading, but was instead considering passages and discussions in several different parts of the *Essay*.[7] Moreover, from the fact

---

included "Lock of Education" and "Mr. Locks Four Letters of Toleration" in an earlier part of his list (p. 1, nos. 27 and 37). Of course, the lateness of his listing of Locke's *Essay* may not of itself be significant; Henry More's works are not listed in the "Catalogue" at all, although textual evidence establishes that he studied More as a student. Moreover, the fact that the *Essay* and the *Art of Thinking* are listed together on p. i may give some reason to think that in *this* list JE was recording the books he actually owned. There is some additional reason to think that he did acquire a copy of Locke's work for his own use while he was writing "The Mind."

4. *Essay*, Bk. II, ch. 4.
5. See below, p. 215. Locke criticizes the notion in *Essay*, Bk. II, ch. 23, no. 2.
6. Ibid., nos. 33–35.
7. For example, "The Mind," Nos. 2 and 3 seem to reflect passages in Locke's Bk. II, ch. 23; No. 10 pertains to Locke's discussion in Bk. IV, ch. 1; No. 11 to Bk. II, ch. 27, etc.

that he comments on Locke's views concerning personal identity in "The Mind," No. 11, it is evident that Edwards was using a copy of the second or a later edition of the work; and it might well have been one he had acquired for his own use.[8]

The evidence of Edwards' reading Locke while he was yet a student, then, is mixed and indecisive at best. But the very character of this evidence is, by itself, an indication of a much more important desideratum. *If* Edwards had in fact read the work during this time, as Hopkins has reported, *then* it is obvious that he did not respond to it in the way Hopkins' report suggests. For he certainly did not, in any of his collegiate writings, express any of that greedy zest of the miser for Locke's "way of ideas" that Hopkins' statement has led us to suppose.

Overall, then, Edwards' main interests and endeavors during this time were directed upon two different levels. He explored the new science, particularly that of Newton, for its explanations of natural phenomena, and formed his own general conception of the system of physical nature and its laws from these studies. Again, he addressed himself to metaphysical questions concerning the foundations of physics, and through treating the problem of materialism under the influence of More formed initial views concerning the nature and grounds of matter, space, and physical causation. Some of these views were to be reshaped significantly in later writings; but his main conclusions— that matter neither exists nor acts by itself, but depends immediately on the immaterial divine Being—were to remain fixed centers of his thought.

These conclusions relate to the doctrine of God's absolute sovereignty in the moral and spiritual world, which Edwards came to accept at the time of his religious conversion, during his first year of graduate study. There is no mention of the event in any of his extant writings of that time, but he writes in his "Personal Narrative" about its effect upon his beliefs. From his childhood he had harbored doubts about the sovereignty of God "in choosing whom he would to eternal life, and rejecting whom he pleased, leaving them eternally to perish and be everlastingly tormented in Hell. It used to appear like a horrible doctrine to me." On the occasion in question, however, Edwards found himself entirely ready to abandon his doubts, not as the result of any reasoned proof or

8. The chapter on identity and diversity (Bk. II, ch. 27), with its discussion of personal identity, was added to the second edition of the *Essay* in 1694 (see *An Essay Concerning Human Understanding,* ed. Peter H. Nidditch [Oxford, 1975], p. xxi).

explanation, he writes, for he "never could give an account how, or by what means, I was thus convinced; not in the least imagining at the time, nor for a long time after, that there was any extraordinary influence of God's spirit in it, but only that now I saw further, and my reason apprehended the justice and reasonableness of it. However my mind rested in it, and put an end to all those cavils and objections."[9]

Although Edwards arrived at the one conviction by argument and the other through a spiritual experience, his belief that God is sovereign in the physical order of the world remained as unshakeable as his acceptance of the doctrine of God's sovereignty in the moral and spiritual order. Many of the developments of his later thought may be seen as efforts to define the constitution of these two orders, and to show the manner of their dependence upon divine providence.

FROM NEW YORK TO NORTHAMPTON: 1722–26

During the summer of 1722 Edwards accepted a call from a small Presbyterian church near New York City. He left Connecticut to take up his pastorate there at the end of August. The struggling church survived only until spring, however, and he returned to East Windsor at the end of April. During the following year he preached in various Connecticut churches, sometimes as a ministerial candidate, and engaged himself in private study. He wrote his M.A. thesis during the summer. In November he accepted a call from the church at Bolton, but soon after was released from the commitment. Some part of the winter and spring was perhaps spent in study at New Haven. Finally, on May 21, 1724, he was appointed junior tutor at Yale. Except for a period of serious illness in 1725–26 he remained in his tutorship for the next two years, until he was called to Northampton in the fall of 1726.

When he went to New York Edwards probably left his manuscripts of "Natural Philosophy" and the other essays behind, for there is no evidence of further writing in them until he returned to Connecticut. His sojourn there was primarily a time of moral and spiritual, rather than scientific and philosophical, reflection. He compiled a series of resolutions for the governance of his thoughts and conduct, and maintained a diary to keep account of his progress in the observance of them.[1]

---

9. Hopkins, *Life*, p. 25.
1. JE's "Resolutions" and "Diary" were first published, in part by Samuel Hopkins (*Life*, pp. 6–9, 10–21), and in full by Sereno Dwight (*1*, pp. 68–73, 74–94, 99–106). Except for the cover leaf of the "Diary," which is in the Yale coll., both MSS are now missing.

The "Diary" for January 12, 1723, records his solemn renewal of his baptismal covenant and rededication of himself to God on that day.[2] In his "Personal Narrative" he remembered the time in New York as one in which he was profoundly affected by a sense of divine things.[3]

Neither are there many signs in his "Catalogue" or book list of a continued interest in philosophical and scientific study during this period. Entries at the beginning of the list, which he probably set down just before or soon after going to New York, include (John Harris') "Lexicon Technicum" and "Sir Isaac Newton's Principia and Opticks."[4] Under the heading "Books to be enquired for" he lists "the best Dictionary of the Nature of Bayle's Dictionary,"[5] and "the best History of Lives of Philosophers."[6] It was probably not until he returned to Connecticut that he added "The Gentleman's library and Ladies library Published by Sir Richard Steele," "Lock of Education," "Jenkins's Reasonableness and Certainty of the Christian Religion,"[7] "Mr. Cheyne's Religious Philosophic book,"[8] "Sr. Isaac Newton's Mathematic Philosophy more Easily Demonstrated . . . by Mr. Whiston," "Mr. Whiston's Astronomical Principles of Natural and Revealed Religion," "Mr. Lock's Four Letters of Toleration," "the Earl of Shaftesbury's Characteristics," and "Whiston's Theory of the Earth."[9]

While he was in New York Edwards began his "Miscellanies." He continued to write articles in this series from time to time throughout the rest of his life, until it extended to nine manuscript volumes. Taken together, this series probably comprises one of the most complete and continuous records in existence of the intellectual history of a single person. Edwards regularly drew material from his "Miscellanies" for use in his sermons and lectures. Its articles show the background of

2. Dwight, *1*, pp. 78–79.

3. Hopkins, *Life*, pp. 28–31.

4. These two entries are nos. 11 and 12 on p. 1 of the bound MS, the page on which JE began the list. The first twenty-four entries on p. 1 were probably written before the end of 1722, and nos. 11 and 12 might have been put down just before or just after he went to New York.

5. Pierre Bayle's *Dictionnaire Historique et Critique* was published in 1697. The Dummer collection of books for the Yale library included the English translation of the *Dictionary* (4 vols., London, 1710).

6. The Yale library had received a copy of Thomas Stanley's *The History of Philosophy: containing the lives, opinions . . . of the philosophers of every sect* (3rd ed., London, 1701).

7. Robert Jenkin, *The Reasonableness and Certainty of the Christian Religion* (2 vols., 3rd ed., London, 1708).

8. George Cheyne, *Philosophical Principles of Religion, Natural and Revealed* (London, 1705).

9. Of this latter group of entries, the first is no. 26 and the last is no. 41 on p. 1 of the "Catalogue." Several of these entries appear to have been copied from advertisements.

thought and reading that he brought to his published works, and they reveal aspects of his theological and philosophical ideas that would otherwise have remained undetected. The import of many passages in other private writings, especially in "The Mind," can best be judged by considering them together with related articles in "Miscellanies."

Upon returning to East Windsor in the early summer of 1723 Edwards entered a period of intense study and intellectual growth. He worked upon his M.A. thesis during the summer, regularly added entries in his "Miscellanies," and took up writing in "Natural Philosophy" again. Before the year's end he had also begun three new note series, "Notes on Revelation," "Notes on Scripture,"[1] and "The Mind." The course of development of his philosophical thought during this period can be traced by considering certain articles in "Miscellanies" which are closely related to his renewed activity in "Natural Philosophy" and the beginning of "The Mind."

Edwards' first step in a new philosophical direction may be seen in Miscell. no. pp, which he wrote shortly before his return to Connecticut. "We know there was being from eternity," he writes, "and this being must be intelligent. For how doth one's mind refuse to believe, that there should be being from all eternity without its being conscious to itself that it was."[2] When he returned to East Windsor in the summer he picked up the thread of this idea, and in an addition to "Of Being" in "Natural Philosophy" he developed it more fully and attempted a demonstration of its most provocative consequence, that the material world "can exist nowhere else but in the mind, either infinite or finite."[3] For all the perplexities this claim would generate about such matters as the status of space and time, the nature of causal dependence, and especially the received views concerning the union of mind and body in the human person; and indeed, for all his reluctance to submit the claim to public scrutiny in his published writings, Edwards seems to have remained fast in his conviction that consciousness, involving perception and knowledge, is necessary for the existence of anything whatever.

Shortly after he set forth his new principle in "Of Being," Edwards undertook an examination of the concept of excellency which was to give rise to another, and perhaps even more fundamental, principle.

1. Professor Schafer dates the beginnings of both of these notebooks in the period following JE's New York pastorate.
2. The article is printed in Townsend, p. 74.
3. Below, p. 75. For further discussion, see below, pp. 186–87.

Many "Miscellanies" entries written during the summer of 1723 show that the ideas of order, harmony, and excellency were becoming central to his conception of the relations between God and the world, and his understanding of God's purposes in the creation of it.[4] Sometime in the fall, probably shortly after the commencement in which he received his M.A. degree, Edwards began Miscell. no. 78 on the subject of excellency itself. His purpose was to give an analysis and explanation of it. After writing a few sentences he transferred the discussion to another paper, to make it the first article in "The Mind."[5] After a preliminary analysis of harmony and proportion with respect to their beauty, Edwards turned to the question of why proportion is always "pleasing to the mind" and disproportion always displeasing. In order to explain this fact he introduces a general metaphysical theory, in which the central proposition, as Edwards himself states it, is: "In identity of relation consists all likeness, and all identity between two consists in identity of relation."[6]

The idea expressed in this line seems to have burst upon him as a fresh and fundamental insight. He devoted much of the remainder of the essay to comments upon its ramifications and upon instances that seem to confirm it. He concluded that the relations of a thing to others are the fundamental condition of its existence, and that "being, if we examine narrowly, is nothing else but proportion." After he completed the main essay he made several additions to it through the autumn and following winter, as new implications for the concept arose in connection with the development of his theological views in "Miscellanies."[7]

In the meantime, Edwards resumed his writing in other parts of "Natural Philosophy." He began to form a definite plan for the composition of a general treatise, setting down his memoranda concerning its style and organization on the cover leaf of the manuscript.[8] He advised himself with regard to the presentation of "things exceedingly beside the ordinary way of thinking," and determined to state every matter clearly and distinctly, without confusion and ambiguity, "so that the ideas shall be left naked." The whole would be organized

---

4. For example, Miscell. nos. 29 (see Townsend, pp. 153–54), 32, 34 (ibid., p. 241), 42 (ibid., p. 238), and 64.

5. See below, pp. 325–26.

6. Below, p. 334.

7. See below, p. 320.

8. Below, pp. 192–95.

so that the easiest, most intelligible, and most general propositions came first, "according to the dependence of other things upon them." The several postulata which he added to the essay "Of the Prejudices of Imagination" during this time suggest the manner in which he intended to conduct his arguments.[9] And his fresh additions to both the long series and the short series of "Things to be Considered" in "Natural Philosophy" probably concerned the topics he intended to discuss in the work. In addition to the questions in optics and astronomy that he had commented upon before, Edwards' new entries discuss at length such subjects as the causes of mountains and the valleys among them, the nature of the atmosphere, and the structures and means of propagation of plants.[1] In the meantime, in October 1723 he wrote and sent off his "Spider" letter.[2] This was his first, and ultimately his only, attempt to submit a contribution in natural philosophy for publication. The circumstances and motives concerned in his writing this letter are interesting in themselves, and can be described briefly here.

At some earlier time Timothy Edwards had communicated with Judge Paul Dudley of the Superior Court of Massachusetts, who was a colonial Fellow of the Royal Society of London. Dudley got from the elder Edwards an account of a remarkable pumpkin vine that had flourished untended in his pasture, and had incorporated some of the details of the report into a paper on the powers of vegetation which he communicated to the Royal Society. The paper did not appear in the *Philosophical Transactions of the Royal Society* until 1724,[3] but Dudley apparently wrote Edwards in the summer of 1723, probably to notify him that it was forthcoming and to thank him for his contribution. At any rate, the letter contained a postscript inviting the report of any other wonders of nature that might be worthy of Dudley's attention.

Although Dudley's letter is no longer extant, it is referred to at the beginning of Jonathan's "Spider" letter. He responded to the opportunity, worked up the observations in "Of Insects" in his now famous letter, and presented them with all the modesty his "Natural Philosophy" memoranda had counseled. He began, "If you think, Sir, that

9. Below, pp. 199–201.
1. In the short series, these entries run from No. 22 to No. 28, the last in this series. In the long series, the post-New York entries begin with No. 45.
2. Below, pp. 163–67.
3. "Observations on some of the Plants in New-England, with Remarkable Instances of their Nature and Power of Vegetation," *Philosophical Transactions of the Royal Society of London*, *33* (1724), 194ff. Cited hereafter as *Philosophical Transactions*. TE's contribution is quoted below, p. 163, n. 3.

they are not worthy the taking notice of, with greatness and goodness overlook and conceal," and ended, "Pardon me if I thought it might at least give you occasion to make better observations on these wondrous animals, that should be worthy of communicating to the learned world." He sent the letter on October 31, 1723. A note on the manuscript shows that Dudley received it and kept it among his personal papers. But neither the letter nor its subject is mentioned in any of Dudley's further published papers or communications to the Royal Society.[4]

Edwards joined the Yale faculty as junior tutor in June 1724. Mr. Robert Treat was his senior colleague during this year, and Treat was replaced by Jonathan's cousin, Daniel Edwards, for the next. The college was again without a resident rector, and had been since Cutler and Browne resigned in 1722, when they and Samuel Johnson publicly declared their doubts about New England congregationalism and their intention to take up episcopacy. Hence in 1724 the tutors bore the major burden of the government of the college. During his first year Edwards and Treat gave extraordinary service in organizing and cataloging the library, for which they were paid an additional stipend. In 1725, as he journeyed to East Windsor after commencement, Edwards was overtaken by a serious illness which forced him to stop at North Haven. He remained there for several months, and afterwards had a long convalescence at home, so that he did not resume his teaching duties until the summer of 1726. In the fall he resigned his tutorship and went to Northampton.

From the few entries in his "Diary" for this period, Edwards found his tutorial duties difficult and distracting. Nevertheless he continued to add new articles to his notebooks, during the first year at least. Memoranda added on the cover of "Natural Philosophy" show his further reflections about the treatise he was planning, and the unnumbered series of articles (US) in the last section of that manuscript dates from this time. Several of these articles indicate his further attention to works of Newton, Whiston, and others that he had read during his student years. For the most part, his scientific interests still were directed toward problems in physics; the articles on ice and elasticity, which he produced by periodic additions of passages over quite a long time, show him employing the concept of gravity to explain the phenomena, as he had in earlier discussions. US No. 8, is particularly significant, for

4. For further discussion, see below, pp. 152–53.

the axioms in this entry show how Edwards proposed to apply the principle of sufficient reason to infer an immaterial cause of certain motions of bodies.

"The Mind" includes several articles that show a definite relation to Edwards' teaching of logic during his tutorship. Notes at the back of his copy of Brattle's *Compendium of Logic*, which he probably used in the classroom, are in some instances directly correlated with comments and discussions in "The Mind." It is even more evident, however, that he was engaged in a study of Locke's *Essay*. Many of the articles near the beginning of "The Mind" seem to have been inspired by passages in this work, and "The Mind," No. 11 refers to Locke directly. This article, as has been noted, shows that Edwards was using a second or later edition of the work, for it refers to the theory of personal identity which Locke did not take up in the first edition.[5] Again, there does not seem to be conclusive evidence as to whether Edwards had read the work before, while he was a student at the college. The biographical question thus still seems open to discussion. But if the articles in "The Mind" reflect Edwards' first exposure to Locke's work, then we can no longer think of Locke's influence upon him as though it were the intellectual ravishment of a schoolboy busy at his logic lessons. The discussions in "The Mind" are well anchored by the metaphysical principles that Edwards had already settled, and he was not likely to be blown far from those moorings.

Examination of the articles themselves tends to bear this out. In most questions where Edwards may be seen responding to Locke, we find he either rejects or consciously modifies Locke's express claims. It also appears that Edwards found his more recent insights into the nature of existence demanded some significant revisions in those metaphysical conclusions he had arrived at earlier in "Of Atoms" and "Of Being." Several articles on the existence of bodies and the necessity and reality of space indicate how he accomplished these revisions, and how far he considered and responded to objections to his astonishing doctrine that the whole material world exists nowhere but in the mind.[6] It appears that Edwards might have found the study of Locke to be more pertinent to his efforts to develop a theory of mind. On February 12, 1725, he wrote in his "Diary": "The very thing I now want, to give me a clearer and more immediate view of the per-

---

5. See above, pp. 25–26.
6. For further discussion, see below, pp. 97–111.

fections and glory of God, is as clear a knowledge of the manner of God's exerting himself with respect to spirits and mind, as I have of his operations concerning matter and bodies."[7] But even in "The Mind," No. 11, where he approvingly refers to Locke's theory of personal identity, Edwards shows that he rejects Locke's concept of the status of the mind. Other passages throughout the series indicate that Edwards took a quite different view from Locke's with regard to the acts and operations of the mind, as well.[8]

NORTHAMPTON TO PRINCETON: 1726–58

A brief sketch of the remainder of Edwards' life will be sufficient to complete the history of his composition of the papers in this volume.[9]

In the fall of 1726 Edwards accepted the call to Northampton to become a colleague of his grandfather, the Reverend Solomon Stoddard. He was ordained on February 22, 1727. On July 20, 1727, he married Sarah Pierrepont, daughter of the Reverend James Pierrepont of New Haven. The first of their eleven children was born in August of the following year. When Stoddard died on February 11, 1729, Edwards succeeded to his place as full minister of the Northampton church. In 1731 his sermon *God Glorified in the Work of Redemption*, which he delivered in Boston, was published. During the following years he worked earnestly and with success for the revival of religion; he was a leader in the Great Awakening that was ushered in by George Whitefield in 1740, and all of his published works from 1737 to 1742 are concerned with revival.[1] His *Treatise on Religious Affections* appeared in 1746.[2]

In 1748 a dissension began in his Northampton congregation, which led to his dismissal in 1750. Edwards preached his farewell sermon on July 1, 1750, and in 1751 he settled in the mission church at Stockbridge, Massachusetts. Here he completed his *Enquiry into the Modern Prevailing Notions of that Freedom of the Will*, which was published in 1754.[3] In 1755 he wrote the two dissertations, "The Nature of True

7. Dwight, *1*, p. 105.

8. For further discussion, see below, pp. 119–22.

9. For a more complete and detailed account of Edwards' life from the beginning of his Northampton pastorate, see Winslow, *Jonathan Edwards*, chs. 5–15.

1. These have been edited by C. C. Goen and published under the title *The Great Awakening*, as Vol. 4 of the Yale edition of *The Works of Jonathan Edwards* (New Haven, 1972). This edition is cited hereafter as *Works* (Yale ed.).

2. Edited by John Smith and published as *A Treatise Concerning Religious Affections*, in *Works* (Yale ed. 1959), *2*.

3. Edited by Paul Ramsey and published as *Freedom of the Will* in *Works* (Yale ed., 1957), *1*.

Virtue" and "Concerning the End for which God Created the World" which were published posthumously in 1765.[4] *Original Sin* was completed near the end of the Stockbridge period, and published in 1758, the year of his death.[5] In 1757 he was invited to succeed his son-in-law Aaron Burr as president of the College of New Jersey. He took the oath of office in February 1758. The following month he contracted smallpox from an inoculation against the disease, and died on March 22, 1758.

During the first few years of his residence in Northampton, probably up to the time of Stoddard's death in 1729, Edwards continued to pursue his scientific interests, though at a considerably reduced rate. Several final memoranda on the cover of "Natural Philosophy" indicate that he was still working toward the composition of his treatise in 1726, at about the time he left Yale.[6] Two entries in the unnumbered series in this manuscript were probably written in that year, several more in the next, and the last two in late 1728 or 1729.[7] These last articles were probably connected with his reading of Henry Pemberton's *A View of Sir Isaac Newton's Philosophy*,[8] a work which Edwards cites in the last of the short series of notes he titled "Wisdom in the Contrivance of the World."[9] These notes, which he wrote in late 1732, and the essay "Beauty of the World" that precedes them on the same separate leaf and which was written in 1726,[1] show how Edwards' interests in nature extended beyond what we now regard as the proper domain of the scientist. One of these other interests is in the foreground in the series titled "Images of Divine Things" which Edwards probably began in late 1727 or early 1728 and continued until nearly the end of his life.

Since the manuscript of "The Mind" has been lost, judgments as to the times at which its later entries were made are considerably less certain than for his other notebooks and papers. Comparisons of the content of articles in "The Mind" and those in "Miscellanies" indicate that

4. In *The Works of President Edwards*, ed. by S. Austin (8 vols., Worcester, 1808–09), "The Nature of True Virtue" is in Vol. 2, pp. 395–471, and "Concerning the End for which God Created the World" is in Vol. 6, pp. 9–124.

5. Edited by Clyde A. Holbrook and published as *Original Sin* in *Works* (Yale ed., 1970), *3*.

6. Nos. 15–21 on the inside page. The first of these refers to the Earl of Shaftesbury, whose *Characteristicks* JE might then have been reading. See below, pp. 194–95.

7. These include all the entries numbered 27–40 in this series. See below, pp. 294–95.

8. JE listed the work in his "Catalogue," p. 2, no. 39. It was published in London and Dublin in 1728.

9. See below, p. 309.

1. See below, p. 297.

Edwards had probably written "The Mind," No. 45 by the time he settled in Northampton in late 1726.[2] "The Mind," Nos. 46 through 60 were most likely written by the time of Stoddard's death in 1729 or soon afterward. Several of the articles written during this time indicate that Edwards had read George Berkeley's *An Essay towards a New Theory of Vision*.[3] He might have begun to plan his treatise on the mind during this period.[4] But by 1731 it appears that he had laid "The Mind" aside for the time, because he removed blank paper from the notebook to use in writing sermons.[5]

In the meantime, however, he had begun a rough plan for yet another major work, "A Rational Account of the Main Doctrines of the Christian Religion Attempted."[6] The topics to be handled in this work suggest that he intended to organize the principles he had set forth and explored in his earlier manuscript writings in such a way as to develop a major system of philosophical theology. The plan was still alive for him in the mid-1740s when he jotted a memorandum concerning its preface: "To shew how all the arts and sciences, the more they are perfected, the more they issue in divinity, and coincide with it, and appear to be as parts of it."

By about 1747 he had evidently added several other articles to "The Mind," those numbered 61–69. In that year or the next he formed a new index for the series to correspond with a new organization of the manuscript.[7] Articles up to "The Mind," No. 69 were cited in the original composition of this index; but since the references to Nos. 70 and 71 appear to have been added afterward, and No. 72 is not referred to at all, it seems likely that these three were written after the index was first drawn up. "The Mind," No. 72, in particular, might have been written in Stockbridge when Edwards was developing his argument concerning personal identity for *Original Sin*.[8] One further passage, the quotation from Cudworth's *Intellectual System* which is found at the end of "The Mind," No. 40, was probably added in late 1756 or 1757, when Edwards inserted passages from the same book in his "Images of Divine Things" and in "Miscellanies."[9]

2. See below, p. 327.

3. Listed in JE's "Catalogue," p. 3, no. 24. See below, pp. 123–24.

4. With regard to the "Subjects to be Handled in the Treatise on the Mind," Dwight comments, "The preceding articles were set down from time to time at the close of the work, in two series; the first, ending with No. 26" (Dwight, *1*, p. 664).

5. See below, pp. 327–29.

6. See below, p. 394.

7. See below, pp. 316–22, 328.

8. See below, p. 329.

9. "Images of Divine Things," nos. 208, 209, 210; "Miscellanies," no. 1359.

The untitled piece which we here call "Notes on Knowledge and Existence" was probably also written in Stockbridge, perhaps in 1756 or 1757.[1] These notes might have been set down in planning a philosophical dissertation. They are of particular interest in showing how, at this late date, Edwards was ready to reaffirm that idealistic phenomenalism and the principles underlying it that he had explored so long before in "The Mind" and other manuscript writings. The piece also contains an important and illuminating comment upon immaterial substance and its relation to bodies.

2. *Edwards as a Scientist*

With the above biographical sketch, several mistaken impressions that have been widely held concerning Edwards' scientific interests and objectives may be rectified. In the first place, his early essays, the notes in "Natural Philosophy," and his "Spider" letter were all written at a later time, and his work on them extended over a much longer period, than has generally been supposed. They represent his serious and continued efforts to add his own contributions to the body of current scientific knowledge. His communication of his discoveries concerning the spider's flight to Paul Dudley, and his preparations to compose a treatise on natural philosophy, bear witness to the scope of his ambitions as a scientist.

In the second place, Edwards found no conflict between his scientific interests and his religious convictions and vocation, and his interest in science did not flag after his conversion. On the contrary, the major body of notes and discussions in "Natural Philosophy" were written after his conversion, and he wrote the "Spider" letter and began to plan his treatise at the very time that he was actively seeking a pulpit, during the summer and autumn of 1723. During the same period he was deeply engaged in theological and biblical studies, as is shown by the large number of entries he added to his "Miscellanies," and by his "Notes on Scripture" and his "Notes on Revelation," which he began during this time. He did not finally abandon the treatise on natural philosophy until several years after he had settled in Northampton, when the burden of pastoral duties probably took both his time and interest from the project.

It is hardly likely, in any case, that Edwards could ever have realized the full scope of his ambitions in science. The advent of Newtonian mechanics with its mathematical demands soon brought the age of the amateur scientist, or at least physicist, to an end. In the light of Ed-

1. See below, pp. 394–95.

wards' background, education, and circumstances, it is in fact remarkable enough that he accomplished what he did in his notes and essays. During his student days, the science taught at Yale was still predominantly scholastic. If Samuel Johnson's testimony is to be credited, only the first faltering step was then being made toward the teaching of modern science, and that step was made by tutors whose own formal training in science was minimal and probably thoroughly scholastic in content. What Edwards achieved by way of understanding must have been mainly through his own efforts. Nor did he have the advantage, so important to fostering the valuable contributions of amateurs in England and on the continent, of a circle of collaborators, interested correspondents and critics to whom he could turn for stimulation and direction.

It is likely that the colonial intellectual atmosphere in which he worked was more indifferent than hostile to science. Several prominent New Englanders, indeed, were known correspondents of scientists in England, and some made significant contributions of their own. John Winthrop, Jr., the first governor of Connecticut, a noted chemist and metallurgist, was a charter member of the Royal Society when it was formed in 1663. Thomas Brattle, a Harvard tutor, communicated his observations of the comet of 1680 to the Royal Observatory in Greenwich, whence they were received by Isaac Newton and used by him to compute the comet's orbit.[2] Brattle also published observations of lunar and solar eclipses in the *Philosophical Transactions*. Zabdiel Boylston, a Boston physician, successfully administered inoculation against smallpox, for the first time in the western world, to large numbers of his townsmen during the epidemic of 1720. And Cotton Mather encouraged and publicly promoted the inoculation, even though the other Boston clergymen condemned the practice.[3] Mather's *The Christian Philosopher* greatly encouraged popular acceptance of new ideas, and his communication to the Royal Society of his own and others' scientific observations led to his election as a member in 1713.[4] Paul Dudley, to whom Edwards sent his "Spider" letter, published twelve papers in the *Philosophical Transactions*,[5] mostly on natural history and

2. Brattle was Newton's observer in "Boston, in New-England." See Newton, *Principia*, Bk. III, prop. 41, problem 21, example.

3. Otho Beall, Jr. and Richard Shryock, *Cotton Mather. First Significant Figure in American Medicine* (Baltimore, 1954).

4. See G. L. Kittredge, "Cotton Mather's Election into the Royal Society," *Publications of the Colonial Society of Massachusetts, 14* (1912), pp. 81–114.

5. The complete list of Dudley's papers in the *Philosophical Transactions* is given in *Sibley's Harvard Graduates, 4*, p. 54.

agriculture, and, like Mather, solicited reports of observations of natural phenomena from neighbors and friends. But although almost all these contributors, and other New Englanders who are known to have cultivated scientific interests, lived in or near Boston, they did not form a cohesive circle to whom Edwards could have looked for support and recognition.[6] For all of them, the center of the "learned world" was England. Edwards was well aware of this disadvantage when he reminded himself, in planning his treatise, that "the world will expect more modesty because of my circumstances, in America, young, etc."[7]

Edwards appears to be nearly unique among colonial scientists in the early eighteenth century, in that while their contributions were overwhelmingly in the fields of natural history, agriculture, and medicine, his primary interests and efforts were directed to problems in physics. In his early essays and throughout "Natural Philosophy" he attempts to formulate and apply explanatory hypotheses to account for such phenomena as the appearance of the rainbow and other meteors, the evaporation of water, combustion, respiration, the circulation of blood, the freezing of ice, elasticity, and the reflection, refraction, and diffraction or "incurvation" of light. His "Spider" papers might appear to be an exception; they have been widely praised, not only by students of Edwards' thought but by professional scientists as well, for their contributions to the natural history of the spider. Benjamin Silliman reprinted the draft of the "Spider" letter in his journal as an appendix to an important article on North American spiders by the noted arachnologist N. M. Hentz,[8] and two other well-known entomologists, Henry McCook and Alpheus S. Packard, have credited Edwards with original discoveries in several points in his observations of spiders.[9] But a careful study of "Of Insects," the earliest of the papers

6. In the 1660s Increase Mather had organized a circle in Boston to promote scientific activities in the new world, but it lasted for only a few years. Later efforts to organize a society failed until 1743, when the American Philosophical Society was formed. See Brook Hindle, *The Pursuit of Science in Revolutionary America, 1735–1789* (Chapel Hill, 1956), pp. 59ff.

7. JE's notes for a treatise on natural philosophy, No. 6. See below, p. 193.

8. Appendix to Hentz, "On North American Spiders," *American Journal of Science and Arts, 21* (1832), p. 109.

9. McCook's remarks are in *American Spiders and their Spinning Work* (3 vols., Philadelphia, 1889–93) *1*, pp. 68–69, and *2*, pp. 280–83. See also his paper, "Jonathan Edwards as a Naturalist," *Presbyterian and Reformed Review, 1* (1890), pp. 393–402. A. S. Packard's comments are quoted by Egbert Smyth in "Flying Spider," pp. 2–3. The originality of JE's discoveries has been questioned more recently by David Wilson, "The Flying Spider," *Journal of the History of Ideas, 32* (1971), pp. 447–58. Wilson notes correspondences between Edwards' account and descriptions that had been published in *Philosophical Transactions* by Martin Lister and Francois Xavier Bon. It is highly unlikely that Edwards was acquainted with these papers

and the foundation of the others, shows that Edwards' primary and original concern was to discover the physical principles that would account for the flight of this wingless insect. The essay merits further comment, for it is in many respects typical of Edwards' other scientific efforts, though it is untypical in the respect for which it is best known.

Edwards begins "Of Insects" with a rough classification of spiders, in order to call attention to the bridging and ballooning of the kind that "keep in forests, upon trees, bushes, shrubs, etc." They are often observed to pass from one tree or shrub to another on bridges of web, and Edwards confesses his astonishment at seeing them sail aloft on long strings of web. His objective is to explain these phenomena. The observations that he so admirably describes are not in fact an explanation, but his account of how he arrived at one. He repeatedly watched a spider spin out a web into the air; when the web caught upon a tree or bush it formed a bridge, and when it trailed out free to a great length it carried the spider aloft. From these observations Edwards formed the hypothesis he offers as an explanation: the spider feels, when its web is anchored upon another object, as though the web itself were a nerve, and so hazards to use it as a bridge. And the web must be lighter than air, so that when it has reached a sufficient length the spider is swept aloft by it, according to the principles of buoyancy, as a swimmer is lifted in water by a plank of wood. Further observations discover how the spider expresses the web; these are described in fine detail and illustrated with diagrams. Since Edwards supposed that ballooning and bridging are basically voluntary, he offers a further hypothesis to explain how the ballooning spider controls its descent, and adds a corollary to remark the goodness of God in providing his creatures with such an extraordinary means for their recreation and pleasure.

The observations reported in this part of "Of Insects," as has been mentioned, are quite atypical of Edwards' scientific endeavors. In a few instances elsewhere his descriptions of phenomena are evidently from first-hand experience, for example, the length and varying pitch of the sound of thunder in "Natural Philosophy," SS No. 18, the potholes in river beds in SS No. 23, the flakes of frozen fog in SS No. 26, and the plants he describes in LS No. 48. But none of these involved his conducting experiments, even of the rudimentary sort reported in "Of Insects." In "Of the Rainbow" he mentions several experiments that can demonstrate that a rainbow is caused by sunlight reflected

---

when he wrote "Of Insects" at Yale in 1719 or 1720, though he might have read Cotton Mather's reference to Lister on the subject in *The Christian Philosopher* (London, 1721), p. 149, not long afterward.

from drops of water, and he probably tried some of these, but they were all suggested to him by a few lines in Newton's *Optics*.[1] His casual attitude toward experiments in science is strikingly revealed by US No. 4, where he asserts the compressibility of water solely on theoretical grounds, despite the acknowledged fact that experimental tests indicated the contrary.[2] Again, in SS No. 21b, Edwards' observation of the color of sunlight filtering through the leaves of a tree is striking enough; but though he speaks of it as an experiment, he noticed the phenomenon by chance rather than design. And although it might have suggested several easily contrived experiments, he apparently never considered performing them. Instead, from this single observation he infers a series of very general conclusions about the nature of light, conclusions which are based essentially upon a previously assumed theory.

"Of Insects" is more typical of Edwards' other scientific writings in its pursuit and elaboration of the explanations of phenomena within the framework of acknowledged laws of nature or of a previously accepted physical theory. The principles of hydrostatics are invoked again to explain the ease with which blood can circulate in LS No. 19, and in his treatment of the composition and formation of the atmosphere in LS No. 56. In SS No. 27 he assumes the theory that cold is constituted by frigorific particles, a theory of Pierre Gassendi which Cotton Mather commended,[3] in explaining the cold of the polar regions. Newton's principle that all bodies or parts of matter gravitate toward each other is used by Edwards to explain the size and shape of the world (LS Nos. 1–3), the emission of light and heat (LS Nos. 18 and 19), the cohesion of any two atoms that "touch by surfaces" (LS No. 20), the reflection, refraction, and diffraction of light (SS Nos. 1 and 9; LS No. 46), elasticity (US No. 9), and various other phenomena. The compressibility of water in US No. 4 is deduced from the fundamental conception that water, like any other compound body, is composed of atoms.

Although Edwards addresses himself to a very wide range of topics in his scientific writings, various problems in optics were of particular interest to him throughout. The interest is first manifested in a further passage in "Of Insects." Having noticed that the webs of ballooning spiders are often quite visible at great distances, but nearly invisible

1. Bk. I, pt. 2, prop. 9 (in 1706 ed., pp. 139–40).

2. Dwight speaks of JE's inference as a discovery that was later confirmed and published (Dwight, *1*, p. 53). A sounder and more critical judgment is offered by Clarence Faust in "JE as a Scientist," *American Literature, 1* (1929–30), pp. 399–400.

3. In *Christian Philosopher*, p. 73.

when held near the eye, he proposes to find an explanation for this unusual fact. He first proposes the Cartesian account of why luminous bodies appear larger at a distance as an hypothesis;[4] but because of disanalogies between such cases and the instance of spiders' webs he abandons the account and refers the phenomenon instead to "that incurvation of the rays passing by the edge of any body, which Sir Isaac Newton has proved." At the time he wrote this passage Edwards had probably not yet studied Newton's *Optics*, but had picked up the idea of the "incurvation" of light from his reading of William Whiston or William Derham in connection with his study of astronomy. When he turned to Newton's work soon afterward optics became a central area of his scientific interests, and his reflections upon the theory of light led to a more general conception of the nature of the physical world.

Throughout his discussions of optics Edwards supposes that light consists of small particles of matter, which are emitted at great speeds from luminescent bodies, and are acted upon by other bodies to cause the phenomena of reflection, refraction, and diffraction. To this extent, his conception is like that outlined by Newton in Query 29 in the third book of his *Optics*.[5] In earlier articles, however, his view does not conform to Newton's in specific points, but suggests the prior influence of Cartesian optics. In "Of the Rainbow" Edwards bids the reader to study Newton's account of the reflection and refraction of light, but his own explanation of these phenomena involve the conceptions of "perfectly reflexive" and "imperfectly reflexive" bodies that are foreign to Newton. His illustrations of these notions are reminiscent of the analogies in Descartes' *Dioptrics* of a ball's rebounding from a surface to explain reflection, and its breaking through the surface to explain refraction.[6] Although Descartes rejects the particulate theory of light, he, and Edwards after him, assumes the phenomena follow from the actual impingement of light upon physical surfaces according to the laws of collision; but Newton explicitly rejects this conception and offers a demonstration to the contrary.[7]

4. See René Descartes, *Dioptrics*, Discourse 6. Descartes published *Dioptrics* with his *Discourse on Method* (Paris, 1637). For a recent English translation, see *Descartes: Discourse on Method, Optics, Geometry, and Meteorology,* trans. Paul J. Olscamp (Indianapolis, 1965). JE might have gathered the explanation from Descartes' work, or from Whiston's *Astronomical Lectures,* p. 24.

5. In the 1706 edition JE would have used, this Query was no. 21.

6. *Dioptrics,* Discourses 2 and 3.

7. *Optics,* Bk. II, pt. 3, prop. 8: "The cause of reflection is not the impinging of Light on the solid or impervious parts of Bodies, as is commonly believed."

When Edwards wrote "Of the Rainbow" he apparently had read little more than the beginning sentences of Newton's account of the bow, and studied the diagram which shows how sunlight is reflected from the interior concave surfaces of the raindrops. His own diagram represents the reflections according to his own theory, and imitates Newton's in this respect. But he failed to note the refractions of the rays within the drops, or to understand their importance in determining both the shape of the bow and the arrangement of its colors. At the end of the essay Edwards raises the question of the colors of the rainbow, which he remarks has been "almost answered already," apparently by the hypothesis of reflections he had already given. But he stops short of giving his explanation, and only after several years, in "Natural Philosophy," US No. 2, he notes that the separation of rays into their several colors is the result of refraction within the drops, not reflection from their concave surfaces.

"Of the Rainbow" indicates that Edwards did not read Newton's *Optics* systematically, and that his own theory of light was largely fashioned from ideas gleaned from other sources. He did, however, study the Queries at the end of Newton's work with particular care, and from them he derived the idea of gravity as force by which every body is attracted to every other body. In "Natural Philosophy," SS No. 1, Edwards writes, "To observe that incurvation, refraction, and reflections from concave surfaces of drops of water, etc., is from gravity," probably taking the suggestion from the context of Newton's discussion in the Queries of the role of attractive and repulsive forces in explaining optical phenomena. Edwards follows with SS Nos. 18 and 19, suggesting how the emission of light can be explained by the gravitation of particles of matter. In LS No. 46 he argues that as refraction is caused by the attraction of the rays, and since rays of different colors are differently refrangible, the differently colored rays must have different densities. Differences in density are then explained by differences in the speeds or degrees of vivacity with which the rays proceed. In US No. 23 Edwards explains the selective reflection by which a body appears colored from the same principles.

Despite major differences between Edwards' conception of light and the views of Descartes, Huygens, and Newton, he shares with them the assumption that light is comprised of the same homogeneous matter as gross physical bodies; as he holds a corpuscularean theory, he argues that it differs from other bodies only in the size and speed of the particles of which it is composed. Otherwise, it conforms to the same universal laws of nature as all other material things. In a corollary to LS No.46 he reasons: "Because there is such a difference in the density of rays of light, it appears that the atoms of which the rays of light are compounded are immensely less than the rays themselves." In the earlier fragment, "Of Light Rays," he attempts a calculation of the size of the particles of light that are emitted from a fixed star. As many as there are at the surface of the star "within the space that the least mote [fills]," they still will not fill that space, for they cross each others' paths freely and without mutual obstruction. The rays themselves, he concludes, and the bodies that compose them, must be incalculably small, and the human eye must be exquisitely sensitive to be stimulated by so narrow and rarefied a stream of rays as it receives from the star.

In all these discussions, and in his treatment of other topics, Edwards' chief interest is in developing a reasonable explanation for the phenomena in question, based upon a general theory concerning the fundamental nature of matter and the operation of physical causes. His account of various optical phenomena begins, not with experimental inquiry, but with a conception of the nature of light itself and of the causes of its refraction and reflection. He does not hesitate to introduce apparently arbitrary hypotheses and assumptions into his explanations, provided they conform to the basic theory. In "Of Light Rays" he supposes that 10,000 light rays are received by the eye in a sixtieth of a second of time, without pausing to explain or defend this figure. In US No. 4 he supposes a great abyss of water lying under the earth's crust, and that this water is denser and heavier than that on the surface. In several articles he argues from experience: his account of the growth and propagation of plants arises in part from observations that the seedlings of every species are similar and regular in their arrangements of leaves, buds, etc. (LS No. 48); and he rebuts a theory of the cause of the freezing of water on the ground that it implies that ice has a greater density than water, whereas in fact it floats on water (US No. 12). But even here Edwards does not contrive further experiments or make detailed observations to establish the facts pertaining to his subject. In most instances, the experimentally discovered phenomena to which he refers were gleaned from his reading of Whiston, Derham, and above all, Newton's *Optics*.

The theory of nature upon which Edwards depends in most of his scientific demonstrations is the theory of atomism. All bodies are composed of indivisible, solid particles of a homogeneous matter; they have various sizes and shapes, and various positions and motions in the void of empty space; and they combine and separate, collide and rebound, and otherwise interact according to fixed universal laws. The gross bodies of the world, their properties, and all the observable phenomena in the physical universe are thus determined by the precise character of this system of atoms. Edwards introduces this conception of nature in the earliest pages of "Natural Philosophy," demonstrating its principal ideas by a purely a priori argument drawn largely from the writings of the seventeenth-century Platonist Henry More. Although Edwards' basic physical theory is thus similar to that of such mid-seventeenth-century "Epicurean" mechanists as Gassendi and Charleton, it differs fundamentally from theirs by the introduction of the concept of gravitation.

Upon reading Newton, especially the Queries at the end of the *Optics*, Edwards took up the idea of universal gravitational attraction with enthusiasm, applying it wherever he could in cosmology, physics, and optics. In LS No. 14 he proposed to show "how the motion, rest and direction of the least atom has an influence on the motion, rest and direction of every body in the universe." After applying Newton's law in LS No. 20 to prove that two atoms touching by surfaces must gravitate to each other with an infinite force, he asserts in LS No. 22 that "in some sense, the essence of bodies is gravity." It is therefore folly to seek a mechanical cause of gravity; it is "no way diverse from a principle by which matter acts on matter."

In all these articles Edwards uses the terms "gravity" and "attraction" as equivalent, generally understanding by them any force by which bodies tend toward each other.[8] Like Newton, he regards gravity as universal in nature, and so his conception is very far from that of earlier physicists, who supposed gravity to be a tendency of bodies toward the center of the earth, or a property of only one kind of matter, viz., earth. But Newton hesitated to speculate about the cause of gravity, at least in his published works, and did not rule out the possibility that the forces in nature may have mechanical causes.[9] In letters to Richard Bentley he earnestly denies having ever asserted that gravity is essential to bodies.[1]

The argument of LS No. 20, upon which Edwards' position depends,

8. In *Principia*, Bk. I, prop. 69, Scholium, Newton writes, "I here use the word 'attraction' in general for any endeavor whatever, made by bodies to approach each other."

9. In the famous statement in his General Scholium to the *Principia*, Newton writes, "I have not been able to discover the cause of those properties of gravity from phenomena, and I frame no hypotheses."

1. *Four Letters from Sir Isaac Newton to Doctor Bentley* (London, 1756), Letter II, p. 20; Letter III, p. 25.

gives a good indication of the extent to which he comprehended the specific points of Newton's mathematical formulation and application of the laws of force. He supposes two atoms, equal in size and shape and touching along a common surface, are each divided *ad infinitum* in the same manner into parts in a continued proportion. Each part of one of the atoms, he argues, will attract a corresponding and equal part of the other. By applying Newton's law of gravitational force to these pairs of corresponding parts, he calculates that the members of every such pair will attract each other with the same finite quantity of gravitational force. But since there are an infinite number of these pairs of corresponding parts, he concludes, the whole force with which the two atoms attract each other must be a finite force taken an infinite number of times, or an infinite force. Not only does Edwards err in calculating the force attracting the parts of each of the pairs in the case he describes (the quantity will not be the same for every pair of parts); he also mistakenly assumes that the attraction between two bodies taken as wholes is simply the sum of the attractions of each part of the one to some corresponding part of the other. Among other things, this assumption neglects to take into account the fact that any part of a body is attracted to the other parts of the same body (or atom).[2]

For physicists and philosophers of the late seventeenth and early eighteenth centuries, there were serious conceptual difficulties in the supposition that gravity is an original or essential property of bodies. Edwards himself, in US No. 31, acknowledges that the point is not intuitively evident, for we can conceive a body without conceiving its attracting any other. Nevertheless, he still takes his former arguments to be sufficient for the claim. But the major problem with the doctrine lay in its implication that bodies as such may act upon and affect each other at a distance, even through empty space. This thesis was directly contrary to the mechanistic theory of motion, which, it was held, could only be produced or altered in a body by its actual contact with some other external body. Edwards would not have been moved by this reasoning, for even by the time he read Newton on gravity, he had adopted a very different metaphysical position concerning matter and motion. In essence, his position required that the mechanistic theory be taken merely as the form or manner in which the system of nature operates; it does

2. *Principia*, Bk. I, prop. 88. Newton demonstrates that the attraction of all the parts of a body of whatever size or shape for another external body, is equal to the attraction of a globe of similar and equal matter having its center at the common center of gravity of the parts.

not express the real causes by which natural events occur. Hence, in LS No. 61 he remarks that action at a distance in space has no greater difficulties than action at a distance in time, as when each successive position of a moving body is determined by its position at the preceding but no longer existent moment. Thus Edwards' physical theory, however contrary to the prevailing views concerning the status of attractive forces, was anchored in this respect in more basic metaphysical doctrines.

In its basic conception, Edwards' theory of the nature of the physical world belongs decidedly to the modern rather than the medieval age. Throughout his scientific writings, his masters were Descartes, Gassendi, Boyle, and Newton, though in most cases he knew their contributions through secondary sources. For all his failures to grasp the full ramifications of their theories, to master the necessary mathematical tools for modern physics, and to submit his various hyphotheses to experimental tests in the manner demanded by Baconian science, he nevertheless adopted with a whole heart their conception of a scientific explanation of the phenomena of nature. Although he undoubtedly studied scholastic science to some extent during his undergraduate years, his writings show little or no traces of it. He never appeals to the virtues, qualities, or entelechies of natural bodies in his explanations, nor distinguishes between natural and violent motions, nor even adopts the divisions of things into various natural kinds in the manner of the scholastic textbooks.

In matters of specific information as well, Edwards drew heavily and almost exclusively from modern sources. Even some of the more obscure proposals in the earlier parts of "Natural Philosophy" may be traced to his reading in the various books we have mentioned. There are, indeed, some exceptions, but they have a dubious value in proving him a scholastic. In LS Nos. 32 and 56 (§12) Edwards comments upon the physical basis for judicial astrology, a science that was generally treated with scorn by mechanical philosophers of the early eighteenth century, and, indeed, by Cotton Mather himself.[3] Nevertheless, the physician Richard Mead published a paper in the Royal Society's *Miscellanea Curiosa* in 1708, in which he argued that celestial motions might have medical effects upon the bodies of terrestrial animals.[4]

---

3. *Christian Philosopher*, p. 24.

4. "A Discourse concerning the Action of the Sun and Moon on Animal Bodies, and the Influence this may have in many Diseases," *Miscellanea Curiosa* (3 vols., London, 1708) *1*, pp. 371–401.

A more perplexing instance appears in US No. 4, where Edwards claims that "the water of the sea at a very great depth is found not to be salt." This opinion was attacked by Robert Boyle in a minor tract that Edwards had probably never seen.[5] Boyle attributes the opinion to Julius Scaliger, a sixteenth-century humanist whose work on physics had been used as a textbook at Harvard earlier in the seventeenth century. But probably the oddest of all the remarks Edwards offers concerning the phenomena in nature is that near the end of "Of Insects," that flying insects are "little collections" of "the corrupting nauseousness of our air." Providence has so fashioned them, he tells us, and has suitably arranged for their destruction in the sea at each summer's end.

This passage in "Of Insects," which is devoted to the providential "use" or end of spiders is in some respects typical of Edwards, as it was of many scientists and scientific writers of the early eighteenth century. Similar passages are, indeed, relatively infrequent through most of his writings. He gave much more attention to this aspect of the investigation of nature at a relatively late time, near the end of his tutorship and during the first years of his Northampton pastorate. It was then that he began his series, "Wisdom in the Contrivance of the World"; and Edwards abandoned this series after only seven entries. In his earlier papers his specifically teleological improvements, where they appear, are not offered as causal explanations of the phenomena in question. In "Of Light Rays," for example, he turns to admire God's handiwork in fashioning the rays and contriving the eye only after attempting to calculate how subtle the rays are that we can see.

This manner of treating final causes is, in fact, quite within the spirit of many of the theistic scientists of the time, especially in England. Robert Boyle, for example, writes, "I see not why the admitting that the Author of Things design'd some of his Works for these or those Uses, amongst others, may not consist with the Physical Accounts of making thr·e things."[6] At the end of his *Optics* Newton observes, "So far as we ca·. know by natural Philosophy what is the first cause, what Power he h·s over us, and what Benefits we receive from him, so far our Duty towards him, as well as that towards one another, will appear to us by the Natural Light."[7] When in LS No. 8 and again in US No. 40 Edwards remarks the use of comets, he is probably only offering an im-

5. "Observations and Experiments about the Saltness of the Sea," in *Works*, ed. T. Birch (6 vols., London, 1772) *3*, p. 765.
6. *A Disquisition about the Final Causes of Natural Things* (London, 1688), pp. 22–23.
7. *Optics*, Query 31 (1706 ed.: Q. 23, p. 348).

provement on the theory Newton offered in his *Principia*,[8] which Henry Pemberton repeated in his *A View of Sir Isaac Newton's Philosophy*.[9] Edwards read Pemberton's work in Northampton.

Edwards' thoughts were much more given to reflection upon the power and wisdom of God in contriving the whole system of nature, than to searching out the special benefits brought by particular things in it. "Natural Philosophy" contains a series of articles on this theme, beginning with LS No. 14, where Edwards notes "the great wisdom that is necessary in order thus to dispose every atom at first, as that they should go for the best throughout all eternity; and in the adjusting by an exact computation, and a nice allowance to be made for the miracles which should be needful." Each of the succeeding passages on the theme, like this one, takes its departure from the conception of nature as a system of atoms which is exactly determined by universal laws. In them Edwards celebrates, not only the regularity and beauty of the world, but the manner in which the succession of events has unfolded from the first creation, and will continue to unfold to the end of the world, according to an original plan of providence. Hence, in the original creation of the chaoses of atoms, God so ordered that, "without doing any more, the chaoses of themselves, according to the established laws of matter, were brought into those various and excellent forms adapted to every of God's ends—omitting the more excellent works of plants and animals, which it was proper and fit God should have a more immediate hand in" (US No. 6).

These passages are not merely theological "improvements" upon the scientific conception of nature, in the manner of Cotton Mather's *The Christian Philosopher*. Nor are they expressions of occasional and tangential spasms of religious piety. Edwards rather views the whole course of natural causes, as the scientist investigates them, in a theological setting. His own inquiries set out from the metaphysical position articulated in "Of Atoms": "Hence we see what's that we call the laws of nature in bodies, to wit, the stated methods of God's acting with respect to bodies, and the stated conditions of the manner of his acting" (Prop. II, Corol. 15). Mather undertook to show that "Philosophy is no Enemy, but a mighty and wondrous Incentive to Religion."

8. Bk. III, prop. 41, ex. (in 1713 ed., p. 472): "For the conservation of the seas, and fluids of the planets, comets seem to be required, that, from their exhalations and vapors condensed, the wastes of the planetary fluids spent upon vegetation and putrefaction, and converted into dry earth, may continually be supplied and made up."

9. Pemberton discusses the use of comets in Bk. II, chap. 4, §19.

This view was shared by many scientists of the early eighteenth century,[1] and was publicized in such works as John Ray's *The Wisdom of God Manifested in the Works of Creation,* Whiston's *Astronomical Principles of Religion, Natural and Revealed,* and Derham's *Astro-theology* and *Physico-theology.* Edwards not only endorsed, but went beyond it: in a treatise he planned to entitle "A Rational Account of the Main Doctrines of the Christian Religion Attempted," he would argue that "all the arts and sciences, the more they are perfected, the more they issue in divinity, coincide with it, and appear to be as parts of it." It would probably not be far wrong to suggest that Edwards held to this point of view throughout his scientific inquiries.

But one must be wary of leaping to the conclusion that Edwards' scientific efforts were prejudiced by the doctrines of his Calvinist theology. They certainly were not thereby biased in favor of the scholasticism that still held sway through most of New England. He had no anxiety of the sort that Samuel Johnson mentions, that "the new philosophy would bring in a new divinity and corrupt the pure religion of the country." Nor was Edwards insensitive to the presence of prejudice around him. In "Of the Prejudices of Imagination" he asserts the claims of reason against that habit of thinking that "makes the vulgar so roar out" upon hearing the discoveries of science. "Old men," he observed in his "Diary," "seldom have the advantage of new discoveries, because they are beside the way of thinking to which they have been so long used. *Resolved,* if I ever live to years, that I will be impartial to hear the reasons of all pretended discoveries, and receive them if rational, how long soever I have been used to another way of thinking."[2] Since Edwards pursued science primarily in order to discover "the stated methods of God's acting with respect to bodies," or the laws of nature, he can hardly have made such a resolution naively or casually.

The treatise that Edwards planned to write upon natural philosophy promised to give great weight to his metaphysical doctrines, and it was these that he expected would receive the strongest objections. In a note on the cover of his manuscript of "Natural Philosophy," he advised himself to propose them as modestly as possible by way of questions, and to conceal his real conviction concerning them. In his most developed plan for the treatise he proposed to employ many axioms

1. Richard Westfall treats the subject in detail in *Science and Religion in Seventeenth-Century England* (New Haven, 1958).
2. "Diary" for Monday, Sept. 23, 1723, in Dwight, *1,* p. 94.

to "prepare the way" for his exposition, beginning with the clearest and most general, and adding others as desired at the beginning of each part. The axioms in US No. 8 might well have been intended for the start of the treatise, and his use of axioms in the article on ice, US No. 12, probably illustrates the manner in which he intended to employ them in the several parts of the work. Otherwise, according to his memoranda, he planned to add confirming corollaries after his various propositions, such as we find in many articles in "Natural Philosophy."

The whole treatise, therefore, was probably planned to be organized in the manner of a deductive system, beginning with the most general and fundamental aspects of physical theory, and descending from these to more specific problems. This is, as we have seen, much the way in which Edwards' reasoning proceeds in "Natural Philosophy." He warns himself several times in his memoranda, however, to avoid making undue pretenses to certainty, or including disputable claims, in the course of his reasoning. For the most part, Edwards seems to have developed his conception of the plan of the treatise from the various rules and examples given in Pt. IV of Arnauld's *The Art of Thinking,* though he takes suggestions from other sources as well: he refers specifically to Richard Steele's *The Ladies Library* and Shaftesbury's *Characteristicks.*

The contents of Edwards' treatise can be known only from the notes and articles in "Natural Philosophy" itself. Judging by these, it promised to give considerable space to general physics, beginning with Edwards' theory concerning the nature and reality of matter, and going on to treat gravity and such phenomena as light, heat and cold, cohesion, and elasticity that were to be explained by attractions among atoms. Both optics and astronomy would have been treated at length. Among terrestrial phenomena Edwards would have discussed the atmosphere and such meteors as clouds, the rainbow, lightning, halos and parahelia; the formation and causes of mountains, valleys, and plains, as well as the cycle of seasons on the earth; and the seas, rivers, springs and fountains, which would probably have been treated in connection with the subterranean abyss. In biology Edwards' manuscript contains discussions of the morphology, growth, and propagation of plants, and respiration and the circulation of blood in animals. He would probably have devoted a separate section to man, discussing the organs of perception, the nervous system and animal spirits, the brain, and the union of the soul and the body. In sum, it promised to be a complete system of natural philosophy. Whether Edwards abandoned the project out of timorousness, or loss of interest in it, or from a sense of inadequacy for the task, can hardly be guessed.

Assessments of Edwards as a scientist have varied, some rating him for what he did achieve in these papers, and others for what he would have achieved if he had not abandoned his projects. But it is probably less important to judge Edwards as a scientist, than to find in his papers the manifestation of some significant but as yet unstudied aspects of the reception of the new science in Calvinist and scholastic New England. Thomas Brattle and others were content to contribute the shillings and guineas of their discoveries to the coffers of the learned; Benjamin Franklin worked with his hands as well as his mind to satisfy his curiosity about nature and to draw the worldly profit of his knowledge; Cotton Mather found the discoveries of others "a mighty and wondrous incentive to Religion," and pitched himself against the theistic fatalism of his fellow townsmen in promoting inoculation against smallpox. Edwards was governed by motives of a different character, to undertake a different and more ambitious project: the construction of a complete system of natural philosophy, one which he feared, even from the start, to publish, and which he finally abandoned after several years of work in preparing the considerable body of materials that are presented below.

3. *The Development of Edwards' Philosophical Thought*

Although both "Natural Philosophy" and "The Mind" are connected with Edwards' early efforts to compose major philosophical treatises, neither of these notebooks presents the substance of those treatises in an organized and systematic manner. The contents of the manuscript notebooks, as we know them, were produced by the occasional additions of comments and articles over extended periods of time. They are more properly to be regarded as philosophical journals which show the progress of his thought as he worked forward on his projects, than as even partial drafts of the works as he planned them. Many doubts remain concerning the final form in which he intended to set forth his principles and conclusions in those treatises; but the more accurate dating of the manuscript notebooks and their contents now makes it possible to study the development of his philosophical thought as it is reflected in them. When the passages in "Natural Philosophy" and "The Mind," and other related articles in "Miscellanies," are examined in the order in which they were written, it is possible to discover how Edwards' most fundamental ideas first began to take definite form, and how through subsequent exploration and revision they came to function as fixed principles in his thought. The present chapter will be concerned primarily with this evolution.

From the chronological order and biographical circumstances of these writings, it is evident that they represent at least two major stages in the early development of Edwards' thought. The first is reflected in the beginning portions of "Natural Philosophy," especially in "Of Atoms," the opening part of "Of Being," and several entries in the long numbered series of "Things to be Considered and Written fully about." In this stage, while he was still a graduate student at Yale, he was particularly concerned about the challenge of metaphysical materialism, and about the nature of being in general and the grounds of its necessity. His early treatment of these topics will be examined in the first two sections below.

The idealistic phenomenalism of "The Mind" clearly belongs to the second major stage in the development of Edwards' thought. This stage is introduced by two important passages, both written in the latter part of 1723. One is the addition to "Of Being" in which he argues that nothing can exist without being perceived or known. The other, his first article in "The Mind," examines excellency, or "being's consent to being," as a necessary condition for the existence of any object. The third section of this chapter will examine the content and context of these two passages. The last two sections will then discuss Edwards' subsequent views concerning the physical world, its relation to mind, and the nature and status of mind itself, so far as his thought on these matters is reflected in "The Mind" and in certain related passages in other writings.

THE REFUTATION OF MATERIALISM

In No. 26 of the long series in "Natural Philosophy" Edwards reflects upon the arguments he had formulated in his earlier "Of Atoms." He reminds himself "to bring in an observation somewhere in a proper place, that instead of Hobbes' notion that God is matter, and that all substance is matter, that nothing that is matter can possibly be God, and that no matter is, in the most proper sense, matter."[3] Despite its appearance of expressing a mere afterthought, this remark brings into focus the main conclusions of his earliest philosophical arguments in

3. See below, p. 235.

"Of Atoms," "Of Being," and several earlier notes in the long series: contrary to the materialist claim that there is no substance except matter, Edwards finds God alone is substance while matter is the immediate effect of the exercise of God's infinite power. It follows that God himself cannot be material.

The contrasts between Edwards' early metaphysical conclusions and the claims of the materialists deserve careful study, not only because he himself often calls attention to them, but because he consciously undertook to develop a metaphysics that would be a conclusive answer to materialism. In later life he confessed that he had never read Hobbes,[4] and there is no evidence that he studied the work of any recognized materialist during the period of his collegiate and graduate study when these arguments were drafted. He learned about Hobbes through reading Hobbes' critics, especially Henry More and the theistic followers of Isaac Newton; and he developed his own arguments through reflection upon their rebuttals of materialism. Like them, he was an advocate of the sciences, their procedures, and their well-established conclusions. Also like them, he recognized the threat of materialism to orthodox Christian natural theology, and joined his efforts to theirs to establish by argument the reality and the spiritual nature of God, and to show how the finite world, even as understood in the sciences, depends upon God's infinite wisdom and the free and purposeful exercise of his infinite will for its creation and preservation.

The doctrine that all substance is matter was seen as a direct contradiction to these basic tenets of Christian natural theology. Hobbes' metaphysics was taken by his critics to imply either an outright atheism, or else the radically heterodox thesis that God is material. It denied the independent reality of any intelligent and voluntary spirits, and so, by implication, the independent reality of an omniscient, omnipotent, and beneficent being. Materialism proposed that the universe is a complete, autonomous, and self-sustaining system of unthinking bodies that are subject only to inherent, necessary, and mathematically exact laws of mechanical causation; and so it ruled out the conception of a divine and providential government of the world. And it held that all phenomena whatever are reducible to or explainable by the properties and motions of bodies alone, so that even the moral sciences are to be treated as a special branch of mechanics.

Threatening as the materialist metaphysics was to orthodox natural

---

4. In *Freedom of the Will*, Pt. IV, §6. See *Works* (Yale ed.) *1*, p. 374.

theology, Hobbes' opponents were by no means agreed how it was to be combated. Materialism had achieved a new plausibility in learned circles during the seventeenth century. The rejection of scholastic metaphysics and science, which was everywhere concurred with, had been stimulated in part by the rediscovery and study of the works of the ancient materialists, especially the atomists Lucretius and Epicurus. Even while Hobbes was under attack the works of Pierre Gassendi, the principal modern exponent of atomism, were widely and respectfully read.[5] In England Ralph Cudworth undertook to demonstrate that it was Moses himself who had originally formulated the doctrine of atomism;[6] and even in New England the "corpuscularean philosophy" was openly assented to by some members of the Mather circle.[7] In the meantime the competing Cartesian mechanistic physics was enjoying its greatest vogue throughout Europe. On all hands it was acknowledged that the physical sciences were concerned with the laws of matter and local motion, not with the union of matter and substantial form as the Schools had taught. And with this general agreement the concept of matter itself assumed a new importance in physical theory. Although its real nature and its relation to space and time were the subject of major controversies, matter was no longer considered to be the mere formless substratum, the principle of potentiality and passivity of scholastic theory, but was regarded as having a real essence of its own, and as being sufficient by itself to account for the actual existence and properties of bodies.[8] In addition it was generally conceded that bodies

5. Gassendi was the main figure in the seventeenth-century revival of Epicurus' mechanistic physics of atoms and void. Gassendi's most important work was *Syntagma Philosophiae Epicuri* (Lyons, 1649), which set forth a system of atomistic physics that was the chief competitor to the Cartesian physics in the later seventeenth century. His principal English disciple, Walter Charleton, made Gassendi's views well-known in that country through the publication of *Physiologia Epicuro-Gassendo-Charletoniana* in 1654.

6. In his *True Intellectual System of the Universe* (London, 1678), Cudworth argues that atomism was first propounded by one Mochus, a Phoenician physiologer spoken of by Jamblichus. Cudworth agrees enthusiastically with the conjecture of several others that "this Mochus was no other than the celebrated Moses of the Jews" (ch. 1, §10, p. 12). It is Cudworth's main contention that the original tradition of theistic atomism stemming from Mosaic times gave way in the classical period to two schools, each preserving a part of the ancient truth: atheistic atomism, as in Democritus, Leucippus, and Epicurus, and theism, as in Pythagoras, Socrates, and Plato.

7. Nathaniel Mather argued the thesis, "There is a vacuum" at his master's commencement in 1688, and after his death the same year, his brother Cotton Mather reported that he had demonstrated "his Intimate acquaintance with the *Corpuscularean* (and only right) Philosophy." See S. E. Morison, *The Intellectual Life of Colonial New England* (Ithaca, N.Y., 1960), pp. 268–69.

8. So Descartes contrasts his own conception of matter with that of the scholastics in his

sustain and transmit motion to each other by themselves, without the operation of immaterial causes, according to fixed mathematical and mechanical laws; and that the purely physical world can thus be conceived as an entirely autonomous, self-sustaining, and deterministic system. In view of these admissions it could hardly be denied that matter is fundamental to the physical world, that it is the ground of the objective existence of the bodies that compose that world, and that it is therefore a real substance in a proper and metaphysical sense.

Edwards himself, throughout his scientific writings, appears as an advocate of this new physics. He assumes that phenomena in nature are to be explained by the sizes, shapes, and motions of material particles, by the impulses and other forces that affect their motions, and the universal laws that govern them. He assumes a strictly deterministic universe in which every body affects every other according to those laws, and infers that God must have arranged the atoms with infinite care and wisdom in the first creation in order that all subsequent events, even miraculous ones, should follow according to the divine plan.[9] In view of all this, his denial at the same time that matter is a real substance would have struck most of his informed contemporaries as paradoxical. Edwards' own statement in LS No. 26, that "no matter is, in the most proper sense, matter," is a reflection of the paradox. The significance of his denial, and the background of ideas from which he developed it, can hardly be appreciated without further consideration of the efforts that were made during the later seventeenth century to refute Hobbes' doctrine and to defend the main doctrines of natural theology.

The threat of materialism was primarily felt by those who were ready to grant that matter is a real substance. They generally considered that Hobbes' doctrine was an unwarranted extension of this truth, for he claimed that matter is the only substance. Accordingly, the most widely accepted rebuttals of Hobbes were those that attempted to prove that there is some other substance that is incorporeal and autonomously capable of thinking, willing, and acting. The spiritual nature and perfections of God, as well as the spiritual and moral dignity of man, it seemed, could only be defended through some form of mind-body or spirit-matter dualism.

In the literature Edwards had studied, the arguments that attempted

---

early unpublished essay, "Le Monde" (1633). See in Ralph Eaton, ed., *Descartes: Selections* (New York, 1927), pp. 318–19.

9. See "Natural Philosophy," LS No. 14 (below, p. 231).

to establish or confirm such a dualism tended to exhibit one or the other of two general patterns. The first undertook to show that certain dicoverable phenomena or recognized facts about the world cannot be explained by matter and motion alone, but testify to the presence and operations of a spiritual substance. The Cartesian demonstration of mental substance from one's own conscious thinking was of this sort,[1] and so too were the arguments to confirm God's governing wisdom and power from the general appearances of a contingent order, design, and purposefulness in the world as a whole.[2] The second kind of arguments attempted to prove that, although matter is a substance, it cannot exist absolutely and by itself, but must depend upon an independent, immaterial, and self-subsisting being. Thus, from a theory of time according to which the existence of a temporally enduring substance at one moment is not sufficient for its existence at the next successive moment, Descartes argued that all bodies and all finite minds as well must depend upon God's timeless creative operation for their conservation or continual recreation at every successive moment while they endure.[3] And Henry More maintained that the existence of both minds and bodies depends upon an independent, immaterial, infinite, and necessary space.[4]

1. In *Meditation VI* Descartes argues, "Because, on the one side, I have a clear and distinct idea of myself inasmuch as I am only a thinking and unextended thing, and as, on the other, I possess a distinct idea of a body, inasmuch as it is only an extended and unthinking thing, it is certain that this I [that is to say, my soul by which I am what I am], is entirely and absolutely distinct from my body, and can exist without it." E. S. Haldane and G. R. T. Ross, eds., *Philosophical Works of Descartes* (2 vols., 1955), *1*, p. 190. Cited hereafter as *Philosophical Works*.

2. Henry More's *An Antidote against Atheisme* is devoted to proving the existence of God as an incorporeal being. Bk. II presents his arguments from the phenomena of nature. *Collection of Several Philosophical Writings*, pp. 37–85.

3. In *Meditation III* Descartes writes, "All the course of my life may be divided into an infinite number of parts, none of which is in any way dependent on the other; and thus from the fact that I was in existence a short time ago it does not follow that I must be in existence now, unless some cause at this instant, so to speak, produces me anew, that is to say, conserves me. . . . So far as my parents [from whom it appears I have sprung] are concerned, although all that I have ever been able to believe of them were true, that does not make it follow that it is they who conserve me, nor are they even the authors of my being in any sense, in so far as I am a thinking being." *Philosophical Works*, *1*, pp. 168, 170. In *Principles of Philosophy*, Pt. I, nos. 51–52 he holds that both body and soul are substances in the sense that "they are things which need only the concurrence of God in order to exist." Ibid., *1*, pp. 239–40.

4. In *Divine Dialogues* (2 vols., London, 1668), *1*, p. 106, More writes, "I have always been prone to think of this subtle Extension (which a man cannot dis-imagine but must needs be) to be a more obscure shadow or adumbration, or to be a more general and confused apprehension of the Divine Amplitude. For this will be necessarily, though all matter were annihilated out of the world. Nay indeed this is antecedent to all matter, forasmuch as no

As these examples suggest, the arguments of both sorts involved highly speculative and controversial assumptions about such questions pertaining to the foundations of physics as the essence of matter, the nature of physical causation, the ontological foundation of the laws of nature, and the status of space and time. Edwards was well aware of the importance of these assumptions as they pertained to physical theory and to metaphysics, and he knew and acknowledged those that were implicit in and essential to the developing tradition of rebuttals of materialism. He argued that the design of the world and the regular order of events in space and time cannot be attributed to the nature and operation of purely mechanical causes alone, but presuppose at least an intelligent and purposeful contrivance of the world machine in its original creation. Moreover, although his views on the nature and status of space, time, and the laws of physics changed as his thought developed, he argued from the outset that they are not absolutely grounded in the inherent nature of matter and motion, but are due to the presence and voluntary operations of an omnipotent being. The Newtonians whom Edwards read gave a special emphasis to this latter view. They directly associated the absolute space and time of Newton's theory with the divine Being;[5] and they argued that the principle of universal gravitation cannot be explained by merely mechanical causes, but is a contingent principle by which bodies are ordered in the world that can have arisen only from the voluntary dispensation of an intelligent and omnipotent creator.[6] Edwards echoes these claims in his early comments that "infinite wisdom must be exercised in order that gravity and motion be perfectly harmonious," and that "it is universally allowed that gravity depends immediately on the divine influence."[7]

But these arguments served only to show that the regularity of the world, the "manner of existence" of bodies, depends upon God, whereas

---

matter nor any being else can be conceived to be but in this. In this are all things necessarily apprehended *to live and move and have their being*."

5. In *Optics*, Query 28, Newton writes, ". . . does it not appear from phenomena that there is a Being incorporeal, living, intelligent, omnipresent, who in infinite space, as it were in his sensory, sees the things themselves intimately, and thoroughly perceives them, and comprehends them wholly by their immediate presence to himself."

6. Helene Metzger discusses the arguments of Samuel Clarke, George Cheyne, William Derham, Andrew Baxter, and Joseph Priestley, in *Attraction Universelle et Religion Naturelle chez quelques Commentateurs Anglais de Newton* (Paris, 1938).

7. "Natural Philosophy," LS Nos. 9, 23a. See below, pp. 230, 234–35.

the main point of Edwards' response to materialism is that the "very existence" of bodies depends immediately upon the divine Being, that bodies do not exist by themselves as substances at all. In taking this position Edwards not only fashioned a rebuttal of materialism, but in doing so he undermined the assumptions of the metaphysical dualism of Descartes and the Newtonians as well. The possibility of his doing so arose from considering certain philosophical problems that were generated by dualism itself.

Despite the wide appeal of dualistic theories of metaphysics in the seventeenth century, it soon became apparent that such theories offered major theological and philosophical difficulties. First, not every dualistic metaphysics was satisfactory from a theological point of view. Despite its demonstrations of the existence of God and the immateriality of the soul, the Cartesian metaphysics so extended the scope of the mechanistic system of matter and motion as to explain all animal and the most overt human behavior by mechanistic principles alone; and it so limited the role of God's operations in nature as to rule out all possibility of recognizing divine providence in the world. In England, at least, the new philosophers had a decided preference for a metaphysics that endorsed manifestations of divine government in nature. John Ray pronounced Descartes a "mechanic theist,"[8] and Henry More dubbed the Cartesians "nullubists" for denying that spirit has any amplitude or location in space; they thereby challenge God's omnipresence and even imply God does not actually exist: "Sulking Atheists, on pretense of extolling the Nature of God above the capacity of being so much debased as to be present with anything that is extended, have thus stretched their wits to the utmost extent to lift the Deity quite out of the Universe."[9] Indeed, the Cartesian theory, resting as it did upon the conception that thought and extension are entirely distinct and independent essences, had the consequence of dividing the world into two independent and autonomous systems of things. More's own metaphysical views were largely motivated by a conviction that minds and bodies together belong to a single unified causal order, and that the divine Being is intimately and actually present in that order and continually governs it. His criticisms of both Hobbesian and Cartesian metaphysics, and his own constructive metaphysical views, exercised an important influence upon subsequent English thought.

8. In *Wisdom of God* (5th ed., London, 1709), pp. 43–48.
9. *Divine Dialogues, 1*, p. 137.

Because Edwards' earliest philosophical writings also show the direct influence of More, it is appropriate to devote some further space to More's position.

In More's view, the basic error of Cartesianism lay in the claim that extension is the essence of material substance, and that space and matter are identical. Because space necessarily exists, he argued, it follows that matter too exists necessarily and independent of God. Furthermore, it follows that spirits cannot act upon bodies, that there can be no final causes or divine government in the world, nor any independent power of will to produce good or evil.[1] On the contrary, More maintained, extension and amplitude are necessary for all actual existence, and actual presence in real space is a necessary condition for a causally unified system of things. Bodies and spirits alike, therefore, are extended, present to each other in space, and capable of motion from place to place. They differ in that minds are indivisible ("indiscerpible"), capable of penetrating bodies, and are self-active, capable of moving themselves and causing motion in other things; while bodies are divisible, impenetrable, and passive, capable only of receiving, sustaining, and mechanically transmitting motion.[2] The causal action by which spirits move bodies thus arises from the power of spirits themselves; but the exercise of that power requires the actual presence of a spirit in the place of the body.

More found evidence of such spiritual presence and action, not only in human and animal behavior, but in the apparitions and other psychic phenomena reported to him by others.[3] In addition to this, he argued that the purely mechanistic physics must fail even in its main objectives. A large number of the most regular phenomena in the physical world, for example, the revolutions of the planets, and the presence of weight, elasticity, cohesion, and magnetism in terrestrial bodies, cannot be accounted for mechanistically solely by the motions and transmissions of motion of particles of matter. They must result, he concluded, from the universal presence and regular operations of an immaterial spirit of nature or "hylarchic principle."[4] His inference

1. "Publisher to the Reader," ibid., summarizes many of More's main objections to the Cartesian metaphysics.

2. *Immortality of the Soul*, Bk. I, ch. 3, in *Collection*, pp. 21–22.

3. More devoted Bk. III of *Antidote against Atheisme* to such evidences. See *Collection*, pp. 86–142.

4. See *Divine Dialogues, 1*, pp. 31ff; in *Enchiridion Metaphysicum* (1671), chs. 9–23 are devoted each to a different proof of the existence and operation of an immaterial spirit from some regular phenomenon or property in bodies.

was a prototype of the argument Newtonians later used to infer God as the ground for the principle of universal gravitation. As for space itself, More held it to be real and entirely distinct from matter, omnipresent, penetrable, and immovable, a necessary and infinitely extended being: "This distant Space cannot but be something, and yet not corporeal, because neither impenetrable nor tangible; it must of necessity be a Substance Incorporeal necessarily and eternally existent of itself: which the clearer Idea of a Being absolutely perfect will more punctually inform us to be the Self-Subsisting God."[5]

More's criticisms of the Cartesian philosophy serve to exhibit some of the difficulties that were found in a dualistic metaphysics as such. To the extent that the basis of causation was laid in the essence of a substance, it seemed impossible to explain how substances with different essences, minds and bodies, could have any causal interaction or stand in any other real relation. And to the extent that causation was based upon an interaction between substances, as in More's incorporation of a spirit of nature as causal agent, the assumption of mechanical or mathematical regularity in nature was no longer warranted and the explanatory power of substantialist physics was considerably reduced.

In addition, seemingly unresolvable disputes over the real nature of minds and bodies gave rise to a considerable scepticism with respect to the essence of substance. The development of an empirical methodology in England led scientists away from the Cartesian view that the laws of physics should be derived from a clear concept of the essence of matter, or from any other metaphysical principles. For Newton, the discovery of the presence of gravitational force in all bodies came through an analysis of observed phenomena; it did not depend upon a knowledge of the essence of any substance, which in any case, Newton held, we do not have: "In bodies, we see only their outward figures and colors, we hear only the sounds, we touch their outward surfaces, we smell only the smells and taste the savors; but their inward substances are not to be known by our senses, or by any reflex act of our minds: much less, then, have we any idea of the substance of God. We know him only by his most wise and excellent contrivances of things, and final causes."[6] John Locke pressed the point even further, arguing that from the ideas derived from experience we can form no concept

5. *An Appendix to the Foregoing Antidote against Atheisme,* ch. 7, no. 6; see *Collection,* p. 165.
6. *Principia,* General Scholium (1713 ed., p. 483).

whatever of the substance or real essences of minds and bodies as they are in themselves. We have only a relative notion of substance as an unknown substratum or support of the qualities and powers of things; and neither reason nor experience can discover the real essences of things upon which their perceivable qualities and powers depend.[7]

Despite their scepticism with respect to the extent of our knowledge, Locke and Newton continued to think of matter as a substance. The perceivable properties of bodies cannot subsist by themselves, but must inhere in something else, a substratum or subject which supports them but is not in turn supported by anything else.[8] And the regular coexistence of certain distinct qualities and powers in every body must result from some fundamental property or essence common to them all, a property which does not in turn result from or depend upon any other property of bodies. Hence each body, they supposed, has a fixed ontological structure: it consists in a single subject, a real essence belonging to that subject, and the set of distinct qualities and powers that inhere in the subject and are caused by or depend upon the real essence. A complete knowledge of a body, one which included everything true of the body taken by itself and which showed the connections among the distinct facts, would represent it as having that structure. But our actual knowledge of bodies, as it is derived from experience and observation, extends only to the outer layer of this structure. Locke's and Newton's scepticism with respect to the substances of bodies was not so much directed to the question whether they have this assumed ontological structure at all, as to the question whether it is possible to have scientific knowledge of the inner layers of the structure.

So far from throwing suspicion upon the claims of metaphysical materialism, therefore, such scepticism with regard to our knowledge of substance could only serve to undermine the dualist's arguments against materialism. Locke himself rejected the Cartesian view that

7. *Essay*, Bk. II, ch. 23, nos. 3–4, 30.

8. Ibid., nos. 4, 5: "When we talk or think of any particular sort of corporeal substances, as horse, stone, etc., though the idea we have of either of them be but the complication or collection of those several simple ideas of sensible qualities, which we use to find united in the thing called horse or stone: yet, because we cannot conceive how they should subsist alone, nor in one another, we suppose them existing in and supported by some common subject; which support we denote by the name substance, though it be certain we have no clear or distinct idea of that thing we suppose a support.

"The same thing happens concerning the operations of the mind, viz., thinking, reasoning, fearing, etc., which we conclude not to subsist of themselves, nor apprehending how they can belong to body or be produced by it, we are apt to think these the actions of some other substance, which we call spirit."

thinking is the essence of mental substance, holding instead that it is only an operation of the mind.[9] And since we are as much in ignorance of the substance of mind as of the substance of bodies, it is impossible for us to prove or assert with certainty that matter itself cannot think.[1] George Berkeley summed up the matter both accurately and succinctly in a note in his *Philosophical Commentaries*: "Matter once allow'd. I defy any man to prove that God is not matter."[2] Berkeley's remedy for materialism was to argue that matter does not exist; Edwards' first and major step, on the other hand, was to argue that matter is not a substance.

The ancient problem underlying Edwards' argument in "Of Atoms" is whether matter is infinitely divisible, given that it is continuously extended and that continuous extension is infinitely divisible. Descartes held that extension is the essence of matter, and deduced its infinite divisibility from this.[3] Historically this consequence was seen to involve a paradox, for it implied that the smallest parts of bodies are infinitely small, that is, mere mathematical points which are altogether devoid of extension; but not even an infinite number of such unextended entities could comprise the real extension of a body. Henry More produced a similar argument against the Cartesian view in *The Immortality of the Soul*: what lacks extension altogether, as a mathematical point, is a nonentity, and real matter cannot be composed of nonentities.[4] More concluded that the smallest divisible parts of bodies must have some real extension, though these "indiscerpible" parts are so small that they could not have any less extension, or be actually divided into any lesser parts, and still be real.

Edwards had studied More's argument and depended upon it for some of the main points of his own. A solid body cannot be broken into infinitely small parts, or "in every part," without being annihilated.[5] But while More interprets the notion of solidity in terms of size, that is, the having a finite real extension, Edwards interprets it as the having a continuum of parts. A perfectly solid body is one that is "an absolutely full, a solid body, that has every part of space included within its

9. Ibid., ch. 1, no. 10.

1. Ibid., Bk. IV, ch. 3, no. 6.

2. "Notebook A," no. 626. See A. A. Luce, ed., *The Works of George Berkeley* (9 vols., London, 1948), *1*, p. 77.

3. *Principles of Philosophy*, Pt. II, no. 20. Descartes here demonstrates the falsity of atomism from the simple premise that extension is infinitely divisible.

4. *Collection*, p. 3.

5. "Of Atoms," Prop. 1; below, pp. 208–10.

surface solid or impenetrable." In such a body, all the parts are so conjoined that they touch other parts "by surfaces," and not only in "some particular points or lines of their surfaces."[6] And if two bodies should happen to come together so as to touch by surfaces, they become parts of one single body.[7] Any body whose parts are so conjoined is everywhere equally full and solid, Edwards argues, so that whatever its size or shape, if it could be divided into any of its parts, it could be divided into every part and so be annihilated. Again, because a body perseveres or continues to exist only so far as it resists being divided through its continuously extended parts, its being or essence must consist in such a resistance. Indeed, resistance to division and solidity are the same, and they are the same as body itself. All the real properties of bodies are modes of or dependent upon solidity; the extension of a body, as distinct from that of space, results from solidity; shape is a modification of the extension, and mobility is the communicability of solidity from one to another part of space.[8]

A body in fact perseveres and resists annihilation by any finite force or power, Edwards assumes. Its solidity must therefore consist in an infinite power of resistance to any division or separation through its continuously extended parts. Again, two solid bodies that happen to touch by surfaces so as to become continuous cannot be separated again by any finite power. But at the same time, the mere continuum of parts, their "touching by surfaces," cannot account for such a power, "for it is self-evident that barely two atoms being together, and that alone, is no power at all, much less an infinite power." The power by which the bodies persevere, or by which their solid parts cohere together and resist separation, must be the infinite power of God.[9]

In drawing this last conclusion Edwards evidently follows More's view that matter is completely passive, in itself entirely indifferent to any state of motion or rest, and so by itself incapable of resisting a division into its real or extended parts. It was on this ground that More objected to the Cartesian explanation of cohesion among the particles in compound bodies, namely, that it is only the state in which the particles are at rest relative to each other. More found the solution sophistic, for it does not explain why such a state occurs and persists. The cohesion among particles or indivisible atoms—and in Edwards'

6. Below, pp. 212–13.
7. "Of Atoms," Prop. 2; below, p. 213.
8. Ibid., Prop. 1, corol. 4; below, pp. 211–12.
9. Ibid., Prop. 2, corols. 1–3; below, pp. 213–14.

argument, the cohesion even among the parts of a single atom—cannot arise from passive matter, but must depend upon the active power of an immaterial agent.

In developing his argument Edwards might also have considered Locke's explanation of solidity, the property among all others that Locke considered to be necessary to body.[1] Solidity, he held, is that whereby we conceive a body to fill space, that is, a resistance by which it keeps all other bodies out of the space it occupies so long as it remains there. This resistance, he maintained, is so great that no finite power can surmount it. Furthermore, solidity is that whereby the extension of body is distinguished from the extension of space, and that upon which the mutual impulse, resistance, and protrusion of bodies depends. Edwards goes beyond Locke in this point, however, in maintaining that solidity is the essence of body in a Cartesian sense; all the other real properties are dependent upon it.

It is through his analysis of the essence of body as resistance, and his claim that such resistance can only be accounted for by the power of God, that Edwards finally turns to the question of substance. First, he asserts: "Solidity results from the immediate exercise of God's power, causing there to be an indefinite resistance in that place where it is," and bodies are preserved in being by the constant exercise of God's power. Hence "all body is nothing but what immediately results from the exercise of divine power in such a manner."[2] But because solidity and body are the same, "it follows that the unknown substance, which philosophers used to think subsisted by itself, and stood underneath and kept up solidity and all other properties, which they used to say it was impossible for a man to have an idea of, is nothing at all distinct from solidity itself; or, if they must needs apply that word to something else that really and properly does subsist by itself and support all properties, they must apply it to the divine Being or power itself."[3]

Locke again is the most likely source of Edwards' reflection upon the unknown substance that supports the properties of bodies. Edwards infers that there is no such thing, or else that it be taken to mean God or his power. In either case, his argument seems to be that, because the essence of bodies immediately and continually depends upon the exercise of divine power, there is no other supporting substratum of the properties of bodies. The actual existence of a body involves no

1. *Essay*, Bk. II, ch. 4.
2. "Of Atoms," Prop. 2, corol. 9; below, p. 215.
3. Ibid., corol. 11; below, p. 215.

more than the divine power, the solidity or resistance that immediately
results from the exercise of that power, and the part of real space in
which the power is exercised. The account is remarkably similar to
one proposed as an hypothesis by Isaac Newton in an early unpublished
essay, *De Gravitatione et Equipondio Fluidorum,* in order to represent his
objections to Cartesian metaphysics.[4] Against Descartes, Newton holds
that real extension or space is neither a substance nor the attribute
of a substance, but an infinite, eternal, and immutable "emanent
effect of God." Parts of this space may thus be empty, neither being
nor containing a substance. As we, by our will, can move our bodies
into such empty spaces, so God, by his omnipotent will, can prevent
any body from entering a certain space, and so make that space impervious or impenetrable. Such a space would then manifest all the
properties of a body, even though no substance was there. If the impenetrability were transferred from place to place continuously according to certain laws, all the effects of a moving body would be consequent. "And so if all this world were constituted of this kind of being, it
would seem hardly any different."[5] In order to construct Edwards'
view of bodies, it appears sufficient to add to this of Newton's the
further proviso that any quantity of continuous extension that God so
makes impenetrable should remain the same and undivided throughout all changes or transferences of it.

It is especially important to note that the conception of body that
Newton here briefly proposes, and that Edwards claims to have established, diverges sharply from the traditional concept of substance as
assumed in materialist and dualist theories. The causal basis for solidity
or resistance, and the other properties of bodies that are consequent
upon it, is no longer taken to be the subject to which the resistance and
those properties belong as attributes. It is not God that is solid or
resists, even though solidity or resistance immediately depends upon
the exercise of his power, and does not arise from anything else. So
far as substance is understood to be the subject to which properties
belong and in which they are conjoined, Edwards asserts there is no
such subject apart from solidity itself. At a later point, in "The Mind,"
No. 27, after further reflection upon the concept of resistance itself,
Edwards found it necessary to change this view and to specify the

4. This essay has been published in A. Rupert Hall and Marie Boas Hall, ed. and trans.,
Unpublished Scientific Papers of Isaac Newton (Cambridge, 1962), in Latin, pp. 89–121, and in
English, pp. 121–156.

5. Ibid., pp. 131–140.

thing that can be said to resist. But even then he maintains, as he does at first in "Of Atoms," that the subject that resists does not contain the causal basis of its resisting; nor is that subject something that could exist by itself.[6]

Edwards' reasoning seems to be entirely cogent within the framework of certain generally accepted assumptions about substance and its essence, namely, that the essence of a substance is that upon which all its other properties depend but which in turn neither depends upon nor arises from any other property. The actual resistance of a body, he argues, is something that needs a causal explanation, and therefore cannot be the essence of a substance. Nevertheless, he holds, resistance is the essence of bodies: it depends upon no other property of bodies, but all the other real properties of bodies depend upon it. It follows, therefore, that bodies cannot be substances, and cannot exist by themselves, but must depend upon some other substance which causes their resistance.

Edwards describes this cause as God's infinite power, and resistance is the immediate effect of God's voluntarily exerting his power, or his "acting in that particular manner in those parts of space where he thinks fit." Resistance is not to be conceived as an extraneous product of such action as though something made by it, for it endures only so long as God's action continues. Resistance results immediately from God's acting rather as a performance results from the performing of it, for example, as the raising of an arm results from the act of raising it. It is in this way that Edwards understands God and his power to be the substance of bodies, and indeed to be *ens entium*, the substance of all things. His predecessors thought of substance as the owner of properties; while Edwards thought of substance as the doer of deeds. So he took God to stand to the physical world as its creator, sustainer, and governor; not as something he has made and continues to manage, but as something he has done, and is doing and will do, in a particular manner.

Such a conception of substance and of bodies in relation to substance makes the materialist's notion of mechanical causation among bodies untenable. Bodies and their motions are God's actions, and while those actions may be connected by fixed rules according to the will of the actor, the actions do not affect each other, for actions cannot themselves act. Edwards concludes his argument with just those points: the laws of

6. See below, pp. 95–96.

nature in bodies are "the stated methods of God's acting with respect
to bodies, and the stated conditions of the alteration of the manner of
his acting. . . . Hence there is no such thing as mechanism, if that
word is taken to be that whereby bodies act each upon other, purely
and properly by themselves."[7] He suggests a related point in his long
series, in connection with the argument in LS No. 20 to establish that
the essence of a body is the force of gravity among its parts.[8] Because
the very being of a body therefore depends upon gravity, gravity itself
cannot arise from a mechanical cause as the materialists assert (LS
No. 22). Taken as a principle of order in the physical world, "it is
universally allowed that gravity depends immediately upon the divine
influence" (as in fact such Newtonian followers as Richard Bentley and
George Cheyne argued). Hence again, "we may infallibly conclude that
the very being, and the manner of being, and the whole of bodies depends immediately on the divine power" (LS No. 23a).[9]

Although "Of Atoms" is the earliest of Edwards' philosophical
writings, its main conclusions concerning the ontological status of
bodies and their immediate dependence upon God's power and will
remained fixed points in his metaphysical system. Even when he revised
his views concerning the nature of bodies and their relation to space,
his arguments expressly involved or presupposed these early established
claims. But on almost all occasions Edwards is careful, as he was at
first, to point out that his general metaphysical remarks about substance
and essence were intended to apply to bodies only; minds or spiritual
beings, he implied, should be considered differently. After pointing out
that instead of matter being the only substance it is truly nothing at
all "strictly and in itself considered," he goes on to speak of spirits by
way of contrast. They are "nearer in nature" to God, and so are more
properly beings, and more substantial than matter.[1] Edwards does not
seem to have attempted to form a more detailed theory of mind until
later, after his New York pastorate.

THE NECESSITY OF BEING

In "Of Atoms" Edwards addressed himself to the question of the nature and status of bodies. From the argument there he derived a concept
of God as a real being, the only substance properly so called, and the

7. "Of Atoms," Prop. 2, corol. 16; below, p. 216.
8. Below, pp. 232–33.
9. Below, pp. 234–35.
1. Below, p. 238.

substance of all other things. The absolute sovereignty of God in relation to the world was thereby asserted, and in a manner explained.
Within a short time after he set down that argument, Edwards went on
to another but related philosophical project, the proof of the absolute
and inherent necessity of God's existence. His first effort at a demonstration is found in the early part of the essay "Of Being" in "Natural
Philosophy." Subsequent restatements, refinements, and uses of the
argument followed for years afterward, in later additions to the same
essay, in "The Mind," and in his "Miscellanies." In all these places it
appears as a form of the so-called ontological argument for God's existence, but with differences that are immediately apparent.

The first and most important difference is that, whereas St. Anselm's
original formulation of the ontological argument, and most of the subsequent versions offered in the seventeenth century, turn upon the idea of
God as the most perfect or greatest conceivable being, Edward's argument attempts to demonstrate God from the conception of being per se,
or being in general, alone. Although he affirms the perfection of God in
many other places, this argument does not treat God with respect to
perfection.

In virtue of this difference, Edwards had no obvious need to deal
with one of the major questions raised by the argument in its standard
versions, namely, whether we have in fact an idea of the subject of the
argument. Doubts whether we have an idea of a most perfect conceivable being, and whether this idea is sufficiently adequate and clear for
purposes of the argument, were historically a major source of difficulties
for the ontological argument. But Edwards could hardly have found
occasion to doubt whether we have a conception of being. As a college
sophomore he learned that the idea of being is necessary to all thought
and reasoning. Logic textbooks in the Aristotelian tradition took up the
categories as the most general kinds of being. The account of the categories typically began with the distinction between substance, or what
exists by itself, and accidents, or what exists by inherence in some substance as its subject; the main Aristotelian categories of accidents—
quantity, quality, relation, and so on—were then explained in turn.
The familiar diagram of Porphyry's tree showed the distribution of substance into its several kinds and ranks. Being itself was discussed as a
transcendental concept, not assignable to any one category, but presupposed by all the categories in common.[2] In a note at the back of the

2. William Morris has argued that the Aristotelian logic of Franco Burgersdjck was an
important influence in JE's conception of being. See "The Genius of Jonathan Edwards,"

textbook he used while tutoring in logic at Yale, Edwards takes being to be the most abstract of our ideas.[3] And the central principle upon which Edwards' argument depends, in all his statements of it, pertains to the doctrine that all thought and reasoning are about what is. In short, Edwards might reasonably have claimed that none of the resources needed for his proof involved any inherent obscurity; they were all to be found in a standard logic manual.

In spite of this, Edwards himself found the argument extremely difficult to state coherently; he returned repeatedly to reformulate it and to explain its foundation. Some of the difficulties came from attempting to express the underlying logical principle without asserting an implicit contradiction; and some seem to have arisen from the effort to utilize a logical notion of being in general in order to explain the necessary being of God. The latter difficulties were closely related to traditional semantic problems in speaking or thinking about God. Edwards might well have noted that Charles Morton, in his manuscript manual of logic, discussed 'being' as a term which is not perfectly, but only analogically, univocal: "Analogicalls have the same name and nature (as univocals), but not Equally, and depending one of the other. So being: it is a Common name for Substance and Accident, but Substance hath more of being then Accident, and Accident would have no being but as depending on Substance. So God and Creature are both Said to be beings."[4] Moreover, Morton maintained, only finite things can be distributed under the categories or predicaments, "for infinite are excluded whether they be positive or negative: Positive, as God, who can have no Genus or common nature with any of his creatures; Negative (which may rather be called Indefinite y^n Infinite), as not a man, not a horse, etc. Now these words signifie nothing certain, and therefore can be referred to no certain order of things."[5] Such claims left open to serious question how far the being of God is amenable to logical consideration at all.

In Edwards' earliest form of his argument in "Of Being," the existence of a necessary, infinite, and eternal being is inferred directly from the fact that the concept of being has no contrary; "nothing" or a "state of absolute nothing" is inconceivable and utterly impossible. "It is the greatest contradiction, and the aggregate of all contradictions, to

---

in Jerald Brauer, ed., *Reinterpretation in American Church History* (Chicago, 1968), pp. 37–38.

3. Quoted below, p. 340, n. 2.

4. "Of Antepredicaments," *Compendium Logicae*, Pt. I, ch. 3. This quotation is from the copy in JE's textbooks (discussed above, pp. 14–15).

5. "Of Predicaments in General," ibid., ch. 4.

say that there should not be." Indeed, it is impossible to explain this point, he adds, for " 'nothing' is that whereby we distinctly shew other contradictions. But here we are run up to our first principle, and have no other to explain the nothingness or not being of nothing by."[6] Later, in "The Mind," No. 12, Edwards writes that it sometimes seems strange "that there should be being from all eternity." Nevertheless, "that necessity of there being something or nothing implies it."[7] But the logical problem remains in this statement: if "nothing" is the first principle by which contradictions are shown, we cannot explain how the expression 'there is nothing' is a contradiction. It is this point that leads Edwards to further discussion of the idea of nonbeing in later entries in "Miscellanies" and in his final additions to "Of Being."

In these passages he undertakes to make a distinction. We can indeed conceive of nothing, he allows, when we are thinking of particular things—for example, ourselves or the world—for "there is another way besides these things having existence." So nothing does have a being "when we speak of nothing in contradiction [to] some particular being." But taken in an absolute sense, 'nothing' does not express a logically possible alternative. Because there is therefore no alternative to being, considered absolutely, "the stating the question is nonsense, because we make a disjunction where there is none. 'Either being or absolute nothing' is no disjunction."[8] Hence, with regard to God's existence, "there is no second to make a disjunction; there is nothing else supposable."[9]

From this final form of the argument it is possible to gather a better idea of the logical background of Edwards' conception of the necessity of being, and consequently the necessity of God's existence. When a genus is distributed into its several species, the species may be seen as the several alternative ways for something to belong to the genus. Thus it is possible but not necessary that an animal be a man, because the other species of animals are alternative ways of being an animal. On the same grounds, it is possible but not necessary that there are no men; as Edwards comments in Miscell. No. 880, "What we do when we think of absolute nihility (if I may so speak) is only to remove one thing to make way for and suppose another."[1] In this way, all contingent possi-

---

6. Below, p. 202.
7. Below, p. 343.
8. "Of Being," below, p. 207.
9. Miscell. no. 587, in Townsend, p. 81.
1. Townsend, p. 87.

bilities are understood as applying only to what falls under a genus, where distinct alternatives are rationally conceivable. But being itself is the highest genus; it falls under no other genus and therefore it admits of no rationally conceivable alternative. Above all, "not-being" is not a genus correlative to being.

The conception of God as being in general implies that all reality is included in God, and Edwards himself makes this implication explicit in many places. In Miscell. No. 27a he writes, "We have shewn that absolute nothing is the essence of all contradictions, but being includes in it all, that we call God who is and there is none else besides him";[2] in "The Mind," No. 15, "we always find this, by running of it up, that God and real existence are the same";[3] in Miscell. No. 880, "God is the sum of all being and there is no being without his being."[4] A quite similar treatment of the necessity of God as being in general was given by the seventeenth-century Platonist Nicolas Malebranche in a brief passage in his *Recherche de la Verité*. Malebranche writes that God, or "Being without any limitation, Being infinite, and in general," is necessarily present to the mind, and even affects it more strongly than the presence of finite objects. The mind "cannot divest itself absolutely of this general Idea of Being; since 'tis impossible to subsist out of God. . . . The mind in considering any Being in particular, does not so much separate and recede from God, as approach near some of his Perfections, if I may be so permitted to speak, by removing farther off from others."[5] Both Malebranche and Edwards used the idea of the highest genus to express God's all-inclusive nature; both took this to mean not only that God is the sum of all particular existent things, but that his being includes the contingent possibility of particular things. Edwards also holds that God is not only a necessary being, but the ground of all other necessity: "A state of nothing is a state wherein every proposition in Euclid is not true, nor any of those self-evident maxims by which they are demonstrated; and all other eternal truths are neither true nor false."[6]

But there is a significant dissimilarity between Edwards' statements and the above quoted remarks of Malebranche. Malebranche, in speaking of the manner in which particular things are in God, explains that

2. Ibid., p. 74.
3. Below, p. 345.
4. Townsend, p. 87.
5. *Recherche*, Bk. III, Pt. 2, ch. 8. Quoted from Taylor, *Search after Truth*, p. 124.
6. "Of Being," below, p. 206.

the essences of particular things are a partial and limited presentation of God's unlimited perfections. Being in general, for Malebranche, is the necessary unity of all perfections, and each real thing included in it is some finite and limited set of perfections. In contrast, the language which Edwards uses in speaking of being in general and of God is singularly free of the term "perfection." As will be discussed later, Edwards significantly transforms the concept of reality as a system of beings hierarchically ordered according to their inherent perfections. The theory of excellency, through which Edwards finally comes to terms with the Platonic and Augustinian notion of perfection, differs from it in the fundamental respect that excellency is a relational concept: "One alone, without reference to any more, cannot be excellent."[7] Before that theory can be adequately treated, it is necessary to clarify what, in Edwards' view, is included in infinite and necessary being, and more specifically, in what manner the created world of bodies and spirits is included. These, in fact, were apparently among the questions Edwards put to himself after reaching his first conclusions, that bodies are only the solidity which immediately results from God's exertion of his power in certain parts of space, and that God himself is universal being.

Edwards' earliest answer to those questions is found in the passages in "Of Being" immediately following his opening demonstration of God's necessary existence; they seem to have been written on the same occasion. The attribute by which God is understood is omnipresence. "Absolute nothing" and "where" are contradictory terms, so that being is everywhere, and, by implication, every being is somewhere in space. Space, he continues, is itself necessary, for we can think of any other thing being or not being otherwise, but we cannot remove the idea of space from our thoughts or conceive it not to be. "I had as good speak plain," he concludes, "I have already said as much as that space is God."[8]

Both the argument and its conclusion are a clear reflection of Henry More's doctrines concerning space and God's omnipresence. The view fully agrees with the concept of God as immediately present to the bodies he causes and governs, and it explains how all things are included in the being of God, that is, by having spatial location. But the theory, taking it literally from Edwards' own words, involves equally serious

7. "The Mind," No. 1, below, p. 337.
8. Below, p. 203.

difficulties. More does not claim that space literally is God, but that the concept of space is a confused representation of God. Edwards himself warns against the "gross conceptions we have of space," but does not go on to explain. In any event, the idea of space itself having an infinite power, and of acting to bring about resistance in certain places as it wills, hardly agrees with any recognized concept of space.

Still, for More, actual presence in some part of space is a necessary condition for real existence; and the Newtonian physics posits a real, absolute space as the locus of bodies and the scene of their actual motions and interactions. The laws of motion and gravitation govern those actual motions, and not the relative motions of things as observed by finite perceivers from some fixed point of view. Like More, Newton is ready to ground the reality of this space in the divine Being. But for Newtonian theory, the problem of understanding real space is that of making intelligible the connection between it and the space which is relative to our observations of bodies and their properties and motions. One of Newton's efforts to explain an intelligible connection involves an analogy between real and relative space; as relative space is the presentation of an ordering of objects in the experience of a finite observer, so real space is the ordering of objects in the experience of an infinite observer, namely God. Space, Newton suggests, is God's sensorium: "Does it not appear from phenomena that there is a Being incorporeal, living, intelligent, omnipresent, who in infinite space, as it were in his sensory, sees the things themselves intimately, and thoroughly perceives them, and comprehends them wholly by their immediate presence to himself: of which things the images only carried through the organs of sense to our little sensoriums, are seen and beheld by that in us which perceives and thinks."[9] Both absolute and relative space, Newton suggests, involve the "point of view" and conditions of perceptual experience of observers. They differ in that relative space is the spatial ordering that finite observers perceive among mere images of objects, as these images are caused in their own bodies, located in particular places in real space; absolute space is the spatial ordering that an infinite observer perceives among the very objects themselves.

Edwards may well have pondered these suggestions of Newton during the year or two after he wrote the opening sections of "Of Being," for they seem to form the connecting link between his early declaration that space is God and the alternative thesis he set before himself in the

9. *Optics*, Query 28 (1706 ed.: Q. 20, p. 315).

summer of 1723, namely, that things exist only as they are actually perceived or known, either in the experiences of finite minds, or as they are known by God. During the ensuing years of his tutorship he explored this new conception of being, traced its consequences, and considered some of the main difficulties it presented. From that time forward the proposition that reality consists in knowing and being perceived or known formed a central doctrine of Edwards' metaphysics.

BEING KNOWN AND BEING LOVED: THE STRUCTURE OF BEING

Edwards' earliest statement of the doctrine that nothing can be without being known is found in his "Miscellanies," in the entry numbered pp, which he wrote in early 1723 near the end of his New York pastorate:

> We know there was being from all eternity; and this being must be intelligent. For how doth one's mind refuse to believe, that there should be being from all eternity, without its being conscious to itself that it was; that there should be being from all eternity and yet nothing know, all that while, that anything is. This is really a contradiction; we may see it to be so, though we know not how to express it. For in what respect has anything had a being when there is nothing conscious of its being? For in what respect has anything had a being, that angels, nor men, nor no created intelligence know nothing [of], but only as God knows it to be? Not at all more than there is sound where none hears it, or color where none sees it. Thus for instance, supposing a room where none is, none sees the things in the room, no created intelligence: the things in the room have no being any other way than only as God is conscious [of them]; for there is no color there, neither is there any sound, nor any shape, etc.[1]

A few months later Edwards restated the main points of his doctrine and began to elaborate his defense of it in an addition to the essay "Of Being."[2] It is impossible that anything should exist and nothing know it, he maintained, for "nothing has any existence anywhere else but in consciousness. No, certainly nowhere else, but either in created or uncreated consciousness." Things that are not perceived by created minds can exist only as God knows them. But neither is this simply an

1. Townsend, p. 74.
2. Below, pp. 203–06.

expression of the traditional doctrine of God's omniscience. "Let us suppose, for illustration, this impossibility, that all the spirits in the universe to be for a time deprived of their consciousness, and God's consciousness at the same time to be intermitted. I say the universe, for that time, would cease to be of itself; and not only, as we speak, because the Almighty could not attend to uphold the world, but because God knew nothing of it."

The introduction of the thesis that nothing whatever can be without being known, as Edwards asserts it in these passages, marks a major turning point in his thought. That his most complete exposition of the thesis should be written as an addition to his earlier essay on being in general shows that he considered it to be a fundamental metaphysical principle, one to which our understanding of all things must conform. So far forth, the thesis determined a major philosophical program. Our conception of God must incorporate the idea that he is necessarily conscious of himself; and our understanding of the created universe and its relation to the Creator must conform to the principle that the universe can exist only as it is perceived by finite and created minds, or as it is known by God. Many articles in "The Mind," and others in "Miscellanies," show the extent to which Edwards was occupied with this project during the subsequent years. He reconsidered and revised his earlier views concerning matter, space, and the general constitution of the physical world. He also made a critical examination of certain claims and assumptions concerning the nature of spirits and their relations to bodies, and explored the foundations for a general theory of mind. He failed to accomplish his project of producing a systematic treatise on the mind, but many of the fruits of his efforts found a prominent place in the doctrines and arguments of his other published works. In addition, these inquiries led Edwards to some of his boldest and most interesting, albeit less well-known, philosophical conclusions.

Before taking up the substance of these matters, some attention should be given to the question how Edwards originally came to assert his leading metaphysical principle that nothing can be without being known. It could not have emerged as a logical consequence of his earlier views, for Edwards himself recognized it is incompatible with them. Neither does it seem that he adopted it from the work of any other philosopher or theologian. Various efforts in the past to demonstrate the source of Edwards' idealism in some published work have failed to make a convincing case;[3] in most instances, there is no firm evidence that

3. Georges Lyon, in chapter 10 of *L'Idealisme en Angleterre au XVIIIe Siècle* (Paris, 1888),

Edwards had actually studied the works in question by the time he had formulated his idealist account of the world. In addition, the dissimilarities between Edwards' developed views and those of other early eighteenth-century idealists tell strongly against the hypothesis that he simply took over such a distinctive metaphysical doctrine from any of them.[4]

In fact, Edwards' assertion of idealism, that is, the thesis that physical objects exist only in the mind or cannot exist unless they are perceived, is not his primary claim, as an examination of Miscell. no. pp and the passage in "Of Being" clearly shows. In both places he introduces his idealism as a logical consequence of the much more general metaphysical principle that nothing whatever can be without being known. Edwards recognized, of course, that this consequence of the principle, more than any other, required some further and independent proof or vindication, and he undertook to provide such. But, as will be shown more fully below, the arguments he constructed for this purpose could hardly have been borrowed from the writings of another idealist, for they were shaped very specifically to deal with the peculiarities of his own earlier views concerning the existence of bodies. Above all, Edwards' arguments are not at all concerned with one question that was central to the other idealists of the time, namely, whether bodies are substances, capable of existing by themselves. He had already decided that question in the negative, and did not trouble to reconsider the matter.

How then did Edwards first come to assert that nothing at all can be without being known? The writings of his early New York pastorate, that is, the "Diary" and "Resolutions," and especially the articles in "Miscellanies" preceding no. pp, offer valuable clues. These writings give no evidence that he continued to think systematically about the abstract questions of the nature of being and the ontological status of bodies after leaving college. But they show that he was deeply concerned about the distinctive character and the value of religious life and faith

---

argued that Edwards must have received his idealism from Berkeley. This hypothesis was later disputed by, among others, Egbert Smyth in "Early Writings of JE," pp. 212–47 and H. N. Gardiner, "The Early Idealism of Jonathan Edwards," *Philosophical Review, 9* (1900), pp. 573–96. Clarence Gohdes has argued that the Platonist Theophilus Gale might have been a source of JE's idealism; see "Aspects of Idealism in Early New England," *Philosophical Review, 39* (1930), pp. 537–55. J. H. MacCracken, in *Jonathan Edwards Idealismus* (Halle, 1899), urges that the idealist Arthur Collier, through his *Clavis Universalis* (London, 1713), had a direct influence upon JE.

4. See further below, pp. 94–96, 102–03.

during this time, and his ideas concerning these matters took form in a manner that is very relevant to the claim that nothing can be without being known. Two points emerge from his discussions in "Miscellanies" that are especially important: first, he was convinced that the primary and essential element in religion consists in cognition—a unique consciousness and knowledge of God; second, he became convinced that religion, taken in this sense, is the very purpose of the entire creation.

The view that religious faith consists essentially in the knowledge of God was certainly not peculiar to Edwards, but his understanding of that proposition must have arisen in part from the intense character of the spiritual exercises and experiences that he recorded in his "Diary." In Miscell. no. aa he characterizes faith as a unique awareness of a certain ineffable property, divinity, which might be recognized or discovered through contemplating the idea of God. When this property is disclosed in the idea, he says, it certifies to the beholding mind that the idea is indeed from God.[5] Such an awareness of God requires that the mind be abstracted or turned away from the body and sensual pleasures, but it affords a spiritual happiness which is superior to any bodily good. In Miscell. no. f Edwards notes that, just as Hobbes had mistakenly supposed that matter and not spirit is the only substance, so it would be mistaken to assume that happiness consists only in sensuous pleasures and that there is no real spiritual happiness.[6] The contemplation of God is indeed the highest good for man, and is the end for which he was created.[7]

In Miscell. no. gg Edwards carries these reflections an important step further: the knowledge of God and the spiritual happiness it affords is the purpose of the entire universe. It is certain that the world has a purpose, he argues; but it would be entirely lacking in purpose if there were no intelligent beings:

> For senseless matter, in whatever excellent order it is placed, would be useless if there were no intelligent beings at all, neither God nor others; for what would it be good for? So certainly, senseless matter would be altogether useless, if there was no intelligent being but God, for God could neither receive good himself nor communicate good. What would this vast universe of matter, placed in such excellent order and governed by such excellent rules, be good for, if there was

5. See Townsend, pp. 244–45.
6. See ibid., p. 193.
7. Miscell. no. kk, in Townsend, p. 237; Miscell. no. tt, in ibid., pp. 126–28.

no intelligence that could know anything of it? Wherefore it necessarily follows that intelligent beings are the end of the creation, that
their end must be to behold and admire the doings of God, and to
magnify him for them, and to contemplate his glories in them.[8]

The universe could have no purpose unless it is known by intelligent
beings. This claim may readily be associated with the proposition Edwards asserted quite soon afterward in Miscell. no. pp, that the universe
could have no existence unless it is known by intelligent beings. The
connection is even more apparent when we recall that Edwards had
already denied the substantial and independent reality of the physical
world, and maintained that it depends immediately and necessarily for
its existence upon God's continual creative activity. These views provided a setting that was, at the least, very conducive to a new interpretation of existence. In fact, after he had formulated his new metaphysical principle Edwards occasionally expressed the connection
between his metaphysical and his teleological views of the world. In
Miscell. no. 87, for example, he writes, "Intelligent beings are created
to be the consciousness of the universe, that they may perceive what
God is and does. This can be nothing else but to perceive the excellency
of what he is and does."[9] And in Miscell. no. 247 he strikes the same
note: "For God to glorify himself is to discover himself in his works, or
to communicate himself in his works, which is all one. For we are to
remember that the world exists only mentally, so that the very being of
the world implies its being perceived or discovered."[1]

However important these teleological considerations might have
been in fostering Edwards' later metaphysical views, there is no sufficient reason for saying that he based his metaphysics upon teleology.
On the contrary, his defense of the central principle that nothing can
be without being known contains no direct or even covert references
to the purposes of the world. In both Miscell. no. pp and "Of Being"
he suggests that the principle is necessary and self-evident per se. That
there should be being from eternity but nothing know it, he says,
"is really a contradiction; we may see it to be so, though we know
not how to express it."[2] And again, it "grates upon the mind to think
that something should be from all eternity, and nothing all the while
be conscious of it"; it is not possible to "bring the mind to imagine"

8. Townsend, pp. 236–37.
9. Ibid., pp. 128–29.
1. Ibid., pp. 129–30.
2. Above, p. 75.

that anything should be and nothing know it.[3] It is taken as a necessary consequence of this principle that the physical universe cannot·exist without being perceived or known. But Edwards admits the need for an independent proof of the consequence, for our imagination leads us to think otherwise: "Our imagination makes us fancy we see shapes and colors and magnitudes though nobody is there to behold it."[4] In fact, his earlier conclusion that a body is an infinite resistance produced by God in some part of real space is entirely compatible with the assumption that bodies can exist without being perceived. But again, Edwards does not attempt to refute this assumption by appeal to the supposed purposes of bodies. He bases his argument entirely upon a new analysis of the necessary properties of bodies, especially of solidity or resistance.

Edwards' first formulation of his argument, which is found in "Of Being," is clearly defective; it does not yield the intended conclusion, and it depends upon an account of solidity which he promises to give in another place. Nevertheless, the underlying strategy can be elicited from his reasoning. Various considerations had led Newton, Locke, and other philosophers and scientists to conclude that colors are not really in the objects where they appear, but only in the minds that perceive them. Edwards intended to show that similar considerations apply in the case of solidity, so that it will follow that this property also, the very essence of body, is only in the perceiving mind. Thus he argues that, as color can neither be nor be perceived without light, so solidity or resistance can neither be nor be perceived without motion.[5] From these points by themselves, however, it does not follow that either light or resistance exists only in perceiving minds. Edwards' second formulation of his argument, in "The Mind," No. 27, is a much more plausible and important version of it.

Before taking up this argument in detail, however, it is necessary to examine yet another major development in Edwards' thought, one upon which that argument, and indeed the whole of his subsequent philosophical thought, depends. Shortly after writing the addition to "Of Being" that is discussed above, Edwards turned his attention to the examination of the concepts of excellency, harmony, and proportion which began to play a prominent role in his discussions of the relations of God to his creation and the ends for which he created it.

3. Below, p. 204.
4. Ibid.
5. Below, pp. 204–06.

Miscell. no. 64 indicates the direction his thought was taking. The article begins:

> Thus the matter is as to the Holy Spirit's gracious operations on the mind. We have shewn in philosophy that all natural operations are done immediately by God only in harmony and proportion. But there is this difference: those, being the high[est] kind of operations of all, are done in the most general proportion, not tied to any particular proportion, to this or that created being, but the proportion is with the whole series of acts and designs from eternity to eternity.[6]

This reflection, probably more than any other, led Edwards to see the need for a systematic treatment of the concepts of harmony and proportion as they apply to both physical and mental objects and events, and to the manner in which God acts in producing them. That perfection, goodness, and excellency consist in harmony or proportion, and that the greater excellency belongs to the higher or more general proportion, were for him unquestioned assumptions. Accordingly, when Edwards soon afterward addressed these questions, he did so in connection with an analysis and explanation of excellency. He began in Miscell. no. 78; but after writing a few lines he transferred the opening remarks to a separate paper and continued with the essay which was to become the first article in "The Mind."

The task Edwards set for himself in "The Mind," No. 1 is the definition of excellency and beauty, evil and deformity. He supposes from the start that the same concept—excellency—will account for both moral and aesthetic value, and indeed all value in general. His starting point is with what he takes to be a received view, that "all excellency is harmony, symmetry or proportion." Edwards never seriously questions this view; his concern is with the analysis and explanation of it: "We would know why proportion is more excellent than disproportion, that is, why proportion is pleasant to the mind, and disproportion is unpleasant."[7]

It should be noted that although in this statement of objectives Edwards suggests that excellency is to be considered the same thing as pleasantness, it is by no means clear that he was committed to this assumption. That there is a real and even a necessary connection between goodness and our desire and pleasure, is affirmed by the whole

6. From a transcription of the original, provided by Thomas Schafer.
7. Below, p. 332.

Platonic and Augustinian tradition into which Edwards was born. The *real* good, it holds, is necessarily the *proper* object of will and desire, wherefore the *apparent* good is the *actual* object of our wants and choices. And even though the possession of *apparent* goods can make us suffer, the actual possession of the *real* good necessarily satisfies and pleases us—it could never make us miserable. In Edwards' case, the basis for proceeding is the assumption that real beauty and real good are some one thing, either proportion and harmony, or some more fundamental nature that is essential to them. He further supposes that the explanation why this one thing *is* beauty and goodness will also show why it pleases and satisfies us.

He begins with the reflection that proportion is complex, and that it arises from and depends upon an equality of ratios. This provides the hypothesis that excellency consists in equality, that is, any equality that could enter into a ratio, such as equality of size, shape, or distance. He tests the hypothesis by various examples, and finds, in particular, that when an object is added to an existing composition, the beauty of the result depends upon the extent to which the new element conforms with and adds to the equalities already present. In general, he finds that the more complex the composition, and the more its parts and their arrangement exhibit equalities of relation, the greater is the complex beauty. He concludes, "This simple equality, without proportion, is the lowest kind of beauty, and may be called simple beauty. All other beauties and excellencies may be resolved into it."[8] Further investigation also shows that complex beauty is not merely a combination of simple beauties; in complex objects it is often necessary to "omit" some simple beauties in some parts, "for the sake of the harmony of the whole."[9] That equalities and proportions extending through the whole of a complex have a priority over those that are confined to limited parts, will become an important element in the general theory toward which Edwards is moving.

Having established these general points concerning beauty, equality, and proportion, Edwards turns to the introduction of his explanatory theory. He begins with a new statement of the conclusion so far reached: "All beauty," he writes, "consists in similarness, or identity of relation." Then, to clarify this claim, he adds, "In identity of relation consists *all likeness*, and *all identity between two* consists in identity of relation"(italics added).[1]

8. Below, p. 333.
9. Below, p. 334.
1. Ibid.

It seems evident that the notions of likeness and "identity between two" can only pertain to universals. Accordingly, the most straightforward way of interpreting the sentence is as a statement about universals: all universals, Edwards is plainly asserting—whatever can be common to different things—are relations. All the properties that things may have in common, whether essential or accidental, are constituted by relations which are identical in each, either relations among the constituent parts of each thing, or relations of each to others. But relations alone are universal, and two things can exemplify or partake in the same universal only by virtue of themselves or their constituent parts standing in the same relations.

Other statements in "The Mind," No. 1 make it clear that this is indeed what Edwards intends to affirm. Of bodies having the same shape, he writes, "The bodies are two, the relation between the parts of their extremities is the same, and this is their agreement with them." Even the similarity between two distinct sounds or other sensible qualities, in virtue of which they are pleasant, consists in the proportionate relations in the motions of our sense organs: "The organs are so contrived that upon the touch of such and such sensible particles there shall be a regular and harmonious motion of the animal spirits."[2] It seems evident that Edwards is prepared to account for all sameness of qualities and quantities by a sameness of relations; the Aristotelian distinctions between three different categories of accidents are collapsed into the single category of relations.[3]

But Edwards' view of the centrality of relations among objects extends even beyond this; he brings the Aristotelian category of substance itself under that of relations: "For being, if we examine narrowly, is nothing else but proportion. When one being is inconsistent with another being, then being is contradicted."[4] And again, "Disagreement or contrariety to being is evidently an approach to nothing, which is nothing else but disagreement or contrariety of being, and the greatest and only evil; and entity is the greatest and only good."[5]

2. Below, p. 336. See "Natural Philosophy," US No. 5 on JE's explanation of the pleasure and pain that come by the senses (below, p. 265). This entry was probably written shortly after "The Mind," No. 1. At a later time, in "The Mind," No. 42, he reconsiders this explanation of the agreement among simple sensible qualities, and proposes a very different one (see below, pp. 360–61).

3. John Locke had already gone far toward breaking down the distinction between qualities and relations by treating all so-called secondary qualities of objects as mere "powers to produce various sensations in us" (*Essay*, Bk. II, ch. 8, no. 14).

4. Below, p. 336.

5. Below, p. 335. Roland Delattre, in *Beauty and Sensibility in the Thought of Jonathan Edwards*

Earlier, in "Of Atoms," Edwards had rejected the notion of substance as an underlying support of the properties of bodies, and maintained that their being consists in solidity alone. As we shall find later, his reformulated argument concerning the status of bodies turns upon the consideration that solidity or resistance itself is not an "absolute" property of bodies taken singly and individually, but is a relational property, to be explained by the order and regularity of relations between two bodies or their constituents.[6]

In the context of "The Mind," No. 1, Edwards draws another important consequence from his principle that being itself consists in relations:

> One alone, without reference to any more, cannot be excellent; for in such a case there can be no manner of relation no way, and therefore no such thing as consent. Indeed, what we call one may be excellent, because of a consent of parts, or some consent of those in that being that are distinguished into a plurality some way or other. But in a being that is absolutely without any plurality there cannot be excellency, for there can be no such thing as consent or agreement.[7]

In a brief addition to Miscell. no. 117, which Edwards must have added soon after writing the above, he gives what may be regarded as a corollary to it: "We have shewn that one alone cannot be excellent, inasmuch as, in such a case, there can be no consent. Therefore, if God is excellent, there must be plurality in God; otherwise there can be no consent in him."[8] While this is not the place to discuss Edwards' account of the Trinity as such, it seems evident that his new concept of being, when applied to the divine perfections, stands in sharp contrast to the long tradition of philosophical theology into which he was born. God's goodness is not grounded in the absolute unity and simplicity of his being, but belongs to him only as he constitutes a plurality involving relations.[9]

(New Haven, 1968), has called attention to the central place of beauty in JE's conception of being. The analysis of the statements in "The Mind," No. 1 that is proposed here will be found to support and confirm Delattre's general claim, although it differs in emphasis and in some details from his account.

6. See below, pp. 95–96, for a discussion of "The Mind," No. 27.

7. Below, p. 337.

8. Townsend, p. 258.

9. See Delattre's discussion of beauty in relation to JE's conception of God, in *Beauty and Sensibility*, Pt. II, pp. 117–84.

If the above interpretation of Edwards' statements and their general import is correct, they present a very different view of the formal and intelligible structure of reality from any that had been developed by the major philosophers of the seventeenth century, and even by those of his own time. Edwards' account excludes, not only the concept of a material substance which he had already rejected, but the very notion of substance as it was entertained during this period. The claim that every real being *must*, as a condition of its reality, stand in some relation to other things, and even to all other things, implies that the universe is necessarily pluralistic. Nor does it admit that any one of this plurality of things is an ultimate substance, in the sense that it can exist by itself independently of all others, or that it can have any unity or self-identity apart from the relations in which it stands to others.

Whatever logical or ontological difficulties such a view might prove to involve, it should be noted that from a schematic point of view it is very well suited to avoid some of the most severe and widely debated philosophical problems arising from the concept of distinct and independent substances. A thorough examination and analysis of these problems and the controversies surrounding them would be much too extravagant an undertaking here. But a major source of the difficulties found in the theory of metaphysical dualism concerned the intelligibility, or even the logical possibility, of any real causal or other relations existing between two independent things with such entirely different essences as minds and bodies were conceived to be.[1] Indeed, it seems to have been widely assumed that unless two things have a similar nature or common properties, each in itself, they cannot be said to stand in any relation to each other whatever. But on the other hand, it seems also to have been widely assumed that unless things have a different nature and distinct properties, each in itself, they cannot be really distinct individuals or things. In contrast to this, Edwards' view implies that two things cannot exist unless they stand in some relation to each other, and two things cannot have a similar nature or common properties unless each is a plurality of items that stand in the same relations as those of the other. The logical force of this theory, as against the conception of independent substances with distinct essences, is reflected in a single cryptic comment in "The Mind," No. 1: "Two things can agree in nothing but relations,

1. See above, pp. 59–61.

because otherwise the notion of their twoness (duality) is destroyed."[2]

But this remark, as it stands, is more than a little puzzling. It seems to assert that we cannot conceive there to be two numerically distinct individuals when they agree in all their nonrelational properties, or have all such properties in common. But on the other hand, Edwards suggests, we *can* conceive two individuals to be numerically distinct when they agree in all their relations. At first sight it seems that if the former of these two claims is accepted, the latter should be denied. Certainly, it would appear, if numerical identity follows from the sameness of nonrelational properties, it follows from the sameness of relations as well. By extension of Leibniz' principle of the identity of indiscernibles, that "there cannot be two individual things in nature which differ only numerically,"[3] it could be argued against Edwards that we cannot conceive individuals to be numerically distinct unless we conceive some difference between them, either in their nonrelational properties or in their relations.

A few sentences before this controversial claim, however, and in the same general context, Edwards briefly explains how two bodies at a distance from each other are beautiful. He might well have had this particular case in mind when he suggested that things can agree in their relations and still be conceived to be numerically different. "All identity between two consists in identity of relation. Thus, when the distance between two is exactly equal, their distance is their relation one to another; the distance is the same, the bodies are two, wherefore this is their correspondency and beauty."[4] Because beauty consists in the identity or sameness of relations, Edwards emphasizes that in this case the relation of either body to the other is the *same* as the relation of the other to it; if one is just six feet from the other, the other is just six feet from it. In the case of this and all other symmetrical relations, no individual can stand in it to another unless the other stands in the same relation to it. But "is distant from," "is just six feet from," "is next to," are also relations that nothing can have to itself. Whatever stands in such relations must, as such, be numerically distinct things. In this case, it would appear, numerical difference follows from the relation itself, or as Edwards might say, from the sameness or agreement of the relations; a difference of properties or relations is not logically required. Where

2. Below, p. 335.

3. G. W. Leibniz, "First Truths," in Leroy Loemker, ed., *Leibniz Philosophical Papers and Letters* (2nd ed., Dordrecht, 1969), p. 268.

4. Below, pp. 334–35.

no difference of property or relation is present, of course, the two bodies would be indiscernible, but they would still be numerically distinct.

Edwards discussed the problem of the identity of individuals on at least two later occasions in his published works, in *Freedom of the Will*[5] and in *Original Sin*.[6] In both places his treatment of the problem may be seen to agree in essential respects with the early comment in "The Mind," No. 1. The discussion in *Freedom of the Will* is particularly significant, for in attacking Isaac Watts' conception of the arbitrariness of God's will Edwards seems to take up the very position that Leibniz had argued against Samuel Clarke, one of Newton's most devoted champions.[7] Edwards explicitly states a form of the principle of the identity of indiscernibles as the foundation of his own position, "that in all the various possible things which are in God's view, and may be considered as capable objects of his choice, there is . . . evermore a preferableness in one thing above another."[8] Nevertheless, Edwards interprets and applies Leibniz' principle in a manner that Leibniz himself would reject. Among other things, he concedes what Leibniz frequently and

5. In Pt. IV, §8; see *Works* (Yale ed.), *1*, pp. 384–96.

6. In Pt. IV, ch. 3; see ibid., *3*, pp. 389–412.

7. See in H. G. Alexander, ed., *The Leibniz-Clarke Correspondence* (Manchester, 1956). In his third paper to Clarke, Leibniz attacks the Newtonian concept of absolute space by the following argument (p. 26): "I say then, that if space was an absolute being, there would something happen for which it would be impossible there should be a sufficient reason. Which is against my axiom. And I prove it thus. Space is something absolutely uniform; and without the things placed in it, one point of space does not absolutely differ in any respect whatsoever from another point of space. Now from hence it follows, (supposing space to be something in itself, besides the order of bodies among themselves,) that 'tis impossible there should be a reason, why God, preserving the same situations of bodies among themselves, should have placed them in space after one certain particular manner, and not otherwise; why every thing was not placed the quite contrary way, for instance, by changing East into West."

To this Clarke replies (p. 32): "The uniformity of space does indeed prove, that there could be no (external) reason why God should create things in one place rather than in another: but does that hinder his own will, from being to itself a sufficient reason of acting in any place, when all places are indifferent or alike, and there be good reason to act in some place?"

This correspondence occurred in 1715 and 1716. Clarke himself published it in 1717.

8. *Works* (Yale ed.), *1*, p. 384. The principle of the identity of indiscernibles is explicitly introduced as applying to states of affairs as candidates of possible choice: "'Tis inquired, whether *different* objects of choice mayn't be absolutely *without difference*? If they are absolutely *without difference*, then how are they *different* objects of choice? If there be absolutely *no difference* in any respect, then there is *no variety* or *distinction*: for distinction is only by some difference. And if there be no *variety* among proposed *objects* of choice, then there is no opportunity for *variety of choice*, or difference of determination. For that determination of a thing which is not different in any respect, is not a different determination, but the same" (p. 385).

emphatically denied, that it is "possible for God to make two bodies perfectly alike, and put them in different places."[9] Such bodies, he maintains, would be different only with respect to the "circumstance" of their place; but if each were in the place of the other there would be *no numerical difference* in the particular state of affairs. "If anyone should say . . . that there must be something determined without an end; viz., that of those two similar bodies, this in particular should be made in this place, and the other in the other, and should inquire why the Creator did not make them in transposition, when both are alike, and each would equally have suited either place? The inquiry supposes something that is not true; namely, that the two bodies differ and are distinct in other respects besides their place. So that with this distinction, *inherent* in them, they might in their first creation have been transposed, and each might have begun its existence in the place of the other."[1]

In *Original Sin* Edwards employs other arguments to show that the unity and identity of every created thing through time are founded upon an arbitrary establishment of the divine will by which things are immediately produced. This establishment in turn has its sufficient reason in God's wisdom, according to which there is analogy and harmony among all things, and a good consequence or end obtained by them.[2] Once again, he rejects the basic conception of the world as comprised in various distinct and independent individual things or substances, each with its own nature and inherent properties that belong to it independently of its relations to others. "There are *various kinds* of identity and oneness, found among created things, by which they become one in different manners, respects and degrees, and to various purposes; . . . and every kind is ordered, regulated, and limited in every respect, by divine constitution."[3] This general view of the logical structure of reality, as we have seen, first emerged in Edwards' thought from the analysis of excellency in "The Mind," No. 1.

For purposes of further discussion, it will be helpful to sketch a rough and tentative picture of the formal structure of the world which seems to emerge from Edwards' view that universals, common properties, and the individual identities of things consist in or depend upon relations. We may consider, for a start, that there are various primitive and fully

9. Ibid., p. 388.
1. Ibid., p. 389.
2. *Works* (Yale ed.), *3*, pp. 402–06.
3. Ibid., pp. 404–05.

determinate relations that are logically independent of each other. No individual things will exist except as they are instances of these primitive relations, so that every existing individual will necessarily stand in such a relation to at least one other individual. We might then suppose that these primitive relations are ordered by various other relations which supervene upon them, in such a way that all the instances of any one of the primitive relations will themselves be connected in some determinate way with instances of others. Hence every existing individual will have various determinate relations with every other individual. The general and intelligible structure of the world, including the identities and differences among the objects in it, their natures and common properties, and their regular order in space and time, may be seen as determined according to and following from such ordering relations.

A formal system of relations of this sort might be looked upon in several different ways, each of which can throw some light upon the structural concepts that Edwards brings into regular use in developing his theory of the creation. Such a system might be referred to in describing the order that is actually present in a complex set of objects, as Edwards often uses the terms "regular order," "harmony," and "proportion" in describing the natural world. Again, a system of relations might be expressed as a framework of general laws with reference to which certain particular objects and relations are explained, and others predicted. Furthermore, such a system might be taken as defining a plan or course of action that is adopted and implemented for some purpose, or as a set of fixed rules that are recognized and applied in acting. Taken in this way it might show the formal structure of what Edwards often refers to as the arbitrary constitution of God and his constant and regular manner of acting in the course of his creating.

The notion of a system of relations as defining a rule of action that may be adopted or recognized and applied seems to afford a way of interpreting the explanation by which Edwards finally claims to answer the question with which he began "The Mind," No. 1: "Why is proportion pleasant to the mind, and disproportion unpleasant?" The claim that universals are relations was introduced as the first step in answering this question; and our lengthy elaboration of the implications of that claim may now throw some light upon what is otherwise an entirely obscure argument. Edwards presents it as follows:

All beauty consists in similarness, or identity of relation. In identity of relation consists all likeness, and all identity between two consists in identity of relation . . . . So bodies of exactly the same figure: the bodies are two, the relation between the parts of the extremities is the same, and this is their agreement with them. But if there are two bodies of different shapes, having no similarness of relation between the parts of the extremities, this, considered by itself, is a deformity, because being disagrees with being; which must undoubtedly be disagreeable to perceiving being, because what disagrees with being must be disagreeable to being in general, to everything that partakes of entity, and of course to perceiving being. And what agrees with being must be agreeable to being in general, and therefore to perceiving being. But agreeableness of perceiving being is pleasure, and disagreeableness is pain.[4]

The notions of agreement and disagreement that Edwards introduces in this explanation probably take their rise from the formal disciplines, especially logic, to which he was devoted as a student. In the Ramist system of logic, in particular, these terms had an established use in the classification of "arguments" or reasons that should be searched out and applied to a subject matter in explaining or proving something about it. So-called "simple" arguments were thus divided into those that "agree with" the matter in question and those that "disagree with" it. The former included arguments involving the causes and effects of a thing, or its "subjects" and "adjuncts." The latter included the contraries, "relatives," and contradictories of it.[5] There is no doubt that Edwards was familiar with this classification system from his undergraduate studies. In fact, in the Latin version of the Ramist system in Edwards' own textbook, the terms *consentaneum* and *dissentaneum* are used;[6] and in "The Mind," No. 1 and elsewhere he regularly uses "consent" and "dissent" to express the relations of agreement and disagreement.[7]

John Locke's definitions of truth as "the joining or separating of

---

4. Below, pp. 334–35.

5. Ramus' system of logic is discussed by Wilbur Howell, in *Logic and Rhetoric in England, 1500–1700* (Princeton, 1956), pp. 146–172.

6. *Expositionis Georgii Dounami, in Petri Rami Dialecticam Catechismus.* See further above, p. 14.

7. In "The Mind," No. 45, JE comments, "When we spake of excellence in bodies we were obliged to borrow the word 'consent' from spiritual things. But excellence in and among spirits is, in its prime and proper sense, being's consent to being. There is no other proper consent but that of minds, even of their will; which, when it is of minds towards minds, it is love, and when of minds towards other things it is choice" (below, p. 362). For discussion, see below, pp. 131–32.

signs, as the things signified by them do agree or disagree with one another,"[8] and of knowledge as "the perception of the connection or agreement, or disagreement and repugnancy, of any of our ideas,"[9] seem to have an even more direct bearing upon Edwards' explanation of excellency. According to Locke, ideas might agree or disagree in any of four general respects: identity or diversity, relation, coexistence and necessary connection, or real existence.[1] Edwards holds that all these ultimately consist in the agreement or disagreement of things with respect to relations. But Locke also distinguishes among several sorts of relations according to their basis or foundation, and each sort involves the notions of agreement and disagreement in a somewhat different way. What Locke calls the proportional, the natural, the voluntary, and the moral relations all differ according as they depend upon the ideas or characters of the things themselves, the causes and circumstances of origin of the things, or on the other hand upon some voluntary act by which the relation is instituted, or some general standard or rule which is adopted, recognized, and applied in judging things.[2] In these latter cases, things agree or disagree according as the relation is instituted for them or not, and as they conform or disconform to the established rule. It is with reference to moral relations in particular that moral good and evil are defined:

> Good and evil, as hath been shown, are nothing but pleasure or pain, or that which occasions or procures pleasure or pain to us. Morally good and evil, then, is only the conformity or disagreement of our voluntary actions to some law, whereby good or evil is drawn on us from the will and power of the law-maker.[3]

It seems evident that Edwards understands the notions of agreement and disagreement as applying with respect to the relations among a complex order of objects. Their agreement or disagreement is not determined by the presence or absence of certain particular relations, but by the sameness or difference of the relations among them. An object agrees with others in a given complex order when it is proportioned to them, or when its various relations to them are the same as their relations to each other. We have already noted that, in Edwards' general

8. *Essay*, Bk. IV, ch. 5, no. 2.
9. Ibid., Bk. IV, ch. 1, no. 2.
1. Ibid., nos. 2–7.
2. Ibid., Bk. II, ch. 28, nos. 2–4.
3. Ibid., no. 5.

conception of the logical structure of the world, every existing thing is related in some manner to all other existing things. It has also been suggested that he seems to consider any system of relations among things, not only as being present and observable in some set of objects, but also as constituting a system of laws by which the parts of an order of objects can be explained, and again as defining a course of action by which such an order could be produced for some purpose, or a set of general rules for acting in the production of it. In the latter view, the system of relations may be seen to be analogous to what Locke calls voluntary and moral relations.

If this analogy is admitted, then when Edwards speaks of an object agreeing with others, he should be taken to mean, not only that it is proportioned to others, but also that in being so proportioned it conforms to the general laws obtaining among those others, and even throughout the entire system of the world, and that it accordingly satisfies the rules by which this system is formed, and the purposes for which it is formed. It seems plausible to suppose that when Edwards says in explanation of excellency that an agreement of an object with others is necessarily *agreeable to* being in general and to everything that exists, this agreeableness involves or consists in the necessary conformity of such an agreement with the general laws of the universe, and consequently the satisfaction of the rules and purposes according to which it was·created.

It also seems plausible to interpret Edwards' explanation of excellency as maintaining that it is in this same way that excellency is understood to please us and deformity or disproportion to displease us. He points out how, when we accidentally notice a set of marks, we are very apt "to be ranging of them into regular parcels and figures, and if we see a mark out of its place, to be placing of it right by our imagination; and this even while we are meditating on something else. So we catch ourselves at observing the rules of harmony and regularity in the careless motions of our heads or feet, and when playing with our hands, or walking about the room."[4] In these observations he calls attention to the manner in which even our casual perceptions, imaginings, and overt actions involve the application of rules. In a corresponding manner, Edwards implies that the pleasure we feel when we perceive any proportion or agreement essentially involves the satisfaction of rules of order and proportion that we ourselves apply to the objects of perception and thought. There is at least the suggestion in this that for

4. Below, p. 336.

Edwards the very nature of mental activity consists in the applying of rules to things.

It is clear, in any case, that Edwards holds that the kinds of agreement or consent among the objects that please us are the same as that agreement or consent to being which is necessary for any object to exist. Indeed, he holds, it is just because such relations are necessary for the existence of a thing, that they are necessarily the ones that please us when we perceive them. "The reason why equality thus pleases the mind, and inequality is unpleasing, is because disproportion or inconsistency is contrary to being. For being, if we examine narrowly, is nothing else but proportion."[5] Later, in "The Mind," No. 49, Edwards notes that not only the perception of being's consent to being, but the "mere perception of being" is pleasing to the perceiver, so that "there is in the mind an inclination to perceive the things that are, or the desire of truth."[6]

This supposed correspondence of the mind and its modes of operation about objects, to the manner in which those objects actually exist, is a basic point in Edwards' view that the physical world exists only as a representation or "shadow" of the spiritual. God creates and governs the world according to established rules of order and proportion; and it is in the very regularity and harmonious order of the world that God manifests his nature and so accomplishes his purposes in creating it. In a similar manner, Edwards argues, the spiritual character and attitude of a person are manifested and represented in his countenance,[7] and the mind of the artist is revealed in the harmonious relations among the parts of his work: "The notes of a tune or the strokes of an acute penman, for instance, are placed in such exact order, having such mutual respect one to another, that they carry with them into the mind of him that sees and hears the conception of an understanding and will exerting itself in these appearances. And were it not that we, by reflection and reasoning, are led to an extrinsic intelligence and will that was the cause, it would seem to be in the notes and strokes themselves."[8] Accordingly, Edwards argues that we perceive and enjoy regularity and proportion in the world because the regularity in its relations is the consequence of the manner in which it was actually created by God's

5. Below, p. 336.
6. Below, p. 367.
7. See "The Mind," No. 20, below, p. 346; ibid., No. 62, below, p. 380.
8. Ibid., No. 63, below, p. 382.

mind; and because the very existence and nature of its objects consist in such regularity in its relations.

THE WORLD IN SPACE AND TIME

After completing his long essay upon excellency, and making several additions to it, Edwards apparently found he had exhausted the topic and established a sufficiently firm conception of it, at least for the time.[9] He went on in "The Mind" to treat a variety of other matters pertaining to the relations between minds and bodies, the nature of cognition, the nature and status of space, and the existence of bodies. It is apparent that he had taken up a serious study of Locke's *Essay* during this time, and in doing so he seems to have concentrated upon certain parts of the book rather than worked systematically through it.[1] Most of the following articles were probably written during his Yale tutorship. Several of them suggest that the lessons in logic that he was preparing for his undergraduates gave him occasion for reflecting upon the relations between logic and our performances of reasoning and judgment. He probably used Brattle's "New Logic" and Arnauld's *Art of Thinking* in his teaching, and perhaps also some version of Ramus.[2]

The course of his philosophical inquiries, as they are recorded in "The Mind" and other private writings, suggests that Edwards was working toward the formulation of a coherent system of ideas, which would largely be founded upon the principle that nothing can be unless it is perceived or known. He seems to have had little moral doubt that such a system could ultimately be established and defended. At the same time, he seems to have had no definite plan for proceeding. Instead of setting about it in a systematic manner, he occupied himself with private study and reflection upon what he took to be the central points and problems to be handled. One of these, inevitably, was the construction of a solid proof that bodies cannot exist unless they are perceived or known. In Locke he found just the right language for stating this claim, either expressions he had not before confronted, or whose suitable use for this purpose he had hitherto entirely overlooked and disregarded: bodies are "ideas that exist only in the mind." With this language in hand, and probably with Locke's chapter on ideas and qualities at his

9. Of the remaining articles in "The Mind" that are concerned with excellency, only No. 14 followed No. 1 by less than some three years.

1. For further on Edwards' reading of Locke, see above, pp. 16–18, 24–26.

2. See above, p. 33.

elbow,[3] Edwards finally turned to work out the required proof in "The Mind," No. 27. The argument of this article makes an appropriate starting point for examining how Edwards undertook to develop a new theory of the physical world and its relation to the minds that perceive and know it.

In "The Mind," No. 27 Edwards adopts a strategy similar to the one he used in his earlier argument in "Of Being."[4] He asserts, on the authority of "every knowing philosopher," that colors are "strictly nowhere else but in the mind"; and then adds, "Color may have an existence out of the mind with equal reason as anything in body has any existence out of the mind beside the very substance of the body itself, which is nothing but the divine power, or rather the constant exertion of it." Besides color, he argues, our idea of body includes only solidity or resistance, and this in turn depends immediately upon the exercise of God's power: actual resistance is the actual exertion of that power, whereas the power of resisting is only "the constant law or method of that actual exertion." The question therefore is whether resistance, as so understood, can be conceived to exist unperceived and out of the mind. So far forth, Edwards is concerned just with his own earlier conception of resistance as comprising the very being of body; and that conception seems to imply that bodies can exist unperceived. It asserts that actual resistance exists in certain parts of real space, and that its existence in any one part of space depends immediately and solely upon God's exerting his power there. Now, however, Edwards offers an account of resistance that is incompatible with the idea that it could be produced by itself in any given part of space.

Resistance cannot exist, he argues, unless something is resisted, for there can be no actual resistance unless one thing resists another. Hence we cannot conceive it to exist unless we conceive something that resists and is resisted; and if we conceive resistance existing out of the mind, we must conceive that which resists and is resisted as existing out of the mind as well. But it is obvious that neither actual resistance itself nor the mere power or law of resisting can be what resists and is resisted. Because our concept of body includes nothing else that we can conceive existing out of the mind that could be what resists and is resisted, it follows that resistance itself cannot be conceived as existing out of the mind. Edwards does not even consider whether

3. *Essay*, Bk. II, ch. 8.
4. See above, p. 80.

our concept of body might include the notion of an underlying sub-stratum in which the resistance inheres; his earlier rejection of this thesis is taken for granted here.

The above treatment of resistance not only furnished Edwards with a vindication of his thesis that bodies cannot exist out of the mind; it also set the stage for a brief explanation of how bodies can exist in the mind. At the end of "The Mind," No. 27 he writes, "But now it is easy to conceive of resistance as a mode of an idea. It is easy to conceive of such a power or constant manner of stopping or resisting a color. The idea may be resisted—it may move, and stop, and rebound; but how a mere power which is nothing real can move and stop is inconceivable."[5]

When read in the light of comments and discussions elsewhere in his manuscript notes, this statement can best be interpreted as setting forth a form of idealistic phenomenalism. The things that resist and are resisted are colors (or colored shapes), as they are phenomena presented in visual experience. Because they are colors, he supposes, they are ideas that exist only in the minds that perceive them. These ideas are perceived to move, touch each other, and rebound in a fixed and regular manner, and so are understood to resist and be resisted. Actual resistance is not a property of each idea by itself; it is just that actual succession of observed motions of the ideas in the circumstances described. And the power of resistance is not an inherent cause of those changes of motion, it is only the constant manner in which they occur, or the general law to which they conform. Hence an idea is a solid body when its successive motions follow from its circumstances and relations to other bodies in accordance with that general law.

Edwards closes "The Mind," No. 27 with a very general conclusion: "The world is therefore an ideal one; and the law of creating, and the succession of these ideas, is constant and regular."[6] Evidently he considered this phenomenalistic treatment of resistance to be basic to a larger program of explanations which would show how the whole system of the physical world exists in the mind. All bodies, their properties and relations, their mutual interactions and successive changes are to be accounted for by series of ideas in perceiving minds, and by the laws that govern order and succession among the ideas. In "The Mind," No. 10 he writes, "Truth as to external things is the consistency

5. Below, p. 351.
6. Ibid.

of our ideas with those ideas, or that train and series of ideas, that are raised in our minds according to God's stated order and law."[7] As this passage indicates, Edwards does not suppose that physical objects are merely nominal entities, at least with respect to the knowledge of perceiving minds. Like Locke, whose theory of truth he is evidently considering,[8] Edwards holds that bodies have real natures independent of the ideas and beliefs we form concerning them. But he rejects Locke's view that these real natures are unperceived and unknowable properties of substances; instead he holds that they consist in the general laws that govern the order and regularity of the series of ideas that are "raised in our minds" in the course of sense experience. These general laws, Edwards asserts, are established by God. In "The Mind," No. 15 he reforms his conception of truth with respect to external things in the light of this assumption. Truth, he now holds, is the agreement of our ideas with existence; and the existence of external things consists in "the determination, and fixed mode, of God's exciting ideas in us. So that truth in these things is an agreement of our ideas with that series in God. 'Tis existence, and that is all we can say."[9]

In spite of the major differences between this and Edwards' earliest views concerning the nature of physical objects, it is apparent that he continued to hold some of his earliest metaphysical conclusions, and that these conclusions were fundamental to the formulation of his idealistic phenomenalism. It has been sufficiently noted that he continued to reject the notion that bodies are substances in which properties inhere. He did not neglect to emphasize this point on later occasions, for example, in Miscell. no. 267[1] and "The Mind," No. 61.[2] Beyond this, as he had argued in "Of Atoms" that solidity is the immediate effect of the exercise of divine power, now he maintains that God is the immediate cause of the ideas that are presented to us in sense experience, and that the order of succession of these ideas depends entirely upon God's will. Finally, Edwards continues to maintain that bodies, and indeed all created things, exist in God who is the being of all things. So Edwards concludes "The Mind," No. 15: " 'Tis impossible that we should explain and resolve a perfectly abstract and mere idea of existence: only we always find this, by running of it up, that God and

7. Below, p. 342.
8. *Essay*, Bk. IV, ch. 5.
9. Below, pp. 344–45.
1. Townsend, p. 78.
2. Below, p. 380.

real existence are the same."[3] But it was a corollary of Edwards'
earlier view that all things exist in God by way of being in space. Now,
however, he maintains that bodies are in God by way of his knowledge
or consciousness of them; and this knowledge essentially involves
general laws, or determinations of his will with respect to regularities
in the order of ideas he causes in created minds.

This difference seems to be fundamental in Edwards' understanding
of his principle that nothing whatever can be without being known. He
urged this principle, not merely as a theory about the nature of physical
objects, but as a wholly new account of being in general. In the opening
portion of "Of Being" he had followed Henry More in arguing the
necessary omnipresence of being, and had concluded that space is God.
His first declaration that nothing can be without knowledge or consciousness, however, marks the point of his general rejection of More's
metaphysical system. Bodies are in God as determinations of his will
with respect to order and succession, not as resistance in parts of real
space. In "The Mind," No. 2 Edwards attacks More on another
fundamental point: spirits are not in place in the sense that they are
extended through parts of real space, as More had argued, but only in
the sense that their perceptions and actions are regularly connected
with the perceived positions and motions of phenomenal bodies.
These regular connections are governed by certain general rules that
are established by God.[4] Again, in "The Mind," No. 9 Edwards
strikes at the heart of More's system and his own earlier conception
of reality: space, he contends, is only an external object, and like all
other external things it has only an ideal existence. It is a necessary
being in the sense that it is "a simple idea that is necessarily connected
with other simple exterior ideas, and is, as it were, their common
substance or subject."[5] And in "The Mind," No. 13 he concludes that
the necessity and infinitude of space depends upon "the law of nature,
or the constitution of God."[6] A closer examination of these articles,
and other passages related to them, will show more fully how Edwards
conceives this "constitution of God."

Having rejected the notion that spirits are extended, in "The Mind,"
No. 2 Edwards goes on to propose a phenomenalistic account of the
concept of the place of a mind. In this account he assumes that the

3. Below, p. 345.
4. Below, p. 339.
5. Below, p. 341.
6. Below, p. 343.

concept is basically one which perceivers apply to themselves. That is, the place of a perceiving mind is just the place the perceiver sees or judges *himself* to be with respect to the phenomenal bodies he perceives at a given time. A given perceiver's concept of his own place is to be explained by those regular features of his own experience that lead him to recognize or judge where he is. These features, Edwards holds, concern the differences in the degree of clarity or "strength" among the ideas perceived at a given time, and the connection between the mind's operations and the perceived ideas or phenomenal body that is immediately affected. Some minds, he notes, are united with particular bodies, that is, each finds that it always perceives the same phenomenal body most clearly and strongly and that its operations regularly affect that body immediately. These conditions, in general, constitute the law of the union of mind and body. This is not a law to which every mind conforms, however, but only a law to which all the perceptions and operations of certain minds conform. A mind could have a place with respect to bodies it perceives and affects without being united with one particular body. Hence Edwards concludes that disembodied or separate minds are also in places: "At least a finite spirit cannot thus be in all places at a time equally."[7]

In "The Mind," No. 3, Edwards considers the difference between embodied and disembodied minds more fully. As opposed to Locke's assumption that the ideas we receive in sense perception are caused by events in our bodies, Edwards asserts those ideas are "communicated to us immediately by God while our minds are united with our bodies; but only we in some measure know the rule." There is therefore no difficulty in supposing that separate or disembodied minds also perceive things: "They will be communicated then also, and according to some rule, no doubt, only we know not what."[8] Again, in Miscell. no. 176 he argues in like manner for the possibility that separate spirits can act upon bodies: "We find that from such motions of mind there follows such alterations in such and such matter according to established rules, and these rules are entirely at the pleasure of him that establishes them. And why should we not think that God establishes other rules for other spirits, I cannot imagine."[9]

It was apparently from reflection upon this possibility that other minds might receive ideas or perceive things according to very differ-

7. Below, p. 339.
8. Ibid.
9. From a transcription supplied by Thomas Schafer.

ent laws from the ones we know to obtain in our own case, that Edwards came to reopen the question of the necessity and infinitude of space itself. In "The Mind," No. 13 he suggests that this question, and likewise the question of the reality and duration of time, is to be resolved by arguments similar to those that apply to the "extension" or place of minds. With regard to space, his intention is to evaluate Locke's use of an ancient argument to prove that space is independent of the bodies in it, and extends to infinity beyond the universe of bodies: "If body be not supposed infinite (which I think no one will affirm), I would ask whether, if God placed a man at the extremity of corporeal beings, he could not stretch his hand beyond his body? If he could, then he would put his arm where there was before space without body."[1] Edwards accordingly asks whether an intelligent being could be removed beyond the limits of the corporeal world, and whether a spirit so removed would be "at a distance" from the limit as we are in places and at distances from bodies within the limits of the world. Such questions, he suggests, are actually questions about the rules according to which different minds might perceive things. He accordingly answers, "I cannot tell what the law of nature, or the constitution of God, would be in this case."[2] He seems to infer from this that the necessity and infinitude of space as we conceive them are entirely relative to the special laws by which God communicates ideas to our minds. In a later addendum to "The Mind," No. 13 he argues that the concept of space itself is relative to the kinds of ideas a mind receives; specifically, that the common idea of space is dependent upon the perception of color, and that the ideas of space and motion formed by a person who was born blind must be entirely unlike the common notions, agreeing with them only with respect to proportions and number.[3]

These discussions of place and space reveal certain basic points in Edwards' conception of God's constitution or determination with respect to the order of the ideas he causes. First, he holds that God's determination consists in his acting according to fixed rules in his communication of ideas to each perceiving mind. Hence the course of experience for each mind is constant and regular. But second, God may, and indeed does, communicate ideas to certain different minds

---

1. *Essay*, Bk. II, ch. 13, no. 21.
2. Below, p. 343.
3. Below, pp. 343–44. JE might have been led to this point by reading Berkeley's *An Essay Towards a New Theory of Vision* (Dublin, 1709). For discussion of his reading of this work, see above, p. 36.

according to very different rules. The rules by which he acts are entirely contingent, subject to "the pleasure of him who establishes them." Hence the order of experience for disembodied minds, or minds placed "outside" the limits of the physical world, will be quite different from that for embodied minds or minds placed "within" the system of physical objects. Third, each perceiver can know, or can come to know "in some measure," what rules govern the series of ideas presented to his own mind; but he cannot know what rules might govern the order of ideas in other minds, or at least in minds that are unlike his own in some specified manner. It follows that each perceiving mind is able to form concepts of external objects and their relations that have legitimate and universal application to its own experience, but none of these concepts is thereby logically guaranteed to have a universal application to all the experiences of every perceiving mind.

In these several points it is quite evident that Edwards was influenced both directly and deeply by John Locke's "way of ideas" and his analysis of experience. Despite his rejection of Locke's specific assumptions with respect to the external existence of bodies and their role in causing ideas, he wholeheartedly accepted Locke's view that it is a wholly contingent matter that each mind receives the sensory information it does, and that the content and order of its experience is as it is. Thus Locke argues that we cannot know what ideas might be received by perceivers with more or different sensory capacities than ours,[4] or by angels and other spirits who are not united to bodies as our minds are.[5] Edwards follows Locke in holding that a perceiver knows from his own experience whether his mind is united with some particular body and how that union determines the place and motions of his mind.[6] In these particular points Locke's discussions were most likely a positive influence in Edwards' development of an account of the constitution of God as his established rules for communicating ideas.

Nevertheless, it is clear that Edwards' fundamental commitments throughout these discussions are entirely different from Locke's. He has no interest in the problems of substance and essence as Locke understood them. Instead, his attention is given almost exclusively to the connections between our concepts of physical or "exterior" things, the order of the ideas presented in experience, and the laws or established rules that govern that order. In these points, his treatment

4. *Essay*, Bk. II, ch. 2, no. 3.
5. Ibid., ch. 23, no. 13.
6. Ibid., nos. 18–21.

accords with the principle stated in "The Mind," No. 1, that all universals are relations; and his general account of the nature and status of the physical world seems to have been in part guided by it. Locke is concerned about the question which of the kinds of simple ideas of sensation, if any, are epistemically important as representing real qualities of bodies.[7] Edwards, on the other hand, identifies real qualities with the fixed order and relations among ideas as they are presented in experience, and accordingly finds less explicit use for the notion of a simple idea. The very notion of an idea, as applied to the immediate objects of sensation, is in Locke's account primarily an epistemological one; simple ideas are, for him, the fundamental building blocks of knowledge. But in Edwards' discussions, the term "idea" as applied to given experience has primarily an ontological import; it serves to establish that the objects we perceive cannot exist except in minds. And while Locke supposes that a mind's "union" with a body is an unperceivable antecedent condition for its receiving any ideas of sensation, Edwards undertakes to explain mind-body union in terms of the order and relations of ideas perceived *within* the course of experience.

What of the correspondence between Edwards' general theory and that of George Berkeley? In view of several of Edwards' statements that we have examined, it seems that it would not be surprising to discover the following passage in "The Mind":

> The ideas of sense are more strong, lively, and distinct than those of the imagination; they have likewise a steadiness, order, and coherence, and are not excited at random, as those which are the effects of human wills often are, but in a regular train or series, the admirable connection whereof sufficiently testifies the wisdom and benevolence of its Author. Now the set rules or established methods, wherein the mind we depend on excites in us the ideas of sense, are called the *Laws of Nature*: and these we learn by experience, which teaches us that such and such ideas are attended with such and such other ideas, in the ordinary course of things.[8]

It seems evident that Edwards would agree with the main points of this section from Berkeley's *Principles of Human Knowledge*. Their main differences, it would appear, are concerned with their theories of mind, rather than their general theories of bodies. Apart from this, there are

---

7. This is one of the problems involved in Locke's attempt to distinguish between the secondary and the primary qualities. See *Essay*, Bk. II, ch. 8, nos. 15ff.

8. Berkeley, *The Principles of Human Knowledge* (Dublin, 1710), Pt. I, no. 30.

considerable differences in their perspectives and philosophical objectives. Berkeley was primarily concerned to defeat the scepticism and atheism he believed must follow from the assumption of material substance, and accordingly his presentation of idealism is primarily centered upon the overthrow of this assumption. But Edwards, as we have seen, dismissed the assumption long before he developed his idealism. Thereafter, he was very little concerned about philosophical scepticism. His idealism was apparently not developed to answer it. Moreover, in only one of Edwards' many arguments for the existence of God, in "The Mind," No. 28, which is a brief corollary to No. 27, does he explicitly use his idealism as a premise.

This is not to say that Edwards ignored the challenges of reason and common sense to his view, or that he was not concerned to demonstrate that it preserves and even guarantees our convictions with regard to the objective reality of the physical world. On the contrary, he worked hard to develop the theory in a manner that would accord with and confirm our ordinary beliefs about the places of objects and the assumptions of physical science with regard to the causes of physical change. He believed that the main source of objections, difficulties, and confusions, from the point of view of common sense, is the statement that the material world exists nowhere but "in the mind." In "The Mind," No. 51 he comments, "It is from hence I expect the greatest opposition. It will appear a ridiculous thing, I suppose, that the material world exists nowhere but in the soul of man, confined within his skull."[9] But this problem arises only from the improper and metaphorical use of spatial terminology to express the relation between mind and body. The mind is not the same as the brain, nor is it somehow contained in the brain. The connection between the two is entirely operational: "The seat of the soul is not in the brain any otherwise than as to its immediate operations and the immediate operations of things on it."[1] The connection neither is nor is dependent upon a spatial relation between the two, as the expressions "in the mind" and "in the brain" seem to suggest.

It is therefore improper, Edwards admits, to say that the soul is *in* the brain. "To speak yet more strictly and abstractly, 'tis nothing but the connection of the operations of the soul with these and those modes of its own ideas, or those mental acts of the Deity, seeing the brain exists only in idea."[2] And by the same reasoning, it is improper

9. Below, p. 368.
1. Below, p. 352.
2. Below, p. 355.

to say that bodies do not exist *without* the mind: "For place itself is mental, and 'within' and 'without' are mere mental conceptions. . . . But when I say 'the material universe exists only in the mind,' I mean that it is absolutely dependent on the conception of the mind for its existence, and does not exist as spirits do, whose existence does not consist in, nor in dependence upon, the conceptions of other minds."[3] Once the metaphors are expunged from the theory, it is clear that it does not deny, but rather explains, our ordinary beliefs about the places of things. "Things are truly in those places, for what we mean when we say so is only that this mode of our idea of place appertains to such an idea."[4] Furthermore, "The soul, in a sense, has its seat in the brain; and so, in a sense, the visible world is existent out of the mind, for it certainly, in the most proper sense, exists out of the brain."[5]

These clarifications do not resolve another and more serious objection to idealism, however, which is based upon acknowledged scientific claims about the causal relations between mind and body. Edwards stated the problem most cogently at a later time, in Miscell. no. 1340:

> If it be said that the sensible world has no existence but only in the mind, then the sensations themselves, or the organs of sense by which sensible ideas are let into the mind, have no existence but only in the mind. And those organs of sense have no existence but what is conveyed into the mind by themselves, for they are a part of the world. And then it would follow that the organs of sense owe their existence to the organs of sense, and so are prior to them, being the causes or occasions of their own existence—which is a seeming inconsistence with reason, which, I imagine, the reason of all men cannot explain and remove.[6]

The paradox seems to be as follows. The true scientific explanation of perception asserts that all our ideas of sensation causally depend upon our organs of sense. But idealism asserts that these organs, since they are bodies, exist only as ideas of sensation. From the two assertions he concludes that the organs of sense are the causes of themselves, that they "owe their existence" to themselves, and so are prior to themselves.

However insoluble Edwards might have thought this problem to be at the time he wrote Miscell. no. 1340, certain passages in "The Mind"

3. Below, p. 368.
4. Below, p. 353.
5. Below, p. 369.
6. Townsend, p. 223.

show that he had considered it before and had developed resources for avoiding it, at least in the form stated above. The paradox as given involves two distinct assumptions, neither of which is admitted in those earlier passages. First, it assumes that ideas of sensation causally depend upon the organs of sense in such a way that the former "owe their existence" to the latter. Second, it assumes that the organs which cause ideas in a particular mind must actually exist as ideas of sensation in that same mind. The first of these assumptions pertains to the concept of cause that is employed in scientific explanations, and the second to the concept of existence as it is used by the idealist in interpreting causal inferences made in the context of scientific explanation.

Edwards' treatment of the idea of cause, taken as a relation between objects or events in nature, does not admit that the effect "owes its existence" to the cause. In "The Mind," No. 26 he defines "cause" as "that, after or upon the existence of which, or the existence of it after such a manner, the existence of another thing follows."[7] An effect is thus consequent upon a cause, but need not have a necessary dependence upon its cause or receive its existence from it. Indeed, Edwards holds that all the objects and events in nature receive their existence from God: ideas of sensation are immediately communicated by God,[8] the order of phenomena by which bodies are solid objects is wholly determined by God,[9] and even every new thought in a mind depends for its occurrence upon God.[1] Causation in the context of physical or scientific explanation pertains only to the regular order in which God creates: "To find out the reasons of things in natural philosophy is only to find out the proportions of God's acting."[2] Accordingly, our bodily organs are causes of our ideas of sensation only in the sense that it is "God's constitution that some of our ideas shall be connected with others, according to such a settled law and order, so that some ideas shall follow from others as their cause."[3]

This interpretation of the causal relation does not eliminate the paradox of perception that has been raised for idealism, however. The theory still asserts that the organs of sense are on the one hand ideas of sensation, and on the other are the regular antecedents of all our ideas

---

7. Below, p. 350.
8. "The Mind," No. 3, below, p. 339.
9. Ibid., Nos. 27, 61, below pp. 351, 379–80.
1. Miscell. no. 267, in Townsend, p. 78.
2. "The Mind," No. 34, below, p. 353.
3. Ibid., No. 40, Corol., below, pp. 358–59.

of sensation. Does it not follow that the organs of sense are regular antecedents of themselves, and so must precede their own existence? This conclusion depends on a further assumption, however, that the bodily organs which cause ideas in a particular mind must actually exist as ideas of sensation in that mind. This assumption is contrary to fact; as Edwards notes in "The Mind," No. 40, we do not actually perceive the states of our sense organs from which our ideas of sensation follow. But in making the point he raises an even more serious difficulty for the idealist's effort to explain the connection between mind and body in sense perception: "How can this be, seeing that ideas most commonly arise from organs, when we have no idea of the mode of our organs, or the manner of external objects being applied to them?"[4]

The issue is evident. Our ideas of sensation are explained in science by antecedent modes of our sense organs. The explanation assumes that these bodily states exist; but since they are not actually perceived, the idealist must conclude that they do not exist. Edwards takes this problem to be only one instance of a more general one. In both our common understanding of the physical world and our scientific explantions of it we refer to objects and events even when they are not considered to be perceived by anyone. We believe the furniture of a room exists when no one is present, that there may be as yet undiscovered systems of remote stars, that ideas of sensation arise from unperceived events in our bodily organs, and that observable phenomena in the physical world depend on the properties of and interactions among singly imperceptible elementary particles. Edwards' metaphysical view, so far as it has been treated above, implies that no physical object can actually exist without being perceived. The claim that his view is compatible with common sense and science thus seems to be vitiated.

Edwards devoted several important discussions to this problem, undertaking to show that his idealism can account for the truth of assertions about unperceived objects and events just as well as a realist metaphysics. Idealism even admits that conception of the world as a system of atoms having a fully determined and continuous history of successive changes which he had set forth earlier in his scientific writings: "Though we suppose that the existence of the whole material universe is absolutely dependent on idea, yet we may speak in the old way, and as properly and truly as ever."[5] It does not follow that the system of atoms, its original creation, and all its subsequent history are

4. Below, p. 359.
5. "The Mind," No. 34, below, p. 353.

actually perceived by any mind. It might exist nowhere "perfectly" except in God's mind, and there it exists as "his determination, his care, and his design that ideas shall be united forever, just so and in such a manner as is agreeable to such a series."[6] God does not perceive these objects; rather, "God *supposes* its existence; that is, he causes all changes to arise *as if* all these things had actually existed in such a series in some created mind, and *as if* created minds had comprehended all things perfectly" (italics added).[7]

Edwards' concept of "supposed" existence involves several closely related points. First, he does not consider that the things whose existence is supposed are entities of a different ontological kind from those that are actually perceived—they are not, for example, "the real things" in contradistinction to mere ideas of things. On the contrary, he considers that all material objects and events are comprised by ideas and sequences of ideas. The only objects that actually exist, however, are those that are actually perceived, or that exist in actual ideas in finite and created minds. It is indeed possible, he suggests, that all the objects and events in the material universe are actually perceived, so that even the individual atoms actually exist in some created mind; they are not unperceivable in principle, but only unperceived by us in fact. But even if no one perceives them, and they do not actually exist, Edwards holds that God *supposes* their existence in some mind, and causes all other ideas in us *as if* they actually existed in that way. "The supposition of God which we speak of is nothing else but God's acting in the course and series of his exciting ideas as if they, the things supposed, were in actual idea."[8]

Second, Edwards considers that all the ideas that are actually perceived by any finite mind, together with those that God only supposes, constitute a single order and succession of ideas. This single order of ideas comprises one unique system of material objects with a single continuous history, what he calls "the system of the ideal world."[9] This system is common to all perceivers in the sense that the series of ideas excited in any created mind, however it differs from those in other minds, nevertheless constitutes some of the objects and events in that system. Each perceiver is thereby afforded some partial and limited view of the same material world. Edwards assumes that no created mind

6. Below, p. 354.
7. Ibid.
8. "The Mind," No. 40, below, p. 357.
9. Ibid.

perceives all the objects and events in the material world; but different minds might perceive the same objects and events in the sense that objects and events in the ideal system might be comprised of ideas that are excited in several different minds. In addition, this system might include some objects and events that are not perceived by any mind, for example, the individual atoms and their original arrangement and motions in the first creation. These are the things that do not actually exist, but are only supposed.

Third, Edwards holds that this system of the ideal world is a complete and fully determined whole, in which every object and event is related to all others in accordance with God's constitution. Hence, given the determinations of God's will, all actually existing things may be conceived to follow from some particular thing whose existence is only supposed, for example, a particular atom and its determinate state at the beginning of the creation: "All ideal changes of creatures are just so, as if just such a particular atom had actually all along existed even in some finite mind, and had never been out of that mind, and had in that mind caused these effects which are exactly according to nature, that is, according to the nature of other matter that is actually perceived by the mind."[1] Again, given the objects that are actually perceived and so actually exist, those whose existence is supposed are necessary: "These things must necessarily be put in to make complete the system of the ideal world. That is, they must be supposed if the train of ideas be in the order and course settled by the supreme mind."[2]

One of the most important consequences of this view, and one that Edwards particularly emphasizes, is that every supposed object or event implies some actually existing and actually perceived objects or events in the established order of nature; and again, any difference in supposed objects or events implies some difference in the states of affairs that actually are or eventually will be perceived by some mind. "For upon supposition of these things are infinite number of things otherwise than they would be, if these were not by God thus supposed."[3] Conversely, Edwards holds that any actually perceived state of affairs implies, and in a sense even contains, all the unperceived objects and events that are supposed as antecedents for it: "And these hidden things do not only exist in the divine idea, but in a sense in created idea, for that exists in created idea which necessarily supposes it. . . . So, were our thoughts

1. Below, p. 354.
2. Below, p. 357.
3. Ibid.

comprehensive and perfect enough, our view of the present state of the world would excite in us a perfect idea of all past changes."[4]

Applying this view to the particular matter of accounting for the causal role of our sense organs and brains in sense perception, Edwards writes, "It is hardly proper to say that the dependence of ideas of sensation upon the organs of the body is only the dependence of some of our ideas upon others. For the organs of our bodies are not our ideas, in a proper sense. Though their existence be only mental, yet there is no necessity of their existing actually in our minds, but they exist in the same manner as has been explained [i.e., as supposed]." At a minimum, he argues, this account has the same empirical consequences and serves "exactly the same purpose as can be supposed if our organs were actually existing in the manner vulgarly conceived, as to any manner of benefit or end that can be mentioned."[5] But there can be no doubt that he was genuinely perplexed by the theory. He remarks of it, "But we have got so far beyond those things for which language was chiefly contrived, that unless we use extreme caution we cannot speak, except we speak exceeding unintelligibly, without literally contradicting ourselves."[6] Here, as elsewhere and on many other occasions, the logical framework of his conception was so different from the traditional categories and terms of philosophical discourse, that he could hardly find language with which to express it.[7]

Nothing is more apparent in his theory of supposed existence than that Edwards conceives general laws of nature to be ontologically prior to the objects and events of the world. Although he granted, and even insisted, that no law of nature is ontologically or logically necessary, he also insisted that the laws of nature hold universally in the actual world. He entertained no Humean doubts whatever concerning the strict uniformity of nature. And although he did not address himself directly to the problem of how we know the laws, several comments concerning empirical knowledge, as we shall see, indicate that he had no interest in and little place for inductive reasoning in his epistemological theory. It was as a metaphysical assumption that he considered no particular object can exist except as it is in conformity with some general law

4. Below, p. 354.
5. "The Mind," No. 51, below, p. 368.
6. Ibid., No. 35, below, p. 355.
7. He was particularly distressed by the difficulties of expressing spiritual matters as he understood them in the available language. For example, he searches for the right terms to capture his concept of faith; see "Observations concerning Faith," no. 37, in Worcester ed., *4*, pp. 436–38. See also his comment upon words in "The Mind," No. 18, below, pp. 345–46.

determining its relation to others; nor need those others even actually exist, as the theory we have been examining tells us.

At the same time, Edwards maintains that nature and the actual world contain nothing permanent but the laws of contingent regularity. In "The Mind," No. 61 he argues at length that the solidity of bodies is no less a matter of regularity of motion than is their gravity. It is therefore an error among philosophers and physicists alike to suppose that solidity resides in the unknown substance of bodies, while gravity must be due to some extraneous cause or to God. Both alike have their cause in the operations of an intelligent and voluntary being.[8] In a late passage in "Natural Philosophy," Edwards tries to explain why it is generally thought that there must be some cause of gravity but not of solidity.[9] He likewise finds no basis for the widespread controversy over whether bodies can act upon each other at a distance and without physical contact, as they apparently do by gravitational attraction.[1] In another brief comment he writes, " 'Tis the same thing that distant existence as to place should have influence on bodies, as in gravity, as that existence distant as to time, being past, should have influence on its present existence, as in the successions of motion."[2] Because the past moment of time and everything it contains have ceased to exist for any present moment, it can have no real causal relation to what exists in the present moment.[3] Occurrences in space and time, therefore, whether they are near or remote, are connected only by fixed laws of order. In a much quoted passage in a late addendum to "The Mind," No. 13 Edwards sums up his view of the whole system of physical objects:

> That which truly is the substance of all bodies is the infinitely exact and precise and perfectly stable idea in God's mind, together with his stable will that the same shall gradually be communicated to us,

8. Below, pp. 377–80.
9. US No. 31, below, p. 290.
1. Thus Newton warns Richard Bentley against the assumption that gravity is innate in matter: "That Gravity should be innate, inherent and essential to Matter, so that one Body may act upon another at a Distance thro' a Vacuum, without the Mediation of anything else, by and through which their Action and Force may be conveyed from one to another, is to me so great an Absurdity, that I believe no Man who has in philosophical Matters a competent Faculty of thinking, can ever fall into it. Gravity must be caused by an Agent acting constantly according to certain Laws; but whether this Agent be material or immaterial, I have left to the Consideration of my Readers." Letters to Bentley, no. 4, in *Isaac Newton's Papers and Letters on Natural Philosophy*, ed. I. B. Cohen, (Cambridge, 1958), pp. 302–03.
2. "Natural Philosophy," LS No. 61, below, p. 257.
3. See Miscell. no. 267, in Townsend, p. 78; *Original Sin*, in *Works* (Yale ed.), *3*, p. 400.

and to other minds, according to certain fixed and exact established methods and laws.[4]

THE MIND

From his earliest writings onward Edwards emphasized that minds or spirits have a distinct nature from bodies, and an ontological status superior to them. In an early note in "Natural Philosophy" he comments, "The nearer in nature beings are to God, so much the more properly are they beings, and more substantial; and that spirits are much more properly beings, and more substantial, than bodies."[5] Later, from the impossibility that anything should be without being known, he concludes that "those beings which have knowledge and consciousness are the only proper and real and substantial beings, inasmuch as the being of all other things is only by these."[6] In many other places he asserts that spirits are the end for which God created the world; that "senseless" bodies are only images or shadows of spiritual beings, and are created only for the sake of them.

Despite such repeated claims, however, Edwards rarely addressed himself directly to the most fundamental questions about mind or spirit. Even in the manuscript he entitled "The Mind" he concerned himself more fully with problems about the existence of bodies and the manner of their dependence upon the mind, than with the existence and nature of minds themselves. In planning his treatise on the mind he promised more. There he proposed to discuss human nature in a detailed and systematic way, starting with the most basic metaphysical principles: "Treat first of being in general, and shew what is in human nature necessarily existing from the nature of entity; and then concerning perceiving or intelligent beings in particular, and shew what arises from the nature of such; and then animal nature, and what from that."[7] Most of what can be determined of the account thus outlined must be pieced together and worked out by interpretation and inference from widely scattered passages.

As we have noted, Edwards' earliest writings were deeply influenced by the metaphysical views of Henry More. He accepted More's claim that space is a necessary spiritual being, and probably supposed that all spirits are extended and occupy space. But the doctrine that nothing

4. Below, p. 344.
5. LS No. 44, corol. 3; see below, p. 238.
6. "Of Being," corol.; see below, p. 206.
7. "Subjects," No. 8; below, p. 388.

can be without being known led to his making substantial revisions in
this account. Early in "The Mind" he finds that the supposition that
spirits are extended treats them as "very gross and shadowy and corporeal," and he urges instead that the spiritual be identified by such
notions as thought, love, hate, inclination, and desire.[8] From this
point Edwards' discussions of the mental are particularly marked by
the influence of John Locke. Many articles in "The Mind" were evidently written in response to specific statements in Locke's *Essay*.
Throughout these passages it appears that Edwards agrees with Locke
in assuming that consciousness and immediate self-consciousness are
the characteristic marks of the mental. Yet his discussions show that
Edwards was very far from accepting Locke's general theory of mind,
and that he almost never adopted Locke's claims without significant
revision. In many points he openly rejected Locke's views. In the last
analysis, it will appear that their concepts of mind are as sharply distinct
as their concepts of bodies.

Edwards' phenomenalistic idealism, like that of Berkeley, assumes
that there are many different created minds, each one conscious,
capable of perception, knowledge, and volition, and in each of which
God excites an orderly train of ideas of sensation that comprise the
bodies it perceives and affects. It is tempting to suppose that Edwards,
like Berkeley, considered each mind to be an individual substance in
which these various modes of consciousness inhere and by which they
are supported.[9] The passage previously quoted from "The Mind,"
No. 51, in which Edwards contrasts the status of the material world
with that of the mind, especially lends itself to the view that minds are
substances. The material world, he writes, "is absolutely dependent on
the conception of the mind for its existence, and does not exist as
spirits do, whose existence does not consist in, nor in dependence on,
the conception of other minds."[1]

This interpretation, however, conflicts with Edwards' express doctrine that God alone is substance, and that all created things exist in
immediate dependence upon him. In "Of Atoms" he rejects the notion
that the substance of a body is a distinct but unknown underlying
support of its properties, and thence argues that the substance of bodies
is the divine power exerted in a particular manner. Much later, in
Miscell. no. 267, Edwards argues in an exactly similar way with respect

8. "The Mind," No. 2, below, p. 388.
9. See *Principles of Human Knowledge*, §§89, 91; Luce, *Works of Berkeley, 2*, pp. 79–81.
1. Below, p. 368.

to minds. The "mere exertion of a new thought," he holds, requires some cause that immediately produces and upholds it. This cause cannot be antecedent thoughts, for "they are past, and what is past is not." The cause is therefore a substance, where "substance" means God: "But if it be meant something else that has no properties, it seems to me absurd. If the removal of all properties, such as extension, solidity, thought, etc. leaves nothing, it seems to me that no substance is anything besides them."[2]

The most obvious target of this critical remark is Locke, who gives similar accounts of spirit or immaterial substance and body or material substance:

> By supposing a substance wherein thinking, knowing, doubting, and a power of moving, etc. do subsist, we have as clear a notion of the substance of spirit as we have of body: the one being supposed to be (without knowing what it is) the substratum of those simple ideas we have from without; and the other supposed (with like ignorance what it is) to be the substratum to those operations which we experiment in ourselves within."[3]

For Edwards, on the contrary, a body consists in nothing but the ideas of sensation "from without" that are immediately communicated to the mind by God. And from the argument in Miscell. no. 267, it appears that a mind itself is nothing but various thoughts, perceptions, etc. which are likewise immediately produced and sustained by God.

Edwards' rejection of the Lockean account of spirit is indicated as early as "The Mind," No. 11, where he comments upon Locke's theory of persons and the identity of persons. According to Locke, as one cannot know what the substance or spirit is that thinks in him, so he cannot know whether the same or a different spiritual substance might be thinking in him at different times, or whether the same or different spirits might belong to different persons. Nevertheless, he points out, each *person* is "a thinking intelligent being that has reason and reflection and considers itself as itself, the same thinking thing in different times and places; which it does only by that consciousness which is inseparable from thinking and, as it seems to me, essential to it."[4] Each individual self or person, Locke holds, identifies itself and distinguishes itself from all other persons by its own unique consciousness. "As far as

2. Townsend, p. 78.
3. *Essay*, Bk. II, ch. 23, no. 5.
4. Ibid., ch. 27, no. 9.

this consciousness can be extended backwards to any past action or thought, so far reaches the identity of that person."[5] In "The Mind," No. 11, Edwards seems to approve this account of the identity of persons; but as for Locke's distinction between persons and spiritual substances, he adds, "He might have said that identity of spirits, too, consisted in the same consciousness. For a mind or spirit is nothing but consciousness and what is included in it. The same consciousness is, to all intents and purposes, individually the very same spirit or substance, as much as the same particle of matter can be the same with itself at different times."[6]

Edwards' difference from Locke on this fundamental point seems central to his interpretation and modification of Locke's claims about minds, their nature and their acts and operations. Edwards denies that the conscious thoughts and actions of a mind subsist in an unknown substance, and that they arise from or depend upon the real essence of such a substance. On the contrary, he holds that every state of consciousness is immediately produced by God, and that the existence of individual minds, their natures, properties, and relations to other minds and to bodies, are founded upon the constant method or established rules by which God acts in producing them. In his "Diary" for February 12, 1725, during the first year of his tutorship, Edwards wrote, "The very thing I now want, to give me a clearer and more immediate view of the perfections and glory of God, is as clear a knowledge of the manner of God's exerting himself, with respect to spirits and mind, as I have, of his operations concerning matter and bodies."[7] In his "Subjects to be Handled in the Treatise on the Mind" he comments, "The manifest analogy between the nature of the human soul and the nature of other things: how laws of nature take place alike; how it is laws that constitute all permanent being in created things, both corporeal and spiritual."[8] And again in the same series, "In how many respects the very being of created things depends on laws, or stated methods fixed by God, of events following one another."[9]

His rejection of Locke's conception of the thinking substance may be associated with several other points in which Edwards takes explicit exception to Locke's claims. One instance concerns the question wheth-

5. Ibid.
6. Below, pp. 242–43.
7. Dwight, *1*, p. 105.
8. "Subjects," No. 36; below, p. 391.
9. Ibid., No. 50; below, p. 392.

er matter could think. Followers of Descartes maintained that the essence of matter excludes thinking, so that thought must be the essence of another distinct substance. Locke, on the other hand, held that thinking is not continuous in the mind, but consists in episodes of conscious mental action and operation; hence it cannot be the essence of the thinking substance, but only one of its operations, as motion is of the body that moves.[1] Indeed, he argues, in view of our ignorance as to what substance it is in us that thinks, we cannot prove it impossible that matter should think: "It is not much more remote from our comprehension to conceive that God can, if he pleases, superadd to matter the faculty of thinking, than that he should superadd to it another substance with the faculty of thinking."[2]

But Edwards supposes no such ignorance of the substance that thinks. Accordingly, in "The Mind," No. 21a, he argues in support of the Cartesian position that the nature of matter excludes the possibility of matter itself thinking. All the properties in matter, he holds, have a necessary dependence upon solidity and extension; but thought has no such connection with these or the other properties in matter, and is even "alien" to them. God may, and does, *add* thought (though not a thinking substance) to a body according to certain laws, so that thought is "in the same place" as the body, but he cannot include it *in* the properties of matter in such a way that it would depend upon those properties and so as to make matter itself think.[3]

It should be noted in connection with this argument that Edwards did not work out his phenomenalistic account of solidity, reducing the property to a law governing the order and succession of perceived ideas, until afterward in "The Mind," No. 27. There is no indication that he attempted at any later time to reformulate his argument in terms of relations among the laws governing ideas instead of relations among properties in matter. Miscell. no. 1263, in which he discusses God's immediate and arbitrary operations, contains a suggestion as to how such a reformulation might be given: God's creation of bodies involves a primary and absolutely arbitrary operation by which the laws of resistance, attraction, and inertia were established, and then a secondary operation establishing the dispositions and motions of particular bodies. The secondary operation is also arbitrary, but not absolutely

1. *Essay*, Bk. II, ch. 1, no. 10.
2. Ibid., Bk. IV. ch. 3, no. 6.
3. Below, pp. 346–48.

so, since it follows upon and presupposes or "makes use of" the primary. But the creation of the soul, he holds, is not by any secondary or consequent operation of God: "Most things in the visible world were brought into their present state so as to [be] of such a particular kind, or to complete their species of creatures, by a secondary creation, which is a mixed operation; excepting the creation of the highest order of creatures, viz., intelligent minds, which were wholly created, complete in their kind, by an absolutely arbitrary operation."[4] The passage does not attempt to demonstrate that God's creation of intelligent thought must be by a primary operation, however, and it may well be questioned whether such a demonstration would be possible. However that may be, Edwards continued to accept the proof as originally presented in "The Mind," No. 21a, and in Miscell. no. 361 he jotted down a reminder of the place where he had written it.[5]

Another matter in which Edwards came to differ from Locke pertains to the question of the identity of the self, or, as Edwards would have it, the identity of a spirit. Despite his seeming approval of Locke's account of personal identity in "The Mind," No. 11, Edwards later offers explicit objections to it in "The Mind," No. 72, and implies other criticisms in his extended treatment of the subject in *Original Sin*. In both places Edwards follows Locke in attending to the practical bearings of personal identity, as the self may be concerned in its own future happiness or misery but indifferent to the future condition of others, and as it is subject to reward or punishment for its own past actions but not those of others. And in both places Edwards suggests that Locke is mistaken in proposing that the identity of one's self depends necessarily and entirely upon one's conscious memories of particular past thoughts and actions. In Edwards' own view, the identity of a self or spirit, and indeed of any other created thing, depends entirely upon the arbitrary constitution of God by which he determines the order and course of successive ideas and states of consciousness.

It seems evident that Locke's account of personal identity is developed on the assumption that a self, in any of its present states, knows with certainty which present self it is, and is capable of knowing which past self it was, and of conceiving which future self it will be. Consequently, it can be certain about which past actions it is responsible for and which future state of happiness or misery it is uniquely interested

4. Miscell. no. 1263 in Townsend, pp. 184–93.
5. Miscell. no. 361: "Soul of man. Matter. Thought. Vid. Mind, p. 8."

in, namely, the actions and states of its past and future selves. Locke thus argues that, because our beliefs about our past selves involve memories of past states of consciousness, and our conception of our future self involves the idea of memories of our present states of consciousness, it is memory alone that makes us certain of our unique and continuing personal identity. Moreover, he seems to hold that the very fact of personal identity is founded on memory alone, and consequently determines which past actions and future states we are now responsible for. "For as far as any intelligent being can repeat the idea of any past action with the same consciousness it had of it at first, and with the same consciousness it has of any present action, so far it is the same personal self."[6]

In "The Mind," No. 72 Edwards questions whether memory is sufficient for personal identity, or even sufficient for one's beliefs concerning his identity, especially with regard to his future existence. God might annihilate me and create another self that has my present ideas as its memories, although I should have no reason to concern myself about its welfare. We could reply on behalf of Locke that whatever future self has my present ideas as memories is necessarily identical with me, and is certainly the self whose welfare I am now considering. But, Edwards goes on, that future self is not necessarily unique. God might create two persons with exactly the same memories of past actions and experiences, but differing with respect to their present actions and experiences; one might be happy and the other miserable. Assuming Locke's view, both these persons would be identical with the same past self, and each would be responsible for that self's actions. But neither would be identical with the other, nor even need be conscious of the existence or condition of the other.[7]

The above objections tend to argue that, as opposed to Locke's theory, the sameness of consciousness and memory is not sufficient for self-identity. In *Original Sin* Edwards allows it is necessary, or "one thing essential to it," but adds, "'Tis evident, that the communication or continuance of the same consciousness and memory to any subject, through successive parts of duration, depends wholly on a divine establishment."[8] His subsequent account of identity is intended to show that it would not be unjust or unreasonable for God to impute Adam's sin

6. *Essay*, Bk. II, ch. 27, no. 10.
7. Below, pp. 385–86.
8. *Works* (Yale ed.), *3*, p. 398.

to all subsequent human beings as their own sin, for it is not impossible that God's establishment for all subsequent persons is such as to make each of them truly and in fact identical with him, so that his sin is in fact theirs. The points of this argument concerning Edwards' concept of mind or spirit may be drawn into focus without tracing the whole exposition of it in detail.

His argument depends essentially upon the assumption that every created thing, in any moment when it exists, is immediately and entirely the effect of God's acting in that moment. It follows that every created thing is an effect, and that things existing at different moments in time are numerically distinct effects. "There is no identity or oneness in the case, but what depends on the *arbitrary* constitution of the Creator; who by his wise sovereign establishment so unites these successive new effects, that he *treats them as one*, by communicating to them like properties, relations, and circumstances; and so leads us to regard and treat them as one."[9] It is thus entirely due to an arbitrary constitution that satisfies the divine wisdom, that successive states of consciousness are united in such a way as to be the same, and involve the same memories of one continued self. It is likewise by an arbitrary constitution that each person subsequent to Adam is united to him, or is the same person as he. We may conceive such a constitution applying throughout nature, Edwards holds, so that every individual member of any natural kind is, by divine establishment, one with the first and original parent of that kind, and so that all subsequent members are given properties in accordance with those of the first parent.[1]

In the case of persons, Edwards certainly did not suppose that God unites us with Adam by giving each of us the same conscious memory of Adam's sinful action as being our own, in the manner that Locke's explanation of personal guilt would require.[2] Adam's act of disobedience is ours by virtue of our "innate sinful depravity of heart,"[3] or a

9. Ibid., p. 403.

1. Ibid., p. 406.

2. Locke writes, "For supposing a man punished now for what he had done in another life, whereof he could be made to have no consciousness at all, what difference is there between that punishment and being created miserable? And therefore conformable to this, the Apostle tells us, that at the Great Day, when everyone shall receive according to his doings, the secrets of all hearts shall be laid open. The sentence shall be justified by the consciousness all persons shall have that they themselves, in what bodies soever they appear, or what substances soever that consciousness adheres to, are the same that committed those actions and deserve that punishment for them" (*Essay*, Bk. II, ch. 27, no. 26).

3. *Original Sin*, Pt. I, ch. 1, §1, in *Works* (Yale ed.), *3*, p. 107.

"natural tendency or propensity" to sin.[4] More precisely, it is by virtue of the *first* existence of a corrupt disposition in any of Adam's posterity, "whereby he is disposed to *approve* of the sin of his first father, as fully as he himself approved of it when he committed it, or so far as to imply a full and perfect consent of heart to it."[5]

Edwards' claim that each person possesses a definite innate moral disposition, which is prior to his first conscious experiences and actions and his particular memories of these, indicates an important departure from Locke's conception of the mind as being, in its first existence, a mere "white paper."[6] Nor is Edwards' departure in this matter confined to his admission of innate moral tendencies in accounting for original sin. In "The Mind," No. 54 he asserts that causal reasoning depends upon "an innate principle, in that sense that the soul is born with it; a necessary fatal propensity so to conclude on every occasion."[7] Other passages indicate that Edwards considers much, if not all, of our conscious mental processes in perceiving, reasoning, and judging arise from and are determined by fixed dispositions of the mind, and that he regards at least some of these dispositions to be innate, in some sense of that term.

The nature of the difference between Edwards and Locke with respect to innateness in the mind is not immediately apparent, however. Locke had argued at length that the mind has no innate ideas, that all its ideas arise from and are supplied by its conscious experience, at first by sensation and then by reflection.[8] Edwards seems to agree fully with this doctrine, especially in his "Subjects to be Handled in the Treatise on the Mind," where in No. 29 he sets the topic, "Sensation: How far all acts of the mind are from sensation, all ideas begin from thence, and there never can be any idea, thought or act of the mind unless the mind first received some ideas from sensation, or some other way equivalent, wherein the mind is wholly passive in receiving them."[9] Nos. 30, 31, and 32 of the series continue this theme, with suggestions that even angels and other separate spirits must receive ideas of sensation, and so are "united to some kind of matter."[1] Yet in No. 52 he

4. Ibid., p. 120.
5. Ibid., p. 391.
6. *Essay*, Bk. II, ch. 1, no. 2.
7. Below, p. 370.
8. *Essay*, Bk. II, ch. 1, nos. 3–4.
9. Below, p. 390.
1. Below, pp. 390–91.

promises to discuss "in what respects ideas or thoughts and judgments may be said to be innate and in what respects not."[2] His explanations of original sin and of causal reasoning, as mentioned above, indicate that he does not suppose our consciously perceived ideas or conscious acts of thought and judgment are innate in us, but only that certain dispositions, tendencies, or propensities for such conscious states are innate. And Locke's attack upon innate ideas does not seem to rule out the possibility that dispositions are innate.

Nevertheless, Locke's *tabula rasa* theory of mind does preclude the possibility of our having innate dispositions of the sort that Edwards admits; and as a result, Edwards' discussions of the operations of consciousness in cognition and volition are in disagreement with Locke's in some fundamental respects. A comparison of the two ways of treating these operations will help to clarify Edwards' conception of the nature of the mind. It will also tend to show that, in his lifelong study of the *Essay*, Edwards used Locke's views more as a foil for developing his own conception of the spiritual world than as a source or authority for it.

The *tabula rasa* theory of mind, as asserted by Locke, forms the basis for an extended account of how thinking goes on in us, and how knowledge, belief, and volition come about. According to this account, the mind, before it actually receives ideas and consciously perceives them, possesses nothing but capacities, faculties, or powers for receiving and retaining ideas, and for performing various other acts and operations with and about them. Locke's empiricism consists in the claims that no act or operation of the mind can be performed before it has actually received and passively perceived simple ideas, first by sensation and then by reflection, and that no operation can produce a simple idea that has not already been perceived in this manner.[3] At the same time, he holds that all reflective thinking, cognition, and voluntary action either consist in or depend upon the mind's actually exercising its active powers in performing the various acts and operations of which it is capable about the ideas it perceives. That is, our concepts of objects, our knowledge and beliefs concerning them, and our voluntary actions as well, result from the mind's performing those acts and operations of which it is capable. Thus such knowledge as we have and are able to have results from operations of the understanding, by which we distinguish or compare, combine and separate, abstract from, and connect

2. Below, p. 392.
3. *Essay*, Bk. II, ch. 2, no. 2.

together ideas.[4] All our concepts of individual things and their properties and powers, their kinds, relations, and modes, are formed by performing these operations about the simple primitive ideas originally received by sensation and reflection.[5] Voluntary action depends upon the mind's consciously preferring and choosing or commanding the performance or forbearance of an action, either one of the operations of the understanding itself or some motion in the body.[6]

This account of thinking involves the basic assumption that all states of knowledge, belief, and volition involve the conscious activity of an agent, not of the understanding and will, but of the mind which has the powers of understanding and willing.[7] We cannot know what the mind is, but through introspection and our ideas of reflection we can discover what it does and what it therefore is capable of doing. Although the mind cannot exercise its faculties or capacities without having perceived ideas to exercise them about, the capacities themselves neither consist in nor depend upon ideas. They may thus be said to belong to the mind by nature, and to be innate in it, even though the mind has no innate ideas. In addition, Locke seems to assume that the mind has natural dispositions or propensities to exercise its abilities, to set itself upon the appropriate intellectual tasks, and to perform the due acts and operations of which it is capable on the occasions when it actually perceives ideas. To this extent, Locke's view seems to admit of the mind's having innate dispositions. But these are quite different from dispositions or propensities to choose sin or to infer the existence of a cause, such as Edwards holds to be innate. The former would be manifested in the mind's regularly exercising its powers, while the latter would be manifested in the mind's regularly arriving at or realizing some definite contingent result. In Locke's view, all such dispositions as these must be acquired from the accidental connections of ideas

4. Locke lists the operations of mind in ibid., ch. 1, no. 4, and discusses them at length in ibid., chs. 9–11. In ch. 11, no. 14, he writes, "Observing the faculties of the mind, how they operate about ideas, . . . we may the better examine and learn how the mind abstracts, denominates, compares, and exercises its other operations about those which are complex, wherein we are much more liable to mistake." Accordingly, he remarks of the discerning faculty, "so far as this faculty is in itself dull or not rightly made use of, for the distinguishing one thing from another, so far our notions are confused, and our reason and judgment disturbed or misled" (ch. 11, no. 2). Similar observations are made concerning the proper use of each faculty.

5. Ibid., ch. 12, nos. 1–2.

6. Ibid., ch. 21, no. 5.

7. Ibid., no. 6.

in experience, and they are manifested in the mind's associating or connecting ideas by habit or custom, without reflection or antecedent operations of reason.[8]

It is doubtful how far Edwards supposed that conscious thinking involves our consciousness of our performing such a variety of mental acts and operations as Locke describes. As we have noted, his later comments show that he agreed with Locke that all thinking begins with our passively receiving ideas of sensation, and he supposed that from these ideas and the order in which they are presented we form ideas of external things and come to know the laws of nature that govern them. But Edwards gives no clear account of how such ideas are formed and such knowledge is achieved. The main trends of his epistemological discussions, however, suggest that, instead of the step-by-step operations required in Locke's empiricist account of our acquisition of concepts and knowledge, Edwards consistently assumes that our apprehension, even of complex objects, is direct and immediate, and does not depend upon prior reflection and conscious methodical procedure. In earlier passages he seems to hold that all knowledge is either immediate and intuitive, or arises by necessary inference from what is intuitively known. In later discussions he argues that certain acts of cognition which are neither intuitive nor demonstrative occur immediately and without reflection as they are determined by fixed dispositions, propensities, and habits of the mind.

Edwards' earlier emphasis upon intuition and demonstration shows the important influence of seventeenth-century rationalism upon his thought. The essay "Of the Prejudices of Imagination" is an unmistakable reflection of the Cartesian logics of William Brattle and Antoine Arnauld that he studied in college. He apparently used these logic books again while teaching the subject at Yale, and several articles in "The Mind" show their continuing influence upon his thought.[9] His primary concern in these passages is with the impediments that stand in the way of intuitive and demonstrative knowledge. We are prevented from the certain and rational apprehension of objects, he maintains, by prejudices of the imagination formed from our earliest conscious experi-

---

8. Ibid., ch. 33, especially nos. 5–7. This chapter first appeared in the second edition of 1694.

9. Leon Howard, in *"The Mind" of Jonathan Edwards: A Reconstructed Text* (Berkeley, 1963), comments at length upon the apparent influence of Arnauld's *Art of Thinking* upon various of JE's discussions in "The Mind."

ences,[1] by the ideas of sensation themselves which "clog the mind,"[2] and by the weakness of our minds and the imperfections of our ideas of things. Demonstration itself, he holds, gives only relative assurance, for it depends upon our severely limited ability to keep ideas attentively in order before the mind so as to discern their connections.[3] In one place he asserts that if we were to have perfect ideas of all things at once we would have no need for reasoning, because things would be immediately known and self-evident.[4] And in another he claims that if it were not for the "imperfection and slowness of our minds," the accurate observation of a falling body in one part of its motion would "immediately and of itself" give rise to the idea of the whole of its motion.[5]

Consonant with this view of knowledge as the immediate apprehension of self-evident truths, Edwards maintains at first, in "The Mind," No. 19, that we have immediate and intuitive knowledge of such general facts as that grass is green and honey is sweet, even though the facts themselves consist in regularities among ideas in the constant course of experience.[6] Later, however, in "The Mind," No. 53 he acknowledges that the certainty or fallibility of perceptual judgments depends upon the constancy of our experience and our opportunities for trial and experiment in cases similar to the one being judged.[7] This change of view with regard to perceptual judgment might have been stimulated by his reading of Berkeley's *An Essay Towards a New Theory of Vision*. The influence of that work seems evident in several later articles in which Edwards discusses the role of judgment in cognition, and the manner in which judgment is formed. In "The Mind," No. 57 he follows Berkeley in holding that judgments of spatial distance are not based upon a natural trigonometry of the eyes or on our observation of the angles at which light rays converge to them, "for the mind judges by nothing but the difference it observes in the idea itself, which alone the mind has any notice of."[8] Like Berkeley, he explains these judg-

1. "Of the Prejudices of Imagination," below, p. 196.
2. "The Mind," No. 22, below, pp. 348–49.
3. Ibid., No. 5, below, pp. 339–40.
4. Ibid., No. 10, corol. 3, below, p. 342.
5. Ibid., No. 34, below, p. 354.
6. Below, p. 346.
7. Below, pp. 369–70.
8. Below, p. 372. See Berkeley, *New Theory of Vision*, §§4–13, 19–20; in Luce, *Works of Berkeley, 1*, pp. 171–73, 175.

ments by our recognizing a "particular mode of indistinctness" in the ideas;[9] and he explains judgments of temporal distance, or "pastness," in a similar manner by "a certain peculiar inexpressible mode of fading and indistinctness which I call veterascence."[1] In "The Mind," No. 59 he agrees with Berkeley again in distinguishing between these judgments and intuitive or demonstrative knowledge: "Though the thing is not properly self-evident, yet [the mind] judges without any ratiocination, merely by the force of habit."[2] Our regular experience, he goes on, gives rise to an habitual association of ideas which determines our judgment without antecedent reflection. Similarly, in "The Mind," No. 69, he declares that memory involves the repetition of an idea together with an act of judgment that it was perceived before; "and that judgment not properly from proof, but from natural necessity arising from a law of nature which God hath fixed."[3]

All this suggests a general progression in Edwards' conception of how the mind knows, from an early emphasis upon intuition and demonstration which may be associated with Cartesian and generally rationalist theories of mind, to a later emphasis upon mental habits of associating ideas and propensities for certain acts of judgment, such as may be associated with the post-Lockean empiricism of Berkeley and Hume.[4] Throughout this progression Edwards either disregards or rejects Locke's own analysis of the faculties of mind and the operations by which they are exercised. His treatment of Locke in this matter is nowhere more evident than in the series of articles in "The Mind" concerned with abstract ideas and genus and species.

In "The Mind," No. 7 Edwards assumes with Locke that our abstract ideas are "creatures of the mind," formed by us to expedite reflection and discourse.[5] But in this article Edwards holds these ideas are formed arbitrarily, while Locke holds that our abstract ideas of natural kinds are made by us in conformity with the observed regular features and

9. *New Theory of Vision*, §3, ibid., p. 171.

1. Below, pp. 372–73.

2. Below, p. 373. See *New Theory of Vision*, §45, in Luce, *Works of Berkeley, 1*, pp. 187–88.

3. Below, p. 384.

4. Sang Hyun Lee discusses the importance of habit and disposition in JE's theory of mind in "Jonathan Edwards' Theory of the Imagination," *Michigan Academician: Papers of the Michigan Academy of Science, Arts, and Letters, 5* (Fall, 1972), pp. 233–41, and in "Mental Activity and the Perception of Beauty in Jonathan Edwards," *Harvard Theological Review, 69* (1976), pp. 369–96.

5. *Essay*, Bk. III, ch. 3, no. 11.

common properties of the objects themselves. In Locke's view, only our ideas of modes are formed in a wholly arbitrary manner.[6] The adequacy and truth of these ideas are guaranteed, he holds, for it does not depend upon their correspondence with anything else, but only upon their being formed.[7] Edwards proposes a comparable standard of truth, internal consistency, for all abstract ideas.[8] Yet in "The Mind," No. 17 he recalls the pleasure he had earlier received from studying the abstract system of definitions and distributions of the "old logic," for it taught him to place his ideas in order, and revealed "new and strange dependencies of ideas, and a seeming agreement of multitudes of them in the same thing that I never observed before."[9] Later he maintains that some abstract ideas have a real foundation in nature, not by virtue of the manner in which we form them, but because "God evidently designed such particulars to be together in the mind and in other things."[1] In "The Mind," No. 42 Edwards directly attacks Locke's account of the operation by which abstract ideas are formed: the abstract ideas of color and sound cannot be formed by mentally sifting out the common features of all particular colors and all particular sounds, for these are simple ideas and have no common features.[2] In these cases, he argues, the mind perceives a unique and unanalyzable agreement among some of its simple ideas, from which it is "determined to rank those ideas together in its thoughts; . . . and by the nature, determination and habit of the mind, the idea of one excites the idea of others."[3] In the next article Edwards declares that "the union of ideas is not always arbitrary, but unavoidably arising from the nature of the soul, which is such that the thinking of one thing, of itself, yea,

6. Ibid., ch. 5, no. 3.

7. Ibid., Bk. II, ch. 32, no. 13: "As to the truth and falsehood of our ideas in reference to the real existence of things: when that is made the standard of their truth, none of them can be termed false, but only our complex ideas of substances." But Locke earlier (ch. 32, no. 9) notes that when the truth of ideas is judged by "the conformity they have to the ideas which other men have and commonly signify by the same name," then all ideas might be false; and indeed, our complex ideas of mixed modes are the most likely to be false in this sense (no. 10).

8. "The Mind," No. 10, below, p. 342.

9. Below, p. 345. It remains moot whether the "old logic" to which JE refers in this entry was that of Ramus or that of the Aristotelians (e.g., Burgersdijck or Morton); and whether by the "other logic" he means that of Arnauld (and Brattle) or that of Locke. Clearly, each of these left a characteristic mark upon some important part or aspect of his thought.

1. "The Mind," No. 37, below, p. 355.

2. Below, pp. 360–61. See Locke's account of abstraction, *Essay*, Bk. III, ch. 3.

3. Below, p. 361. Compare JE's earlier discussion of the agreement of sense qualities in "The Mind," No. 1, below, pp. 335–36.

against our wills, excites the thought of other things that are like it."
God himself thus distributes things into kinds, not only by manifesting
agreements among them, but by "making the soul of such a nature that
those particulars which he thus made to agree are unavoidably together in the mind, one naturally exciting and including the others."[4]

The above examination indicates that in his later discussions of the
manner in which we make causal inferences and perceptual judgments,
and form memories and abstract ideas, Edwards finds that our performances are not reflective and procedural, and they do not depend
upon our recognizing intrinsically necessary connections among the
ideas concerned. Instead, although the mind acts in a constant and
regular manner in these cases, it typically acts without antecedent
conscious reflection. And it connects or unites ideas, and forms judgments concerning them, even in the absence of perceived evidence or
demonstrated proof of their actual connection. The mind's operations
in these cases, Edwards holds, are nevertheless not at random, but are
determined according to its fixed habits and dispositions, either innate
or natural, or developed from earlier experiences.

It is important to note that, although these habits and dispositions
are manifested in certain states and acts of the mind, they do not themselves consist in mental states or acts; they are not treated simply as felt
constraints upon or inclinations of our mental endeavor. Instead,
Edwards uses the terms "habit," "disposition," "tendency," "propensity" to mean any general law governing the regular order of antecedent and consequent occurrences. Thus in Miscell. no. 241, in the
context of a discussion of the habit of grace, he writes:

> All habits being only a law that God has fixed that such actions,
> upon such occasions, should be exerted, the first new thing that
> there can be in the creature must be some actual alteration. So,
> in the first birth, it seems to me probable that the beginning of the
> existence of the soul, whose essence consists in powers and habits,
> is with some kind of new alteration there, either in motion or
> sensation.[5]

In "The Mind," No. 69 he notes the difficulty of discovering the laws
of nature which govern our mental acts;[6] in his "Subjects to be Handled
in the Treatise on the Mind" he proposes that they might be reduced

---

4. "The Mind," No. 43, below, p. 362.
5. Transcription of the original supplied by Thomas Schafer.
6. Below, p. 385.

to three principles, namely, "association of ideas, resemblance of some kind, and that natural disposition in us, when we see anything begin to be, to suppose it owing to a cause." These laws, he says, are "a kind of mutual attraction of ideas," by which "one idea suggests and brings in another."[7]

These references to laws governing the order and sequence of thoughts, and Edwards' statement that "laws of nature take place alike" in the mind and in other things,[8] can give rise to a misleading interpretation of his theory of mind. He does not suppose that our mental lives consist solely in successive episodes of conscious perception, following each other according to fixed rules. In his treatise on the mind he intended to discuss "wherein there is an agreement between men and beasts; how many things in men are like instincts in brutes."[9] According to "The Mind," No. 59, the habitual association of ideas is one respect in which human and animal intelligence are alike. But in his addendum to that article Edwards points out that animals are capable of no more than perception, memory, and habitual association, whereas the human mind can consciously reflect upon its acts and voluntarily and actively arrange and dispose its ideas. It is thereby capable of rational will, while animals have only instinct and sensual appetite; and the human mind is capable of knowing spiritual things and hence capable of religion.[1]

All this notwithstanding, self-conscious reflection and volition do not give the mind an absolute governance over its thoughts and judgments. We find, in some cases, that "the thinking of one thing, of itself, yea, against our wills, excites the thought of other things that are like it,"[2] and that the supposition "that anything should start up into being without any cause, itself or anything else, is what the mind, do what we will, will forever refuse to receive, but will perpetually reject."[3] The discovery in ourselves of the unavoidability of these associations and the inability of the mind to think otherwise, through trial and failure, gives us knowledge of the laws or the constant manner in which God acts with respect to our minds. Moreover, Edwards holds that our recognized inabilities to think or believe otherwise are, by themselves, grounds for

---

7. "Subjects," No. 43, below, pp. 391–92.
8. Ibid., No. 36, below, p. 391.
9. Ibid., No. 49, below, p. 392.
1. Below, p. 374.
2. "The Mind," No. 43, below, p. 361.
3. Ibid., No. 54, below, p. 393.

the assurance of what is thought or believed. In his treatise on the mind he intended to discuss a two-fold ground of the assurance of judgment: "a reducing things to an identity or contradiction, as in mathematical demonstrations, and by a natural, invincible inclination to a connection, as when we see any effect, to conclude a cause; an opposition to believe a thing can begin to be without a cause. This is not the same with the other and cannot be reduced to a contradiction."[4]

Edwards recognizes that in admitting our self-conscious intellectual inabilities and our "invincible inclination to a connection" of ideas as evidence sufficient to justify belief, he is making a profound and fundamental departure from Locke's theory of knowledge, and indeed from the whole rationalist tradition. In "The Mind," No. 71 he specifically lays aside Locke's definition of knowledge: "Knowledge is not the perception of the agreement or disagreement of ideas, but rather the perception of the union or disunion of ideas, or the perceiving whether two or more ideas belong to one another."[5] The perception of union or disunion, as Edwards speaks of it, is not the recognition of a relation among the ideas themselves, but a recognition of the mind's own inability to act otherwise with regard to them. Hence he adds, "Perhaps it cannot properly be said that we see the agreement of the ideas unless we see how they agree, but we may perceive that they are united and know that they belong to one another, though we do not know the manner how they are tied together."[6] Accordingly, we may know the truth even of propositions that we cannot understand, on the basis of our fixed inclination to believe them and our inability to believe the contrary.

Thus the mysteries of faith become evident to the saint through a divine influence which alters the disposition of his mind and affords him a view of divine things that convinces him of their truth. In his attacks upon the deists Edwards repeatedly argues that our ordinary and scientific convictions about the natural world are no more founded upon absolutely indisputable argument than the doctrines of religion; but on the other hand, he maintains, the saint's convictions about God rest upon evidence as compelling for him as the evidence of scientific or philosophical truths is for one whose beliefs are governed by natural dispositions of the mind.[7] In Miscell. no. 1297 he takes note of Hume's treatment of the causal argument for God's existence, an argument to

4. "Subjects," No. 10, below, p. 388.
5. Below, p. 385.
6. Ibid.
7. This is the substance of JE's argument in Miscell. no. 1340; see Townsend, pp. 219–35.

which Edwards himself was committed. Hume undertakes, he writes, "to shew that there is no real connection between cause and effect, and that there can be no certain or even probable reasoning from one to the other. He endeavors to subvert all proofs of a particular providence, of a future state, and of an intelligent cause of the universe."[8] Edwards himself supposes that our belief in the causal relation and the necessity of a cause does not rest upon intuition or proof of that connection, but only upon a fixed propensity of the mind. But in "The Mind," No. 54 he argues that this propensity underlies a rational belief about God's existence and nature.

This discussion of Edwards' theory of mind should end with some remarks about his views concerning the will. His most detailed and important discussions of volition are found in his *Freedom of the Will* and in the manuscript writings, letters, etc. that are associated with the work.[9] "The Mind," Nos. 21b, 60, 67, and 70, and several comments in his "Subjects to Be Handled in the Treatise on the Mind," virtually exhaust the passages in this volume that are specifically concerned with the topic. But these few discussions and remarks are of particular interest for what they suggest concerning Edwards' concept of the will as part of his general theory of the mind.

One of the most important points that these passages make clear is that Edwards wholly rejected the traditional distinction between the will and the affections. Among the "Subjects" for his treatise he included, "Of the nature of the affections or passions: how only strong and lively exercises of the will; together with the effect on the animal nature."[1] In the same series he also proposes to discuss "how far the love of happiness is the same with the faculty of the will; it is not distinct from the mere capacity of enjoying and suffering, and the faculty of the will is no other."[2] And in "The Mind," No. 67 he asserts the direct opposite of Locke's account of pleasure and pain:

> Pleasure and pain are not properly ideas. Though pleasure and pain may imply perception in their nature, yet it does not follow that they are properly ideas. There is an act of the mind in it. . . . All acts of the mind about its ideas are not themselves mere ideas.
>
> Pleasure and pain have their seat in the will, and not in the under-

8. Townsend, p. 216.
9. See in *Works* (Yale ed.), *1*.
1. "Subjects," No. 7, below, p. 388.
2. Ibid., No. 44, below, p. 392.

standing. The will, choice, etc. is nothing else but the mind's being pleased with an idea, or having a superior pleasedness in something thought of, . . . or a pleasedness in such a state of ourselves and a degree of pain when we are not in that state, or a disagreeable conception of the contrary state at that time when we desire it.[3]

In these passages it is clear that Edwards understands pleasure and pain in general, not as being perceived states or sensations in the mind, but as being intentional acts; pleasure and pain are the acts of being pleased or displeased *with* or *in something* that is perceived or contemplated. Moreover, he holds that whatever it is that the mind is inclined to or disposed to be pleased with is that mind's apprehension of good. In "The Mind," No. 60 he writes, "It is utterly impossible but that it should be so, that the inclination and choice of the mind should always be determined by good as mentally or ideally existing. It would be a contradiction to suppose otherwise. For we mean nothing else by 'good' but that which agrees with the inclination and disposition of the mind; and surely that which agrees with it must agree with it."[4] To this extent, the much exercised question whether the will is determined by the apprehension of good is settled by definition. The problem Edwards deals with in this article is not primarily whether good determines the will, but which perceived good determines a particular act of will. The particular act of will as distinct from the faculty, general inclination or disposition of will, is "the mind's inclination with respect to its own immediate actions."[5] In No. 12 of his series of "Subjects" he asserts more plainly, "Imperate acts of the will nothing but the prevailing inclination, concerning what should be done that moment; so God hath ordained that the motions of the body should follow that."[6]

It is not difficult, in the light of these passages, to understand the nature of Edwards' criticism of Locke in "The Mind," No. 70. Locke considered "uneasiness" to be a felt state or sensation of the mind, which is antecedent to the act of will and distinct from it. That this state, or the mind's perception of it, determines the will was, for Locke, an empirical fact which he took great pains to establish.[7] But for Edwards, on the contrary, uneasiness should be regarded as a disposition

3. Below, p. 384.
4. Below, p. 376.
5. Ibid.
6. Below, pp. 388–89.
7. *Essay*, Bk. II, ch. 21, nos. 33–40. Locke added these sections to his chapter on power in the second edition of the *Essay*.

or act of the will itself, so that the question whether it determines the will when it occurs is settled by definition. Edwards' point in this passage is that uneasiness in our present state cannot determine, or constitute, every particular act of will; our will and choice to remain in the same state can never be determined by, or consist in, our uneasiness in it.[8]

The will, then, is "nothing else but the mind's being pleased with" ideas or states of ourselves, or, on the other hand, its being displeased with them. The assertion of this point in "The Mind," No. 67 leads us directly to that feature of his theory of excellency according to which, as we found earlier, he claimed that it is necessary that the perception of agreement be pleasing to the mind, and the perception of disagreement be painful. Accordingly, we should expect that Edwards' account of the nature and dynamics of the will is largely founded upon his theory of excellency, that his very concept of will is inextricably tied to some account of how we perceive excellency and deformity, and that will is to be understood as the necessary agreeableness or disagreeableness of such perceptions.

An examination of other passages in "The Mind" indicates that this is certainly the case. In "The Mind," No. 45, his second major treatment of excellency in the series, he begins, "When we spake of excellence in bodies we were obliged to borrow the word 'consent' from spiritual things. But excellence in and among spirits is, in its prime and proper sense, being's consent to being. There is no other proper consent but that of minds, even of their will; which, when it is of minds towards minds, it is love, and when of minds towards other things it is choice."[9] What Edwards here speaks of as a matter of correct terminology actually involves a major development in his theory of excellency. When someone perceives excellency in an object or set of objects, we are told, he not only is pleased with or by that excellency, but his being so constitutes a consent with or to it. As the remaining discussion in "The Mind," No. 45 makes clear, this consent itself involves a relation between the consenting person and the object that pleases him and that he consents to; a relation that may be beheld by some other mind, and found to be agreeable and lovely, or deformed and odious. Edwards thus turns from an account of how the will works to an account of what makes its workings virtuous or vicious. It is the former account that we are presently

8. See below, p. 385.
9. Below, p. 362.

concerned with; but we may note in passing that he here takes his general theory of excellency to be the basis for his moral theory. That is, the moral theory is worked out by considering how one mind's love for or hate of another (or indifference to another), as it is related to that other mind, may be agreeable or disagreeable, lovely or odious, to one that beholds it.[1] But the entire exposition of "The Mind," No. 45 presupposes that will, whether as love or as choice, consists in a mind's being pleased with an excellency that is perceived.

The consequence of such a view may be seen to give rise to a serious problem, and one which had long been considered central to the theory of the will. If good is the proper object of the will, what accounts for the clear and evident fact that we choose what is evil? The most straighforward explanation for the partisans of such a theory is that we choose what appears to the intellect at that time to be good; that it is in fact evil that we choose is fundamentally an error in the mind's factual judgment about the object. But this explanation is not easy to defend; in many cases, perhaps even most, we choose the evil or less good even though our factual judgments as to goodness are not mistaken, or at least are contrary to the choice. It was this, indeed, that led Locke to set aside the theory that the perception of goodness determines the will, and to propose that it is determined instead by our feeling of uneasiness in our present state.[2] But as we have noted, Edwards treats such feelings as easiness and uneasiness as being, not what determines the will, but what constitutes the will as it is determined by something else, that is, by what is perceived. According to what appears so far, Edwards thinks that our perception of excellency necessarily determines the will. In an earlier discussion, it was proposed that the necessity here is akin to that by which a rule, when it is applied, is necessarily satisfied or unsatisfied.[3]

Such a view immediately raises an ancient problem in moral psychology: Why do we sometimes, perhaps even usually, perceive excellency or good, but nevertheless fail to choose and act in accordance with it; and perceive deformity and evil, but nevertheless choose it? If our interpretation is so far correct, it would appear that Edwards' account of the will gives rise to it in its most extreme form, for it considers that it is by logical necessity that the will is determined by the

---

1. See below, pp. 362–66. Clyde Holbrook discusses this aspect of JE's moral theory in *The Ethics of Jonathan Edwards* (Ann Arbor, 1973), esp. pp. 97–112.

2. *Essay*, Bk. II, ch. 21, no. 37.

3. See above, p. 92.

perception of good. The remaining passages in "The Mind" that pertain to the will are directly concerned with the issue.

In "The Mind," No. 39, Edwards brings up an important consideration, which permits him to distinguish between will and conscience:

> Beside the two sorts of assent of the mind called will and judgment, there is a third, arising from a sense of the general beauty and harmony of things, which is conscience. There are some things which move a kind of horror in the mind which yet the mind wills and chooses; and some which are agreeable in this way to its make and constitution which yet it chooses not. These assents of will and conscience have indeed a common object, which is excellency. Still they differ: the one is always general excellency, that is, harmony taken in its relation to the whole system of beings; the other that excellency which most strongly affects, whether the excellency be more general or particular.[4]

Both will and conscience have excellency as the object; both consist in the being pleased by the perception of excellency. But the passage calls to mind Edwards' basic view that excellency and deformity are *relational* properties; they consist in relations of agreement and disagreement of a thing with others. Consequently, the same thing can be and be perceived to be excellent with respect to its relations to a limited number of things, and yet be and be perceived to be deformed with respect to its relations to the system of all things. In this case it has a false or limited beauty.[5] Our conscience, Edwards holds, is our "horror" in viewing the true deformity; but our will might be a choice of its limited and therefore false beauty. How could this be, when both the limited beauty and the extended deformity are perceived, and can be accurately judged? Edwards closes "The Mind," No. 39 with a suggestion: "The degree wherein we are affected by any excellency is in proportion compounded by the extensiveness and the intensiveness of our view of that excellency."[6]

Edwards had broached the idea of intensiveness of view in "The Mind," No. 21b, where he claims, "It is not merely by judging that anything is a great good that good is apprehended or appears; there are other ways of apprehending good. The having a clear and sensible idea of any good is one way of good's appearing, as well as judging that

4. Below, p. 356.
5. "The Mind," No. 14, below, p. 344.
6. Below, p. 356.

there is good."[7] Later, in "The Mind," No. 60, he gives more form to
the distinction by representing motivation or the determination of will
as a compound of three distinct "proportions." The degree of good
apprehended or represented by an idea, he notes, "used to be reckoned
by many the only thing that determined the will." But in addition to
that, he argues, motivation involves some *degree of apprehension* of the
good, which itself depends upon the degree of certainty or assurance of
the judgment of the goodness, and upon "the deepness of the sense of
the goodness, or the liveliness and sensibleness of the goodness or sweetness, or the strength of the impression on the mind." Finally, the will's
determination is affected by "the proportion or degree of the mind's
apprehension of the propriety of the good, or of its own concernment in
it," as whether it is a near or a remote pleasure that is perceived.[8]

We thus see Edwards moving away from the traditional concept of
will and intellect as distinct powers or faculties of the mind, and toward
the conception of distinct kinds or modes of apprehension or perception
of objects; the one kind he sees as generally terminating in judgments
of truth or falsity that have varying degrees of assurance, and the other
as terminating in some degree of that agreeableness or disagreeableness
that at first he had claimed was the necessary consequence of all perception of excellency. It may, in fact, be questioned how far Edwards kept
these two modes of apprehension entirely distinct in his later writings.
In his major essay on the "sense of the heart" in Miscell. no. 782, for
example, he treats this sense of the heart as a sensible knowledge of an
object which, when the object is spiritual, involves a conviction of its
reality and truth, as well as a delight in and warm agreeableness toward
its goodness.[9]

For our present purposes, it appears that there is at hand at least
some evidence for proposing that Edwards' general conception of the
will developed through his writings in "The Mind" in a manner similar
to his conception of the intellect. From the very start, in "The Mind,"

7. Below, p. 348.
8. Below, pp. 375–76.
9. Townsend, pp. 113–26. JE's conception of the synthesis of intellect and will in his account of the affections and the sense of the heart has been carefully examined by John Smith
in his introduction to *A Treatise Concerning Religious Affections*, in *Works* (Yale ed.) *2*, pp. 11–17.
See also the discussion in Smith's recent paper, "Jonathan Edwards as Philosophical Theologian," *Review of Metaphysics, 30* (1976), pp. 321–24. Norman Fiering's paper, "Intellect and
Will in the New England Mind," *William and Mary Quarterly, 29* (1972), pp. 515–58, gives an
excellent account of the history of the intellectualist-voluntarist controversy in colonial
thought, and of JE's place in relation to it.

No. 1, he saw will and intellect as necessarily conjoined in our perception of objects, and as being concerned about and directed to relations within and among the several individuals present rather than the properties of each individual taken separately. Both truth and goodness, he thought, are born to the mind by such relations, and indeed the very existence and natures of the objects themselves are comprised in such relations and in laws governing them.

But in the course of investigation Edwards found and became increasingly convinced that we humans, at least in our fallen state, do not and cannot actually apprehend those relations that bear truth and goodness; they are not disclosed either to intuition or by demonstration. At the same time, he found that we all generally do form concepts, judge objects, and reason about them in much the same ways. And again, though perhaps to a considerably lesser extent and degree, we share the same natural tendencies to approve benevolence and disapprove malice, to enjoy proportion and symmetry but feel uneasy about disproportion and irregularity, to admire a rose or tree but shrink from a snake or spider. In all these cases, he still supposes, our mental states and acts are about relations; but they do not occur in accordance with our actual and full recognition of the relations concerned, and so we cannot explain how and why they occur except by reference to dispositions, propensities, and habits of the mind itself. These dispositions and habits constitute the general and particular laws according to which our ideas are united and our judgments and affections about them occur. Such laws, it seems, might vary greatly from one to another mind, and might be altered in any one mind by circumstance, or especially by the regeneration extended from God, upon whose constant operation all our conscious thinking immediately depends in any case.

How far this hypothesis is confirmed by Edwards' discussions of our cognitive and moral psychology in other places must at present be left an open question. But what he set down in the late fragment we have titled "Notes on Knowledge and Existence" seems to support the interpretation. In a list of topics to be discussed he includes:

How real existence depends on knowledge or perception. From hence shew how all real union and all created identity is arbitrary. How God is as it were the only substance, or rather, the perfection and steadfastness of his knowledge, wisdom, power and will.

And then, with regard to the mind, he writes:

Answer to that objection, that then we have no evidence of immaterial substance. Answer: True; for this is what is supposed, that all existence is perception. What we call body is nothing but a particular mode of perception; and what we call spirit is nothing but a composition and series of perceptions, or an universe of coexisting and successive perceptions connected by such wonderful methods and laws.[1]

4. *Preparation and Editing of the Texts*

The principal objective of the Yale edition is to present the authentic texts of Edwards' writings in a clear and readable form. In the case of works published during Edwards' own lifetime, this objective is satisfied by following the words of the first-edition texts which he himself saw into print. Eighteenth-century printing conventions with respect to spelling, capitalization, punctuation, use of italics, etc. are revised in specified ways so as to preserve the style and flavor of Edwards' writing, but at the same time render it in a printed form more acceptable to the modern reader.[2] The same objectives are sought in the publication of his manuscript writings; but the means of achieving them are necessarily very different. The various special problems confronted in preparing texts of the writings in this volume, and the ways they have been handled, call for some further explanation.

From the point of view of the editor, each of the writings presented below is in many ways unique in the problems it presents. None of them was written to be published, and only one, the "Spider" letter, was intended for an eye other than the author's. Each was produced for its own particular purpose, and accordingly they vary greatly in form and content from extended essays to mere topical outlines and lists of memoranda. Some were written with careful attention to style and grammatical form, while others were composed in careless haste; some were written from corrected drafts, others are themselves mere drafts with various amounts and kinds of revision on the page. All texts except that of "The Mind" are based upon the original manuscripts, each of which presents special problems according to the manner in which it was formed and organized, the time at which it was written, and its present physical condition. And although "The Mind" is based upon Sereno Dwight's published version, this can hardly be treated as a first-edition text prepared by Edwards himself. Discussion of the special

1. See below, p. 398.
2. See Ramsey's account in *Works* (Yale ed.), *1*, pp. 118ff.

problems of editing that are peculiar to each of the writings will be reserved for the headnotes preceding each of the texts or set of related texts below. The present concern is with those problems that are common to many or all of the writings, and with the manner in which they have been resolved.

The first major problem is that of establishing an authentic and verbally accurate text of the manuscript writings. Various difficulties in this matter are due to the present condition of the manuscripts, the nature of Edwards' chirography, the quality of his pen and ink, and the degree of caution with which he wrote and amount of revision he made either in the course of writing or afterward. Each of these calls for particular comment.

Several of Edwards' manuscripts are now badly deteriorated through much handling (and mishandling), both by Edwards himself and by later readers. Some pages have become so badly rubbed, marked, torn, and frayed at the edges that portions of the original text have been destroyed altogether or made entirely illegible. Where there are copies or published versions made at earlier times when the manuscripts were in better condition, the missing and illegible words have been taken from these. In all such cases, the words in question are set in square brackets, and the source from which they were taken is explained in an editor's footnote.

These earlier copies and published versions have also been used to assure the accuracy of the editor's transcriptions of the manuscripts. Edwards' handwriting is notoriously difficult to read, especially in many of the earlier papers where he wrote in a very small, hurried, half-printed script, crowded his lines on the page, and wrote to the extreme margins of the paper. In many places where his chirography was adapted to writing speed and the conservation of space rather than readability, it is difficult to tell by the eye where the words begin and end, not to speak of discerning what words they are. The same small loop, dot, or curved dash might represent any vowel or even diphthong, and the same curved vertical stroke could stand for quite different consonants. Many words can be read only by scrutinizing the marks under a microscope or by photo-enlargement, and the context is often as much a factor in finding the correct reading as Edwards' inscription of the word itself. These difficulties are exacerbated further in passages in which he wrote with a blunt quill, or used ink that faded so rapidly that he himself was occasionally forced to touch it up afterward.

In preparing the texts presented below, the editor's transcriptions of the manuscripts have been systematically compared with the readings of others who have copied or published them, and often to good purpose. Such comparisons have led to the correction of innumerable errors, even obvious ones, both in the earlier published versions and in the editor's own initial transcriptions. While such comparison afforded the means for resolving many problematic readings, it also called attention to others and to plausible alternative readings that might deserve mention. Not every doubtful case is sufficiently uncertain or significant to demand editorial annotation, but where there is a substantial question of meaning or style the matter has been explained in a footnote to the text, and plausible alternative readings given in other published versions have been noted. In one or two cases where neither I nor any other reader has found an intelligible reading the wholly illegible part of the text is represented by an ellipsis and annotated.

The problem of establishing an authentic text for publication goes beyond the question of making verbally accurate transcriptions of the manuscripts. Most of the writings included here were actually composed on the pages from which our text is derived, rather than copied from corrected drafts. Consequently, the most accurate transcriptions contain all the inadvertent verbal omissions, redundancies and repetitions, slips of the pen, and grammatical infelicities, both major and minor, that may be committed in the act of composition. Moreover, most pages show some number of Edwards' revisions of his writing, made either at the time of composition or afterwards. Apart from making the manuscripts more difficult to read, these revisions sometimes complicate and confuse the text. Many revisions are made by deleting words or phrases; occasionally Edwards struck through more or fewer words in deleting than the meaning or form of his sentence would permit. Other revisions consist in words or phrases written above the line; sometimes these do not conform to the grammatical structure of the sentence, and sometimes Edwards left it unclear at what point in the sentence they were intended to be inserted. He usually wrote longer additions to a discussion in available space elsewhere on the same page or on another page of the manuscript, with key marks or marginal and parenthetical notes to explain the place he intended them to be introduced. Some of these organizational instructions are ambiguous, and some lead to unnecessary awkwardness in the flow of a discussion.

Most of the problems of wording, word order, and organization of the text that arise from these causes can be handled by silent editing.

The objective is to present the text that results from Edwards' composition and revision, so that his deletions are omitted and his additions are incorporated in course without comment. Moreover, wherever his meaning and intentions are perfectly clear the mistakes that result from his incomplete or grammatically faulty revisions have been silently corrected, as have similar trivial mistakes in unrevised text, for example in the tense or number of a verb, or the inadvertent repetition of a word. Words that are not actually present in the manuscript text, but are required for the meaning of a sentence, are put in square brackets in the conventional manner. Annotation is provided only in cases where Edwards' meaning and intentions are ambiguous or obscure. In these cases, the actual wording of the manuscript and the nature of Edwards' revisions are presented in the editor's footnotes. The purpose of these notes is to explain the state of the manuscript as fully as possible at every point where Edwards' meaning or style is not entirely clear. In this way, it is hoped the reader will be adequately informed about relevant difficulties with the text, without being burdened with an excess of editorial annotation.

Nevertheless, the footnotes to the texts as given below are almost entirely those of the editor. Many of Edwards' notes in his manuscripts consist in comments in the margins concerning the organization of the text, and these have been presented in editor's footnotes together with explanations of their purpose and location. Otherwise, Edwards' notes consist in parenthetical remarks, cross-references to other passages in his writings, and citations of published works and passages of Scripture. These are most appropriately printed within the text where they apply and at the places where Edwards wrote them, rather than as separate footnotes at the bottom of the page. Where further information is needed to complete or explain Edwards' notes, it is given in footnotes of the editor. Relevant information pertaining to the dates and chronological order of passages and the sources of particular ideas or statements of fact presented in them is also given in the editor's notes.

Despite the numbers of silent and annotated decisions concerning the correct wording of these texts, they have not been "improved" in substance or style by the editor's emendation. Verbal inconsistencies, awkwardness of phrasing, redundancies of expression, and errant syntax all stand as Edwards wrote and left them, even though he himself would not have approved their publication. All undeleted passages have been preserved in the text below, however obscure their meanings might be. And substantial passages that Edwards himself deleted are given in footnotes when they reveal significant points in the way his ideas developed and his expression of them was altered after critical reflection. In this way, it is hoped, the reader will not only be presented with an authentic final text, but will be informed about the most significant steps in Edwards' composition of it.

The policies of the Yale edition call for silent editing with respect to the modernization of spelling and capitalization, the expansion of Edwards' abbreviations, and the regularizing of his various references to published works and passages of Scripture. Certain words and contractions familiar to Edwards but no longer current, for example, "spake," "lien" and "shewn"; "ben't," "han't," " 'tis," and " 'em," have been retained as authentic to his style, but the y-contractions that are frequent in his earlier writing are lengthened to their modern forms. Edwards' own abbreviations, for example "SS" for Scriptures, "G." for God, "X" for Christ and "Xtian" for Christian have been silently expanded. On the other hand, the abbreviations "Fig." for Figure, "Prop." for Proposition, "Corol." for Corollary, "Ax." for Axiom, "Obj." for Objection, and "N.B." for *Nota Bene* have been retained where these are used nongenerically.

The text has been punctuated in conformity with the standards of this edition, in a generally eighteenth-century style but somewhat less densely than an eighteenth-century editor would have done. Almost all punctuation is that of the editor, because in his manuscript writings Edwards rarely pointed in the conventional manner, and his occasional dot might equally represent a comma, a colon or semicolon, or a period, or in some cases, as it appears, it might have been produced entirely by accident. In the flow of his composition Edwards often developed his thought through long sequences of independent and subordinate clauses, with little regard for the conventional form of the complete sentence. Where his compound structures have proved to be inordinately long, cumbersome, and confusing to the modern reader, they have been divided into sentences, although doing so has produced numerous sentences beginning with a conjunction. Often an appropriate punctuation could be supplied only by applying a range of marks, inserting them according to their degree of relative strength, the comma being used as the weakest and the semicolon, colon, and period as relatively stronger in an ascending order. Where clarity required, the dash and parentheses have been used as well. The many notes and memoranda that begin with such words as "how," "to shew that," and "relating to," have been treated as much as possible on an analogy with sentences.

The organization of the text and sequence of passages is presented as it appears in the source, but with certain notable exceptions that should be explained here. Edwards' paragraphs have been retained, except that inordinately long paragraphs have been silently divided by the editor. His numbering of entries (and Dwight's, in the case of "The Mind") has also been retained. Where two items are found with the same number, they have been distinguished by the use of "a" and "b." Series of entries that Edwards himself did not number have been given numbers by the editor for convenience of reference. These numbers, and Dwight's numbers in "The Mind," have been put in square brackets in the text itself, though the brackets are omitted in the editor's citations of them. In the last series of notes in "Natural Philosophy," the unnumbered series, numbering has proceeded according to the chronological order in which the articles were composed; in other cases, it is according to the sequence of items as they appear in the manuscript. Other special details of organization that require explanation are treated in the editor's headnotes to the texts, and in footnotes at the appropriate points.

In volumes of the Yale edition dedicated to Edwards' published works, most of the footnotes to the text are Edwards' own, and the relatively few editor's notes are distinguished from these by bein printed in brackets. In the case of his manuscript writings, however, almost all of Edwards' notes are contained within the text, while the need for annotation results in a relatively large number of editor's notes. In this volume, therefore, the editor's notes are printed without brackets; and where Edwards' statements, his marginalia, certain deleted passages, and the like form the content of a footnote, they are given in an editor's note together with appropriate annotation.

5. *Acknowledgments*

This volume could hardly have been completed without the generous assistance and support of many friends and colleagues. I am especially indebted to Thomas A. Schafer of McCormick Seminary for offering his time, skill, and knowledge in so many instances, and for sharing so much of the best fruit of his own study of Edwards' manuscripts. He contributed most of the information concerning the dating of the early writings that is presented here, and also prepared Edwards' many drawn illustrations for reproduction with the texts below. The contributions of my wife, Ruth Mastin Anderson, have been equally great. She gave invaluable help with aspects of the background research, offered expert criticism of the writing and editing, and spent many unrewarded hours in the tedious work of typing and proofreading. Above all, she lent her constant support to this project, shared the moments of excitement and satisfaction it has afforded, and patiently endured my seasons of anxiety and frustration as well.

The advice and assistance of John E. Smith of Yale University has helped me to avoid many pitfalls as the work progressed, and I have benefitted greatly from our discussions of Edwards' thought. I am also indebted to Wilson Kimnach of the University of Bridgeport for many rewarding conversations, and for his timely help in expediting steps toward the completion of the project. Discussion with Sang Hyun Lee of Hope College, and with the Reverend Chalmers Coe of Columbus, has helped my understanding and appreciation of various aspects of Edwards' work. Edmund S. Morgan and Sidney E. Ahlstrom of Yale University, and Paul Ramsey of Princeton University, read and helpfully commented upon the Introduction. I received other help from the late Rev. John Mastin, Shirley Niebanck, Pamela Coe, and Helen Mastin.

Throughout the preparation of this volume I enjoyed the help and cooperation of Marjorie Wynne, Suzanne Rutter, and the other members of the staff of the Beinecke Rare Book and Manuscript Library at Yale. My work has also been facilitated by the collections and facilities of the Sterling Library at Yale, the New York Public Library, the Library of Congress, the libraries of the Massachusetts Historical Society, the New York Historical Society, the Ohio State University, the University of Minnesota, and Macalester College, and in England by the libraries of Cambridge University, Sheffield University, and the British Museum. The New York Historical Society has given permission to publish Edwards' "Spider" letter here, and supplied the photograph of Edwards' illustration in that letter.

I received special support from the Ohio State University in the form of a period of assigned research duty in 1967–68, and two grants-in-aid. Robert and Harriett Balay generously opened their home to me and my family during several brief and extended periods of work in New Haven. I have also enjoyed the hospitality of David and Beverley White,

Gunter and Sarah Garbe, and Martin Einhorn at various times while working on this project.

Wallace E. Anderson

Columbus, Ohio
August 1978

PART ONE

The "Spider" Papers

NOTE ON THE "SPIDER" PAPERS

The "flying" spider is the subject of three closely related manuscripts: an essay titled "Of Insects," the draft of a letter based upon this essay, and the finished letter itself which Edwards wrote from his draft. The first two of these are preserved in the Andover collection of Edwards' manuscripts. Both have been previously published, the letter-draft by Sereno Dwight in 1829 in his *Life of President Edwards*,[1] and the essay by Egbert C. Smyth in 1890.[2] The finished "Spider" letter has only recently been discovered by George Claghorn in the manuscript collection of the New York Historical Society. It is presented here for the first time.

Inasmuch as the "Spider" letter is now available, Edwards' draft of this letter is of considerably less importance for the critical study of his early life and work. Accordingly, only the letter and "Of Insects" are presented in this section of the volume. Readers who have a particular interest in the letter-draft will find it, newly edited from the manuscript, in Appendix B at the end of this volume.

The newly discovered manuscript not only furnishes the finished text of Edwards' celebrated letter; it provides important information about the dates of his early writings. In the opinion of Dwight and Smyth, Edwards wrote his "Spider" letter at the age of twelve, prior to his matriculation at Yale College.[3] This date has been assumed almost without question by later biographers and commentators. But the letter itself was dated by Edwards from Windsor, October 31, 1723, more than seven years later, and after he had completed both his bachelor's and master's degrees at Yale College.

"Of Insects"

"Of Insects" is clearly the earliest of the "Spider" papers. Edwards used

---

1. Dwight, *1*, pp. 23–28. Dwight's version is, in effect, an attempt to reconstruct JE's sent letter from the draft. Because JE worked out his opening and concluding remarks together on a separate page of the draft, Dwight presented them together as a separate letter which he supposed was written to accompany that containing the substance of the discussion, and to serve as an apology for it.

2. "Flying Spider," pp. 5-13. Smyth's edition is, as nearly as he could make it, a facsimile transcription from the manuscript. In the same article he presents a new edition of JE's letter draft prepared in the same manner.

3. Dwight, *1*, p. 28; Smyth, "Flying Spider," pp. 3–4.

it as the primary if not the only basis for his account of spiders in the letter.[4] It is written on both sides of a single folio leaf of paper. Alterations in the color and composition of the ink in the course of the essay indicate that Edwards did not write the whole at once, but in several distinct sittings. The last four lines of the essay, in particular, are identical in ink and the character of the handwriting to the draft of the "Spider" letter; Edwards must have added them in October 1723 while the draft was being prepared. Throughout the rest the handwriting is very uniform in size and style, but quite different from that in the letter-draft. These appearances suggest that the whole of the essay, except for those last lines, was written within a relatively short period of time, and at a significantly earlier date than the "Spider" letter. The question is, how much earlier. The approximate date of "Of Insects" can best be judged by comparing it with other early manuscript writings.

The paper Edwards used for the essay gives no positive clue to its date, for its London Arms watermark is unlike any other found among his early papers. The handwriting, however, is quite similar to that found in the earliest parts of "Natural Philosophy," that is, in the propositions on atoms and in the first entries of the long numbered series of notes in "Things to be Considered and Written fully about" in that manuscript.[5] Edwards wrote these passages in a fairly smooth cursive hand, and formed many of his capital letters with ornamental flourishes. Although the hand of "Of Insects" is smaller, it presents similar features. The inks in the essay also appear to have a general similarity to those in the early passages of "Natural Philosophy." Most of the first page of the essay, down through the first unnumbered corollary, is written in a brownish gray ink similar in composition to that found in the first entries of the long numbered series. The paragraph concerned with explaining the visibility of spiders' webs at great distances is written in a glossy reddish brown ink somewhat similar to that in "Of Atoms" in "Natural Philosophy."

Edwards' discussion of the optical problem presented by the appearance of spiders' webs offers an even firmer basis for associating "Of Insects" with the earlier portions of "Natural Philosophy," and with the scientific studies of his college years. Both show that he had some acquaintance with Newtonian optics, and with Newton's theory of light diffraction in particular. Edwards refers to this theory by the word "incurvation" both in "Of Insects" and in the first entry in the short numbered series of "Things to be Considered" in "Natural Philosophy." It is significant inasmuch as this term is

---

4. A comparison of the contents of the essay and the letter shows that several revisions were made in the letter; but the letter contains only one significant point that is not mentioned at all in "Of Insects," viz., that many people wrongly suppose that spiders spin their webs at night.

5. Below, pp. 208–17 and 229–30.

not used in Newton's *Optics*, nor is its cognate used in the Latin edition of the work. Edwards might have gotten the term "incurvation" from reading William Whiston's *Sir Isaac Newton's Mathematick Philosophy more easily Demonstrated*, or perhaps some other secondary account of Newton's optical theories, but he could not have learned it from Newton's own writings.[6] Also, his explanation in "Of Insects" of the large appearance of the fixed stars to our naked eye was probably gleaned from Whiston's *Astronomical Lectures*. This work seems to have been the basis for at least one entry in the long numbered series in "Natural Philosophy" as well.

These points by themselves are sufficient to overthrow the opinion of Egbert Smyth, that Edwards wrote "Of Insects" about a year before he entered college.[7] Whiston's *Astronomical Lectures* was used by tutors Samuel Johnson and Daniel Browne to introduce the Copernican astronomy to the Yale students at New Haven in 1717.[8] The copy they used was brought from England in the collection of books gathered there for Yale College by Jeremiah Dummer. So far as we know, neither it nor any other work presenting Newton's discoveries had been used in any American college before this date. And since Edwards spent almost all of his first three collegiate years in Wethersfield, it is improbable that he would have had an opportunity to study Whiston's books or learn about Newton's theory of the "incurvation" of light before he came to New Haven for his senior year in June 1719.

Comparisons of the orthography of "Of Insects" with that of Edwards' other early manuscript writings, especially his dated letters and letter-drafts, give additional evidence for the probable date of the essay. In both the earliest portions of "Natural Philosophy" and "Of Insects" are found numerous spelling irregularities and inconsistencies involving double letters. The final 'l' is often doubled, as in "equall" and "severall," where in later writings Edwards uses the standard single 'l' spellings. In both manuscripts we find both "immediately" and "imediately," and in "Of Insects" Edwards spells both "webbs" and "webs." In both there are several instances where "of" is written for "off." Such irregularities become considerably less frequent through successively later passages in "Natural Philosophy."

Edwards' early letters show a particularly significant change in his spelling of the first person personal pronoun with the lower-case 'i'. In his earliest letter, dated May 10, 1716, he writes the pronoun "i" four times out of the eleven instances. In the two extant letters dated in 1719 and a draft dated

6. Throughout *Optics* Newton uses the term "inflection," and in the Latin edition of 1706, the cognate *inflectio*. But Whiston and several others occasionally adopt the term "incurvation" when referring to light diffraction.

7. "Flying Spider," pp. 3–4. Smyth dates the essay in the year 1715, largely on the basis of Dwight's erroneous conclusion that JE wrote the "Spider" letter in 1716.

8. So Johnson reports in his autobiography, in Schneider and Schneider, *Johnson: Career and Writings*, 1, p. 9.

November 1, 1720, there are a total of thirty-two "I" but no "i" at all. Yet the lower-case form appears, though infrequently, somewhat after this time: there are two "i" and thirty-two "I" in the second November 1, 1720, draft; twenty-eight "I" in the letter of March 1, 1721; and then an "i'll" together with thirteen "I" in the draft of December 12, 1721. But there is none of the lower-case form in the "Spider" letter of October 31, 1723, or thereafter. The count in "Of Insects" is forty-nine "I" to one "i." Clearly, in this respect the essay appears to be closer in date to the letters between 1719 and 1721 than to the letter of May 10, 1716.

Occurrences of Edwards' spelling "verry" in these writings are just as significant. In the three extant letters written before the draft of November 1, 1720, Edwards spells "verry" nine times, and "very" only once. In this draft, however, he spells the word "verry" once, but corrects it to "very"; and this is the last occurrence of "verry" in any of his dated manuscripts. In "Of Insects" we find twelve occurrences of "very," but also three of "verry"— and Edwards did not correct any of these. The relatively low incidence of "verry" in "Of Insects" suggests a later date than Edwards' July 24, 1719, letter in which all five occurrences of the word have that spelling; but the fact that he did not correct the spelling in "Of Insects" suggests a date before, or at any rate not long after, the November 1, 1720, draft in which he did correct it. With respect to the spelling "verry," in fact, "Of Insects" reflects a somewhat earlier orthography than the first parts of "Natural Philosophy," where sixteen occurrences, all spelled "very," are found in "Of Atoms," the opening parts of "Of Being" and "Of the Prejudices of Imagination," and the first entries of the two numbered series.[9]

There is considerable evidence, then, for the conclusion that "Of Insects" was written after Edwards came to New Haven in June 1719 for his senior year in college, and some evidence that he wrote it somewhat before he began any of the notes or essays in "Natural Philosophy." The most probable date to assign to it would be between the summer or autumn of 1719 and the summer or autumn of 1720. With the exception of the letters and letter-drafts mentioned above, "Of Insects" is still properly considered the earliest of the extant manuscripts in Edwards' hand.

The "Spider" Letter

Edwards' letter of October 31, 1723, is one of the most carefully written and best preserved of all his extant manuscripts. It is written on a folded full

---

9. On the other hand, at the beginning of the long numbered series JE writes "starrs" more often than "stars," but by the end of the first page of that series he uses the latter spelling regularly; and in the one instance of the word in "Of Insects," it is spelled "stars." Again, in "Of Atoms" and early entries in the longer numbered series JE often spells "bodys," and even "bodise." But in the shorter series and the second page of the longer he regularly writes "bodies." This is the spelling in the one instance of the word in "Of Insects." While in both cases the words in "Of Insects" conform to the later spellings, the single instances of each word hardly support a judgment that "Natural Philosophy" was begun earlier.

sheet of foolscap with London Arms/crowned GR watermarks, a paper which is found elsewhere only in a series of six sermons. The letter fills the first three pages of the folded sheet.

Edwards obviously took extraordinary pains to write the letter as neatly and legibly as possible. The hand is fairly large, uniform, printlike cursive with each letter carefully formed. The lines are well spaced and margins are ample and even. The punctuation is much more complete than in any of his private writings, but even here his use of capital letters is erratic. There are only a few corrections on the page. We find nine cross-outs, mostly for stylistic improvements in passages where he revised the wording while copying from his draft. In several interlined corrections he supplied words that had been omitted while copying. For the most part his corrections were made on the draft, and the letter was copied directly from this.

On the last verso of the letter, which Edwards had left blank, are three notations written in three different hands. One of these is simply the surname "Lister"; another is an identifying caption, "Spiders—Mr. Edwards." These two appear to have been added at an early time in the history of the manuscript, for they are written with quill pens and homemade inks that have turned brown like much of Edwards' own ink. The third notation, "Historical Society, New York. Presented by Geo. Adlard, May, 1861," proves to have been written on the manuscript by Mr. Adlard himself. These three notations furnish significant clues to the identity of the person to whom Edwards wrote his letter, as will be shown below.

Neither the letter nor Edwards' draft of it gives the name of the person to whom it was addressed. Sereno Dwight conjectured that he was a gentleman living in England,[1] and until the discovery of the letter the matter had not been pursued further. Now, however, there is sufficient evidence to establish that the recipient of Edwards' "Spider" letter was the Honorable Paul Dudley, Associate Justice of the Superior Court of Massachusetts, and Fellow of the Royal Society of London.[2]

Dudley was a frequent contributor to the *Philosophical Transactions of the Royal Society*, writing on such topics as the manner in which maple sugar is procured, the method New England farmers used to locate the hives of honeybees, and the characteristics of the "moos-deer" and the "poison-wood tree." In many of these papers he followed the common practice of including accounts of observations reported to him by friends and acquaintances together with his own. In the paper "Observations on some Plants in

---

1. Dwight, *1*, p. 23.

2. An account of Dudley's career may be found in *Sibley's Harvard Graduates, 4*, pp. 42–54. According to Sibley, both Timothy Edwards and Dudley entered Harvard as members of the class of 1690. Edwards apparently left Cambridge in 1688, however, to continue his studies under the Reverend Pelatiah Glover of Springfield. He received his B.A. and M.A. from Harvard in 1694, and then was listed as a member of the class of 1691 (*Sibley's Harvard Graduates, 4*, pp. 93–94).

New-England, with remarkable Instances of the Nature and Power of Vegetation," which appeared in 1724, Dudley included an account of a prolific
pumpkin vine which, he assured his readers, "I have well attested from a
worthy Divine." This unimpeachable witness is identified in a footnote as
"The Reverend Mr. Edwards of Windsor."[3]

It is clear in both the "Spider" letter and the draft that Edwards was
writing in response to an invitation to his father to report "any thing else
that he has observed in nature worthy of remark."[4] The form of words implies that the senior Edwards had already, before the end of October 1723,
communicated some notable instance. It is highly unlikely that the report
thus referred to was any other than that of the pumpkin vine which Dudley
credited in his paper of 1724 to the Reverend Mr. Edwards. In fact, the
invitation to report any further observations was most likely added to a
letter from Dudley bearing the news that the account of the pumpkin vine
had been sent to the Royal Society and would shortly be published.

Two of the notations that were jotted on the blank last page of the manuscript of Edwards' sent letter lead to an independent confirmation that the
letter was addressed to Paul Dudley. One of these identifies Mr. George
Adlard as the person who donated the letter to the New York Historical
Society in 1861. In the following year Mr. Adlard published a genealogy of
the Dudley family, tracing both its English and American branches.[5] In addition to Edwards' letter, Adlard also donated several papers that must have
been preserved among Dudley family effects. They include three letters from
Lord Cornbury to Joseph Dudley, and two papers written by Paul Dudley,
one the draft of a letter to John Chamberlayne and the other a scrap containing rough notes with the title "Christ's forty days' Abode on the Earth after
His Resurrection." All these manuscripts resemble Edwards' letter in another
respect. Each has an identifying caption added later on an outside margin,
in the same hand as the caption "Spiders—Mr. Edwards" on the "Spider"
letter. In fact, the hand of these notations is so like that of Paul Dudley in
the two manuscripts written by him, that it was probably Dudley himself
who wrote them, perhaps at a time when he was organizing various loose
family papers, including some of his own.

In asking Timothy Edwards for further observations of natural phenomena, Dudley was openly soliciting materials to include in his further communications to the Royal Society; and it is clear from the language of the
"Spider" letter that Jonathan was almost painfully conscious of this when
he wrote it. If Dudley found his account of spiders worthy, he would present

3. Dudley's paper may be found in *Philosophical Transactions*, *33* (1724), pp. 194–200.
Timothy Edwards' contribution is given and credited on p. 197. It is quoted below, p. 163,
n. 3.

4. See below, p. 163.

5. George Adlard, *The Sutton-Dudleys of England and the Dudleys of Massachusetts in New
England. From the Norman Conquest to the Present Time* (New York, 1862).

it for publication in the *Philosophical Transactions* and it would thus come before the "learned world." There is nothing to show what Dudley thought of the letter, but no part of it was published by the Royal Society, and Dudley made no reference to it or its subject in any of his later communications to the Society. From the appearance of the surname "Lister" jotted on the last page of the manuscript, however, it is evident that the letter was read by someone besides Dudley, and that this person was familiar with other writing on the subject. The name is undoubtedly a reference to the seventeenth-century English naturalist Martin Lister, who published three papers on spiders in the *Philosophical Transactions* between 1669 and 1684.[6] The first and last of these report Lister's observations of spiders "darting" webs and sailing upon them, the very subject of Edwards' letter. The person who jotted Lister's name on the manuscript, whoever he was, might have intended to call attention to the priority of Lister's work; and this in turn might explain why Edwards' observations were not published.

Editing of the "Spider" Papers

Texts of the three "Spider" papers have been prepared from Edwards' manuscripts. Readings of "Of Insects" have been checked against the edition of Egbert Smyth, and those of the draft of Edwards' "Spider" letter have been compared with both Smyth's and Dwight's versions. Where readings are doubtful, explanations and alternative readings are given in footnotes. A fragment torn from the edge of the manuscript has removed several words from the original of "Of Insects." These have been recovered from Smyth's edition, which was prepared before the damage occurred.

No serious problems are presented to the reader of the manuscript of the sent "Spider" letter. A handwritten copy in the New York Historical Society library provided a useful check, despite its several errors.

The texts of "Of Insects" and the sent "Spider" letter have been edited in accordance with the regular practices of the Yale edition.[7] The punctuation of "Of Insects" has been supplied almost entirely by the editor. In the letter, however, Edwards' own punctuation has been preserved, with a few exceptions, and supplemented by the editor only where necessary.

The "Spider" letter-draft, which is presented in Appendix B, is printed in such a way as to indicate the state of the text as it appears in the manuscript, including Edwards' various revisions and corrections. Further details may be found in the note at the beginning of the Appendix.

6. "Some Observations concerning the odd turn of some Shell-Snailes, and the Darting of Spiders," *Philosophical Transactions*, *4* (1669), pp. 1011–16; "A Letter . . . concerning a kind of Fly that is Vivaporous, together with a Set of curious Inquiries about Spiders, . . ." *Philosopical Transactions*, *6* (1671), pp. 2170–75; and "A Letter . . . containing the Projection of the Threds of Spiders," *Philosophical Transactions*, *14* (1684), pp. 592–94. There is no evidence that JE was acquainted with any of these papers when he wrote his letter.

7. See above, p. 136.

"OF INSECTS"

OF all insects, no one is more wonderful than the spider, especially with respect to their sagacity[1] and admirable way of working. These spiders, for the present, shall be distinguished into those that keep in houses and those that keep[2] in forests, upon trees, bushes, shrubs, etc.;[3] for I take 'em to be of very different kinds and natures (there are also other sorts, some of which keep in rotten logs, hollow trees, swamps and grass).

Of these last, everyone knows the truth of their marching in the air from tree to tree, and these sometimes at five or six rods distance sometimes. Nor can anyone go out amongst the trees in a dewy morning towards the latter end of August or the beginning of September,[4] but that he shall see hundreds of webs, made conspicuous by the dew that is lodged upon them, reaching from one tree and shrub to another that stands at a considerable distance; and they may be seen well enough by an observing eye at noonday by their glistening against the sun. And what is still more wonderful, I know I have several times seen, in a very calm and serene day at that time of year, standing behind some opaque body that shall just hide the disk of the sun and keep off[5] his dazzling rays from my eye, multitudes of little shining

1. A large fragment has been broken from the top margin of the MS. The words "respect to their sagacity," which were contained on this fragment, have been taken from Smyth's edition ("Flying Spider," p. 5). Another fragment from the upper left corner, with the end of "admirable," was missing even when Smyth transcribed the essay. He consulted an earlier copy of the text for a missing word at the corresponding place on the verso side of the leaf (see Smyth, p. 10, n. 3; and below, p. 159, n. 3), and it is probable he used this copy to confirm "admirable" as well. The copy to which Smyth refers has not been located.

2. The words "those that keep" have been taken from Smyth's edition ("Flying Spider," p. 6); they are lost with the fragment broken from the MS.

3. The words "and those that keep in rotten logs" are interlined at this point. Although JE did not delete them, he repeats them in the next sentence, which he also added above the line.

4. JE revised the text, deleting "the beginning" and altering "of" to "in"; but the interlined words which complete the revision are illegible.

5. At this point in the MS there is a marked change of ink color, from a brownish gray to a truer gray. The change might mark the beginning of a second "sitting" after JE had laid the essay aside for a short time.

webs and glistening strings of a great length, and at such a height as
that one would think they were tacked to the sky by one end, were it
not that they were moving and floating. And there often appears at
the end of these webs a spider floating and sailing in the air with them,
which I have plainly discerned in those webs that were nearer to my
eye. And once [I] saw a very large spider, to my surprise, swimming in
the air in this manner, and others have assured me that they often
have seen spiders fly. The appearance is truly very pretty and pleasing,
and it was so pleasing, as well as surprising, to me, that I resolved to
endeavor to satisfy my curiosity about it, by finding out the way and
manner of their doing it; being also persuaded that, if I could find out
how they flew, I could easily find out how they made webs from tree
to tree.

And accordingly, at a time when I was in the woods, I happened to
see one of these spiders on a bush. So I went to the bush and shook
it, hoping thereby to make him uneasy upon it and provoke him to
leave it by flying, and took good care that he should not get off from it
any other way. So I continued constantly to shake it, which made him
several times let himself fall by his web a little; but he would presently
creep up again, till at last he was pleased, however, to leave that bush
and march along in the air to the next; but which way I did not know,
nor could I conceive, but resolved to watch him more narrowly next
time. So I brought [him] back to the same bush again; and to be sure
that there was nothing for him to go upon the next time, I whisked
about a stick I had in my hand on all sides of the bush, that I might
break any web going from it, if there were any, and leave nothing
else for him to go on but the clear air, and then shook the bush as before; but it was not long before he again to my surprise went to the
next bush. I took him off upon my stick and, holding of him near my
eye, shook the stick as I had done the bush, whereupon he let himself
down a little, hanging by his web, and [I] presently perceived a web
out from his tail and a good way into the air. I took hold of it with my
hand and broke it off, not knowing but that I might take it out to the
stick with him from the bush; but then I plainly perceived another
such string to proceed out at his tail.

I now conceived I had found out the whole mystery. I repeated the
trial over and over again till I was fully satisfied of his way of working,
which I don't only conjecture, to be on this wise, viz.: They, when they
would go from tree to tree, or would sail in the air, let themselves hang
down a little way by their web; and then put out a web at their tails,

which being so exceeding rare when it first comes from the spider as to be lighter than the air, so as of itself it will ascend in it (which I know by experience), the moving air takes it by the end, and by the spider's permission, pulls it out and bears it out[6] of his tail to any length, and if the further end of it happens to catch by a tree or anything, why, there's a web for him to go over upon. And the spider immediately perceives it and feels when it touches, much after the same manner as the soul in the brain immediately perceives when any of those little nervous strings that proceed from it are in the least jarred by external things. And this very way I have seen spiders go from one thing to another, I believe fifty times at least since I first discovered it.

But if nothing is in the way of those webs to hinder their flying out at a sufficient distance, and they don't catch by anything, there will be so much of it drawn out into the air, as by its ascending force there will be enough to carry the spider with it; or, which is all one, till there is so much of this web which is rarer than the air as that the web, taken with the spider, shall take up as much or more space than the same quantity [of air]. Of which, if it be equal they together will be in perfect equilibrium or poise with the air, so as that when they are loose therein they will neither ascend or descend, but only as they are driven by the wind; but if they together be more, will ascend therein: like as a man at the bottom of the sea, if he has hold on a stick of wood, or anything that is lighter or takes up more space for the quantity of matter than the water. If it be a little piece, it may not be enough to carry him and cause him to swim therein, but if there be enough of it, it will carry him up to the surface of the water (if there be so much as that the greater rarity shall more than counterbalance the greater density of the man); and if it doth but just counterbalance,[7] put the man anywhere in the water and there he'll keep, without ascending or descending. 'Tis just so with the spider in the air as with the man in the water, for what is lighter than the air will swim or ascend therein, as well as that which is lighter than the water swims in that. And if the spider has hold on so much of a web that the greater levity of all of it shall more than counterpoise the greater

6. Smyth: "and draws [?] it out."

7. Smyth: "if it be Doth but just Cause to balance." JE neglected to delete "be" when he revised his original wording.

A slight change of ink color is found at this point in the MS. The following portion through the unnumbered corollary below is in a thinner gray ink, and is written with a sharper pen. It might have been written in a third "sitting."

gravity of the spider, so that the ascending force of the web shall be
more than the descending force of the spider, the web, by its ascending,
will necessarily carry the spider up unto such a height, as that the air
shall be so much thinner and lighter, as that the lightness of the web
with the spider shall no longer prevail.

Now perhaps here it will be asked how the spider knows when he
has put out web enough, and, when he does know, how does he get
himself loose from the web by which he hung to the tree. I answer:
there is no occasion for the spider's knowing, for their manner is to
let out their web until the ascending force of their web and the force
the wind has upon it, together with the weight of the spider, shall be
enough to break the web by which the spider hangs to the tree, for
the stress of all these comes upon that, and nature has so provided,
that just so much web as is sufficient to break, that shall be sufficient
[to] carry the spider. And [this] very way I very frequently have seen
spiders mount away into the air, with a vast train of glistening web before them, from a stick in my hand, and have also shewed it to others.
And without doubt they do it with a great deal of their sort of pleasure.

There remain only two difficulties. The one is, how should they
first begin to spin out this so fine and even a thread of their bodies?
If once there is a web out it is easy to conceive how if the end of it were
once out, how the air might take it and so draw it out to a greater
length. But how should they at first let out of their tails the end of a
fine string, whereas[8] in all probability the web, while it is in the spider,
is a certain liquor with which that great bottle tail of theirs is filled,
which immediately upon its being exposed to the air turns to a dry
substance and very much rarifies and extends itself. Now if it be a
liquor, it is hardly conceivable how they should let out a fine string,
except by expelling a small drop at the end of it; but none such can
be discovered. To find out this difficulty I once got a very large spider
of the sort; for in lesser ones I could not distinctly discern how they
did that, nor can one discern their webs at all except they are held up
against the sun or some dark place. I took this spider and held him
up against an open door, which, being dark, helped me plainly to
discern, and shook him. Whereupon, he let himself down by his web—
as in the [first] figure, by the web *cb*—and then fixed with his tail one
end of the web that he intended to let out into the air to the web by
which he let himself down, at *a*; then, pulling away his tail, one end of

8. Smyth: "when."

the web was thereby drawn out, which being at first exceeding slender, the wind presently broke it at *d*, and drew it out, as in Figure the second, and it was immediately spun out to a very great length.

The other difficulty is, how when they are once carried up into the air, how they get down again, or whether they are necessitated to continue, till they are beat down by some shower of rain, without any sustenance—which [is] not probable nor agreeable to nature's[9] providence. I answer: there is a way whereby they may come down again when they please by only gathering in their webs in to them again, by which way they may come down gradually and gently. But whether that be their way or no, I can't say—but without scruple, that

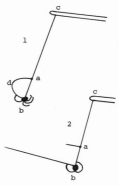

Figs. 1, 2

or a better, for we always find things done by nature as well or better than [we] can imagine beforehand.

Corol. We hence see the exuberant goodness of the Creator, who hath not only provided for all the necessities, but also for the pleasure and recreation of all sorts of creatures, and even the insects and those that are most despicable.

[1]Another thing particularly notable and worthy of being inquired into about these webs is that they, which are so exceeding small and fine as that they cannot be discerned except held in a particular position with respect to the sun or against some dark place when held close to the eye, should appear at such a prodigious height in the air when near betwixt us and the sun, so that they must needs some often[2] appear as big as a cable would do, if it appeared exactly *secundum rationem distantiae.* To solve, we ought to consider that these webs, as they are thus posited, very vividly reflect the rays of the sun, so as to cause them to be very lightsome bodies; and then see if we can't find any parallel phenomena in other lightsome bodies. And everybody knows

---

9. Smyth: "natural."

1. The following paragraph is written in a distinctive reddish-brown ink. JE might have inserted it into the essay at this point at some time after the rest was written (see above, p. 148); it is related in content to the beginning entries in the shorter numbered series in "Natural Philosophy" (see below, p. 219).

2. Smyth: "of 'em."

that a candle in the night appears exceedingly bigger at a distance than it ought to do, and we may observe in the moon towards the new,[3] when that part of it that is not enlightened by the sun, is visible, how much the enlightened part thereof is enlarged and extended beyond the circumference of the other parts. And astronomers also know how exceedingly the fixed stars are beyond their bounds to our naked eye, so that without doubt they appear many hundreds of times bigger than they ought to do. The reason may be that the multitude and powerfulness of the rays affects a greater part of the retina than their share,[4] that which they immediately strike upon. But we find that a light that so does when it is alone, and when no part of the retina is affected by anything else but that, so that the least impression is felt by it, won't do so—or at least not so much—in the midst of other perhaps greater light, so that other parts of the retina are filled with impressions of their own. But these webs are instances of the latter, so that this reason does not seem fully to solve this so great a magnifying, though without a doubt that helps. But the chief reason must be referred to that incurvation of the rays passing by the edge of any body, which Sir Isaac Newton has proved.[5]

One thing more I shall take notice of, before I dismiss this subject, concerning the end of nature in giving spiders this way of flying; which, though we have found in the corollary to be their pleasure and recreation, yet we think a greater end is at last their destruction. And what makes us think so is because that is necessarily and naturally[6] brought

3. Where the large fragment is missing from the top margin of the MS, Smyth's edition supplies the words "lightsome bodies and everybody knows," and the words "may observe in" in this and the preceding sentence. Also, the word "do" in the phrase "ought to do" is missing from the MS because of a fragment broken from the upper right corner. Smyth supplied the word from an earlier copy of the MS (see above, p. 154, n. 1).

4. Smyth: "their space"; JE crowded the words between the lines. The explanation JE suggests here is that proposed by Descartes (*Dioptrics*, discourse vi. See also Jacques Rohault, *Physica*, Pars I, cap. 32, sec. 25–26). He might have received it from reading Whiston, *Astronomical Lectures*, Lect. III, Phenomenon 4, pp. 24–25.

5. I.e., the diffraction of the rays. Newton discussed diffraction in *Optics*, Bk. III; but used the word "inflection" to refer to the phenomenon in the *Optics* and elsewhere, except in the *Principia*, 1713 ed., Bk. I, prop. 96, Scholium, where he uses "inflectio." JE probably received "incurvation" from Whiston, *Newton's Mathematick Philosophy*, p. 266. See discussion of Whiston's influence on JE, above, p. 32.

Between this and the next paragraph there is a blank space about three-centimeters wide across the page, which JE might have left for a more complete discussion of Newton's optical theory. The ink of the following paragraph and the two numbered corollaries is probably the same as the gray ink in the unnumbered corollary on the first page of the manuscript.

6. Smyth: "actually."

to pass by it, and we shall find nothing so brought to pass by nature but what is the end of those means by which is brought to pass; and we shall further evince it by and by, by shewing the great usefulness of it. But we must show how their destruction is brought to pass by it.

I say then, that by this means almost all the spiders upon the land must necessarily be swept first and last into the sea. For we have observed already that they never fly except in fair weather; and we may now observe that it is never fair weather, neither in this country nor any other, except when the wind blows from the midland parts, and so towards the sea. So, here in New England, I have observed that they never fly except when the wind is westerly, and I never saw them fly but when they were hastening directly towards the sea. And [the] time of the flying being so long, even from the middle of August to the middle of October—though their chief time here in New England is in the time as was said before, to wit,[7] the latter end of August and the beginning of September—and they keep flying all that while towards the sea, [they] must needs almost all of them get there before they have done. And the same indeed holds true of all other sorts of flying insects, for at that time of year the ground, trees and houses, the places of their residence in summer, being pretty chill, they leave 'em whenever the sun shines pretty warm, and mount up into the air and expand their wings to the sun. And so, flying for nothing but their ease and comfort, they suffer themselves to go that way that they find they can go with greatest ease, and so wheresoever the wind pleases. And besides, it being warmth they fly for, and it being warmer flying with the wind than against it or sideways to it—for thereby the wind has less power upon them—and as was said of spiders, they never flying but when the winds that blow from the midland parts towards the sea bring fair weather, they must necessarily, flying so long a time, all the while towards the sea, get there at last. And I very well remember, that at the same time when I have been viewing the spiders with their webs in the air, I also saw vast multitudes of flies, many of 'em at a great height, all flying the same way with the spiders and webs, directly seaward. And I have many times, at that time of year, looking westward, seen myriads of them towards sun setting, flying continually towards the sea; and this, I believe, almost everybody, if not all,[8] of my own country will call to mind that they have also seen. And as to other sorts of flying insects,

7. Smyth: "towards."
8. Smyth: "specially."

such as butterflies, millers, moths, etc., I remember that, when I was a boy, I have at the same time of year lien on the ground upon my back and beheld abundance of them, all flying[9] southeast, which I then thought were going to a warm country. So that, without any doubt, almost all manner of aerial insects, and also spiders which live upon them and are made up of them, are at the end of the year swept and wafted into the sea and buried in the ocean, and leave nothing behind them but their eggs for a new stock the next year.[1]

Corol. 1. Hence also we may behold and admire at the wisdom of the Creator, and be convinced[2] that is exercised about such little things, in this wonderful contrivance of annually carrying off and burying the corrupting nauseousness of our air, of which flying insects are little collections, in the bottom of the ocean where it will do no harm; and especially the strange way of bringing this about in spiders (which are collections of these collections, their food being flying insects) which want wings whereby it might be done. And what great inconveniences should we labor under if there were no such way. For spiders and flies are so exceeding multiplying creatures that if they only slept or lay benumbed in [winter] and were raised again in the spring, which is commonly supposed, it would not be many years before we should be as much plagued with their vast numbers as Egypt was. And if they died for good and all in winter they, by the renewed heat of the sun, would presently again be dissipated into those nauseous vapors which they are made up of, and so would be of no use or benefit in that [in] which now they are so very serviceable.

Corol. 2. Admire also the Creator in so nicely and mathematically adjusting their multiplying nature, that notwithstanding their destruction by this means and the multitudes that are eaten by birds, that they do not decrease and so, little by little, come to nothing; and in so adjusting their destruction to their multiplication that they do neither increase, but taking one year with another, there is always just an equal number of them.

Another reason why they will not fly at any other time but when a

9. MS: "very all flying"; Smyth: "busy all flying."
1. About one centimeter of blank space was left on the MS between this paragraph and the corollary below.
2. In the MS two words or abbreviations, perhaps "from Pvd," are jotted in the blank space above this first line of the corollary and encircled. They do not appear to be intended as an interlineation at this point, although Smyth took them to be such. He read the construction as, "be convinced from providence there is exercised. . . ."

dry wind blows, is because a moist wind moistens the web and makes it heavier than the air. And if they had the sense to stop[3] themselves, we should have hundreds of times more spiders and flies by the seashore than anywhere else.[4]

3. Smyth: "fly."
4. These last two sentences are in the hand and ink of JE's draft of his "Spider" letter of Oct. 31, 1723, and were evidently added at the time he wrote the draft.

THE "SPIDER" LETTER

Windsor, Oct. 31, 1723[1]

Sir:[2]

In the postscript of your letter to my father you manifest a willingness to receive anything else that he has observed in nature worthy of remark;[3] that which is the subject of the following lines by him was thought to be such: he has laid it upon me to write the account, I having had advantage to make more full observations. If you think, Sir, that they are not worthy the taking notice of, with greatness and goodness overlook and conceal. They are some things that I have happily seen of the wondrous and curious works of the spider. Although everything pertaining to this insect is admirable, yet there are some phenomena relating to them more particularly wonderful.

Everybody that is used to the country knows of their marching in the air from one tree to another, sometimes at the distance of five or six rods, though they are wholly destitute of wings: nor can one go out in a dewy morning at the latter end of August and beginning of September but he shall see multitudes of webs reaching from one tree and shrub to another; which webs are commonly thought to be made in the night because they appear only in the morning by reason of the dew that

1. Published through the courtesy of the New York Historical Society, New York City.
2. The letter was almost certainly addressed to Judge Paul Dudley, Fellow of the Royal Society of London, and Associate Justice of the Superior Court of Massachusetts (see above, pp. 151–53).
3. In his paper, "Observations on some of the Plants in New-England, with remarkable Instances of the Nature and Power of Vegetation," Paul Dudley reports the following instance of the power of vegetation, citing "The Reverend Mr. Edwards of Windsor" as his source: "In the year 1669, a single Pumpkin Seed was accidentally dropp'd in a small Pasture where Cattle had been fodder'd for some Time. This single Seed took Root of itself, and without any Manner of Care or Cultivation; the Vine run along over several Fences, and spread over a large Piece of Ground far and wide, and continued its Progress till the Frost came and kill'd it. This Seed had no more than one Stalk, but a very large one; for it measured eight Inches round; from this single Vine, they gathered two hundred and sixty Pumpkins; and, one with another, as big as an half Peck; enough to fill a large Tumbrel, besides a considerable Number of small and unripe Pumpkins, that they made no Account of." *Philosophical Transactions*, 33 (1724), p. 197.

hangs on them, whereas they never work in the night, they love to lie
still when the air is dark and moist; but these webs may be seen well
enough in the daytime by an observing eye, by their reflection of the
sunbeams; especially late in the afternoon may those webs that are
between the eye, and that part of the horizon that is under the sun,
be seen very plainly, being advantageously posited to reflect the rays,
and the spiders themselves may be very often seen traveling in the air
from one stage to another amongst the trees in a very unaccountable
manner. But, Sir, I have often seen that which is yet more astonishing.
In a very calm serene day in the forementioned time of year, standing
at some distance between the end of an house or some other opaque
body, so as just to hide the disk of the sun and keep off his dazzling rays,
and looking along close by the side of it, I have seen vast multitudes of
little shining webs and glistening strings, brightly reflecting the sunbeams, and some of them of a great length, and at such a height that one
would think that they were tacked to the vault of the heavens, and
would be burnt like tow in the sun, making a very pleasing as well
as surprising appearance. It is wonderful at what a distance these webs
may plainly be seen in such a position to the sunbeams, which are so
fine that they cannot be seen in another position, though held near to
the eye; some that are at a great distance appear (it cannot be otherwise) several thousands of times as big as they ought: They doubtless
appear under as great an angle as a body of a foot diameter ought to do
at such a distance; so greatly doth coruscation increase the apparent
bigness of bodies at a distance, as is observed in the fixed stars. But that
which is most astonishing is that very often there appears at the end of
these webs, spiders sailing in the air with them, doubtless with abundance of pleasure, though not with so much as I have beheld them and
shewed them to others. And since I have seen these things I have been
very conversant with spiders. Resolving if possible to find out the mysteries of these their amazing works, and pursuing my observations, I
discovered one wonder after another till I have been so happy as very
frequently to see their whole manner of working; which is thus:

When a spider would go from one tree or branch to another, or
would recreate himself by sailing or floating in the air, he first lets himself down a little way from the twig he stands on by a web, as [in] Fig. 1;
and then taking hold of it by his forefeet as in Fig. 2, and then separates
or loosens the part of the web *cd* from the part *bc* by which he hangs;
which part of the web *cd*, being thus loosened, will by the motion of the
air be carried out towards *e*, which will by the sufferance of the spider

be drawn [out] of his tail with infinite ease by the moving air, to what length the spider pleases, as [in] Fig. 3: And if the further end of the web *de,* as it is running out and moving to and fro, happens to catch by a shrub or the branch of a tree, the spider immediately feels it and fixes the hither end of it, *d,* to the web *bc,* and goes over as by a bridge by the web *de.* Every particular of this, Sir, my eyes have innumerable times made me sure of, saving that I never could distinctly see how they separated the part of the web *cd* (Fig. 2) from the part *bc,* whether it be done by biting of it off or how, because so small a piece of so fine a web is altogether imperceptible amongst the spider's legs, and because the spider is so very quick and dexterous in doing of it all. But I have seen that it is done, though I have not seen how they do it. For this, Sir, I can see: that the web *bc* (Fig. 3) is

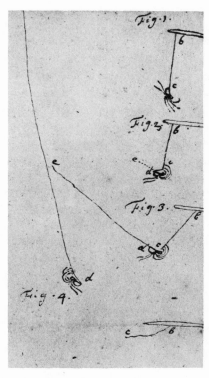

separated, and not joined to the spider's tail, while the web *de* is drawing out.

Now, Sir, it is certain that these webs, when they first come from the spider, are so rare a substance that they are lighter than the air, because they will immediately ascend in a calm air, and never descend except driven by a wind: and 'tis as certain that what swims and ascends in the air is lighter than the air, as that what ascends and swims in water is lighter than that: So that if we should suppose any such time wherein the air is perfectly calm, this web is so easily drawn out of the spider's tail, that barely the levity of it is sufficient to carry it out to any length. But at least its levity, or ascending inclination, together with so much motion as the air is never without, will well suffice for this. Wherefore, if it be so that the end of the web *de* (Fig. 3) catches by no tree nor other body till it be drawn out so long that its levity shall be so great as to be more than equal to the gravity of the spider, or so that the web and the spider taken together shall be lighter than such a quantity of air as takes up equal space, then according to the universally acknowledged laws of nature the web and the spider together will ascend and not descend in the air. As when a man [is] at the bottom of the water, if he has hold of a piece of timber so great that the wood's tendency upwards is greater than the man's tendency downwards, he together with the wood will ascend to the surface of the water. Therefore, when the spider perceives that the web *de* is long enough to bear him up by its ascending force (which force the spider feels by its drawing of him towards *e*), he lets go his hold of the web *bc* (Fig. 4) and, holding by the web *de*, ascends and floats in the air with it. If there be not web more than enough just to equal with its levity the gravity of the spider, the spider together with the web will hang *in equilibrio*, neither ascending nor descending, otherwise than as the air moves; but if there be so much web that its ascending tendency, or rather the buoying force of the air upon it, shall be greater than the descending tendency of the spider, they will ascend till the air is so thin, till they together are just of an equal weight with so much air. But if the web be so short as not to counterpoise the weight of the spider, the web and spider will fall till they come to the ground.

And this very way, Sir, I have multitudes of times seen spiders mount away into the air with a vast train of this silver web before them from a stick in mine hand; for if the spider be disturbed upon the stick by shaking of [it] he will presently in this manner leave it. Their way of working may very distinctly be seen if they are held up in the sun, in a calm day, against a dark door or anything that is black.

And this, Sir, is the way of spiders' working. This is the way of their going from one thing to another at a distance, and this is the way of their flying in the air. And although I can say I am certain of it, I don't desire that the truth of it should be received upon my word, though I could bring others to testify to it to whom I have shewn it, and who have looked on with admiration: But everyone's eyes who will take the pains to observe will make them equally sure of it; only those who would make experiment must take notice that it is not every sort of spider that is a flying spider, for those spiders that keep in houses are a quite different sort, as also those that keep in the ground, and those [that] keep in swamps upon the ground amongst the bogs, and those that keep in hollow trees and rotten logs; but those spiders that keep on branches of trees and shrubs are the flying spiders. They delight most in walnut trees, and are that sort of spiders that make those curious, network, polygonal webs that are so frequently to be seen in the latter end of the year. There are more of this sort of spider by far than of any other.

Corol. 1. Hence the wisdom of the Creator in providing of the spider with that wonderful liquor with which their bottle tail is filled, that may so easily be drawn out so exceeding fine, and being in this way exposed to the air will so immediately convert to a dry substance that shall be so very rare as to be lighter than the air, and will so excellently serve to all their purposes.

Corol. 2. Hence the exuberant goodness of the Creator, who hath not only provided for all the necessities, but also for the pleasure and recreation of all sorts of creatures, even the insects.

But yet, Sir, I am assured that the chief end of this faculty that is given them is not their recreation but their destruction, because their destruction is unavoidably the constant effect of it; and we find nothing that is the continual effect of nature but what is the end of the means by which it is brought to pass: but it is impossible but that the greatest part of the spiders upon the land should every year be swept into the ocean. For these spiders never fly except the weather be fair and the atmosphere dry, but the atmosphere is never clear and dry, neither in this nor any other continent, only when the wind blows from the midland parts, and consequently towards the sea; as here in New England, the fair weather is only when the wind is westerly, the land being on that side and the ocean on the easterly. I scarcely ever have seen any of these spiders flying but when they have been hastening directly towards the sea. And the time of their flying being so long, even from about the middle of August, every sunshiny day till about the end of October (though their chief time, as was observed before, is the latter end of August and beginning of September). And they, never flying from the sea but always towards it, must get there at last. And it seems unreasonable to think that they have sense to stop themselves when they come near the sea, for then we should [see] hundreds of times more spiders on the seashore than anywhere else. When they are once carried over the water their webs grow damp and moist and lose their levity and their wings fail them, and let them down into the water.

The same also holds true of other sorts of flying insects, for at those times that I have viewed the spiders with their webs in the air there has also appeared vast multitudes of flies at a great height, and all flying the same way with the spiders and webs, direct to the ocean. And even such as butterflies, millers, and moths, which keep in the grass at this time of year, I have seen vastly higher than the tops of the highest trees, all going the same way. These I have seen towards evening, right overhead, and without a screen to defend my eye from the sunbeams, which I used to think were seeking a warmer climate. The reason of their flying at that time of year I take to be because the ground and trees and grass, the places of their residence in summer, begin to be chill and uncomfortable. Therefore when the sun shines pretty warm they leave them, and mount up into the air and expand their wings to the sun, and flying for nothing but their own ease and comfort, they suffer themselves to go that way that they can go with the greatest ease, and so where the wind pleases: and it being warmth they fly for, they never fly against the wind nor sidewise to it, they find it cold and laborious; they therefore seem to use their wings but just so much as to bear them up, and suffer themselves to go with the wind. So that it must necessarily be that almost all aerial insects, and spiders which live upon them and are made up of them, are at the end of the year swept away into the sea and buried in the ocean, and leave nothing behind them but their eggs for a new stock the next year.

Corol. 1. Hence [there] is reason to admire at the wisdom of the Creator, and to be convinced that it is exercised about such little things in this wonderful contrivance of annually carrying off and burying the corruption and nauseousness of the air, of which flying insects are little collections, in the bottom of the ocean where it will do no harm; and especially the strange way of bringing this about in spiders, which are collections of these collections, their food being flying insects, flies being the poison of the air, and spiders are the poison of flies collected together. And what great inconveniences should we labor under if it were not so, for spiders and flies are such exceedingly multiplying creatures, that if they only slept or lay benumbed in winter, and were raised again in the spring, which is commonly thought, it would not be many years before we should be plagued with as vast numbers as Egypt was. And if they died ultimately in winter, they by the renewed heat of the sun would presently again be dissipated into the nauseous vapors of which they are made up, and so would be of no use or benefit in that in which now they are so very serviceable and which is the chief end of their creation.

Corol. 2. The wisdom of the Creator is also admirable in so nicely and mathematically adjusting their plastic nature, that notwithstanding their destruction by this means and the multitudes that are eaten by birds, that they do not decrease and so by little and little come to nothing; and in so adjusting their destruction to their multiplication they do neither increase, but taking one year with another, there is always an equal number of them.

These, Sir, are the observations I have had opportunity to make on the wonders that are to be seen in the most despicable of animals. Although these things appear for the main very certain to me, yet, Sir, I submit it all to your better judgment, and deeper insight. I humbly beg to be pardoned for running the venture, though an utter stranger, of troubling you with so prolix an account of that which I am altogether uncertain whether you will esteem worthy of the time and pains of reading. Pardon me if I thought it might at least give you occasion to make better observations on these wondrous animals, that should be worthy of communicating to the learned world, from whose glistening webs so much of the wisdom of the Creator shines.

> Pardon, Sir, your most obedient humble servant,
> Jonathan Edwards[4]

4. The letter ends on the second recto of the folded sheet of foolscap. JE left the last verso blank, but three notations were afterward written on it by three different hands. A notice of presentation, "Historical Society, New York. Presented by Geo. Adlard, May 1861," was written by Mr. Adlard himself. A caption, "Spiders—Mr. Edwards," was probably written by Paul Dudley. The surname "Lister," probably in reference to Martin Lister, the seventeenth-century English naturalist, is in an unknown hand.

PART TWO

"Natural Philosophy" and Related Papers

NOTE ON "NATURAL PHILOSOPHY"

The manuscript of "Natural Philosophy" now exists in several detached sections, all of folio size. The three main sections, having a total of sixteen leaves, are located in the Andover collection. These contain the various essays and series of scientific notes as follows: Two single folio leaves, tied loosely together with a piece of thread, contain the two essays "Of Being" and "Of the Prejudices of Imagination." A quire of four infolded sheets of foolscap contains on its first three leaves the untitled series of propositions and corollaries which will here be called "Of Atoms." The last five leaves of the quire contain two distinct series of numbered scientific notes following the title "Things to be Considered an[d] Written fully about"; these will be referred to as the short series (SS) and the long series (LS). The third of these sections consists of three separately folded sheets,[1] on which Edwards wrote another series of unnumbered notes; it will be referred to as the unnumbered series (US). In addition to these three sections, the Yale collection includes a single folio leaf which Edwards used for writing memoranda concerned with his preparation of a treatise on natural philosophy which he hoped to offer for publication.

These papers were apparently discovered by Sereno Dwight in about 1820.[2] Except for the passages in shorthand which he was unable to transcribe, and a few other short passages, Dwight published the entire contents of the manuscript in his *Life of President Edwards* in 1829.[3] Since then several items from "Natural Philosophy" have been reedited from the manuscript: Egbert Smyth published "Of Being" and the note titled "Colors" from the unnumbered series in 1895.[4] Harvey Townsend's editions of "Of Being," "Of the Prejudices of Imagination," and "Of Atoms" appeared in 1955.[5] Another edition of "Of Being" was prepared by Leon Howard and published

---

1. The first two of these sheets are now torn apart into separate folios, and the third is nearly so, because of frequent handling of the MS.

2. In his draft of the advertisement for his edition of Edwards' *Works*, Dwight mentions repeated trips to East Windsor, Northampton, and Stockbridge to gather materials for his *Life*. The manuscripts he collected at that time formed the main portion of the Andover coll. The draft of his advertisement is also in the Andover coll.

3. Dwight, *I*, app. I, pp. 702–61.

4. "Early Writings of JE," pp. 241–47.

5. Townsend, pp. 1–20.

in 1963.[6] Edwards' shorthand passages were transcribed and published by William Upham in 1902.[7]

Because Edwards' own title for the manuscript does not appear on any of the extant parts, it has come to be generally referred to by the title Dwight invented for it, "Notes on Natural Science." But "Natural Philosophy" is used as a title in several places among Edwards' other manuscript writings. In some cases he might have intended to refer to the treatise which he planned to write using the materials in this collection. But in one place in his "Miscellanies" it is evident that "Natural Philosophy" was his title for the manuscript collection itself. Miscell. no. 146 begins with the heading "Satan Defeated," followed by the reference, "Vid. in Natural Philosophy." The article here referred to, also headed "Satan Defeated," is found in the un-numbered series in the last section of the manuscript.[8]

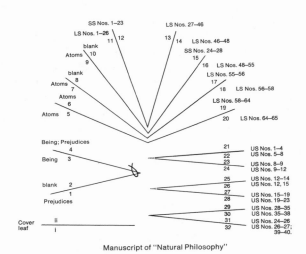

Manuscript of "Natural Philosophy"

As the diagram shows, each section of "Natural Philosophy" has a different physical structure. Also, the contents of each section are independent, at least formally, from those of the others. The sections seem, in fact, to be so many separate manuscripts, rather than parts of a single one.[9] Still, it is evident that Sereno Dwight, who discovered the papers, regarded them as belonging to a single volume. The appearance of nearly corresponding thread

6. "*The Mind*" *of JE*, pp. 139–46. Howard also presents the first paragraph of "Prejudices," pp. 146–48.

7. "Shorthand Notes of JE," pp. 514–21.

8. The passage titled "Satan Defeated" has been omitted from the unnumbered series in the text below.

9. See Townsend, pp. xii–xv.

holes in the paper of each section indicates that they were at one time sewn together into a single notebook, although from Dwight's description this notebook had already come apart, at least to some extent, by the time he examined it.[1] Other details show, however, that the sections were not sewn together before Edwards had written all, or nearly all, the notes and essays contained in them. Before that, it appears the manuscript was a loose collection of separate but related papers, which came through various stages of continued composition and rearrangement to comprise the separate sections as we now have them. The three sections of the manuscript in the Andover collection have been paginated together as one, according to the order of sections as they are represented in the diagram. This was probably the order in which Edwards sewed them together in his notebook, as well. But the pagination is not in Edwards' hand. The numerals are written in pencil by a later editor, perhaps by Dwight. This pagination will be adopted here in making references to particular pages of the "Natural Philosophy" manuscript, but with one exception: on the manuscript itself the sixth and seventh pages have been numbered in reverse, probably because of a peculiarity in the arrangement of text on those pages. A correct serial pagination will be assumed here, however. The leaf containing Edwards' memoranda for the writing of his treatise, which Dwight referred to as the cover of the manuscript, is not paginated. Although it probably was not the outside cover of Edwards' notebook, we will continue to call it the cover leaf. What Dwight called the outside and the inside pages of the cover will be referred to as its first and its second pages respectively.

The dates set by Dwight for "Natural Philosophy" have been accepted almost without question by successive generations of readers. Dwight writes, "Edwards' class pursued their mathematical and philosophical studies, during their last two years of college; and many of the articles in this collection, as is plain from the hand-writing, were obviously written at this time; others during his tutorship, and a few at a still later period."[2] More specifically, in a footnote to the passage in "Of Being" where Edwards asserts that "space is God," Dwight remarks, "this was written at fifteen or sixteen years of age,"[3] that is, during Edwards' sophomore or junior year. Finally, with reference to the long numbered series of "Things to be Considered," Dwight comments, "Several of the articles, in the second series, are in a hand more formed, and were probably written, while he was a Tutor in the college."[4] The articles meant here are very likely some of those in the unnum-

---

1. "The little collection of papers, which I have denominated 'Notes on Natural Science,' consists of eight sheets of foolscap, several of them detached, and containing, each, a series of notes and observations, entirely independent of the others." Dwight, *1*, p. 41.

2. Ibid.

3. Ibid., p. 45, n.

4. Ibid., p. 49.

bered series on the three separately folded sheets, most of which Dwight printed with numbers as a continuation of the long series (his "second series").[5]

A more careful study of the dating of the manuscript was conducted by Egbert Smyth, primarily in an attempt to determine whether "Of Being" could have been written under the influence of a reading of Berkeley's work.[6] That Smyth's conclusions confirmed the dates that Dwight had given is probably due to the fact that he was able to examine only a few manuscripts, most of them undated and most of them from Edwards' earlier period.[7] The erroneous dating of the "Spider" letter-draft by Dwight, and its acceptance by Smyth, also gave considerable impetus to the belief that all Edwards' writings in a comparable hand must belong to a very early period in his life.

Recent investigations of Edwards' early undated manuscripts by Thomas Schafer have demonstrated[8] that Dwight and Smyth not only misjudged the dates of particular manuscripts, but that some of the assumptions upon which they relied led to systematic errors and misrepresentations with respect to the whole corpus of early writings. The correct dating of "Natural Philosophy" is particularly important because it is the largest and most important collection of manuscripts from the earliest period of Edwards' literary activities, and because our understanding of other writings of this and later periods is so intimately related to it. The following study therefore is as complete and detailed as is necessary to set forth all the essential points of evidence considered in reaching the conclusions here presented. Many of the problems of dating arise from the fact that during some periods Edwards was writing in several parts of the manuscript concurrently. Hence an arrangement of the passages into an approximate chronological order, while it is a fairly complex procedure, is a necessary preliminary step to the dating of the manuscript.

Chronology of "Natural Philosophy"

An examination of Edwards' handwriting and ink in "Natural Philoso-

5. Of the forty entries in the unnumbered series, Dwight prints US No. 14 in "Of Atoms" as *Prop. 2, Corol. 18*. He makes US Nos. 3, 5, and 21 to be nos. 30–31 of his "first series"; the remaining entries are added to his "second series" as no. 53, nos. 66–88, and three additional unnumbered entries.

6. Smyth, "Early Writings of JE," pp. 212–36.

7. Smyth lists the manuscripts he examined as including "letters, sermons, plans, a large volume written in the author's later years" ("Early Writings of JE," pp. 212–13). Smyth apparently did not examine the MS of JE's "Miscellanies" in this connection, and he did not know the date of JE's "Spider" letter.

8. Thomas Schafer has graciously contributed his discoveries concerning the dating of "Natural Philosophy" for use in the following discussion. The details of the evidence have been corroborated by the editor.

phy" shows that none of the distinct parts of its contents was written in a single sitting. Entries in the three series of scientific notes, and in his memoranda on the cover, were evidently added as ideas occurred to him in the course of his continued studies. Changes of ink and hand in successive passages of the essays show that he also made additions to them, in some cases apparently after considerable lapses of time.

An initial chronological arrangement of the parts of the manuscript can be accomplished by considering the brands of paper Edwards used in it, as distinguished by their watermarks. The two single leaves containing "Of Being" and "Of the Prejudices of Imagination," and the four-sheet quire with "Of Atoms" and the two numbered series, were evidently its earliest part. These are composed of paper with an initialed English watermark and a countermark showing a crown with "GR" enclosed in a wreath. The same paper was used for his essays "Of the Rainbow" and "Of Light Rays," and one dated sample of the paper is found among Edwards' letters. The cover leaf was probably added to the manuscript next. It has a Seven Provinces watermark, with "HTV" on the countermark, a paper found in three leaves in the manuscript of the first book of Edwards' "Miscellanies."[9] The paper with London Arms watermarks and "PVL" countermarks, that he used for the three separately folded sheets containing the unnumbered series, is found in the "Miscellanies," immediately after the Seven Provinces leaves. These are apparently Edwards' latest addition of paper to "Natural Philosophy."

Of the three essays in the earliest parts of the manuscript, "Of Atoms" shows the least variation in hand and ink in its successive passages. The ink is a glossy reddish brown, uniform in color and composition throughout the composition. There is a change in the form of the handwriting, however, after Proposition 2, Corollary 16, which occurs on the third recto of the quire (p. 9 of the manuscript). Down to this point Edwards wrote in a fairly large sprawling hand, whereas the hand of Corollary 17 and the objection and replies at the end is smaller and more compact. After Corollary 16 Edwards originally wrote "Prop. 3rd" in the earlier hand. This was deleted before he went on to write Corollary 17 (which he then also deleted). The alteration of his intention with respect to adding a third proposition, together with the change of handwriting at that point, suggests that there was at least a brief lapse of time while Edwards reconsidered the course of his argument.

The first three paragraphs of "Of Being" and the beginning portion of "Prejudices" down through the *nota bene* following the second proposition are written in a hand very similar to that at the end of "Of Atoms." The next passages in "Of Being" and "Prejudices," however, were apparently added after a considerable lapse of time. They are in a very small, some-

9. The MS of "Miscellanies" is in the Yale coll.

what angular and rapidly written hand, and the ink is a dull brown in color with quantities of black particles that form crusts in the blots. A generally similar hand and ink occur in the draft of his "Spider" letter, in a long series of entries in his "Miscellanies," and in entries after the beginning portions of the two numbered series of notes in the "Natural Philosophy" quire. The final paragraph of "Of Being" is in still a later hand and ink. Comparisons of it with passages in "Miscellanies" show that this paragraph is probably the last that he wrote in "Natural Philosophy."

A peculiarity in the arrangement of the text of the "Prejudices" essay on the two single leaves suggests that the order of these leaves was reversed in the manuscript at some time after Edwards finished the essay. In the present order, the main portion of the essay down through the statement of Postulatum 7, is found on the recto of the first leaf (MS p. 1), and the verso of this leaf is blank. "Of Being" begins on the recto of the second leaf (MS p. 3), and later additions to this essay are written there and on the verso (MS p. 4). On this same page, below these additions, and separated from them by a line across the page, Edwards wrote the last two paragraphs of "Prejudices." When he put them there, it is likely that the two leaves stood in the reverse of their present order, so that the verso page on which he was writing his additions preceded and faced the beginning part of the essay. This inference is confirmed by the arrangement of text in "Of Atoms." Edwards originally wrote this series of propositions and corollaries only on the recto pages at the beginning of the quire. The verso pages were left blank, presumably for later additions, since the first verso contains added passages keyed for insertion into the discussions on both the first and second rectos. Hence, by following the same practice in "Prejudices," and with the supposed reversal of the two leaves, Edwards would have written his last part of the essay where we find it, on the verso of the leaf with "Of Being."

Edwards began his "Things to be Considered and Written fully about" with the long numbered series (LS), starting on the first recto of the central sheet of the quire (MS p. 11). From the appearance of the ink and hand he wrote several entries at each sitting. The ink of the first part of the series, and also of the beginning of the short series (SS) on the next page, is gray in color, varying in intensity according to the amount of black material in its composition. Although this ink has no kinship with that in "Of Atoms," it is probable that the first entries in the long series were written at nearly the same time as it was begun.[1] LS Nos. 1–8 are in an almost identical large

---

1. There is some evidence that JE kept two inks on hand during much of the general period to which these writings belong. One now appears brown, and the other gray. Among jottings on the back of a letter draft dated Nov. 1, 1720, there is a crude diagram of the left and right optic nerves showing them to be joined in the manner suggested in SS No. 5. This diagram is drawn in a brown ink (though not of the same shade or texture as that of "Of Atoms"), while the labels for the diagram are in a gray ink similar to that with which he began both the long and the short series of "Things to be Considered."

sprawling hand, and LS Nos. 9–14 and 15–19 are in progressively smaller versions of the same hand. In LS No. 20 the hand becomes slightly larger again, but is also more compact, like that at the end of "Of Atoms" and the beginnings of "Of Being" and "Prejudices." From its content, and especially from the note at the end, LS No. 20 was almost certainly written after "Of Atoms" was finished.

From investigation of the chronological order of "Natural Philosophy" thus far, it appears that Edwards began the manuscript with "Of Atoms" and that he probably wrote LS Nos. 1–8 at about the same time, with LS Nos. 9–19 written in two further sittings soon afterward. At about the time he wrote LS No. 20, he began "Of Being" and "Prejudices," though further passages were added to both at a somewhat later date. This succession is further confirmed by the changes in Edwards' orthographic tendencies in the course of writing these passages, as they will be discussed in connection with the problem of dating.

From comparisons of the handwriting and the intensities of the gray ink, Edwards appears to have started the short numbered series on the central verso of the quire (MS p. 12) at about the same time as he wrote LS No. 27 on the preceding page. Minor variations in the ink, pen, and hand of entries thereafter show that he continued writing in both series concurrently, adding a few entries to each at each sitting. Hence SS Nos. 1–6 are concurrent with LS Nos. 27–36, SS Nos. 7–13 with LS Nos. 37–38, and SS Nos. 14–16 with LS Nos. 39–41. SS Nos. 17–21b (two entries are numbered 21) and LS Nos. 42–44 are written in a dark brown ink, which Edwards also used for touching up the faint gray of earlier entries. From SS No. 17 and LS No. 42 Edwards also began by degrees to increase the size of his handwriting, so that SS No. 21b and LS No. 44 are in a hand almost as large and sprawling as that in the first page of "Of Atoms."

In the entries immediately following, however, there is a radical change in the hand and ink in both series, indicating once more that Edwards had probably laid the manuscript aside for a period of time. SS Nos. 22–23 and LS No. 45, at the bottoms of the two inside pages of the quire's central sheet, are written in a small angular hand and dull brown ink very similar to that in Edwards' draft of the "Spider" letter. These entries undoubtedly belong to the same period as his later additions to "Of Being" and "Prejudices."

Edwards continued the short series from SS No. 24 on the sixth recto of the quire (MS p. 15) where it ends with SS No. 28 at the bottom of the page. The long series is continued on the fifth verso, that is, the second verso of the central sheet (MS p. 14), and then on the sixth verso and succeeding pages thereafter to the end of the quire (MS pp. 16–20). Before discontinuing the short series Edwards seems to have had some difficulty in distinguishing it from the long one. LS No. 49 was at first written, with that number, in the short series after SS No. 24. Soon after, he recopied the entry with minor revisions in its proper place in the long series, and at the same time the version in the short series was deleted. SS No. 26 proved to be a false start for an entry on fog, which Edwards deleted after writing SS No. 27. This and SS No. 28, the last of the short series, are in the gray ink of LS No. 50, and are probably contemporaneous with it. LS Nos. 62–65 differ from the earlier entries in either series, in that Edwards began them with subject headings. There are some uncertainties about the chronological relation of these five entries to those in the unnumbered series, which will be discussed in connection with efforts to estimate their dates.

Edwards probably added the cover to the manuscript, and began his lists of memoranda on it, soon after the dormant period we have inferred following the beginning passages of "Of Being" and "Prejudices," and after LS No. 44 and SS No. 21b in the two numbered series. The first five numbered items on the second page of the cover and the first four unnumbered ones on the first page agree in ink and hand with the passages in these places that mark his resumption of writing in the manuscript. From comparisons of the ink with entries in his "Miscellanies" it appears that No. 6, which is written in shorthand, and Nos. 7–14 were entered a short time later on the second page. The fifth entry on the first page of the cover and Nos. 15–21 were written much later. Five of these last seven memoranda are partially or entirely written in shorthand. Two shorthand passages in the unnumbered series of notes in "Natural Philosophy" prove to fit with the memoranda on the cover, because they also concern his plan for a treatise on natural philosophy. By comparisons of ink, these appear to be earlier than Nos. 15–21 on the cover. In the text below they are printed at the end of the cover memoranda, instead of at the places where they actually occur in the unnumbered series.

The unnumbered series of notes on the three separately folded sheets presents further problems. The first of these concerns its relation to the other parts of "Natural Philosophy." In most respects, this series appears to be a continuation of the long numbered series, and in fact, there is no evident reason why Edwards might have wished to distinguish them. The fact that the entries lack numbers can be accounted for by assuming that Edwards began it when the quire containing the numbered notes was not at hand. This assumption is confirmed by several additional points. The last quarter of a page of the quire, after LS No. 65, is left blank, whereas in his other notebooks Edwards' usual practice was to fill each page to the bottom, even when the article extended beyond to the pages of newly added leaves. Furthermore, US No. 3 contains an uncompleted reference in which Edwards probably intended to cite one or more of the corollaries to the second proposition in "Of Atoms." He left a blank space as if to add the citation later, suggesting that "Of Atoms" and the quire containing it were not at hand at the time. Finally, when he drew the diagrams for US No. 12, headed "Ice. Cold," on the first verso of the second sheet, the point of his compasses punctured holes in corresponding patterns through the cover leaf, the two leaves containing the essays "Of Being" and "Prejudices," and the third of the separately folded sheets, which was still blank. From the relative sizes of the holes in each piece, they were piled in the order mentioned underneath the leaf Edwards drew on, in order to serve as a backing for his compasses. There are no such patterns of holes in any of the leaves of quire; thus it was evidently detached from the other parts of the manuscript at the time, and might have been altogether absent. Hence it is reasonable to suppose that Edwards wrote the unnumbered articles as additions to his long numbered series. Nevertheless, even though he must have had all the parts of "Natural Philosophy" together at some later time, he never troubled to number these entries or to complete the unfinished citation.

There is also a problem in establishing the exact chronological relation between the beginning of the unnumbered series and the end of the long numbered series of articles. This arises because of some uncertainty as to the time at which LS Nos. 62–65 were written. By comparisons of hand and ink with entries in "Miscellanies," it is evident that US No. 1 was written quite soon after LS No. 61; it is probable, but not entirely evident, that it followed LS No. 65. This problem will be taken up fully in connection with the dating of these entries.

Edwards wrote US Nos. 1–23 on the first two separately folded sheets (MS pp. 21–28) in the order of their present pagination. On the third sheet, however, comparisons with "Miscellanies" entries show that he continued with US Nos. 24–26 on what is now its second recto (MS p. 31). After finishing US No. 26 which is carried to the top of the next page (MS p. 32), he reversed the fold of the sheet and wrote US Nos. 27–37 on what became the first recto and verso of the sheet (MS pp. 29–30). Finally, he returned to the last verso to write US Nos. 38–40 just below US No. 26. As the above citations indicate, these articles have been numbered in accordance with their chronological order, and not in the order of their position in the manuscript. They are arranged accordingly in the text of the unnumbered series below.

Dating of "Natural Philosophy"

In the light of the above discussion, it will be convenient to divide Edwards' writing in "Natural Philosophy" into four distinct chronological strata, representing the periods of his most concerted efforts in the manuscript. The first stratum consists of "Of Atoms" and the first eight entries of the long numbered series of "Things to be Considered," followed soon after by LS Nos. 9–20 and the beginning passages of "Of Being" and "Of the Prejudices of Imagination," then by LS Nos. 21–44 and SS Nos. 1–21b. The second begins after a period when the manuscript apparently lay dormant, and includes the first additions to "Of Being" and all the "Prejudices" additions, the first fourteen numbered memoranda and the first four unnumbered ones on his cover leaf, SS Nos. 22–28 and LS Nos. 44–50, and finally the end of the long series, LS Nos. 51–65. The third stratum includes US Nos. 1–23 on the first two of the separately folded sheets. And the fourth contains the remaining articles of that series, US Nos. 24–40, as well as all of the remaining memoranda on the cover and the final addition to "Of Being." In estimating the dates of Edwards' writing, these strata may now be considered in order.

Comparisons of the passages in these four strata of "Natural Philosophy" with other dated or independently dateable manuscripts is essential in the process of judging their approximate dates. Unfortunately, there are all too few such manuscripts. Only eight survive from the entire period preceding August 1722, the beginning of his New York pastorate. Five of these are letters dated May 10, 1716, March 26, 1719, July 24, 1719, March 1, 1721, and December 12, 1721. Two are letter drafts, one dated November 1, 1720, and the other undated, both written on the same page of a folio leaf. The last is the valedictory oration Edwards wrote for his commencement in September 1720.[2] Three such manuscripts come from the ensuing four year period, 1722 to 1726, including the New York pastorate, the following year in Connecticut, and his two years of tutorship. These are the "Spider" letter dated October 31, 1723, his draft of that letter written just before that date, and the M.A. thesis written in the summer of 1723 which he submitted for his degree at the Yale commencement in September.[3] In the fall of 1726 he settled in Northampton.

To the above we must add the manuscript of his "Miscellanies," the series of notes which Edwards began during the New York pastorate and continued to write for the remainder of his life. While none of the articles in "Miscellanies" is dated by Edwards, the manuscript affords the most complete and continuous series we have of samples of his handwriting and inks and the brands of paper he used at different times, and is in an almost entirely accurate chronological order. Furthermore, many of the articles in this series are independently dateable in virtue of their similarities to dated items, their suggestions of incidents in Edwards' life, and by other means. Hence the recognition of the approximate contemporaneity of an undated passage with an article in "Miscellanies" is a significant clue to its date. In the following study, I will assume the dating of articles in "Miscellanies" that has been given by Thomas Schafer, and will often refer to his conclusions in these matters.[4]

2. MSS of all the above letters and letter-drafts are in the Andover coll. The MS of JE's valedictory oration is in the Yale coll.

3. The dated "Spider" letter, and JE's draft of this letter, are described above, pp. 150–51, and below, p. 407. The draft of his M.A. thesis is in the Andover coll.

4. Schafer's dating of "Miscellanies" will be presented in full in his introduction to his edition of that series in a forthcoming volume of *Works* (Yale ed.).

Comparisons of passages in "Natural Philosophy" with these manuscripts show close parallels between those in the second chronological stratum, as described above, and the writings belonging to the summer and fall of 1723. We have already noted the great similarity in hand and ink of the additions to "Of Being" and "Prejudices" and of entries in the two numbered series after LS No. 44 and SS No. 21b to that in his draft of the "Spider" letter. More specific and exact parallels may be found with entries in "Miscellanies" that are to be dated 1723–24 following the end of his New York pastorate. These will be examined in detail below. For the present, however, these correspondences in general are evidence that the period of Edwards' inactivity in "Natural Philosophy" between the first and second strata occurred during his nine months in New York. This is confirmed by the fact that "Miscellanies," begun in New York,[5] contains no entries in a hand or ink similar to that in the first stratum of "Natural Philosophy." Nor does it have any of the initialed English paper that is found in the earliest components of "Natural Philosophy." We therefore draw this important preliminary conclusion: the first chronological stratum of passages was composed before August 2, 1722, and the second begun after April 30, 1723.

A major point of evidence in determining the time at which Edwards first began "Natural Philosophy" appears in comparing its brand of paper with that of the dated and dateable pre-New York manuscripts. The same initialed English watermark is found on the folio he used for a letter to his father from Yale, dated March 1, 1721. Another dated sample of this paper is a letter written from New Haven by Edwards' classmate Daniel Dwight to his parents on April 11, 1721. The letter Edwards wrote to his sister dated December 12, 1721, also appears to be on paper of the same brand.[6] The letter drafts dated November 1, 1720, and all the manuscripts of earlier date, however, are on paper with other watermarks. These letters show that a quantity of the paper he used in beginning "Natural Philosophy" was available in New Haven during the spring of Edwards' first graduate year, and that he probably had not exhausted his own stock of it before the middle of his second graduate year when he wrote the December 12, 1721, letter. The absence of the watermark in earlier manuscripts makes it seem unlikely that Edwards acquired this paper before the fall of 1720. And from the quantity of writing and the nature of the contents in the first, pre-New York stratum of "Natural Philosophy" it probably was not begun later than the fall of 1721.

5. JE quotes from the first entry of "Miscellanies" in his "Personal Narrative," where he speaks of it as having been written in New York.

6. No watermark appears on the paper of this letter, which is a short section cut from one end of a folio leaf. The impressions of the chain lines and wire lines of the deckle on which it was made, however, seem to correspond to those on the top portions of countermarked folios of the English paper in "Natural Philosophy."

Further comparisons of handwriting and ink with the dated manuscripts are of little help. His handwriting seems to have changed quite rapidly during this time, and the dated pieces do not provide enough samples to afford reliable comparsions. Moreover, Edwards' letters and his valedictory oration are written in a careful, formal hand intended to be read by others, while "Natural Philosophy" was apparently a private project and is written in a more casual hand. Nor do any of the inks in the dated manuscripts match those in "Natural Philosophy" closely enough to establish a definite conclusion. That of his valedictory oration of September 1720 is quite similar to the smooth reddish-brown ink in "Of Atoms" and the beginnings of "Of Being" and "Prejudices," but no more so than that of two sermons in the group with which he began his preaching career, which were probably written no earlier than the summer of 1722.[7] The faint gray ink in the early entries of his long numbered series has some similarity to that in the letter drafts dated November 1, 1720, but is just as similar to that in his December 12, 1721, letter. Both are similar in composition to the "Natural Philosophy" ink, but are tinged with yellowish-brown. That of the letter of March 1, 1721, has an even deeper shade of brown. The inks of his letters of March 26 and July 24, 1719, are at best only remotely related to any of these.

Comparisons of Edwards' orthography in these dated manuscripts, however, reveal several points in which his spelling practices were changing during this period, so that his orthography in the early portions of "Natural Philosophy" proves to be a fruitful basis for dating its passages. Examination of Edwards' spellings of certain words also tends to confirm our earlier judgment, that he began the manuscript with "Of Atoms" and the first eight entries of the long numbered series.

Some characteristics of Edwards' orthography in the early writings are continued through later life, e.g., his use of contractions such as "'em," "don't" and "ben't." In other points all these writings differ from those coming after his New York period: "thereof," "wherein," etc. are later usually spelled "therof," "wherin," etc. "Whether" is later more often spelled "whither," "remarkable" is later "remarkeable," and "eternall," "naturall," etc. give way to "eternal," "natural," etc. (though the later spellings of all these words may occasionally be found in the earlier writings). In a few cases, however, the change occurred in the course of the pre-New York letters. Two of these are of relatively minor importance for "Natural Philosophy," but three other cases are quite significant.[8]

---

7. Sermons on Matt. 16 : 26 and Heb. 9 : 27, two of a group of five that are written on paper with Vreyheyt watermarks. Another sermon, on Isa. 3:10, also has ink similar to that in "Of Atoms," and is written on the same brand of paper. The Isa. 3:10 sermon is probably of earlier date than any of those in the Vreyheyt group.

8. Both the minor cases concern spellings of the first-person forms of personal pronouns. In the few instances of these pronouns in "Natural Philosophy," all spellings conform with his

In the May 10, 1716, letter, there are three cases of the spelling "verry" and only one "very." All six occurrences in the two letters dated March 26 and July 24, 1719, are "verry." In the first draft of November 1, 1720, the one occurrence is first written "verry," but then altered to "very." Two in the March 1, 1721, letter are both "very." The correction in the first November 1720 draft suggests that Edwards was then deliberately reforming his spelling of the word, and the regular appearance of "very" thereafter indicates that this spelling had become a settled habit in his writing. Except for one instance, the later spelling is found throughout the pre-New York passages in "Natural Philosophy." Three are in "Of Atoms," two in "Of Being," eight in "Prejudices," and five in the two numbered series. The exceptional "verry" appears in LS No. 34, and is evidently an accidental reversion.

A similar change is found in the incidence of his spelling of "att." In the May 10, 1716, letter the one occurrence is "at," but the next two, one each in the July 24, 1719, letter and the first November 1, 1720, draft, are spelled "att." In the second draft on that leaf, the one occurrence is "at," and thereafter the other spelling declines in incidence. Out of the nine cases of the word in the March 1, 1721, letter six are "at." The latest discovered "att" is in the December 12, 1721, letter, where there are also two "at." In "Natural Philosophy" there are no occurrences of the spelling "att," whereas "at" occurs twenty-one times in "Of Atoms," "Of Being," and "Prejudices."

A third point of interest in Edwards' orthography concerns his use of y-contractions from mid-1719 to about mid-1722. These include "y^t" for "that," "y^e" for "the," "y^m," for "them," etc. The earliest instance is in the July 24, 1719, letter, and thereafter there are two in the second November 1720 draft and three in the March 1, 1721, letter. The greatest incidence of y-contractions in "Natural Philosophy" is in "Of Atoms," where there are twelve. Only one occurs in "Of Being," however, and none in either "Prejudices" or the two numbered series. Through this time Edwards might have deliberately inserted y-contractions in writing he considered more formal. They abound in two sermons which he wrote for the New York pulpit, and in one of these they were inserted after the noncontracted forms were written. While the practice did not last long after he went to New York, there are two y-contractions in his "Spider" letter of October 1723, though none in the "Spider" draft.

All these orthographic features tend to confirm the judgment that Edwards began "Natural Philosophy" during his first year of graduate study, between the fall of 1720 and the spring of 1721. All the spellings of "very" in "Natural Philosophy" conform to his settled usage after November 1, 1720, and while his spelling of "at" seems to have changed more gradually, it there conforms to the later rather than the earlier tendency. "Of Atoms" is more

---

later practice. Word counts in the cases discussed below include occurrences in JE's deleted passages, which are usually omitted in the edited texts of these writings.

closely associated with the writing of the fall of 1720 and the spring of 1721 in frequency of y-contractions, while "Of Being" and "Prejudices" follow his later tendency in this usage.

A further change in orthography occurs only in "Natural Philosophy"; but it provides additional evidence for the assumption that "Of Atoms" and LS Nos. 1–8 are the earliest writing in the manuscript and are nearly contemporaneous. Edwards spells "bodys" in five out of eight uses of the word on the first manuscript page of "Of Atoms." In the last of these five he seems to have made a correction of the spelling, and in the remaining fourteen instances thereafter in "Of Atoms," he regularly spells "bodies." The word does not occur in the beginning of "Of Being," while in all five cases in the early part of "Prejudices," it is spelled "bodies." In the long numbered series, however, the earlier "bodys" occurs in LS Nos. 3 and 8; in LS No. 11 and thereafter he spells "bodies."

In the light of these findings, it is most probable that Edwards wrote "Of Atoms" and LS Nos. 1–8 some time in his first year of graduate study, perhaps about the end of 1720. The beginning portions of "Of Being" and "Prejudices," and LS Nos. 9–20, followed soon afterward, probably by the next spring. He began the short numbered series contemporaneously with LS No. 27, but considering the similarities in ink and hand to the preceding entries in the long series, this was probably before the end of the school term, or very early in the second graduate year. Since the short series begins with evidences of his current study of Newton's *Optics*, he was almost certainly in New Haven at the time.[9]

Successive sets of entries written concurrently in both the long and short series have a similar ink and hand down to LS Nos. 42 and 43 and SS Nos. 17 and 18. These entries are in a dark brown ink, very different from the faint gray earlier in the two series. Edwards might have changed his ink because of the faintness of the gray; he touched up earlier entries, including all of SS Nos. 1–6 in this ink. His references to mountains and journeys in LS Nos. 42 and 43, however, suggest time spent in travel away from New Haven, and the optical phenomenon described in LS No. 44 was probably observed in the summer of the year. LS Nos. 42–44 and SS Nos. 17–21b, all of which are in the brown ink, thus were probably written during the spring and summer before his departure for New York on August 2, 1722. These are the latest passages in the pre-New York stratum.

By the time Edwards had returned to Connecticut on April 30, 1723, it is probable that he had written all the lettered and double lettered entries at the beginning of "Miscellanies," and was beginning the numbered en-

---

9. For a discussion of JE's early study of Newton's works and other scientific writings, see above, pp. 21–23. While many passages in "Natural Philosophy" give evidence of the books he was currently reading, this is usually of help only in confirming the general period to which the passages belong.

tries. From comparisons with the draft of his "Spider" letter, he had reached Miscell. no. 88 by the end of October 1723. The additions to "Of Being" which belong in this second stratum of "Natural Philosophy" must have been written before this time. These consist in an initial sentence which he deleted, four paragraphs containing his argument for idealism and the corollary in which he draws his conclusion, all on the recto side of the leaf under the beginning of the essay; and one paragraph on the top of the verso side, in which he picked up again the argument of his first beginning paragraph in the essay. In ink and hand they are most similar to Miscell. nos. 41–44, which were probably written around late July 1723.

Shortly after his return from New York, Edwards also added his third Proposition to "Prejudices," followed it with a sentence mentioning the introduction of the laws of gravity and of motion as a postulatum, and then added seven numbered postulata, all on the same page as the beginning of the essay. He also added a final paragraph on the verso of the leaf containing "Of Being," leaving a blank space between that paragraph and the addition to "Of Being" at the top of the page, which he filled much later with the final paragraph of "Of Being." Of these additions to "Prejudices," Proposition 3 and the next sentence appear contemporaneous with the additions to "Of Being" discussed above, and were probably written in July or August 1723. The seven postulata and final paragraph appear to be contemporaneous with Miscell. nos. 82–88, written probably in September or early October of that year.

Edwards also began to write in the two numbered series again during the summer. LS Nos. 45–48 and SS Nos. 22–23 are very similar to the additions to "Of Being," and so should also be assigned to late July or early August 1723. SS No. 24 closely resembles Miscell. no. 65, and SS No. 26 and LS No. 49 agree with Miscell. nos. 85 and 86. The last two entries of the short series, SS Nos. 27–28, and LS No. 50 are written in the gray ink that first appears in the late 80s in "Miscellanies." They most closely resemble that of Miscell. no. 94, of the end of 1723.

The remaining entries in the long series were probably written during the following winter, before Edwards began his tutorship at Yale at the beginning of June 1724. LS Nos. 51–55 correspond with Miscell. nos. 95–114, and the inks of LS Nos. 56–61 appear in Miscell. nos. 115–117. The inks of the last four entries in the series are considerably varied, and more difficult to locate accurately in "Miscellanies" and other manuscripts. No other dateable sample of the thick dark ink of LS No. 62 has been located; it could be the last heavy dregs of his earlier ink. LS No. 63 and the beginning part of No. 64 are written in a very smooth, faint gray ink, apparently a version of that in Miscell. no. 118. A more similar ink is found on a page of manuscript in "Notes on Revelation," which Edwards transferred there from his "Notes on Scripture." The discussion on this page is referred to in Miscell. no. 133.

LS No. 64 is completed in a lustrous brown ink, the same used for LS No. 65, the last of the longer series. Again, no exact parallels are found in other manuscript writings of this time, but the ink could be a version of that in "Miscellanies" entries in the late 130s. In the judgment of Professor Schafer, Edwards had reached about Miscell. no. 120 at the time he began his Yale tutorship.

Apart from the difficulty of locating the inks of LS Nos. 62–65 in other manuscripts of this period, there is a further detail that makes the dating of these four entries somewhat uncertain. These are the only entries in either of the two numbered series that Edwards began with subject headings written in a large, bold hand. He had followed this practice in "Miscellanies" from its beginning, and it is found elsewhere in "Natural Philosophy" only in the unnumbered series. There it starts after US No. 6 with an article headed "Satan Defeated," which Edwards obviously wrote there by mistake, having intended it for "Miscellanies." After writing a long paragraph he discovered his error, and went on in Miscell. no. 146 to finish the discussion, beginning there with a back reference to its opening portion in "Natural Philosophy." If the above dating of LS Nos. 62–65 is correct, it appears that Edwards began the practice of titling his articles in "Natural Philosophy" with these entries, and then inexplicably discontinued it for a time in beginning the unnumbered series, only to resume it again at the point where he mistakenly thought he was writing "Satan Defeated" on a page of "Miscellanies."

The titling of LS Nos. 62–65 could be more adequately explained if those entries were assumed to have been written at a later time, after he had begun the practice of titling in the unnumbered series in order to avoid further mistakes in the identity of his manuscript. Such an assumption allows for far greater latitude in the search for inks similar to those in the four entries. Comparison with later "Miscellanies" entries still finds the ink of LS No. 62 unmatched, but the gray ink of LS Nos. 63–64 resembles that of Miscell. nos. 203–05. The earliest appearance thereafter of an ink like the brown in LS Nos. 64–65 is in Miscell. nos. 267–78, probably written in 1727 after about the first year of his Northampton pastorate. The almost overwhelming evidence against this dating of the LS entries is the handwriting of LS Nos. 62–65. It is quite distinguishable from that of "Miscellanies" of the early Northampton period, and closely resembles that at the beginning of the unnumbered series in "Natural Philosophy," which was probably written soon after.

The third chronological stratum of "Natural Philosophy," consisting of US Nos. 1–23 on the first two of the separately folded sheets, was almost certainly written during the two years of Edwards' Yale tutorship from June 1, 1724, to August or September 1725. We have already discussed evidence that when he began the unnumbered series the quire containing "Of Atoms" and the two numbered series was not at hand. According to his "Diary" for

June 6, 1724, he traveled to New Haven to take up his post a week previously,[1] and since he had probably resided with his family for a time before this, he might have left the "Natural Philosophy" quire and other manuscripts at home in East Windsor.

Comparisons with "Miscellanies" give further evidence that the unnumbered series was started during his tutorship. The paper of the final three separately folded sheets in "Natural Philosophy," like that of the six sheets added to 'Miscellanies" for Miscell. nos. 82–235, has London Arms watermarks and "PVL" in the countermarks. Dimensions and position of the marks on each of the three sheets are somewhat different, and comparable differences are found on the "Miscellanies" sheets. The first "Natural Philosophy" sheet is the same as the third "Miscellanies" sheet which contains Miscell. nos. 126–146. The second agrees with the fifth containing Miscell. nos. 170–199. The third corresponds to the sixth "Miscellanies" sheet containing Miscell. nos. 200–235. These correspondences of paper help considerably to narrow down that portion of "Miscellanies" which should be considered in our investigation of the third and fourth strata.

The entries on the first page of the unnumbered series (US Nos. 1–4) are written in an uneven gray ink very similar to that in Miscell. nos. 132–141 which he probably wrote during the summer of 1724. The smooth gray ink of LS Nos. 63 and 64 seems to be an earlier stage of this. The brown ink of US Nos. 5–23, which continue to the end of the second sheet, is used in "Miscellanies" entries up to about Miscell. no. 180. The beginning of his article on "Satan Defeated," following US No. 6, agrees exactly in ink and hand with its continuation in Miscell. no. 146, and was probably written well before his illness in the fall and winter of 1724–25. The faded appearance of the ink in US No. 23 is also found in Miscell. nos. 178–180, written in the summer of 1726 when he was an active candidate for the position in Northampton as assistant to his grandfather, the Reverend Solomon Stoddard.

The fourth chronological stratum of "Natural Philosophy" includes the entries on the third separately folded sheet of the unnumbered series (US Nos. 24–40), the remaining numbered and unnumbered memoranda on the manuscript cover, and the last paragraph of "Of Being." These were written more infrequently over a period of several years, mostly during the early part of his ministry in Northampton.

The arrangement of US Nos. 24–40 on the third sheet has already been discussed. US Nos. 24–26 are similar in ink and hand to "Miscellanies" entries in the 180s, and must have been written in the summer or early autumn of 1726, probably just before Edwards moved to Northampton. US Nos. 27 and 28 agree in hand and ink with Miscell. nos. 200–206, written in

1. "Diary" for June 6, 1724, in Dwight, *1*, p. 103.

the fall of that year. The last of the cover-leaf memoranda are written in a very similar ink, and were probably written at about the same time. After this final spurt of interest in his projected treatise, however, Edwards laid the manuscript aside for increasingly longer periods at a time. US Nos. 29–31 are similar in hand and ink to Miscell. nos. 226–31, written in early 1727. US No. 32 might be contemporaneous with Miscell. no. 248, or again with Miscell. no. 301. US Nos. 33–38 agree with Miscell. nos. 311–28, written about the end of 1727. The ink and hand of the series' final entries, US Nos. 39–40, does not appear in "Miscellanies" entries before the early 400s. These entries show evidence of his reading of Henry Pemberton's *A View of Sir Isaac Newton's Philosophy*, which was published in London in 1728.[2] It is probable that US Nos. 39–40 were written late in the following year, 1729.

The only later passage in "Natural Philosophy" is the final paragraph of "Of Being." This was added at about the same time that Edwards wrote Miscell. no. 587, probably during the summer of 1732.

Editing of "Natural Philosophy"

In the following text of "Natural Philosophy" the memoranda on the cover of the manuscript are presented first, followed by "Of the Prejudices of Imagination," "Of Being," and "Of Atoms" in that order. This is the order in which these three essays presently stand in the manuscript, and is probably the way Edwards finally arranged them when he sewed the sections together into his notebook. Of the two numbered series of "Things to be Considered," the shorter begins second in the manuscript, but it is presented first below. The unnumbered entries in the last component of the manuscript are presented as a distinct series, and are assigned numbers in brackets.

For the most part, passages in "Prejudices," "Of Being," "Of Atoms," and the two numbered series are presented in the order in which they appear on the pages of the manuscript. In the case of "Of Being" this differs from the arrangement of text in most previous editions where the section containing Edwards' argument for idealism is placed at the end. Passages that Edwards later added to "Of Atoms" and keyed for insertion into his previously written text have been inserted at the places indicated. In LS No. 48, a long entry on the growth and propagation of trees, Edwards added marginal notes directing the rearrangement of certain passages; the text is printed below in the order indicated by these notes. In the short series Edwards numbered two successive entries 21, and in the long series two are numbered 23. In each case the entries are distinguished below as [a] and [b]. Following SS No. 26 Edwards began another on fog which he also numbered 26. After

---

2. JE quotes from this work in his "Wisdom in the Contrivance of the World." See below, p. 309.

writing only a few words, he deleted the whole. This deleted beginning has been silently omitted in the text below.

The editor has made more extensive revisions in the order of text in the unnumbered series. The entries have been numbered in the chronological order in which they were written. In the case of US Nos. 24–40 this is quite different from their arrangement on the sheets of the manuscript as it is now paginated. The article headed "Satan Defeated," which Edwards mistakenly began in the series after US No. 6, has been omitted from this edition of the text. He intended the discussion for his "Miscellanies," and upon discovering his mistake he completed it there as Miscell. no. 146. Two other entries, both in shorthand, evidently were meant to go with the memoranda Edwards wrote on the cover of the manuscript. They have been omitted from the unnumbered series, and printed instead at the end of the cover memoranda, where they are indicated by [a] and [b]. In some cases in the unnumbered series, Edwards wrote additional passages to an entry at a point one or two entries below in the manuscript, and used key marks to show their relation to the earlier one. In these cases, the later additions have been silently moved and printed with the entries to which they belong.

Edwards' illustrations have been redrawn for the text below. They have been numbered consecutively in each part of "Natural Philosophy," and Edwards' references to them in the text have been silently revised to conform to this numbering.

Footnotes have been added by the editor to explain the special problems in reading and interpreting the manuscript, to indicate significant features of the various passages that have been considered in dating them, and to mention the probable sources of the ideas Edwards expressed. In matters of spelling and punctuation, and in otherwise preparing the text of "Natural Philosophy" for publication, the standard practices for editing from manuscript originals, as prescribed for the Yale edition, have been followed. These practices are described above in Section 4 of the Introduction.

"Natural Philosophy"

COVER-LEAF MEMORANDA

Side i:[1]

[Remember] to set down the order [in which] I would have the particulars stand, a mark here denoting the paragraphs.

Remember to set down this and the propositions following only as postulated, in short, without standing to prove them.

Place in the beginning definitions, as the definition of an atom or perfect solid, what I mean by touching by points, touching by lines, and by surfaces.

In the second place let there be postulata, which let be either axioms or principles exceeding plainly deduced from them.

Let there not only be definitions and postulates at the beginning of the whole, but at the beginning of the particular chapters and sections as there is occasion; which postulates and definitions may be referred to from other parts if it suits best. These may be put before even the sections in the midst of a chapter.

Side ii:[2]

[1.[3] Try] not only to silence but to gain *readers.*

[2. To give but] few prefatorial admonitions about the style and

1. Sereno Dwight refers to this as the "first page" of the cover (Dwight, *1*, p. 702). All five memoranda on this side of the leaf were written between late 1723 and 1726 (see above, pp. 181–82). The leaf has become badly frayed at the top, so that some words are now entirely missing or illegible. Dwight's readings for these words have been inserted in brackets in the text below.

2. Dwight refers to this as the "inside page" of the cover. The words and passages in shorthand were first transcribed by William Upham ("Shorthand Writings of JE," pp. 514–21). These have been newly transcribed for this edition, and are printed below in italics. Conjectural readings and illegible symbols are explained in footnotes at the appropriate points.

3. Nos. 1–5 appear to have been written within a short period of time, perhaps in a single sitting, probably in the late summer or fall of 1723.

method. It doth an author much hurt to show his concern for those things.

[3. What is] prefatorial, not to write in a distinct preface or introduction, but in the body of the treatise. Then I shall be sure to have it read by everyone.

[4. Let much] modesty be seen in the style.

[5.] Not to insert any disputable things, or that I will be likely to be disputed by learned men, for I may depend upon it they will receive nothing but what is undeniable from me, that is, in things exceedingly beside the ordinary way of thinking.

6.[4] *The world will expect more modesty because of my circumstances—in America, young, etc. Let there then be a superabundance of modesty, and though perhaps 'twill otherwise be needless, it will wonderfully make way for its reception in the world. Mankind are by nature proud and exceeding envious, and ever jealous of such upstarts; and it exceedingly irritates and affronts 'em to see 'em appear in print. Yet the modesty ought not to be affected and foolish, but decent and natural.*

7.[5] When I would prove anything, to take special care that the matter be so stated that it shall be seen most clearly and distinctly by everyone just how much I would prove; and to extricate all questions from the least confusion or ambiguity of words, so that the ideas shall be left naked.

8. In the course of reasoning, not to pretend to be more certain than everyone will plainly see it is, by such expressions as "it's certain," "it's undeniable," etc.

9. To be very moderate in the use of terms of art. Let it not look as if I was much read, or conversant with books or the learned world.

10. In the method, in placing things first, respect is to be had to the easiness and intelligibleness, the clearness and certainty, the generality, and according to the dependence of other things upon them.

[11.] Never to dispute for things after that I cannot handsomely retreat upon conviction of the contrary.

[12.] In writing, let there be much compliance with the *reader's* weakness, and according to the rules in *The Ladies' Library*, Vol. 1, p. 340 and seq.[6]

4. This, the first complete entry to be written in shorthand, might correspond in time to Edwards' writing of his "Spider" letter for Judge Paul Dudley. The letter is dated Oct. 31, 1723.

5. Nos. 7–14 appear to have been written in 1724, just before or during the early months of Edwards' Yale tutorship.

6. *The Ladies' Library: Written by a Lady* (2 vols., London, 1714) was published by Sir Richard

[13.] Let there always be laid down as many lemmata or preparatory propositions as are necessary to make the consequent propositions clear and perspicuous.

[14.] When the proposition allows it, let there be confirming corollaries, inferences for the confirmation of what had been before said and proved.

[15.][7] Oftentimes it suits the subject and reasoning best to explain by way of objection and answer, after the manner of dialogue, like the Earl of Shaftesbury.[8]

16. Always, when I have occasion to make use of mathematical proof, to acknowledge my ignorance in mathematics, *and only propose it to 'em that are skilled in that science whether or no that is not a mathematical proof.*

17. *Before I venture to publish in London, to make some experiment in my own country; to play at small games first, that I may gain some experience in writing. First to write letters to some in England, and to try my [hand at][9] lesser matters before I venture in great.*

18. If I publish these propositions *that are so metaphysical that 'tis probable will be very strange to many learned divines and philosophers, to propound 'em only by way of question, as modestly as possible, and the reasons for 'em; not as if I thought them anything well demonstrated, but only as worthy to bring the matter into consideration. Entirely submit 'em to the learned in nature and [. . .][1] and if it be possible, to conceal my determination.*

19. *Lest I may mention a great many things, and places of Scripture, that*

Steele. JE's reference is probably to the third edition of this work (1722). In the chapter "On Ignorance" (Vol. 1, pp. 323–25) Steele sets forth six rules for the conduct of inquiry and the governance of judgment. He goes on to counsel the reader to make the discovery and acceptance of truth the first objective in any controversy, rather than the conquest of an opponent. The proper end of rhetoric is "to remove those Prejudices that lie in the way of Truth, to reduce the Passions to the Government of Reason, to place our Subject in a right Light, and excite our Hearers to a due Consideration of it" (p. 336). The most suitable style for a writer is one which would have such an effect upon the writer himself: "To guess what Success we are like to have, we need only suppose ourselves in the Place of those we address to, and consider how such a Discourse would operate on us, if we had their Infirmities and Thoughts about us. In doing this, we shall find there is nothing more improper than Pride and Positiveness, nor anything more prevalent than an innocent Compliance with their Weakness: Such as pretends not to dictate to their Ignorance, but only to explain and illustrate what they did or might have known before, if they had consider'd it" (p. 340).

7. Nos. 17–21 appear to have been written in 1726, probably soon after the end of JE's Yale tutorship.

8. JE probably refers to Shaftesbury's *The Moralists, a Philosophical Rhapsody*, in *Characteristicks*, 2.

9. MS is torn. Upham: "hand in."

1. Two symbols in the MS, the first one cancelled, seem to be ill-formed.

the world will judge but frivolous reasons for the proof of what I drive at, not to mention such as I fear it of as what I depend on for proof, but to bring 'em in so that the force of the reasons will naturally and unavoidably be brought to the mind of the reader.

20. *To bring in those things that are very much out of the way of the world's thinking as little as possible in the beginning of a treatise. It won't do, for mayhap it will give an ill prejudice and tincture to the readers' mind in reading the treatise. Let them be given a good opinion of the others first, and then they will more easily receive strange things from me. If I tell it at first, it will look something like affectation of telling something strange to the world. They must be pleased with seeing what they believed before cleared up before they will bear to see their opinions contradicted. Let the way be so paved that they may be unavoidably confirmed* [. . .]² *a belief.*

[21.] Use as few terms of art as I can conveniently.

[The following two notes, which are also concerned with the preparation of a treatise, are found among the entries in the unnumbered series in "Natural Philosophy." Both are written in shorthand. The first appears at the end of the axioms in US No. 8 (p. 000 below), and the second immediately precedes US No. 12 (p. 000 below)]

[a.] *Preface: Here are some things in this philosophy that have been published to the world before, perhaps, and I did not leave out because they were* [*pertinent*]³ *to the orderly continuity of the treatise. If I come to 'em, I will not stand to quote. Others, they that are acquainted with the learned world, will be able to distinguish.*

[b.] *Order: Let there be axioms not only at the beginning of the treatise, but at the beginning of every part, to prepare the way for the easy reception of what follows. Let 'em be such as are very evident and plain, either in* [*themselves*],⁴ *or from what men proved before. Let there also be corollaries at the end of every part that will make way for what is otherwise.*

2. MS is torn, and one or two shorthand words are missing.
3. A conjectural reading. The shorthand symbol in the MS appears to be ill-formed.
4. A conjectural reading. The shorthand symbol appears to be ill-formed.

"OF THE PREJUDICES OF IMAGINATION"

Lemma to the Whole[1]

OF all prejudices, no one so fights with natural philosophy, and prevails more against it, than those of imagination. 'Tis that which makes the vulgar so roar out upon the mention of some very rational philosophical truths. And indeed, I have known of some very learned men, that have pretended to a more than ordinary freedom from such prejudices, so overcome by them that merely because of them they have believed things most absurd. And truly, I hardly know of any other prejudices that are more powerful against truth of any kind than this. And I believe it will not give the hand to any, in any case, except those arising from overruling self-interest, or the impetuosity of human passions. And there is very good reason for it: for opinions arising from imagination take us as soon as we are born, are beat into us by every act of sensation, and so grow up with us from our very births; and by that means grow into us so fast that it is almost impossible to root them out, being as it were so incorporated with our very minds that whatsoever is objected to them, contrary thereunto, is as if it were dissonant to the very constitution of them. Hence men come to make what they can actually perceive by their senses, or by immediate and outside reflection into their own souls, the standard of possibility and impossibility: so that there must be no body, forsooth, bigger than they can conceive of, or less than they can see with their eyes; nor motion either much swifter or slower than they can imagine. As for the greatness or

---

1. Though this essay stands at the front of the "Natural Philosophy" MS according to the pagination given it by a later editor (probably Dwight), JE probably did not begin "Prejudices" until after he had written "Of Atoms" and the first entries in the long numbered series of "Things to be Considered and Written fully about" (LS). The first portion, through the note following Prop. 2, was probably composed in late 1721 or early 1722 (see above, pp. 183–86). JE jotted the notation "Lemma to the whole" next to the title shortly after this part was written; the hand appears quite similar, and the ink, though different from the reddish brown of the essay, is very similar to the gray ink of LS Nos. 18 and 19.

distances[2] of bodies, the learned world have pretty well conquered their imagination with respect to that. Neither will anybody flatly deny that it is possible for bodies to be of any degree of bigness that can be mentioned. Yet imaginations of this kind among the learned themselves, even of this learned age, hath a very powerful secret influence, to cause them either to reject things really true as enormously false, or to embrace things that are truly so. Thus some men will yet say they cannot conceive how the fixed stars can be so distant as that the earth's annual revolution should cause no parallax among them, and so are almost ready to fall back into antiquated Ptolemy, his system, merely to ease their imagination.[3] Thus also, on the other hand, a very learned man and sagacious astronomer, upon consideration of the vast magnitude of the visible part of the world, has, in the ecstasy of his imagination, been hurried on to pronounce the world infinite; which I may say, out of veneration, was beneath such a man as he.[4] As if it were any more an argument, because what he could see of the universe were[5] so big as he was assured it was. And suppose he had discovered the visible world, so vast as it is, to be a globule of water to another—the case is the same, I say. As if it would have been any more of an argument that it was infinite, than if the visible part thereof were no bigger than a particle of the water of this: I think one is no nearer to infinite than the other. To remedy this prejudice, I will, as the best method I can think of, demonstrate two or three physical theorems which, I believe, if they

2. The words "or distances" are added above the line, but without a mark showing where they should be inserted in the original construction. Their position suggests the alternative reading, "the greatness of bodies or distances."

3. On the hypothesis of the earth's annual revolution, the absence of a discernible parallax of the fixed stars makes it necessary to suppose they are at such an immense distance from the earth that "the *magnus orbis* is as a point compared with it." As Gassendi points out (in *Institutio Astronomica, lib.* III, *cap.* 8), Aristotelian astronomers argued the supposed absurdity of this consequence against the Copernican theory. See Gassendi, *Opera Omnia* (6 vols., Lyons, 1658), *4*, p. 57. In the letter to his father dated July 21, 1719, JE asks for a copy of Gassendi's *Astronomy* as a book required for his senior year at Yale.

4. JE might be referring to William Derham, who writes, "But now after this account of this so prodigious space as that of our *Solar System* is, what is it to the nearly infinite *Expansum* occupied by the rest of the heavenly bodies!" *Astro-Theology,* Bk. I, ch. 3. Christian Huygens goes further, but in a less ecstatic frame of mind. Noting that Bruno's arguments to prove the number of the fixed stars is infinite are inconclusive, he adds, "Not that I think the contrary can ever be made out. Indeed it seems to me certain, that the Universe is infinitely extended; but what God has bin pleas'd to place beyond the Region of the Stars, is as much above our Knowledge, as it is our Habitation" (*The Celestial Worlds Discover'd* [London, 1698], p. 156). In "Of Light Rays" JE mentions Huygens, and uses his calculation of the distance of Sirius given in that book.

5. Possibly "wasn't," as in Townsend's reading.

are clearly understood, will put every man clean out of conceit with his imagination; in order whereunto, these two are prerequisite: as,

First, *Prop. 1*: There is no degree of swiftness of motion whatsoever but what is possible. That you may not doubt of this, suppose any long piece of matter to move round any point or center, to which one end shall be fixed, with any given degree of velocity. Now that part of this piece of matter that is farthest from the center to which one end is fixed must move swiftest. And then suppose this piece of matter to be lengthened out, and that part of it that moved swiftest before to move on still with the same degree of velocity. 'Tis evident that the farther end moves swifter than the farther end did before, by so much as the piece of matter is longer. And suppose it to be made longer still, the farther end moves still just by so much swifter. So that as the parcel of matter can be protracted to any degree of length whatsoever, so the farther end of it can be moved with any degree of swiftness whatsoever: so that there is no degree of swiftness whatsoever but what is possible.

Secondly, *Prop. 2*:[6] There may be bodies of any indefinite degree of smallness. Let two perfect spheres, *A* and *B*, touch each other in some point of their surfaces at *I* [Fig. 1]. 'Tis evident that there can be a globule of matter just so big as to reach from the surface of one sphere to the surface of the other sphere at any given distance from the point of contact *I*: suppose at *e*. Let the spheres be greater or smaller: since, therefore, that the distance *og* between the surface of one sphere and the surface of the other is

Fig. 1

less according as the spheres are greater, and since the touching spheres can be of any degree of magnitude, and since consequently the distance *og* can be of any degree of smallness, and since the body that fills up that distance is small accordingly, it follows that there can be a body of any degree of smallness.

N.B. This I take to be all that is meant by the divisibility of matter *in infinitum*.[7]

Prop. 3: That it is possible for a body as small as a ray of light to strike the surface of a body as big as the earth, or any indefinite magnitude,

6. This is JE's second version of *Prop. 2*. The first is written immediately above on the page; it is heavily revised and finally deleted with a large "X." The two versions are further separated by a line drawn across the page. They are substantially the same in content, except that no diagram is used in the deleted version.

7. This note concludes the earliest portion of the essay. *Prop. 3*, which is written immediately below it on the page, is in a hand and ink most similar to that of other MS writings of the summer or early autumn of 1723 (see above, p. 187).

supposing it be hard enough to hold the stroke, so as to impel it along with any indefinite degree of swiftness.

Let the laws of gravity and motion be mentioned, and let it be a postulatum inserted that these laws hold universally in all bodies great or small at how great distance soever and however disproportionate.

Postulatum 1.[8] In all bodies or parts of bodies, however small, there is a middle between the two extremes of that body or that part of a body.

Postulatum 2. That there may be bodies of any indefinite degree of smallness. That is, in any of those infinite divisions of matter, it is possible that matter or body may extend so far as the extremes of that part and no further, and then that part will be a distinct body. For instance: let the body *AB* [Fig. 2] be by you supposed to be as small as 'tis possible for a body to be. No doubt but there is a middle between the two extremes of that body, how small soever it is, at *C*. Now we mean that 'tis possible that matter may not extend any further than to the extremes of the half of that body, as far[9] only from *B* to *C*; so that 'tis possible there may be a body smaller than *AB*, however small that is.

Fig. 2

Postulatum 3. That there is no degree of swiftness of motion whatever but what is possible. For instance: suppose the body *AB* to be fixed at the point *B* [Fig. 3], and to move round the point *B* in an hour. If the body *AB* be made as long again, yet 'tis possible it may be moved round in an hour. So let it be made never so long; though it is manifest that the longer it is, the swifter doth the further extreme move.

Fig. 3

Postulatum 4. That the separating of bodies or the parts of bodies that touch each other, is always by divulsion or pulling asunder. That is, if, of the body *AD* [Fig. 4], the parts *AC* [and] *CD* [are separated] it must be by a force pulling one from another. It cannot be by protrusion, because nothing can be between them at that very place where they

8. JE deleted the first of his postulata, but copied out its main point again for the next. The deleted item reads: "*Postulatum.* That there may be an infinite division of body. I do not mean that the parts of body may be separated one from another *in infinitum*, but I mean that in all bodies however small there is a middle between the two extremes of that body." JE seems to have numbered the other postulata after the whole series was written. They all appear to have been written at the same time, probably in the early fall of 1723 (see above, p. 187).

9. Possibly "in fact," as in Townsend's reading.

touch before they are separated. Thus if we suppose them to be separated by the driving in a wedge at *C*, yet the parts must be separated before the wedge could get between them; not but that protrusion or impulsion in another place might cause divulsion in that. Or, if we suppose the parts of the body *D* to be broken thus: let the two ends, *A* and *D*, [be][1] laid upon two other

Fig. 4

bodies, *G* and *H*, and broken by the striking of the body *O* in the middle at *C* [Fig. 5]. Even then 'tis manifest that the parts *AC* and *CD* were pulled asunder. The extreme *e* of *AC* was pulled from the extreme *f* of *CD*. This is all I mean by divulsion.

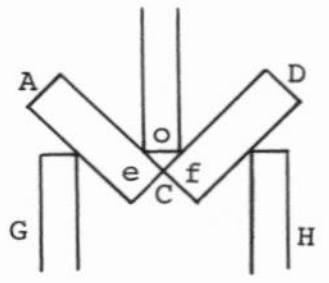

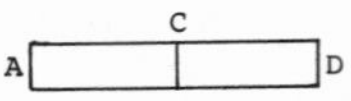

Fig. 5

Postulatum 5. A body, everywhere and in every respect equal, if there be a possibility of separating the parts, may be most easily separated where 'tis least. For instance, the body *IK* [Fig. 6] may be most easily pulled in two at *L* than at *M*. And it is least where 'tis most easily separated.

Postulatum 6. A body whose parts may be separated by such a degree of force, that same body, still retaining the same degree of inseparableness, or another body with an equal degree of inseparableness, will evermore be separated when that degree of force is applied.

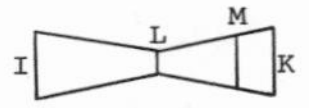

Fig. 6

Postulatum 7. Every body, and every part of body, has length and breadth and thickness.[2]

Suppose the body *AB* to be an absolute plenum, and the parts *AC* and *CB* to be frustrums of a cone [Fig. 7]. I say, the parts of the body could never be separated; to prove which, let us suppose it separable. Let us suppose it fixed at *B*, and every part pulled with equal force towards *A*. 'Tis manifest, by the fifth postulate, that it will break first at *C*. Let there be another absolute plenum, *DB*, being a cone equal that of which *CB* was the frustrum [Fig. 8]. Let it be fixed at *B*, and every part of it be pulled with equal force towards *D*, and with a force equal to that which broke the

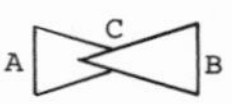

Fig. 7

---

1. JE's word is problematic; Townsend: "baited."

2. The essay to this point is written on the recto page of a single folio leaf. The verso of this leaf is blank; the final two paragraphs are found on the verso of a second single leaf, sewn to the first, and containing the essay "Of Being."

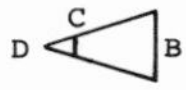

body *AB* at *C*. 'Tis manifest, by the sixth postulate, that the body *DB* would be broken at *C*, where 'tis equal to *C* of the body *AB*. But if so, it would also be broken by the same force in every point betwixt *D*[3] and *C*, by the fifth postulate; because in every point it is less than at *C*. But this is impossible, for it if breaks at every point, the broken parts have no length, breadth and thickness, contrary to the seventh postulate. Such breaking would be annihilation. All these are certain consequences from the supposition that the parts *AC* and *CB* of the body *AB* can be pulled asunder. But we see that these are impossible; therefore that[4]

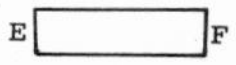

Fig. 8

Again, let the cylinder *EF* [Fig. 9] be an absolute plenum and fixed at *F*, and let all the parts be pulled towards *E* with equal force. I say, that with how great force soever it is pulled, it will nowhere break. If it break, it will break either in some parts only, or in every point; not in some parts only and not in others, for if so it will be because some parts were more easily broken than others (for it is supposed that the force is equal everywhere). But some parts would not be more easily broken than others, by the fifth postulate; not in every point, for then 'tis manifest the broken parts would be without length, breadth and thickness.

Fig. 9

3. JE wrote "B," but the argument clearly requires reference to the point *D* in the diagram.
4. JE left the sentence unfinished.

"OF BEING"

THAT there should absolutely be nothing at all is utterly impossible. The mind can never, let it stretch its conceptions ever so much, bring itself to conceive of a state of perfect nothing. It puts the mind into mere convulsion and confusion to endeavor to think of such a state, and it contradicts the very nature of the soul to think that it should be; and it is the greatest contradiction, and the aggregate of all contradictions, to say that there should not be. 'Tis true we can't so distinctly shew the contradiction by words, because we cannot talk about it without speaking horrid nonsense and contradicting ourselves at every word, and because "nothing" is that whereby we distinctly shew other particular contradictions. But here we are run up to our first principle, and have no other to explain the nothingness or not being of nothing by. Indeed, we can mean nothing else by "nothing" but a state of absolute contradiction. And if any man thinks that he can think well enough how there should be nothing, I'll engage that what he means by "nothing" is as much something as anything that ever [he][1] thought of in his life; and I believe that if he knew what nothing was it would be intuitively evident to him that it could not be. So that we see it is necessary some being should eternally be. And 'tis a more palpable contradiction still to say that there must be being somewhere, and not otherwhere; for the words "absolute nothing" and "where" contradict each other. And besides, it gives as great a shock to the mind to think of pure nothing in any one place, as it does to think of it in all; and it is self-evident that there can be nothing in one place as well as in another, and so if there can be in one, there can be in all. So that we see this necessary, eternal being must be infinite and omnipresent.

(Place this as a lemma where it suits best, and let it be more fully demonstr[ated]:)[2] This infinite and omnipresent being cannot be solid. Let us see how contradictory it is to say that an infinite being is solid; for solidity surely is nothing but resistance to other solidities.

1. MS: "the."
2. JE's note is written above the paragraph. Another, which he wrote in the margin beside the paragraph, reads, "Place this somewhere else."

Space is this necessary, eternal, infinite and omnipresent being. We find that we can with ease conceive how all other beings should not be. We can remove them out of our minds, and place some other in the room of them; but space is the very thing that we can never remove and conceive of its not being. If a man would imagine space anywhere to be divided, so as there should be nothing between the divided parts, there remains space between notwithstanding, and so the man contradicts himself. And it is self-evident, I believe, to every man, that space is necessary, eternal, infinite and omnipresent. But I had as good speak plain: I have already said as much as that space is God.[3] And it is indeed clear to me, that all the space there is not proper to body, all the space there is without the bounds of the creation, all the space there was before the creation, is God himself. And nobody would in the least stick at it, if it were not because of the gross conceptions that we have of space.[4]

And[5] how doth it grate upon the mind, to think that something should be from all eternity, and nothing all the while be conscious of it. Let us suppose, to illustrate it, that the world had a being from all eternity, and had many great changes and wonderful revolutions, and all the while nothing knew; there was no knowledge in the universe of

3. JE was undoubtedly influenced by Henry More's discussion of space. In his *Appendix to the Antidote against Atheism*, More writes: "If after the removal of corporeal Matter out of the World, there will still be Space and Distance in which this very Matter, while it was there, was also conceived to lye, and this distant Space cannot but be Something, and yet not corporeal, because neither impenetrable nor tangible; it must of necessity be a Substance Incorporeal, necessarily and eternally existent of itself: which the clearer Idea of a Being absolutely perfect will more fully and punctually inform us to be the Self-subsisting God." (*Collection*, p. 165)

4. At this point JE put a small cross-mark or dagger like a key mark, suggesting that a passage written elsewhere should be inserted in the essay at this point. No other passage in "Natural Philosophy" has a corresponding mark, however. Townsend took the mark as indicating that "Of the Prejudices of Imagination" should be inserted here (see his edition, p. 2. n. 4). It is more likely that JE intended to indicate that the passages concerning the necessity of being which he added on the verso page of the same leaf should be read as a continuation of the essay at this point (although these passages also lack the characteristic corresponding mark).

5. This and the following paragraphs through *Corollary 1* were added in the summer of 1723. JE left a blank space between the addition and the earlier part of the essay, as though reserving it for further discussion of his opening themes. He began the addition with the following statement, which he then deleted before continuing: "Neither can be any such thing without consciousness. How is it possible there should something be from all eternity and there be no consciousness of it? It will appear very plain to everyone that intensely considers of it, that consciousness and being are the same thing exactly." For JE's earlier statement of this principle, see Miscell. no. pp, quoted above, p. 75.

any such thing. How is it possible to bring the mind to imagine? Yea, it is really impossible it should be, that anything should be, and nothing know it. Then you'll say, if it be so, it is because nothing has any existence anywhere else but in consciousness. No, certainly nowhere else, but either in created or uncreated consciousness.

Supposing there were another universe only of bodies, created at a great distance from this, created in excellent order and harmonious motions, and a beautiful variety; and there was no created intelligence in it, nothing but senseless bodies. Nothing but God knew anything of it. I demand in what respect this world has a being, but only in the divine consciousness. Certainly in no respect. There would be figures and magnitudes, and motions and proportions—but where? Where else, but in the Almighty's knowledge. How is it possible there should? Then you'll say: For the same reason, in a room close shut up, that nobody sees nor hears[6] nothing in it, there is nothing any other way than in Go'ds knowledge. I answer: Created beings are conscious of the effects of what is in the room; for perhaps there is not one leaf of a tree, nor spire of grass, but what has effects all over the universe, and will have to the end of eternity. But any otherwise, there is nothing in a room shut up, but only in God's consciousness. How can anything be there any other way? This will appear to be truly so to anyone that thinks of it with the whole united strength of his mind. Let us suppose for illustration this impossibility, that all the spirits in the universe to be for a time deprived of their consciousness, and God's consciousness at the same time to be intermitted. I say, the universe for that time would cease to be, of itself; and not only, as we speak, because the Almighty could not attend to uphold the world, but because God knew nothing of it. 'Tis our foolish imagination that will not suffer us to see. We fancy there may be figures and magnitudes, relations and properties, without anyone's knowing of it. But it is our imagination hurts us. We don't know what figures and properties are.[7]

Our imagination makes us fancy we see shapes and colors and magnitudes though nobody is there to behold it. But to help our imagination let us thus state the case: Let us suppose the world deprived of every ray of light, so that there should not be the least glimmering of light in the universe. Now all will own that in such a case, the universe would be immediately really deprived of all its colors. One part of the universe is no more red, or blue, or green, or yellow, or black, or white, or light,

---

6. Townsend: "sees can have."
7. JE drew a line across the entire page between this and the following paragraphs.

or dark, or transparent or opaque than another. There would be no visible distinction between the world and the rest of the incomprehensible void—yea, there would be no difference in these respects between the world and the infinite void. That is, any part of that void would really be as light and as dark, as white and as black, as red and green, as blue and as brown, as transparent and as opaque as any part of the universe. Or, as there would be in such case no difference between the world and nothing in these respects, so there would be no difference between one part of the world and another. All, in these respects, is alike confounded with and indistinguishable from infinite emptiness.

At the same time, also let us suppose the universe to be altogether deprived of motion, and all parts of it to be at perfect rest (the former supposition is indeed included in this, but we distinguish them for better clearness). Then the universe would not differ from the void in this respect; there will be no more motion in one than the other. Then also solidity would cease. All that we mean or can be meant by solidity is resistance—resistance to touch, the resistance of some parts of space. This is all the knowledge we get of solidity by our senses, and, I am sure, all that we can get any other way. But solidity shall be shewn to be nothing else more fully hereafter.[8] But there can be no resistance if there is no motion. One body cannot resist another when there is perfect rest amongst them. But you'll say, though there is not actually resistance, yet there is potential existence,[9] that is such and such parts of space would resist upon occasion. But this is all I would have: that there is no solidity now; not but that God would cause there to be on occasion. And if there is no solidity, there is no extension, for extension is the extendedness of the solidity. Then all figure and magnitude and proportion immediately ceases.

Put both these suppositions together, that is, deprive the world of light and motion, and the case would stand thus with the world: There would be neither white nor black, neither blue nor brown, bright nor shaded, pellucid nor opaque; no noise or sound, neither heat nor cold, neither fluid nor wet nor dry, hard nor soft, nor solidity, nor extension, nor figure, nor magnitude, nor proportion; nor body, nor

8. JE's account of solidity in "Of Atoms" preceded this discussion by one or two years. In this remark he probably expresses his intention to give another account of that property which would more fully support his argument. Such an account was given later in "The Mind," No. 27.

9. JE might have intended to write "resistance."

spirit. What then is[1] become of the universe? Certainly, it exists nowhere but in the divine mind. This will be abundantly clearer to one after having read what I have further to say of solidity, etc. So that we see that a world without motion can exist nowhere else but in the mind, either infinite or finite.

Corollary 1. It follows from hence, that those beings which have knowledge and consciousness are the only proper and real and substantial beings, inasmuch as the being of other things is only by these. From hence we may see the gross mistake of those who think material things the most substantial beings, and spirits more like a shadow; whereas spirits only are properly substance.

A[2] state of absolute nothing is a state of absolute contradiction. Absolute nothing is the aggregate of all the absurd contradictions in the world, a state wherein there is neither body, nor spirit, nor space: neither empty space nor full space, neither little nor great, narrow nor broad, neither infinitely great space nor finite space, nor a mathematical point; neither up nor down, neither north nor south (I don't mean as it is with respect to the body of the earth or some other great body, but no contrary points nor positions nor directions); no such thing as either here or there, this way and that way, or only one way. When we go about to form an idea of perfect nothing we must shut out all these things. We must shut out of our minds both space that has something in it, and space that has nothing in it. We must not allow ourselves to think of the least part of space, never so small, nor must we suffer our thoughts to take sanctuary in a mathematical point. When we go to expel body out of our thoughts, we must be sure[3] not to leave empty space in the room of it; and when we go to expel emptiness from our thoughts we must not think to squeeze it out by anything close, hard and solid, but we must think of the same that the sleeping rocks dream of; and not till then shall we get a complete idea of nothing.

A state of nothing is a state wherein every proposition in Euclid is not true, nor any of those self-evident maxims by which they are demonstrated; and all other eternal truths are neither true nor false.[4]

---

1. Smyth: "to." JE might have intended to write "is to become."
2. JE added the following two paragraphs on the verso side of the leaf containing the essay in the summer of 1723.
3. Dwight: "must be careful." Smyth and Howard: "must cease."
4. Dwight omitted this paragraph from his edition of the essay.

When[5] we go to inquire whether or no there can be absolutely nothing we speak nonsense. In inquiring, the stating of the question is nonsense, because we make a disjunction where there is none. "Either being or absolute nothing" is no disjunction, no more than whether a triangle is a triangle or not a triangle. There is no other way, but only for there to be existence; there is no such thing as absolute nothing. There is such a thing as nothing with respect to this ink and paper. There is such a thing as nothing with respect to you and me. There is such a thing as nothing with respect to this globe of earth, and with respect to this created universe. There is another way besides these things having existence. But there is no such thing as nothing with respect to entity or being, absolutely considered. And we don't know what we say, if we say we think it possible in itself that there should not be entity.

5. This final paragraph, probably written in 1732, is the latest of JE's additions to "Natural Philosophy." A parallel discussion occurs in Miscell. no. 587 (see in Townsend, pp. 81–82).

["OF ATOMS"][1]

Prop. 1. All bodies whatsoever, except atoms themselves, must of absolute necessity be composed of atoms, or of bodies that are indiscerpible,[2] that cannot be made less, or whose parts cannot by any finite power whatsoever, be separated one from another. And this will be fully seen as soon as it is seen what bodies those are that are indiscerpible, or what is requisite in a body in order to cause it to be so. And here we shall lay down this proposition: that that body that is absolutely plenum, or that has every part of space included within its surface impenetrable, is indivisible; and that the parts thereof can by no means [be] separated from each other, by any force how great soever. As for instance, suppose the body *B* [Fig. 1] to be what we call an absolute plenum, and suppose the two bodies *A* and *C* to come as impetuously and with as great force as you please, and strike on each side of the body *B*: I say the two bodies *A* and *C* could cause no fraction[3] in the body *B*.

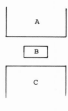

Fig. 1

For if the two bodies *A* and *C* should cause any fractions in the body *B*, those fractions must be in some certain places or parts of the body, and not in others; for there cannot be fractions in every part. For I suppose everybody will own, that after the body is supposed to be broken, that there remain parts of the broken body which are unbroken. And so it will be—let the body be broken into as fine parts as you please, those fine parts are still unbroken. The fraction is not through the midst of those parts, as it is between them. So the fraction must be, if at all, in some places and not in others; and indeed, breaking of a body all over, or in

---

1. Sereno Dwight titled this series "Of Atoms and of Perfectly Solid Bodies." See Dwight, *1*, pp. 708–15.

2. In the MS Edwards spells "indisserpible." Henry More uses the term in *Immortality of the Soul* to signify the indivisibility of spirits, and of the least real parts of bodies. More's influence is apparent in the argument JE develops here (see Introduction, above, pp. 63–64).

3. Dwight reads "fracture" both here and in several other occurrences of the word below.

every part, is the same as to annihilate it. We say, then, that the body B cannot be broken in some parts and not in others by the bodies A and C. For if it is broken in this part and not in that, it must be because it is easier broken in this than in that. But in a body perfectly solid and that is absolutely full, it is everywhere equally full, equally solid, and equally strong, and indeed everywhere absolutely alike, so that there is nothing that should cause a fraction in one place sooner than in another.

And again,[4] suppose the body D [Fig. 2] to be a perfectly solid body, and to be as pressingly jammed up as you please between the two bodies E and F, which are supposed not in the least to give way to the body D; and the surfaces of them which touch the body D are supposed everywhere per- fectly even and plain, and to continue parallel to each other, and to be every way infinitely

Fig. 2

extended. I say the body D could not be broken by the pressure of the bodies E and F. For suppose the body D to begin to be broken and crumbled into parts by the pressure of the bodies E and F. If the whole body D can be broken by that pressure, then the parts of the body D can still be broken again by the pressure of the same bodies with equal reason (supposing the bodies still to continue pressing towards each other). And then, too, their parts can still be broken into other parts, and so on, and that as fast as the motion of the bodies E and F towards each other shall require. And truly, I think if it be so that the parts can be broken still finer and finer, they can be broken so fast as not to retard the motion of the bodies E and F at all; and if so, surely the bodies E and F will presently meet so as to touch intimately everywhere, inasmuch as it was said the surfaces of the bodies were perfectly even and continued parallel. And then I ask what is become of the body D? I think there can be no other answer but that it is annihilated, since it was said the two bodies were infinitely extended. So that we see, if the body D can be broken by the bodies

4. This paragraph was written somewhat later, and on the following (verso) page of the MS. According to JE's key marks, he intended it to be inserted at the end of the first para- graph above. The introduction of it at that point, however, would destroy the continuity of the discussion. Hence it is inserted here, as in Dwight's version. It should be noted, how- ever, that the objection which is introduced in the paragraph below was intended to refer to the point just made, that "there is nothing that should cause a fraction in one place sooner than another."

E and *F*, then it can be annihilated by them—which I believe nobody will own. And the case is all one, let the body *D* be of whatsoever figure. Q.E.D.

But here I foresee that it will be immediately objected, to render what has been said invalid, "But what if the body *B* [Fig. 1] should begin first to be broken off at the corners, where pieces would be more easily cracked off than in other places? And what if it were less in some places than others, or what if the bodies *A* and *C* were applied with much greater force in some places than others?" These objections seem at first quite to render all good for nothing. But I must say that, notwithstanding these objections, what has been said does prove that, suppose the perfectly solid body were everywhere equally bulky, and the bodies *A* and *C* were all along applied with equal force, the perfectly solid body could never be broken. And to them that say it would first break at the corners, I ask how near the corner the first fraction would be. If they tell me, So near, I ask, Why was it not nearer still, since that the nearer the corner, the easier and sooner broken? If after that the place for the first fraction be assigned nearer yet, I ask still, Why not nearer still? So that at last they must be forced to say that the first fraction would be infinitely near the corner, or that the first piece that would be broken off would be infinitely little. And they had as good say that none at all would be broken off first; for as I take it, an actually infinitely little body and no body at all are the same thing—or rather, the same nothing.

And as to the other two parts of the objection, it is enough for them if we can discover it to be the nature of perfectly solid bodies not to be broken, or to resist any however great force; as it will appear rather more plain by another instance, as: Suppose the body *e* [Fig. 3] to be a perfect solid in that shape (wider at the upper, and by degrees to come quite to a point at the lower), and to be thrust with indefinitely great force towards the corner *g* against the sides *fg* and *gh*, which are supposed not at all to give way. It has been proved already that, if it would break anywhere, it would be at the lower point first; and what we have said concerning the corners of the body *B* [in Fig. 1] proves that it would [not] break there. Now since that nothing but the perfect solidity can hinder the body *e* from breaking, we have certainly found

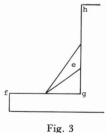

Fig. 3

out that a perfectly solid body cannot be broken. For the body *e* may be as great or as small, as long and as slender as you please; the case is the same. And let the force that *e* is to withstand be as great as you please—if the weight of the universe falling against it from never so great a distance, and as much more as you please—we can prove, and what is said above does prove, that it would neither bend nor break, but stiffly bear the shock of it all.

Corol. 1. From what was said concerning the first and second figures, it plainly appears that breaking of a perfectly solid body and the annihilation of it are the same thing, so far that the breaking of it would be the annihilating of it.

Corol. 2. Hence [it] appears that solidity and impenetrability and indivisibility are the same thing, if run up to their first principles. For, as in the first figure, the solidity of the body *B* is that whereby it so far resists the bodies *A* and *C* that they shall not be able, till the body *B* is out of the way, closely everywhere to touch each other. That is to say, the force of the two (*A* and *C*) endeavoring to meet could not be the annihilating of the body *B*, for the meeting of them would be the annihilating of it. By the second case also. The indivisibility of the body *B* in the first figure, and the body *D* in the second figure, has been proved to be that also whereby the bodies *B* and *D* resist that the bodies pressing upon them should touch each other; inasmuch as the breaking of them would certainly admit of it, and would be their annihilation.

Corol. 3. It appears from the two demonstrations and the two first corollaries that solidity, indivisibility and resisting to be annihilated are the same thing, and that bodies resist division and penetration only as they obstinately persevere to be.

Corol. 4.[5] Since that, by the preceding corollary, solidity is the resisting to be annihilated, or the persevering to be of a body, or, to speak plain, the being of it—for being and persevering to be are the same thing, looked upon two a little different ways—it follows that the very essence and being of bodies is solidity; or rather, that body and solidity are the same. If here it shall be said, by way of objection, that body has other qualities besides solidity, I believe it will appear to a nice eye that it hath no more real ones. What do you say, say they, to extension,

5. This corollary was written somewhat later (but before *Prop. 2, Corol. 9*, where JE refers to it), on the preceding page, i.e., the facing verso, and keyed for insertion here. The last sentence, which is added in the smaller and later hand of *Prop. 2, Corol. 17*, was begun as *Corol. 6* (of *Prop. 1*). By later deleting this designation, JE joined the sentence to *Corol. 4*.

figure and mobility? As to extension, I say, I am satisfied it has none more than space without body, except what results from solidity. As for figure, it is nothing but a modification of solidity, or of the extension of solidity; and as to mobility, it is but the communicability of this solidity from one part of space to another.

Or thus: Since that (by Corol. 1) annihilation and breaking are the same, their contraries, being and indivisibility, must also be the same; and since (by Corol. 2) indivisibility and solidity are the same, it follows that the solidity of bodies and the being of bodies is the same, or that body and solidity are the same.

Corol. 5. From what has been said, it appears that the nature of an atom, or a *minimum physicum* (that is, if we mean by those terms a body that can't be made less—which is the only sensible meaning of the words) does not at all consist in littleness, as generally used to be thought. For by our philosophy, an atom may be as big as the universe; because any body, of whatsoever bigness, were an atom if it were a perfect solid.

N.B. It will be needful here a little to explain what it is that we mean by "perfectly solid," "absolute plenum," etc., for that we have laid down—that that is an absolutely full, a solid body, that has every part of space included within its surface solid or impenetrable. Our meaning is very liable to be mistaken, unless a little explained. We intend not but that a perfect solid may be very full of pores, though perhaps improperly so called, interspersed up and down in it, as in the perfect solid *L* [Fig. 4]. It is only requisite that every part of the body *L* should be intimately conjoined with some other parts of it, so as not only barely to touch in some points or lines thereof (I mean mathematical points or lines), as two perfect globes do, or as a cylinder, when it lies on one side, does a plane, and as all atoms do each other except the surfaces where they happen to be infinitely exactly fitted to join each other. So that the body *L*, although it may have some little holes in it, yet it

Fig. 4

has an absolute plenum continued all along between these holes, so that it is as impregnable as a body that has no holes at all; and this will be understood more fully after we have proved that two atoms touching each other by surfaces can never be separated.

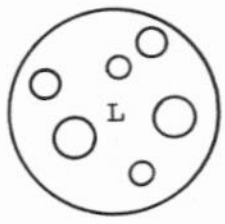

Now 'tis time to apply what we have said concerning atoms, to prove that all bodies are compounded of such. For if we suppose that all those bodies which are any way familiar to our senses yet have interstices so interspersed throughout the whole body that some parts of [it] do only touch others, and are not conjoined with them, by which they are rendered imperfectly solid, yet we must allow that those parcels of matter that are between the pores (that is, betwixt this and the next adjacent pore) have no pores at all in them, and consequently are plenums or absolute solids, or atoms; and surely all bodies that have pores are made up of parcels of matter which are between the pores—which we have proved to be atoms.

Prop. 2. Two or more atoms or perfect solids touching each other by surfaces—I mean so that every point in any surface of the one shall touch every point in some surface of the other, that is, not only barely in some particular parts[6] or lines of their surfaces, how many soever (for whatsoever does touch in more than points or lines toucheth in every point of some surface)—by that become one and the same atom or perfect solid; which will be abundantly clear by the figure: As, suppose the perfect solid *AB* and the perfect solid *CD* [Fig. 5] to be precisely like to the halves of the perfect solid *AD*, to wit, *Af* and *eD*; and then suppose the atom *AB* to move up to the body *CD*, so that the surface *gB* shall touch in every point of the surface *Ch*. Now since that these two bodies, when separate, were precisely every way like the two halves of the body *AD*, it follows that after they are joined together after the same manner as the two halves of the body *AD* are, they must make up a body every way precisely like the body *AD*, as if it were the same; and consequently must be a perfect solid as the body *AD* is.

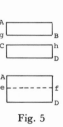

Fig. 5

But perhaps, it will be answered, the halves of the body *AD* are joined and continued, but the two bodies *AB* and *CD* only touch each other. But I affirm that the latter are as much joined and continued as the former; for all the way as the former are joined and continued is only as solidity is all along continued from one to t'other without the least intermission, so as there is not the least vacuity betwixt them. Just so also it is in the latter after they touch; for they are supposed to touch in every point of their surfaces, and then, I am sure, solidity is continued from one to the other without intermission or vacuity. Neither does the [bodies] *AB* and *CD* being once separate make any alteration.

Corol. 1. Hence it follows that all atoms that ever happen to touch

6. Townsend: "points."

each other in any surfaces, or more than barely in some certain points or lines (millions of millions of which don't make so much as the least surface), can never again be separated by any finite power; since it has been proved that the parts of atoms cannot be torn asunder, and since it has been proved that atoms so touching become the same atom.

Corol. 2. From Prop. 1 and the preceding corollary we learn that it must needs be an infinite power that keeps the parts of atoms together, or, which with us is the same, that keeps two bodies touching by surfaces in being. For it must be infinite power, or bigger than any finite, that resists all finite, how big soever; as we have proved these bodies to do.

Corol. 3. We have already as much as [proved][7] that it is God himself, or the immediate exercise of his power, that keeps the parts of atoms or two bodies touching, as aforesaid,[8] together. For it is self-evident that barely two atoms being together, and that alone, is no power at all, much less an infinite power. And if any say the nature of atoms is an infinite power, [they] say the same that I do; for all the nature of them that is not absolutely themselves must be God exerting his power upon them.

Corol. 4. Since, by the foregoing corollary, the exercising of the infinite power of God is necessary to keep the parts of atoms together, and since, by the first corollary of [Prop. 1], the dissolution of them would be annihilation, it follows that the constant exercise of the infinite power of God is necessary to preserve bodies in being.

Corol. 5. Hence, an incontestable argument for the being of God.

Corol. 6. Since, by Corol. 4 foregoing, there is need of the exercise of infinite power in order to keep bodies in being, it clearly follows that there was need of an infinite power to bring them into being; so that it was a divine, and no created being that created and preserves the world.

Corol. 7. Hence, also an incontestable argument for the being, infinite power, and omnipresence of God: of the two latter, inasmuch as we see that the infinite power [is] actually exerted in an infinite number of places at once, even in every part of every atom of the universe. And since that where his power is exercised, there his essence must be, his essence can be by nothing excluded.

Corol. 8. Since, by Corol. 3 of the first proposition, solidity [and] indivisibility are the same, and since, by Corol. 3 foregoing, indivisi-

7. Townsend interpolates "said."
8. Dwight: "tending by surfaces."

bility is from the immediate exercise of God's power, it follows that solidity results from the immediate exercise of God's power, causing there to be indefinite resistance in that place where it is.[9]

Corol. 9. Since, by the fourth corollary of the first proposition, body and solidity are the same, and, by the preceding corollary, solidity is from the immediate exercise of divine power, it follows that all body is nothing but what immediately results from[1] the exercise of divine power in such a particular manner.

Corol. 10.[2] It follows, by the same corollaries, that creation is the first exercise of that power in that manner (vid. No. 47).[3]

Corol. 11. Since, by Corol. 4 of the first proposition, body and solidity are the same, and by the eighth foregoing, resistance or solidity are by the immediate exercise of divine power, it follows that the certain unknown substance, which philosophers used to think subsisted by itself, and stood underneath and kept up solidity and all other properties,[4] which they used to say it was impossible for a man to have an idea of, is nothing at all distinct from solidity itself; or, if they must needs apply that word to something else that does really and properly subsist by itself and support all properties, they must apply it to the divine Being or power itself. And here I believe all those philosophers would apply it, if they knew what they meant themselves. So that the substance of bodies at last becomes either nothing, or nothing but the Deity acting in that particular manner in those parts of space where he thinks fit. So that, speaking most strictly, there is no proper substance but God himself (we speak at present with respect to bodies only). How truly, then, is he said to be *ens entium.*

Corol. 12. Since, by the eighth and ninth foregoing, solidity or body is immediately from the exercise of divine power, causing there to be resistance in such a part of space, it follows that motion also, which is the communication of body, solidity, or this resistance, from one part of space to another successively (that is, from one part of space to the next

9. JE originally wrote *Corol. 8* as follows: "Since, by Corol. 3 of the first proposition, solidity, indivisibility and persevering to be are the same, and since by Corol. 3 foregoing indivisibility is the immediate exercise of God's power, it follows that solidity is the immediate exercise of God's power causing there to be indefinite resistance in that place where it is."

1. The words "what immediately results from" are added above the line.

2. JE crossed out "*Corol. 10*," perhaps intending to join the text to *Corol. 9* preceding.

3. "Things to be Considered and Written fully about," LS No. 47. JE added this reference at the time that he wrote LS No. 47.

4. JE originally wrote "it follows that the opinion that philosophers used to have concerning a certain unknown substance."

immediately adjacent, and so on to the next, etc.) is from the immediate exercise of divine power so communicating that resistance, according to certain conditions which we call the laws of motion. How truly then is it in him that we live, move and have our being.

Corol. 13. From all which, we find that what divines used to say concerning divine concourse had a great deal of truth lay at the bottom of it.

Corol. 14. We by this also clearly see that creation of the corporeal universe is nothing but the first causing resistance in such parts of space as God thought fit, with a power of being communicated successively from one part of space to another, according to such stated conditions as his infinite wisdom directed; and then the first beginning of this communication, so that ever after it might be continued without deviating from those stated conditions.

Corol. 15. Hence we see what's that we call the laws of nature in bodies, to wit: the stated methods of God's acting with respect to bodies, and the stated conditions of the alteration of the manner of his acting.

Corol. 16. Hence we learn that there is no such thing as mechanism, if that word is taken to be that whereby bodies act each upon other, purely and properly by themselves.

Corol. 17.[5] Since, by Corol. 1, atoms that happen to touch each other in surfaces, or more than barely in points and lines, can never by finite force be separated, it follows that all those compound bodies in the universe which can be divided and broken have their parts only touching each other in some points or, at most, lines. Not but that those points and lines in which they touch may be of any number whatsoever; as many (if you please) as a man can note down with his pen in his lifetime. Yet these points and lines fall infinitely short of the least surface, and two bodies touching each other in all those points don't touch each other so much, by an infinite deal, as two bodies touching in the least surface; and although perhaps, *ceteris paribus*, the more points bodies touch each other in, the more difficultly separated, yet it must be allowed that those that touch in most points can be separated infinitely easier than bodies touching in surfaces.

Obj. But, you will say, if so we should surely experience something of

5. At first JE followed *Corol. 16* with *"Prop. 3rd."* Sometime later he deleted this heading and went on to write *Corol. 17*. This corollary was in turn deleted before JE went on to consider the objection which follows. Despite the deletion (a single cross mark over the text) the corollary is presented here as an integral part of the argument.

JE's deletion covers not only *Corol. 17*, but his first partial statement of the objection following: "Strange (you will say) that if two atoms touching each other in more than points or lines can never be separated, that we never find any bodies."

it. A thousand to one but that some of the atoms of those compound bodies with which we converse, in all their infinite jumbles and different colligations and collisions, would happen to touch each other by their surfaces so as not, by any finite force, to be separated. Why then do we never find any bodies but what we can divide and divide again as often as we please? Why do the surfaces of two bodies never happen to touch each other so as never to be hauled asunder again? For who can imagine but that some atom in the surface of one body in so many innumerable applications should happen to touch some atom in the surface of another body by surfaces.

I answer: 1. I do not think it to be at all rash or absurd to suppose that the Almighty might take care, in the first creation, sufficient to prevent any such fatal or inconvenient consequences, by creating of the atoms of which the universe was to be composed, of such figures as that no surface of any one should be so suited to the surface of any other as to be able to touch it by surfaces, which would prevent all that is objected.

2. If we suppose that the Almighty took no care at all of that matter, yet it is a thousand to one, if, of all the atoms in the universe, there happened to be ever a two whose surfaces were so exactly and nicely suited and adapted to each other as that they should precisely coalesce. For is it not infinity to one that one surface should be so as to be precisely fitted to another surface, when there are infinite other different ways that it could have been as well? And it is all one, let the surfaces be greater or less; and the odds is the same betwixt infinity and one atom, and infinity and all the atoms in the universe.

3. Suppose there should be some atoms in the universe which had their surfaces exactly adapted; it is a thousand to one if ever they come together or, if they did, that they should touch on that side where were the correspondent surfaces.

4. If those that had surfaces exactly adapted to each other should come together, a thousand to one if there are not some prominences or some such things that shall hinder their being exactly applied.

5. If there should happen to get together some of those atoms—yea, many millions of them—in a heap so as never again to be got asunder, and if such heaps should be frequent, it need not hinder but that bodies may be divided more than ever we yet experienced, and into finer parts than we can perceive with our senses, either naked or assisted by the best instruments; for what hinders but that a compages of millions of millions of atoms should be so little as to be out of the reach of the microscope?

6. Neither would there be any such fatal adhesion if one atom in the surface of one body should happen to touch an atom in the surface of another in this manner, for 'tis but the taking of an atom from the surface of one of those bodies and the separation is made. And I conceive, if it were three or four millions of atoms, it could be done with infinite ease.

"THINGS TO BE CONSIDERED AN[D] WRITTEN FULLY ABOUT"

[Short Series][1]

1.[2] To observe that incurvation,[3] refraction, and reflections from concave surfaces of drops of water, etc. is from gravity.[4]

2. To observe that 'tis like that the attraction of particles of heat[5] contributes as much towards the burning of bodies as the impulse.

3. To observe how water may quench fire by insinuating into the pores and hindering the free play of the particles, and, by reason of that softness and pliableness, deadening that motion like throwing a stone upon a featherbed.

1. Dwight labeled this the "first series," although JE began it after he had written at least the first nineteen entries of the other, the long numbered series of "Things to be Considered," on the preceding page. The short series is begun on MS p. 12, and continued on p. 15. Parallels in hand and ink show that JE wrote the entries concurrently with those in the long series on MS pp. 11, 13, 14, and 16.

2. Nos. 1–6 were originally written in a very faint gray ink, the same as that of LS Nos. 20–26 on the preceding page of the MS. JE later touched up these six entries in the ink of Nos. 17–23 below.

3. I.e., the diffraction of light. Newton discussed the phenomena of diffraction in *Optics*, Bk. III, where the word "inflection" is used. JE could have received the word "incurvation" either from the Latin of Newton's *Principia*, Bk. I, prop. XCVI, Scholium, or, as is more probable, from Whiston's *Newton's Mathematick Philosophy*, p. 266. He also uses the word in "Of Insects," which was probably written at a somewhat earlier date.

4. In the Queries at the end of *Optics* Newton argues that, in the phenomena of reflection, refraction, and inflection, rays of light and pellucid bodies act upon each other at a distance, and that this action "very much resembles an attractive Force between Bodies" (Bk. III, Q. 29; see also Q. 1, 4). But he never supposes this force to be gravity, and in fact urges that as gravity, magnetism, and electricity are several kinds of attraction which act among bodies at readily observable distances, there may be other sorts which are manifested only at very small distances: "For we must learn from the Phenomena of Nature what Bodies attract one another, and what are the Laws and Properties of the Attraction, before we enquire the Cause by which the Attraction is perform'd" (Bk. III, Q. 31).

5. See SS No. 27 (below, p. 228). Pierre Gassendi argued that heat and cold are produced by frigorific and caloric particles (in *Physica*, Sectio I, Lib. 4, Cap. 6; in *Opera Omnia*, I, pp. 394–401). The more widely accepted account of "corpuscularean" physicists, e.g., Newton and Boyle, was that heat is rapid motion of the constituent particles of the hot object.

4. To observe that if we do suppose an infinite number of surfaces in the universe,[6] yet, according to the number of them, so must the smallness of them be.

5. To observe that the cause that an object appears not double, being seen with two eyes, [is that] all the parts upon the retina that exactly correspond end upon the same spot of the surface in the brain which receives the images.[7]

6. To observe that one end of respiration is that the motion in [the] ribs may be communicated to the parts of the body.[8]

7.[9] To consider whether one use of air in preserving fire be not that the particles of it may be to counteract the fiery particles of the burning body; and whether that be not the reason that nothing shines, rotten wood, glowworms, nor coals, in the exhausted receiver;[1] and that may be one use of air in respiration among the rest.[2]

8. To shew that the probable reason why the light of *ignis fatuus,*

6. See "Of Atoms," Objection and answers, above, pp. 216–18.

7. This is probably JE's synopsis of Newton's account, viz., that the fibers of the optic nerves from corresponding sides of the two retinas meet before they enter the brain (*Optics,* Bk. III, Q. 15). Derham quotes Newton in *Physico-theology,* Bk. IV, ch. 2, n. 15. See also SS Nos. 16, 21b below.

8. Seventeenth-century physiologists of a generally Cartesian persuasion understood respiration as a purely mechanical process, and attempted to explain its role accordingly in the functioning of the body machine. Among more widely accepted views were that respiration cools the blood, or helps circulate the blood. The discussion in Derham's *Physico-theology,* might have been the basis for JE's comment. Derham reports fourteen other "uses" of respiration reckoned by one Malachai Thurston, including speaking, singing, crying, coughing, sneezing, yawning, hawking and spitting, propelling the feces, expelling the embryo, promoting the motion of the contents of the stomach and intestines, and passing the blood through the lungs (Bk. IV, ch. 7, no. 1, pp. 146–49).

9. SS Nos. 7–13 are written in a denser gray ink, the same as in LS Nos. 37 and 38, and in the fragment "Of Light Rays."

1. Robert Boyle reported that when such luminous materials as rotten wood, putrefying meat and fish, and the tails of glowworms were put into a vacuum in the "exhausted receiver," their light was sensibly diminished or ceased altogether ("New Experiments concerning the relation between Light and Air," *Philosophical Transactions,* 2 [1667–68], pp. 581–600). On the other hand, JE either had not read or had failed to take note of cases showing the contrary effect; e.g., Newton, in *Optics,* Q. 30 (1706 ed.: Q. 22), points out that mercury, when agitated in a vacuum, shines like a fire.

2. Before Lavoisier's discoveries, the explanation for the necessity of air for combustion and respiration was largely conjectural. Newton, e.g., writes, "The air abounds with acid vapors fit to promote fermentations, as appears in the rusting of iron and copper in it, the kindling of fire by blowing, and the beating of the heart by means of respiration." *Optics,* Bk. III, Q. 31 (1706 ed.: Q. 23, p. 326).

rotten wood, glowworms, etc., are not accompanied with heat[3] is because of the exquisite smallness of the rays; and to shew that if that were the reason the rays need not be the thousandth part so small as that of the sun.

9. To shew that the different refrangibility of rays must of necessity be either their different velocity or different magnitudes; because there can be no other reason of their different attractability, which indeed is refrangibility.

10. To shew the parvity of the rays of light, the elasticity of air, how wisely the eye is contrived so a man may see[4] things colored.

11. To shew, from Isaac Newton's principles of light and colors, why the sky is blue; the sun not perfectly white, as it would be if there were no atmosphere, but something inclining to a yellow even at noonday; why the sun is yellow rising and setting, and sometimes, in smoky weather, of a blood red; why the clouds and the atmosphere that is near the horizon appear red and yellow before sun rising and after setting; why mountains at a distance are blue, etc.

12. Belonging to clouds, and rain, dew, etc.:[5] to shew how, when the rarified air contained within the bubble begins to cool and condense and be contracted into a narrower compass, the water of the skin, being too much for it, necessarily will begin to gather at the bottom, as in [Fig. 1]; and how by that means the destruction of the cloud and production of rain is brought to pass.

Fig. 1

13. To observe that, all the rays of one sort being obstructed by any medium and others still proceeding, as by the air in smoky weather, etc.—to inquire how it can be; and to

---

3. Newton discusses at length the relation of light and heat, in ibid., Q. 8–11. He suggests that *ignis fatuus* is a vapor that shines without heat, and stands to flame as shining rotten wood stands to burning coals. (1706 ed.: Q. 10, pp. 294–95).

4. MS: "a man may see" is the most plausible reading. JE's words are crowded and carelessly written at the end of the line, and the ink has faded. Dwight omits the entire clause.

5. If JE had written anything earlier on the subject of clouds and vapors, it is no longer extant. Morton's *Compendium Physicae* has a chapter on the "watery meteors," in which he sets forth the commonly accepted explanation that clouds are formed of hollow bubbles of water (in JE's copy, "A System of Physicks extracted from Mr. Morton, his Body of Physicks," Chap. 15, MS Partridge, pp. 210–11). In this entry JE seems to be elaborating upon the explanation of precipitation given by Derham in *Physico-theology*, Bk. I, ch. III, note. See also LS Nos. 56 and 57, below, pp. 248–56.

observe that its so doing makes it probable that there are some other properties in light and mediums yet wholly unknown; and to observe that the unaccountable phenomena of reflections[6] prove the same: and to inquire what it is. And also to seek out other strange phenomena, and compare them all together and see what qualities can be made out of 'em; and if we can discover them, it's probable we may be let into a new world of philosophy.

14.[7] Relating to the foregoing: to observe that if there be no new qualities in the medium nor rays, that it must arise from an infinitely fine and artful contrivance in these bodies.

15. Relating to the rainbow: to instance in many that will not reflect light perceptibly except it be obliquely.[8]

16. Relating to No.13: Why also are not rays reflected at any imaginary surface of water as well as at the true one?[9]

17.[1] To observe that the cause why thunder that is a great way off will sound very grum, which near is very sharp, and other noises (instances of which are to be given), is because the further waves go, the wider they grow and further asunder, as it is in water. Several of the little undulations, by traveling near together, incorporate into one great one.

18. To give the reason why the lightning, which is all at once, has a noise of long continuance, to wit: that although the lightning be all at once, yet some parts of it are much further than others, and the noise caused by that which is furthest off is a much longer time in coming; and we hear the noise successively, from that end which is nearest to us to that which is furthest off. So that it may often happen that we hear that which is really the beginning of a clap, a long time

---

6. See SS Nos. 16, 21b below. JE probably refers to phenomena reported and discussed by Newton in *Optics*, Bk. II, especially those mentioned in pt. 3, prop. 8, etc.

7. SS. Nos. 14–16 are written in a very faint version of the gray ink of Nos. 7–13. The same ink is found in LS Nos. 39–41 on the facing page of the MS.

8. JE probably intended this for "Of the Rainbow," which was written at about the time of this entry (see below, pp. 298–301).

9. Newton raises this question, and gives an answer, in *Optics*, Bk. II, pt. 3, prop. 1.

1. SS Nos. 17–21 are written in a deep brown ink with dense black solids. The hand of Nos. 17 and 18 remains relatively small, but thereafter becomes increasingly larger and more sprawling. LS Nos. 42–44 are in the same ink, and show a similar development of the hand. The entries were probably the last JE wrote before beginning his New York pastorate in August 1722. Nos. 22ff were evidently not written until his return to Windsor in May 1723. See discussion above, pp. 186–87.

after that which is really the end: Which is the reason that in claps which are very near us, the first of it seems to be down amongst us, and the last a rumbling in the heavens above us; when in reality that rumbling among the clouds which we hear afterwards is only the beginning of the clap there, and that severe noise close by us, the end of it. And the reason of this is because the lightning is incredibly swifter than the sound. These things are so far certain and demonstrable that it is impossible that it should happen otherwise.

19. To observe that the weight of the descending blood in the veins completely answers to the weight of the ascending blood in the arteries, in parts above the heart, so that the weight of one exactly balances the weight of another; and the descending blood in the veins pulls up the blood in the arteries, and the weight of the blood in the arteries restrains the impetuosity of the descending blood in the veins, so that the blood in both, ascending and descending, runs as easily and uniformly as if it ran all the while parallel to the horizon. So in the parts below the heart, where the arterial blood descends and the venal ascends, barely the weight of the blood in the arteries is sufficient to raise the blood in the veins even with it, as high as the beginning of the arteries, according to the laws of hydrostatics; and the weight of the blood in the veins restrains the motion of that which descends in the arteries, so that the blood in these also moves just as if it moved on a plane, neither up nor down. And the heart has no more labor to impel the blood up the ascending trunk of the aorta, nor ease in impelling of it down the descending trunk, than if it ran in a trunk parallel to the horizon. Neither doth the blood ascend with more difficulty than it descends, but with equal facility, both in arteries and veins, above and below the heart: and to shew the philosophy of this.[2]

20. To shew the grand use of respiration; and to shew how it keeps nature in a circulation and the blood in motion, and why the course of nature so immediately ceases on the ceasing of respiration.

21[a].[3] To shew that the reason why the fixed stars twinkle, and not the planets, is because the stream of rays by which we see the fixed stars is infinitely less than that by which we see the planets (however,

2. The application of the mechanical principles of hydrostatics to explain the circulation of blood was first made by Galileo's pupil, Giovanni Borelli, in *De Motu Animalium* (Rome, 1680–81). There is no evidence of this work at Yale as late as 1742. In fact, it is uncertain from what source JE acquired his basic knowledge either of physiology or of hydrostatics.

3. MS: JE numbered both this and the following item "21."

some of the fixed stars appear much bigger than some of the planets), and therefore much more liable to be obstructed, and the continuity of it to be broken by anything in the atmosphere.

21[b]. Relating to the thirteenth: to observe that it is certain that the stopping of one sort of rays, and the proceeding of others, is not because that sort of rays alone are stopped by striking against the particles of the medium, from this experiment, viz.: as I was under the trees I observed that the light of the sun upon the leaves of the book I was reading in, which crept through the crevices of the leaves of the tree, to be of a reddish-purplish color; which I supposed to be because many of the green rays were taken up by the leaves of the tree and left all the rest tainted with the most opposite color; which could be no otherwise than by the stopping those green rays which passed near to the edges of the leaves.

N.B. That this light of the sun would not appear colored except the crevices through which the rays came was very small.

Corol. 1. Hence it is certain that bodies do attract the same sort of rays most strongly that they reflect most strongly.

Corol. 2. Hence bodies do attract one sort of rays more than another.

Corol. 3. Hence it is probable that bodies do reflect and attract by the same force, because that they both attract and reflect the same sort of rays.

22.[4] To observe that the motion of no animals is by any power they have of impelling their bodies forwards, but only by the mere sending forth of animal spirits and filling the muscles and thereby shortening of them (*A*, the figure for man's motion. *B*, the motion of serpents and fishes [see Fig. 2]). Also to give the reason of the motion of hawks, etc., without any visible motion of their wings.

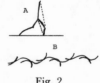

Fig. 2

23. In the plain flat rocks that rivers run over there are commonly holes, sometimes for a considerable depth into the rock, smooth on the sides, having a stone at the bottom something less than the diameter of the hole. That stone doubtless is the cause of the hole, but the diffi-

---

4. SS Nos. 22 and 23 are written in the small angular hand and the brown ink of Miscell. nos. 41–44. JE probably wrote these articles in midsummer 1723, just after he returned to Connecticut from his New York pastorate. Parallel entries are LS Nos. 45 and 46.

culty is to know how the stone should sink down so far into the firm rock. It must be thus: the stone lying on the surface of the rock, and being a little moved by the water, gently rubs the rock it lies on and doubtless rubs off some particles of the rock, and continuing so to rub for a long time, perhaps hundreds of years, it wears down to such a depth into the rock.

24.[5] It need not make us think that our soul is in our fingers, and so all over the body, because our feeling seems to be in them; for if we hold a staff in our hand we seem to feel in the staff, but only we learn better by experience.[6]

25. The cause of that vast disparity of heat in summer and winter cannot be because that the perpendicular ray is at all more rapid in its motion than the oblique, for there is no reason why that ray which comes sideways should not fly as swiftly as that which comes right down. The one and the other are sent forth from the sun with an equal degree of velocity; and because one happens to meet a surface sideways, doth it move the slower for it, nor the other obtain a new velocity because it is like to strike the earth perpendicularly? Indeed, the perpendicular ray makes a stronger impression on the surface of the earth, because it stands fairer for the stroke. But how should this make any difference in the air that is near? But the reason why the perpendicular ray causes the greatest heat is because the reflex ray is more opposite to the direct, and thereby raises a much hotter war, and more vehement agitation of the particles of the air; for while some rays fly one way, others fly directly contrary. For the agitation must needs be much greater than where the direct ray and reflex partly coincide in the same course. Indeed, the surface of the earth, with respect to its minute parts which reflect the sunbeams, is so infinitely un-

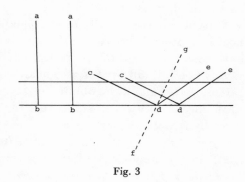

Fig. 3

---

5. SS Nos. 24–28 are written on MS p. 15, separated from the earlier entries of the series by two pages of articles in the long series. SS Nos. 24–25 are parallel in hand and ink with LS Nos. 46–48.

6. Cf. "The Mind," No. 2 (below, pp. 238–39).

even that the reflex ray has equally all directions. That is, the ray *cd* [Fig. 3] is not only reflected towards *ed*, as it would be if the surface of the earth were as a looking glass, but is also reflected back again towards *c*, and every way else indifferently, so that there is a direct opposition in the oblique ray as well as perpendicular. But yet there is not so much opposition, for all the reflections of the perpendicular ray *ab* are in some measure opposite to the direct. They are all reflected by less than a right angle, whereas all the reflections of the oblique ray that are on the other side of the line *fg*, perpendicular to *cd*, are by an angle greater than a right.

Another reason why winter is so much colder than summer is because the rays of the sun when near the horizon travel longer in the atmosphere than when the sun is more over our heads. Thus the ray *be* [Fig. 4] travels much longer in the atmosphere from *f* to *e* before it comes to *e*, the eye, than the ray *ae*. Therefore the light and heat of the sun will be much less. Another reason is because the sun in winter is so much less time above the horizon than in summer. The cold that prevailed in the night is not chased away by the short sunshine of the next day. The next

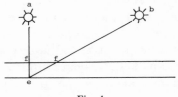

Fig. 4

night there is a new addition of the cold of another night, and every night there is a new increase, and the sun stays too little a time to give a check to this progress.

But another reason why the perpendicularity of the rays adds to the heat is because the rays that fall upon the earth obliquely fall not near so thick as those that fall perpendicularly; as it is very manifest that the rays *ef* [Fig. 5] fall thicker and nearer together perpendicularly on the surface *LM* than on the oblique surface *AB*. This makes a difference as to the heat two ways: first, because the reflection of rays from the surface *AB* is not near so thick as from the surface *LM* because there are not so many rays that fall on *AB* to be reflected. I acknowledge that, notwithstanding their falling thinner, yet the reflection would be as thick if the surface were a speculum, and the angle of reflection were the same as that of incidence, for it is manifest the rays *ef* are at no greater distance from each other after they are reflected towards *n* than they were when they struck the surface *LM*. But seeing by reason of the unevenness of the surface they are reflected every

way indifferently, the spissitude of this reflection must be in exact proportion to the spissitude of this
incidence. For it is manifest that
if the rays *ef* had been reflected towards *o*, they would have been
reflected much thinner than if
they were reflected by the same angle from the surface *LM* [towards
d], in proportion as they fall
nearer together on the surface *LM*

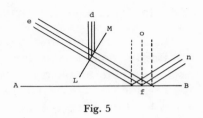

Fig. 5

than on the surface *AB*. 'Tis also manifest that if they are reflected
from the surface *LM* towards *d* in the same angle as they are reflected
from the surface *AB* towards *n*, the reflection is then also thicker in
the same proportion.

And secondly, rays falling thicker when they fall perpendicularly
makes it hotter because the thick rays (it is plain) heat the ground more.
The ground don't cause heat in the incumbent air only by reflection
of the rays of the sun, but as a stone or bar of iron, when it is hot, heats
the air round about it; for the ground that is heated by the summer
sunbeams will continue to cast a heat though the rays of the sun are
for a short time interrupted.[7]

26.[8] It appears that those visible particles of a morning fog are not
single bubbles of water. I have seen a frozen fog, a fog of which those
particles were all frozen as they floated in the air, which were all little
stars of six points as the particles of snow, only very small, and were
not joined together, many of them into one flake, as in snow, but floated
single; at a little distance looked very white like other fog, only not so
thick as another fog often is, not so thick as to hinder the sun from shining bright. T'was evident it was not a fine snow, for t'was otherwise a
a very clear morning and there was not a cloud anywhere to be seen

7. JE might have written this after reading Derham's account in *Astro-theology*, Bk, IV, ch.
4, note, pp. 87–89. Derham gives two causes of the disparity of heat in summer and winter;
first, the different lengths of the day, and second, the oblique direction of the sun's rays in
the winter, because these are "weaker" and strike with less force than the perpendicular rays
of summer. See also JE's later discussion in LS No. 58 below, p. 256.

8. Preceding this entry JE wrote another, numbered 49, which he intended for the long
series. He corrected the mistake by copying the entry in its proper place as LS No. 49 (see
below, p. 246), and then deleted the item from the short series. SS No. 26 is in the same
ink as LS No. 49. Because these two entries agree in hand and ink with that in Miscell. no.
78, they were probably written at about the same time. Miscell. no. 78 also marks the beginning of "The Mind" (see below, p. 326).

above the horizon. 'Tis therefore evident that before they were frozen they were not single bubbles, inasmuch as a single bubble will not make one of those stars; no, not less than seven.

27.[9] The reason why there are so many more frigorific particles[1] towards the poles and in the winter and where the sun is absent, than near the equinoctial and in summer and in the presence of the sun, is not because that the heat of the sun drives the frigorific away towards the poles; for all that the rays can do is to disturb—they have not sense to drive them one way more than another. Neither do they shun them because of an antipathy. But when the sun has great influence, they are disturbed and loose, kept from settling; but at the poles they are fixed. Only this is sufficient to solve their flying from under the sun and gathering at the poles, for seeing all or the most that come to the poles, there they settle and fix, the rays of the sun not disturbing of them. But if all that come there fix there, there will necessarily most of them be gathered there in time. And seeing those that are under the sun are unfixed, and all that got by any means from under do fix, it necessarily follows that all in time will get from under him: because they continually accidentally are getting from under him, and those that get from under fix and return not again.

This, therefore, is undoubtedly a reason why the sun, when returning from the south tropic, does no sooner get the victory of the cold: because those frigorific particles that were brought down in winter return back into their own country again no otherwise than as they happen to be driven by winds.

28. It ought not to be judged that all the blood in the body goes through the heart in the same time that as much blood as [is] in the body goes through. The blood in the smallest branches of the veins and arteries cannot move near so fast as in the greater, for the same force will not make it move near so swiftly. The blood had need to be impelled with a much greater force to move it through a small vein as swift as through a great one; yea, though the blood be in proportion to the smallness of the passage. For 'tis the blood's bearing against the sides

---

9. Preceding this entry JE began another, numbered 26, with the words "the fog that appears." He deleted this beginning before continuing with No. 27. SS Nos. 27 and 28 are parallel in hand and ink with LS No. 50. JE probably wrote them after the end of October 1723.

1. JE accepted Gassendi's theory that cold consists in frigorific particles. For a full discussion of freezing, see US No. 12, below, pp. 270–77; also, SS No. 2, above, p. 219.

of the vein that stops the blood. But a small vein has much more of sides in proportion to the quantity of blood it contains than a greater; and then the blood is something of a thick substance which will move but slowly in a narrow passage. 'Tis by these small veins and arteries the body receives nourishment, but the blood would have no time orderly and regularly to communicate proper nourishment to each part which requires different aliment; as, nothing to the brain but what is suitable to that for animal spirits and other uses, one kind to the various membranes, kinds of flesh, marrow, humors, and the like. If the blood moved so very swiftly in these pipes as in greater, when one part of the body is diseased it would forthwith be communicated to all others. We find that when a person is bit by a serpent, if it be in a great vein, it is immediately communicated to all parts; but if not, perhaps the quantity of all the blood in the body may go through the heart many times before the body in general feels much of the effect of the poison. If the stream of blood was so swift in every small vein, the coldness of our extreme parts, before it would come to such a degree, would kill the man, the shifting of the cold blood would be so quick. Physicians are wont to chafe the limbs before they let[2] blood, to fill the veins, thereby causing the blood in the little veins to move swifter in the [place] wherein the orifice is made.

[*Long Series*][1]

1.[2] To prove the world one vast spheroid.

2. To demonstrate that all the matter that is without the spheroid is so disposed as that there should be an equal attraction on all sides, and so probably an equal quantity of matter.[3]

3. To prove that this world cannot be a small body, for instance, a

2. The word is obscured in the manuscript. Dwight: "before they let blood" (p. 721).

1. Sereno Dwight called this the "second series," although JE began it before the short series. It is written on pp. 11, 13–14, and 16–20 of the "Natural Philosophy" MS.

2. Nos. 1–26, on MS p. 11, are written in a thin gray ink. Changes of shade and density of the ink show that JE wrote several entries during each sitting. Nos. 1–8 are in a large sprawling hand like that in "Of Atoms." These might be the earliest writing in the "Natural Philosophy" MS. Nos. 9–14 and 15–19 were added in at least two further sittings; and Nos. 20–26 are in the same ink as the first entries in the short series on MS p. 12.

The cosmological ideas expressed in the first few entries of this series probably arose from JE's study of Gassendi's *Institutio Astronomica* during his senior collegiate year, and probably also from studying Whiston's *Astronomical Lectures*. The series might have been started near the end of his senior year or during his first year of graduate study at Yale.

3. This entry is referred to in LS No. 25 below.

particle of water of some greater; because if it were so, the greater attraction on one side more than another would immediately put all the bodies contained in it out of order. And so also to prove that there cannot be another world in a particle of our water.

4. To know the shape of the spheroid of the world by observation of the Milky Way, and to know whereabout our system is in it: first, with respect to the plane of the greatest circle, from observations of the ratio of the brightness of the opposite sides, compounded with several other ratios; second, with respect to the latitude or the axis of this spheroid, by observing how much the Milky Way differs from a great circle.

5. To shew that the starry world cannot be infinite because it is a spheroid.

6. To write concerning the lens about the sun.

7. To write concerning the distance of the sun, by observation of the enlightened part of the moon when exactly in the quadrature.[4]

8. To write concerning the use of comets to repair the wastes of heavenly bodies.[5]

9. To shew how infinite wisdom must be exercised in order that gravity and motion be perfectly harmonious;[6] and that, although the jumble of the Epicureans be allowed—although that be impossible.

10. To find out a thousand things by nice observation of the spheroid of the world.

4. The method of determining the distance of the sun by observation of the *luna dichotoma* is explained by Whiston (*Astronomical Lectures,* Lect. VI, pp. 64ff).

5. The idea originated with Newton: "For the conservation of the seas, and fluids of the planets, comets seem to be required, that, from their exhalations and vapors condensed, the wastes of the planetary fluids spent upon vegetation and putrefaction, and converted into dry earth, may be continually supplied and made up. . . . I suspect, moreover, that it is chiefly from the comets that spirit comes, which is indeed the smallest but the most subtle and useful part of our air, and so much required to sustain the life of all things with us. . . . So Fixed stars, that have been gradually wasted by the light and vapors emitted from them for a long time, may be recruited by comets that fall upon them; and from this fresh supply of new fuel those old stars, acquiring new splendor, may pass for new stars." *Principia,* Bk. III, prop. 41, prob. 21 (1713 ed., pp. 473, 480).

6. In Newton's system, the laws of motion are distinct from and independent of the principle of universal gravitational attraction. By the harmony of motion and gravity JE might mean either that all these laws are logically consistent, or, what is more likely, that the world which fulfills these laws is also well ordered to realize God's purposes. See No. 14 below.

11. To shew that however thin we suppose the enclosure of the spheroid of the world or of the whole universe to be (if there be one), if it be perfectly solid, the most violent shocks of the greatest bodies in the world would not be able to break it, or in the least to stir it.

12. To consider whether or no some of the telescopical stars be not the reflection of real stars from such an enclosure, that is, from the common enclosure of the starry world.

13. To consider thoroughly the objections that may be made from more little stars appearing in the Milky Way than elsewhere.

14. To shew how the motion, rest and direction of the least atom has an influence on the motion, rest and direction of every body in the universe. And to shew how, by that means, everything that happens with respect to motes or straw, and such little things, may be for some great uses in the whole course of things throughout eternity. And to shew how the least wrong step in a mote may, in eternity, subvert the order of the universe. And to take notice of the great wisdom that is necessary in order thus to dispose every atom at first, as that they should go for the best throughout all eternity; and in the adjusting by an exact computation, and a nice allowance to be made for the miracles which should be needful. And then to shew how God, who does this, must necessarily be omniscient and know every least thing that must happen throughout eternity. Vid. No. 49. Vid. "The Mind," p. 12, 13, 14.[7]

15. To shew how it must, not only for the present, have such an influence, but forever after.

16. To shew how all nature consists in things being precisely according to strict rules of justice and harmony.

17. To shew how the least wrong step in the least atom, happening never so seldom, if it returns at a certain period, would most certainly, throughout eternity so returning, totally subvert the order of the universe; or if it be supposed, taking one time with another, to be equally frequent (as without doubt it will be, if there is any): and thence to

7. JE added his reference to No. 49 at the time that entry was written in late 1723 or early 1724. His reference to "The Mind" was added much later, in a gray ink of a shade and composition most like the ink of LS Nos. 63 and 64, and Miscell. nos. 200–06. "The Mind," pp. 12, 13, and 14, probably included the entry No. 40 (see below, p. 332).

shew that there is very good philosophical reason to think the hairs of our head are all numbered. Vid. No. 52.

18. To endeavor to shew how two particles [or] atoms whose surfaces are nearly adjusted to each other may, only by the force of gravity, meet each other with incredible celerity. And to shew how by that means an heat may be begotten without any external enkindling, and also rays of light emitted. And to consider what may arise from the different shapes of the particles, with respect to colors or otherwise.[8]

19. To shew that if a congeries of particles of matter were cast together which had their surfaces thus fitted, they would meet each other with such a great celerity, and would of themselves bound back to the same place with an equal degree of celerity, and so would, of themselves, continue to do forever; but that celerity being increased by their mutual impulses and repulses and continual repercussions, till at length they had brought it to an immense degree, sufficient to send them to the end of the world with an almost infinite velocity. And this velocity will receive increase a thousand ways, as by bounding upon their flat surfaces, and striking another in their rebound by round surfaces, etc.

To solve by this method the light and heat of the sun and stars; solving the grand question of kindling fires; firing of powder, etc.; enkindling of mixed liquors, etc. To show also how that it must necessarily and unavoidably be so as [stated in] this paragraph, in a congeries of particles, if the particles are suitable and are so disposed that they can have fair play without hindrance.[9]

20.[1] To absolutely demonstrate that two atoms touching by surfaces tend with infinite force of gravity to adhere together, on this wise: viz., let the atoms *ab* and *cd* [Fig. 1] touch each other by surfaces at *cb*. Now I say the atoms *ab* and *cd* tend to adhere together by an infinite gravity. Let the atom *ab* be supposed to be divided in the middle,

8. This entry is referred to in LS No. 39 below.

9. JE was apparently pondering suggestions of Newton in *Optics*, Bk. III, in Q. 31 (1706 ed.: Q. 23, pp. 323–27), that various phenomena of fermentation and combustion are caused by the powers or forces by which the small particles of bodies act upon each other at a distance. No. 19 is referred to in LS Nos. 24, 33, and 35 below.

1. Nos. 20–26 are written in gray ink, probably the same as that in the preceding entries and in SS Nos. 1–6, but it has become so thin and faint that JE himself later touched up some of the writing in the dark ink of Nos. 42–44 below. Also, almost all the letters referring to the diagram in No. 20 are rewritten in the dense black ink and neat hand of Sereno Dwight.

JE probably composed the first portions of "Of Being" and "Of the Prejudices of Imagination" at about the time that he wrote these entries.

between the two extremities of [it] at *fe*; in like manner let the atom *cd* be divided at *ut*. And then let the innermost half of the atom *ab* be divided again in the middle at *hg*, and the half of that at *ki*, and the half of that at *ml*, and again the half of that and so on *in infinitum*. In like manner let the atom *cd* be divided. It is evident that I may so go on *in infinitum*, because if I go but halfway at a time, I shall never come to the end. It is also evident that the parts of the atom *ab* tend to the corresponding parts of the atom *cd*, according to the squares of the distance, and the quantity of matter in the parts attracting and attracted. And it is again evident, that the part *fg* has half the quantity of matter of the part *ae*, because it is half of a part (*fb*) that is equal to *ae*; and so also, the part *st* has but half the matter that *ud* hath. And it is likewise evident, that the part *fg* is just as near again to the part *st*, as the part *ae* is to *ud*. That is, all the corresponding parts of the parts *fg* and *st* (viz. the extremities and the corresponding extremities, the middle and the middle) are just as near again to each other as the corresponding parts of the parts *ae* and *ud*, as any body may easily see. It must needs be so, that [it] may be said in the general, that the one of the two parts are as near again to each other as the other two parts; yea that *fg* is as near again to *st*, as *ae* is to *ud*. And consequently, because attraction is as the square of the distance, the attraction [of *fg* to *st*] would be four times as strong [as that of *ae* to *ud*] if the quantity of matter [of *fg*] were equal [to *ae*]. But because the quantity of matter of *fg* (which we at present call the body attracted) is but half so much, therefore if the quantity of matter of the attracting part *st* were equal [to *ae* or *ud*], still the gravity of the part *fg* would be but twice as much. But seeing the quantity of matter of *st*, the attracting body, is also but half so much, therefore the gravity is but just equal. So we have proved that the gravity of *fg* and *st* towards each other is just equal to the gravity of *ae* to *ud*. And after [the same] manner, it is proved of the remaining parts: that the gravity of *hi* and *qr* is just equal to the gravity of *fg* and *st*, and consequently to *ae* and *ud*; and that the gravity of *kl* is equal to that; of *mb* to that; and consequently, the gravity of all of them equal [to] the gravity of the first; and so of all the rest of the infinite divisions that might be made. Whence it follows, that the gravity of the first part, *ae* to *ud*, is an infinite number of times in the atom *ab*,

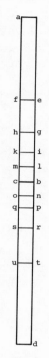

Fig. 1

and so in the atom *cd*; and consequently, that the gravity of the whole put together is actually infinite. For certainly, any small quantity of attraction, let [it] be never so small—if it be a millionth or a million millionth—an infinite number of times repeated, will amount to an infinite gravity. Wherefore, the atoms *ab* and *cd* tend to each other with an infinite force of gravity.

N.B. From this again to prove our whole scheme.

21. The adhesion of bodies arising from gravity proved from the adhesion of two polished marbles in the exhausted receiver.[2]

22. Solidity is gravity; so that, in some sense, the essence of bodies is gravity: and to shew how the very bare being of body, without supposing harmonious being, necessarily infers gravity. And to observe that folly of seeking for a mechanical cause of gravity;[3] but to observe that this has as much a mechanical cause as anything in the world, and is as philosophically to be solved, and ought no more to be attributed to the immediate operation of God than everything else, which indeed arises from it; and that gravity is no way diverse from a principle by which matter acts on matter.

23[a].[4] Because it is universally allowed that gravity depends immediately on the divine influence;[5] and because it may be proved that

2. The adhesion of two polished marbles that have been laid together in the open air was a well-known illustration of the force of atmospheric pressure. Robert Boyle reported experiments in which polished marbles adhered even in a vacuum. JE probably learned of the phenomenon from Newton's *Optics*, Bk. III, Q. 31 (1706 ed.: Q. 23, p. 336).

3. Newton's view of the status of the force of gravity, as expressed in the second edition of the *Principia*, is that gravity, unlike inertia, is not essential to bodies, and is not an immutable property of them (Bk. III, "Rules of Reasoning in Philosophy," Rule III, 1713 ed., pp. 357–58). He declines to give a cause for gravity, but points out that "it must proceed from a cause that penetrates to the very centres of the sun and planets, without suffering the least diminution of its force; that operates not according to the quantity of the surfaces of the particles upon which it acts (as mechanical causes used to do), but according to the quantity of the solid matter which they contain, and propagates its virtue on all sides to immense distances, decreasing always as the inverse square of the distance" (Bk. III, General Scholium, 1713 ed., p. 484).

4. JE numbered both this and the next entry 23.

5. A view made popular by Richard Bentley, who argued that, because gravity is not innate and essential to bodies, "it is consequently most manifest (seeing it doth not depend upon Motion or Rest or Figure or Position of Parts, which are all the ways that Matter can diversify itself) that it could never supervene to it, unless impress'd and infused into it by an immaterial and divine Power." *The Folly and Unreasonableness of Atheism* (London, 1693), Lect. VII, p. 29. See also William Whiston, *Astronomical Principles of Religion, Natural and Revealed* (London, 1717), pp. 45–46.

solidity and gravity are in a good sense the same, and resolvable into each other; and because solidity has been proved to be the very being of a body:[6] therefore we may infallibly conclude that the very being, and the manner of being, and the whole of bodies depends immediately on the divine power.

23[b]. To shew how, that if gravity should be withdrawn, the whole universe would in a moment vanish into nothing; so that not only the well-being of the world depends, but the very being.

24. Relating to No. 19: To shew how a congeries of secondary particles, if rightly compounded, may do likewise, though not so well.

25. Relating to No. 2: Except we suppose a revolution. And to shew that, being of such a figure, it cannot be without causing great confusions; and to shew that, let the figure be what it will, there will be great alterations among the stars, the same as the tides.

26. To bring in an observation somewhere in a proper place, that instead of Hobbes' notion that God is matter and that all substance is matter; that nothing that is matter can possibly be God, and that no matter is, in the most proper sense, matter (relating to the eleventh corollary of Prop. 2).[7]

27.[8] To observe, in a proper place, that since creation is the first causing such resistance, and upholding the causing successively, therefore the same person who created upholds and governs. Whence we may learn who it is that continually governs this noble fabric of glorious bodies: and to expatiate much upon it.

28. To demonstrate that everything does, or at least may, depend upon an infinite number of causes concurring, or the alterations of them, upon an indefinitely little alteration or turn, especially in men's minds. And thence, in a proper place, to shew that no finite spirit can predict such things.

29. In definition of an atom: Such a body whose parts are no ways

6. See "Of Atoms," *Prop. 1, Corol. 4* (above, pp. 211–12).

7. In "Of Atoms," above, p. 215.

8. LS Nos. 27–47 are found on MS p. 13. Nos. 27–41 are written in a gray ink, apparently a denser and darker version of that just preceding. Some brown tones appear in LS Nos. 37–38, so that the color in these entries is the same as that in the fragment "Of Light Rays." LS Nos. 37–38 correspond in ink to SS Nos. 7–13, on the facing verso page 12; and LS Nos. 39–41 agree with SS Nos. 14–16.

separated by pores, but has all its parts conjoined by an absolute continuity of matter.[9]

30. Relating to the note of Corol. 5 of Prop. 1 [in "Of Atoms"]: Hence we may learn that an absolutely solid body may have as much vacuity within its surface as any body whatsoever that is not absolutely solid.

31. Remember to place all about motion under the head of the manner or harmony of existence.

32. To observe how the planets may act upon sublunary things, as plants, animals, bodies of men, and, indirectly, upon their souls too, by that infinitely subtle matter diffused all round them, which in all probability is so subtle as to permeate the air and any bodies whatsoever: but more especially the moon; but most of all the comets, because of the great quantity that is diffused from them. And to tell how it is probable the ancients got the notion from the long experience of the antediluvians.[1]

33. Relating to No. 19: To compute how much motion there may be in an inch square of gunpowder when set on fire, compared with some solid body moving straight forward; and from the prodigious quantity of it, to prove that it could not neither take that motion from any circumambient body, nor have it in itself before; and that it was actually created at that very time. And to shew the only way whereby motion is created is by gravity, and therefore that this must be from gravity.

34. To shew how, by our laws, a compound body of any degree of rarity may have any degree of hardness or inseparability, and vice versa, a very dense body and of little vacuity may be, in comparison of it, very soft and separable.

35. Relating to No. 19: Shew how fiery and shining [bodies] are inflamed or enlightened on this manner.

36. And to shew, if I think fit, how Sir Isaac Newton was very sensible that all spontaneous enkindling was from a certain attraction.[2]

9. See "Of Atoms," N.B., pp. 212–13.
1. See also LS No. 56, pars. 11, 12.
2. Newton discusses combustion and the causes of the light and heat of flame in *Optics*, Bk. III, Q. 10.

37. To shew that it is not only highly probable, but absolutely certain, that the fixed stars are so many suns. For it is certain, in the first place, that they shine by their own light, that is, not by the sun's. For although we don't exactly know how far distant they are, yet we know that they are so far distant at least, that the annual revolution of the earth makes no sensible alteration in their position; and we know certainly that the light of the sun at such a distance will be no more than about so much as the light of a fixed star is here (let anybody calculate and see). And now I ask whether or no it be not certain, that no body will reflect the light of another body which don't shine upon it brighter than a single fixed star does upon the earth, so much as to cause it to shine, with its reflected light, so bright as the fixed stars do at such a distance.

And then, in the second place, it is certain they must be pretty near about so big [as the sun], and shine nearly with as bright a light; or else they could never appear so bright at such a distance. This we may also be certain of by calculation. Which three things are all that are needed to make a sun.

Corol. 1. From the foregoing, that our sun is a fixed star is as certain as that any one particular star in the heavens is one.

Corol. 2. 'Tis as probable that the fixed stars have systems of planets about them, as it would be that ours had, to one that had seen another every way like it have.[3]

38. To bring in, if there happens a good place for it, that it is equally probable in itself that all or the greatest part of the universe was created at the time of the Mosaic creation, as that all or the greatest part of the universe was created at once at any other time.

39. Relating to No. 18: To shew that the motion will be made by rebounding if the particles are elastic, and how that a motion will be otherwise begotten if they be not elastic, but perfectly hard.[4]

40. To observe that, for ought we know, the most dense bodies we

3. The article is primarily founded on ideas and arguments in Huygens' *Celestial Worlds*. JE cites Huygens and uses material from this book in the fragment "Of Light Rays," which judging from ink and hand was written at very nearly the same time, probably during his second graduate year, 1721–22.

4. JE appears to have noticed Newton's comment that "Bodies which are either absolutely hard, or so soft as to be void of Elasticity, will not rebound from one another. Impenetrability makes them only stop." *Optics*, Bk III, Q. 31 (1706 ed.: Q. 23, p. 341).

are acquainted with do not take up above the 10,000,000,000th part of the space they are in (if there shall be need of taking notice).

41. Relating to No. 14: To instance how all and every of the particles here upon earth do follow a particular particle in the atmosphere of a planet of a fixed star, etc.

42.[5] To observe about all the mountains being pitched over to the westward.

43. To observe about all stones being broken pieces of stone, and instances seen in journeys to [. . .].[6]

44. To observe that, as bodies have no substance of their own, so neither is solidity, strictly speaking, a property belonging to body; and to shew how. And if solidity is not so, neither are the other properties of body, which depend upon it and are only modifications of it. So that there is neither real substance nor property belonging to bodies; but all that is real, it is immediately in the first being.

Corol. 1. Hence see how God is said, still more properly, to be *ens entium*; or, if there was nothing else in the world but bodies, the only real being: so that it may be said, in a stricter sense than hitherto, "Thou art and there is none else besides Thee."

Corol. 2. Hence see that, instead of matter being the only proper substance, and more substantial than anything else because it is hard and solid; yet it is truly even nothing at all, strictly and in itself considered.

Corol. 3. The nearer in nature beings are to God, so much the more properly are they beings, and more substantial; and that spirits are much more properly beings, and more substantial, than bodies.

45.[7] To observe it is something difficult to know how it comes to pass that there are, in all continents, however uneven and confused, hilly

5. LS Nos. 42–44 are written in a dark brown ink with heavy solids. These entries are parallel to SS Nos. 17–21(b). They were probably written in the spring or summer of 1722, near the end of JE's second graduate year at Yale.

6. The two words stating the destination of these journeys are very carelessly written; they have defeated the eyes and wits of everyone who has attempted to interpret them. They may refer either to journeys taken by Edwards, or to a work of travel literature. Both Nos. 42 and 43 appear to have been written at the same time; and No. 42 suggests that the journeys were in a mountainous region.

7. In No. 45, and in Nos. 46–48 on MS pp. 14 and 16, JE's hand is small and angular, and the ink is a brown color with black particles that form crusts in heavy blots. They are nearly identical in these respects to entries in JE's Miscell. nos. 41–44. He began to write these soon after returning to East Windsor from his New York pastorate. LS No. 45 was probably composed at the same time, about a year after LS No. 44.

and jumbled, that seem to have mountains and valleys indifferently and undesignedly, everywhere dispersed, yet that there are such convenient channels, whereby water may be conveyed from the middle of these continents, and from all parts, into the ocean. The reason is, when the world was first created, the water covering all the earth, the surface of the earth must needs be very soft and loose, and easily worn or altered by the motions of the water. And afterwards, the water retiring in such a vast body unto one place from off the continents: and some places of them being higher and others lower; some more easily worn, others more difficultly; in some places the water moving with more force, in other with less; some places would necessarily be worn deeper than other, from the middle of the continent to the ocean. And as the water decreased, as going off from the earth, all would retire into these channels; and the waters still decreasing, the remainder [would] run in the deepest places of these channels. And after they were gone, they left channels everywhere, into which the waters, afterwards gushing out in the various parts of the continent, would naturally find their way. Thus also after the Flood, when the surface of the earth was again loosened.

By this means it comes to pass, that generally our large rivers have campaign countries without stones on each side of them, before we come to the ridges of mountains that commonly run parallel to them at some distance on each side. And yet nearer the river still, there are meadows on each side, lower than the plain; and last of all, the channel itself, as here in the Connecticut River: because the water, when it first began to de-flow from the land, it moved [in] vast quantities, enough to fill the whole space between the parallel mountains; so that the reason why the country is so plain, is because it was all once the bottom of a river. But afterward the water, decreasing, was confined to a narrower compass and wore the meadows; but at last, still narrower, was confined to the space between the banks. But there being still a remainder of water in the campaign and country between these greater channels, and flowing off by degrees into them, [it] wore the lesser channels for our little rivers.

46. The reason of the different refrangibility of rays must be either the different figure, or magnitude, or hardness, or internal texture, or different density of the rays. There can be no other differences between one ray and another except the difference be in some of these. Now first, it cannot be the different figure that causes the different refrangibility. This would not cause some rays to be more attracted towards

the edge of bodies; for all bodies equal in other respects are equally attracted, let them be of what figure soever. Nor will this serve to explain how some rays are easier reflected than others. Different magnitude is alike insufficient for these purposes. The different hardness can cause no difference in the attractability. The internal texture can make no manner of difference, either in refraction or reflection, if the quantity of matter and the surface be the same. The different swiftness of motion can't be the reason.[8] Wherefore, there remains nothing now that can be the cause but the different density, the different quantity of matter in the rays in the same room. Then we'll suppose there to be a great deal of difference between the rays of the sun in this respect— some more dense, some more rare, as in all other bodies. Now there will be these other differences arising from this, to wit: that the densest rays will come from the sun with the most rapid motion, not because they are less obstructed by the medium they go through, but because, as everybody may see, their mutual repercussions in the sun, before they leap out into the vast circumambient expanses, will be much more violent because of their greater gravity, which we have shown to be the reason of these repercussions.[9]

Now in the first place, we have no reason to think but that there is a difference in the density of the rays of the sun; and if so, we are certain that that will cause a difference in the rapidity of their motion, and therefore, certainly would cause a difference in their refrangibility. For it is certain that those rays that move swiftest by a body will be attracted least by it, and those that move slowest by it will be attracted most. This will also certainly cause a difference in the reflexibility of the rays; for those rays that strike on a body with greatest force will be most difficultly reflected, and those that strike with least force will be reflected most easily. Those that strike the most forcibly are most likely to make their way forward without reflection, and those bodies that are most likely to stand a stroke of the weaker rays, so as to reflect them, will give way to the stronger rays. Now whether this difference in the density of the rays be the reason of the different refrangibility or no, I think we may be sure of this: that if the true reason were re-

8. JE deleted the following passage, which originally continued his sentence: "Why the angle of reflection should not be the same in all rays, for the slowness of motion never causes the angle of reflection not to be the same with that in incidence. For this may be altered; at this rate, red may be turned into blue: But the property of the rays is found to be unalterable."

9. See LS Nos. 18 and 19, above.

moved, and there be a difference in the density of rays, this would certainly be a new reason of difference in the refrangibility.

It may be objected to this, that there is an infinite variety in the density of bodies, and so, doubtless, in rays; and at that rate there would be an infinite variety of simple colors. I answer: so there is, and multitudes have been distinguished, and more might be if we had instruments and senses enough accurate. The progression there is, from the highest to the lowest colors, is through an infinite variety. But the reason why there are no colors below blue, is because if there are any rays rarer than the blue, they are so weak that they degenerate into shade and are undistinguishable from darkness, and because they han't gravity enough to beget a motion in them sufficient to cause them to leap out at such a distance.

This explication very well agrees with experience. Red is the highest, strongest, harshest color, because it is caused by the densest and most rapid rays; blue is more gentle and weak. Red gives the most light because the rays have more of vivacity, and more strongly affect the organ; blue is the nearest approaching to darkness. Red, long beheld, is painful to the eyes. Green and blue are pleasing, easy, gentle and inoffensive, and healthful to the organ. Blue is so weak a color, the rays are so weak, that they are reflected from the weakest bodies, such as air and thin exhalations; as in the blueness of the skies, which are so weak that they let through the stronger rays. Thus sometimes at sun setting, all the rest of the rays are stopped but the red, which fight their way through all the exhalations the air is full of, and the sun looks as red as blood.

Corol. Because there is such a difference in the density of the rays of light, it appears that the atoms of which the rays of light are compounded, are immensely less than the rays themselves.

47. Since, as has been shewn,[1] body is nothing but an infinite resistance in some part of space caused by the immediate exercise of divine power, it follows that as great and as wonderful a power is every moment exerted to the upholding of the world, as at first was to the creation of it; the first creation being only the first exertion of this power to cause such resistance, the preservation only the continuation or the repetition of this power every moment to cause this resistance. So that the universe is created out of nothing every moment; and if it were not for our imaginations, which hinder us, we might see that wonderful

1. In "Of Atoms," *Prop. 2, Corols. 8, 9.* Above, pp. 214–15.

work performed continually, which was seen by the morning stars when they sang together.

48. There is that which is peculiarly wonderful in trees, beyond anything that is to be found in the inanimate world, even the manner of their growing from seed, their amazing diversification, into such curious branches, leaves, flowers, fruits and seeds, and so successively from one seed after another, in the same manner from age to age, forever.

The discovery of the little tree in the seed has opened a door for the finding out of these wonders,[2] but without that we might have known that the parts of the tree are in miniature before they are in perfection. For the bud, which is but another sort of seed, is nothing but the leaves, twigs, flowers and fruits, folded up together, which we see by degrees to unfold themselves.

But the tree being in embryo in the seed don't seem to solve the difficulty; for the tree most certainly don't keep to its rule, don't exactly follow its copy in the seed. For we may make the tree grow almost as we please; if we lop the tree, there will peep out new branches from the body of the tree where there was no sign of a branch.

But if the branches of the tree did really grow exactly in the same form as their pattern in the seed, this might indeed solve for the growing of one tree, but not for that infinite succession and endless offspring of trees that may proceed from it, except we suppose that in one seed are actually contained an infinite number of trees and seeds, one within another. For this makes actually an infinite number of trees twice over in the same seed: first, an infinite number of successions of one tree less than another; and by that time we are come to the least (we must be allowed to speak contradictions here), the offspring will be so numerous that there will be actually an infinite number of trees of the same size and standing.[3] Wherefore this matter of the growth of trees still remains very difficult.

The reason of it would not be altogether so difficult and perplexing if

2. Reported by Nehemiah Grew in *The Anatomy of Vegetables Begun* (London, 1672) and by Marcello Malpighi in *Anatome Plantarum* (London, 1672). Malpighi was the principal spokesman for the so-called "pre-formation" theory, that the entire delineation of the offspring is actually contained in the seed. In the Colonies, Cotton Mather noted this theory with approval (*Christian Philosopher*, Essay xxvi, p. 128); JE's discussion suggests an acquaintance with it.

3. JE seems to mean that the seed must contain trees "one less than another" for an infinite number of generations, of which the last generation, "the least," actually contains an infinite number of individuals "of the same size and standing."

they always grew in the same regular order. We don't despair of finding out the reason of that which always happens alike and in the same order (thus, when we have reduced the motion of the planets to a rule, we have got above halfway towards giving the reason of their motions), but the branches of the trees seem not capable of being reduced to any rule at all, but there is an infinite variety; one branch grows out here, another there, without any order.

But we shall be helped in this matter if we consider that all trees and plants universally, when they first sprout out [of] the ground, while there is as yet but one twig, are exactly regular; that is, having the buds that grow out of [them] (which are branches in little) standing in a regular and uniform manner, a leaf always growing under the bud. In some, two come out together, one right opposite to the other, always standing transverse to the last two, as in the twig *AB* [see Fig. 2] as in the maple tree; in others, but one at a time, standing at regular distances on different sides, in such order as to stand round the twig in the form of a screw, so that the branches

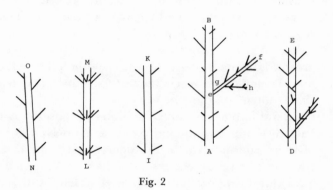

Fig. 2

shall stand out on every side, as in the twig *DE*, as in apple trees, pear trees, cherry trees, etc.; in others, having two together growing out of opposite sides, but not standing transverse as the maple, as in the twig *IK*; in others, having four or five standing round the twig together, as in *LM*; in others, having but one at a time standing always opposite to each other, as in *NO*; and innumerable other ways, but yet always regular.

And as the first sprouts of a tree are always regular, so are all the young sprouts of the tree afterwards, when the tree comes to be divided into many branches; yea, always as long as the tree lives, all the twigs that are of that year's growth are regular. So that it follows that the body, the main branches, and the little twigs, and every part of every tree in the world, in their first beginnings, were regular. So that if all the trees had continued as they were in the year that they grew, the whole tree with all the branches, small and great, would be regular. And now we are sure, that if the sap did not flow more easily into one bud or branch than another, or one were no otherwise advantaged above another, if all the buds and branches had, in all respects, exactly equal advantages for growing, the tree would be most exactly regular. It follows clearly and certainly. For if the common trunk *AB*, when it first grew, was regular, and if the branches *ef* at first were regular, and the branches of the branches *gh* were also regular, and so on, it is certain if all these branches continued as they were at first, and every bud or branch expanded itself alike, the whole tree *AB* will always continue to grow regularly. Thus far we are clear, that the miniatures of all plants are regular; and that there is no provision made in the seed and bud for any but a regular growth; and that if it were not for some accidental causes that promoted or hindered the growth of one of the branches or buds (*ef*) more than another, that all the trees in the world would be regular.

We need not perplex ourselves to find out what should give one a greater advantage of growth than another. The least thing in the world may be sufficient, when they are so small and tender: ten thousand things might be thought of.

There[4] is but here and there one of those buds that grows thus regularly, that grows out and expands themselves. Perhaps some die. Most of them continue in their littleness and imperfect state, the sap not running plentifully enough into them, having more free passage elsewhere or being by some means diverted. And so, the part growing bigger and bigger, they are at last covered in it, and lie latent till by some means the passage of the sap elsewhere is stopped, as by lopping off the tree or otherwise; and then, the sap flowing more plentifully into them causes them to spring forth and make their way out of this bark. It may lie like a seed in the tree for many years, and upon such an occasion spring forth. Hence it is that those little twigs, how small soever—though but of one year growth—that grow out of great trees, yet always have their beginning and rise close by the very heart of the tree; because all the rest that is above it has grown and been added since the tree was so small as to bear buds at that place. We had as good think the trees grow out of the ground without seeds, as that branches grow

---

4. JE jotted instructions for the rearrangement of the final paragraphs. They are presented here, as nearly as possible, in the order of these instructions, rather than as they actually appear in the MS.

out of the trunk without buds. For the buds are but another sort of seeds, that cleave to the tree; and the seeds are but another sort of buds, that drop into the ground.[5] So that when the seeds drop off, it is only a continuation of those branches dropped into the ground. Though the continuation is interrupted, yet, receiving sap from the ground, it will not cease to grow; which is no more strange than that the branch of an apple tree, if cut off and cast into the ground, will continue to grow.[6]

Many plants do actually always continue to grow regular: herbs and weeds that are but of one year's growth, and some trees. And of those that err from that seminal pattern, some keep nearer to it than others.

We therefore conclude that the first seeds that ever were, were regular trees or at least regular parts of trees, each so contrived with vessels, pipes and valves, that as it receives more sap, it continually desires still to shoot forth towards *B*. And infinite wisdom so contrived the curious workmanship of the inlets, receptacles, passages and outlets, pipes and orifices from *A* to *B*; that that which is by degrees added at *B*, by the gentle motion of the sap from *A* to *B* through the pipes, shall be cast into the same form, and shall come out in the same fashion, as if it were cast in a mold. It is also so contrived, that as it continues to proceed towards *B*, the course of some of the passages shall be diverted so as to cause it to shoot forth at the side at *e*, and at every such a regular distance, as the engineer contrives his clock to strike at such uniform distances, and the sap proceeds forwards in the branch *ef* in the same manner as it did in the trunk *AB*, and in like manner breaks out at the sides at regular distances from *g* to *h*, and then breaks forth in like manner at the sides of *gh*, and so *in infinitum* to the world's end. And the trees that grow now are nothing but the branches of those first trees; which, although the

5. JE deleted the following sentence: "So it is contrived that at such due and uniform distances these little continuations of the branches of the tree, while they are very tender, shall be wrapped in curious covering and shelter of leaves, flowers and fruits (and some only of leaves and flowers), and shall drop off."

6. JE deleted the two following paragraphs: "A leaf is still nothing but branches of the tree that grow not so big, and so contrived as to cleave together after such a manner. So likewise is the flower and the fruit too is a compages of branches, and all that the first trees God created had to do was to proceed to the end of the world in such regular branches having various stated periods at the same stated distances: at which periods there happens remarkable changes and unusual phenomena among the branches, as there may be various periods in an engine of human contrivance, some for returning every second, every minute, every quarter of an hour, hour, day, month and year.

"As for the leaves, flowers and fruits, they are not to be looked upon as a continuation of those regular branches, but part of the substance of the trunk to which they grow. I take it there is a threefold substance in the trunk: the exterior and more coarse, leaves are the extremities of this, and one more fine."

communication with the original trunk is ceased, yet still continue to grow, and to be diversified into more and more branches, in the same regular and uniform method *in infinitum*. And the seeds from whence our trees proceed are no new plants, but branches of the old; a continuation of the same plant, in its infinite, regular progress; branches not yet expanded. The trees, or seeds, or whatever they were that God first created, were only the beginning of this progress—enough to set it going.

49.[7] See No. 14. In order to this, 'tis not only necessary that God should tell the number of the stars and know the exact bigness, weight, density, number and distance of these greater bodies of the universe; not only weigh the mountains in exact scales and the hills in perfectly even balances, and measure the seas as in the hollow of his hand; but he must comprehend the dust of the earth in a measure, he must measure the dust of the earth in all these respects. He must know the exact number of particles of dust, the exact dimensions and weight of every atom, the exact distance of every, yea, of every part of every one from every other; yea, from every part of all others in the universe. Thus infinite wisdom is as much concerned, not only in the excellent creation of the world, but merely the creation of it, as infinite power. Yea, one single atom cannot have a being without it. One single atom could not move without it, inasmuch as we have shewn motion cannot be without infinite wisdom; and again, that no body could have a being, without motion, any otherwise than as the world had a being from all eternity.

50. All the way that the soul can influence the body, is only by emitting of animal spirits from the brain; yea, when the soul retracts animal spirits from some parts, it is by emission in others. This emission is either natural (which follows merely from the presence of the soul in the brain, or that which follows of itself from thoughts and passions), or voluntary. And all the way that body has influence upon the soul is by the influx of animal spirits to the brain or efflux from it.

51.   When I come to speak of the body of man, let the demonstration of the soul's being distinct from matter be inserted.

52.   See No. 17. That is, the least wrong step would thus disorder

---

7. No. 49 is written in a thin brown ink with heavy black solids, like that in Miscell. nos. 85–86; No. 50 has a gray ink comparable to Miscell. nos. 88–93; Nos. 51–61 have basically the same brownish gray ink as that in Miscell. nos. 95–117. All these entries were probably written during the winter and spring of 1723–24.

all things and quite overthrow the universe, except God from time [to time] set the whole going anew: which would be necessary, because the least wrong turn in one atom causes a wrong motion in every atom in the universe; and this also, at the end, if returning at such a period of time or continuing at intervals of time, longer or shorter, equal or unequal, would at length overthrow the universe.

53. See No. 14. To the words, "making exact and nice allowance for the miracles which should be needful," [add] "and other ways whereby the course of bodies should be diverted."

54. If the fixed stars moved round the earth once in twenty-four hours, none of them would be seen here upon earth; none of their rays would ever reach the earth. For although it cannot be demonstrated how far distant they are from us, yet they must needs be so far distant that such a motion would be at least ten times so swift as the motion of the rays of light (according to the ordinary computation of their distance, it would be several thousand times swifter; but we suppose it to be ten).[8] Wherefore I say that if the motion of the star at S [Fig. 3] round the earth T be ten times so swift as the motion of bodies emitted on all sides from the body S, none of these emitted bodies will ever reach the body T. In such a case 'tis evident that bodies emitted would have a twofold motion, viz. a motion whereby they are emitted from S, and also the motion that it received with the body while it was with it. Thus, the ray R, emitted from S towards T, would besides have a motion towards W (which it

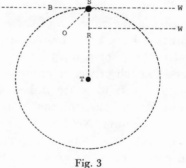

Fig. 3

had while it was in the body) equal to the motion of the body S, which it don't lose when emitted. Wherefore 'tis manifest that the motion of R towards W will be ten times so swift as is its motion towards T.

8. In "Of Light Rays" JE "under-reckons" the distance of Sirius to be 2,000,000,000,000 miles, and that of the most remote stars to be 100 times greater. He assumes the speed of light to be 150,000 miles per second. Using these figures, the speed of Sirius revolving diurnally about the earth in a circular orbit would be about 145,500,000 miles per second, or about 970 times the speed of light, and the remote stars would travel 97,000 times the speed of light.

So that by that time it has got the distance from S to T in the direction ST, 'tis manifest it will have got ten times as far towards W, or in that direction. So that 'tis most manifest that it would never reach T. And even the ray B that is sent out right behind the star S, moves nine times as swiftly towards W, as towards E; so that 'tis evident that all the rays that can be emitted from the star S, move at least nine times so swiftly towards W as they go out towards the earth. 'Tis therefore evident that they all will fall on that side of the earth that is towards W.

But we'll one instance more: let the emission of the ray O be towards O. 'Tis evident that this ray will never gain one inch towards E (or the east), being carried at least nine times so swiftly towards W (or the west), the contrary point; because, being carried at least nine times so swiftly towards W, by that time 'tis got halfway of the distance in that direction, it will have got nine times as far to the west, and therefore will miss the globe of the earth.

55.   *Prop.* The cleaving of bodies or the parts of bodies, one to another, can be from nothing else but their tendency or gravity one to another; so that all cohesion in the world arises from this, and this is the only reason why every least part of all bodies don't move perfectly at liberty, without any respect one to another. For instance, the only reason of the cohesion of the bodies or the parts of bodies *ab* [Fig.4], must be from their tending or gravitating to each other. For it must be either because they tend to each other, or because the parts of the body *a* next to *b* are linked and fastened in amongst the parts of the body *b*. I can think of no medium. Neither is the second another case different from the first, why all the

Fig. 4

corporeal parts below the plane *cd* cleave to any of the parts above [the] plane. Let some of the corporeal parts be particles conceived as coming out of the body *a*: and linked and hooked[9] into the parts of the body *b* or no, it is all one as if they are conceived as only parts of the body *b*, only cleaving to the body *a*. 'Tis evident, therefore, that this is not the reason. Therefore the other must be it.

N.B. When bodies are pressed together by circumambient bodies, the proposition don't call that cohesion.

56.   (1) The parts which constitute the atmosphere are three-

9. MS: possibly "locked," as in Dwight's reading.

fold. First are the parts of the ether, drawn and pressed together by its gravity to the earth, which is nothing but exceeding minute, subtle and active particles; which parts are the most penetrating. Now 'tis certain if there be any ethereal matter at all, however little, this is one part of the atmosphere. For if there be any, that which is round about the earth, or any other celestial body, will be very much condensed and pressed together by its tendency to the earth; so that although it be almost infinitely rare at the distance of four or five diameters of the earth, yet it will, according to the laws of gravity, be thick enough at the surface of the earth. So that there are no proper bounds to this part of the atmosphere, inasmuch as it is nothing but the ether, pressed together, according as 'tis nearer or further from the center of the earth. 'Tis in vain therefore to pretend to asking bounds to the atmosphere.

(2) Second, another part are the vapors and exhalations that ascend from the globe—parts of liquids rarefied so as to ascend from the earth by means of the gravity of the rest of the atmosphere. These vapors are wholly constituted of small bubbles, as is now said by philosophers; these bubbles being lighter than the atmosphere, not because the liquid of it, which makes the skin or walls of the bubble, is rarer than the air; but because the air or subtle matter that is in the bubble is, by the sunbeams or otherwise, made more rare than the circumambient air; so that take the skin of the bubble all and together, and it is lighter than a part of the air that is round about of the same dimension. When we say that air within the bubble is rarer than that without, it must [be] the ethereal part of the air, or at least another part of the air that is not constituted of these bubbles. For that which is in all the bubbles is not the bubbles. Now here, in the first place, it is certain these exhalations do constitute a part of the atmosphere that is about; and second, 'tis certain they[1] don't wholly constitute it, as has been by some thought. For it's contrary to the supposition that these bubbles are lighter than the air and therefore ascend in it. Than what air are these bubbles lighter? It is not meant that these bubbles are lighter or rarer than these bubbles, and therefore ascend among them. So that these are not the primary parts of the air. Yea, 'tis certain that the matter of our atmosphere is the very same with the ether, the same with that which is in the spaces between the heavenly bodies; and that there is a certain subtle matter in these spaces, and that it is the same with, [or] at least partly constituted of the air (only the

1. MS: "it."

air is the ether much compressed), if it has been proved that the self-expanding quality of the air is so great as has been said by the late philosophers.[2] For if one inch square of it, when free and nothing incumbent to press it together, will expand itself so much, 'tis certain that the whole atmosphere, free and having nothing incumbent, will expand itself into all the solar system. And if an inch square of air at the distance of a semi-diameter of the earth will expand itself so as to fill the solar system, then there is nothing that is incumbent upon the atmosphere sufficient to hinder its free expansion, so that the matter of our air is abroad in the heavenly spaces.

(3) The ethereal part of the air that is here near the earth is much more compressed, by reason of the exhalations, or that part that is made up of bubbles floating in the air. For though they in themselves are lighter than the air, yet they have some weight, and must therefore necessarily add to the weight that is incumbent upon that lower part of the atmosphere; whereby the air below, in general, is denser and heavier and so more able to bear up more such exhalations.

(4) Third: There is yet another way whereby the rays of the sun do doubtless cause particles to ascend off from terrestrial bodies, besides this of rarefying of liquids, and making of them lighter than the air so as to be buoyed up thereby. For as the air or ether is nothing but exceeding subtle and agile particles, made so exceeding elastic and diffusive by their lively motion one among another; so when the rays of the sun separate particles so subtle as they are, and like unto them, from terrestrial bodies, and give them as brisk a motion as the particles of ether have, such particles thereby do become—some of them are become, in all respects whatever, particles of ether; and will move up and down, on one side or another indifferently in the ether, as other particles of ether do. Now there is no doubt but that there are great plenty of particles in terrestrial bodies that are as fine as the ether but only are fixed, adhering to other particles by gravity, and want nothing to make them become parts of ether but to be disengaged and loosened, to have a sufficiently active motion given them. We have shewed that all bodies are constituted of atoms,[3] which are, 'tis probable, finer than

2. JE originally wrote "if the self-expanding quality of the air is so great as Sir Isaac Newton has shewn," then revised the clause so as to delete his reference to Newton. The phenomenon is in fact discussed in *Principia*, Bk. III, prop. 41, prob. 21, Ex. (p. 470), and the information that JE mentions here evidently originated from this discussion. But because JE deleted Newton's name, it appears that the *Principia* was not his source directly, and he was not certain of the Newtonian origin.

3. In "Of Atoms," *Prop. 1.* Above, pp. 208–10.

any ethereal particles. And 'tis not to be doubted therefore, that all bodies are capable of being dissolved into parts as fine as ethereal ones. But this is what I would: that doubtless there are great plenty of particles in bodies proper for ethereal matter, and want nothing but to be loosened and set in motion. And if it be so, I think it cannot be doubted but that the rays of the sun do daily disengage and loosen plenty of these particles, and set them into a motion sufficiently lively and brisk so that there is continually rising ethereal matter from off the surface of the earth; and that this in considerable measure constitutes the atmosphere, and is not specifically different from the first constituent parts.

(5) And seeing these particles are so very active, and therefore diffusive and move indifferently any way in the ether, no doubt but those that are daily raised from off the earth[4] diffuse, many of them at immense distances in a very short time; though not so quick as rays of light, nor in right lines as they move.

(6) There is doubtless the like ethereal particles continually diffused from the other planets as from the earth, and *caeteris paribus,* the more any planet has of the sun's influence, the more of these particles are diffused from it;[5] and therefore there are abundantly more from comets than from any of the planets. And seeing there is such subtle matter diffused around from all the heavenly bodies into the ethereal spaces, 'tis probable that the ether is chiefly composed of them.

(7) We have these two reasons to think the motion of those subtle particles is exceeding rapid: *1,* because they receive this motion from the rays of the sun, which move so swiftly as to come from the sun in seven or eight minutes; and *2,* it can absolutely be proved by their great elasticity—so great that an inch square of air can by its elasticity be of such great force, that if sufficiently compressed, it will be of force sufficient to move a prodigious weight; which could not be except the motion of these particles were prodigious swift.

(8) This matter that arises from the heavenly bodies will diffuse itself abundantly faster at a distance from those bodies than very near them, both because they are so much less retarded by their gravity to the bodies from whence they came, and because they have millions of times more liberty and their motion less resisted by circumambient particles.

4. JE deleted "those that are daily raised from off the earth." The words are restored here to clarify the point made in the paragraph.
5. MS: "them."

(9) There may be a great difference in the kinds of particles diffused from different planets, even as there is a great difference in the particles that are diffused from particular bodies upon the earth which cause different odors.

(10) Those effluvia that are diffused from the bodies of the universe, diffusing themselves so fast and being so fine and penetrating, and of different kinds, may cause considerable and different effects in the other planets: being diffused into all parts of the ethereal spaces, and mixing themselves with their atmosphere, and being so very active, [they] may produce considerable effects in the temperature of their air, and of their plants and animals, which have so much to do with their air.[6] And those effects will be different at different times, according as the bodies are nearer or further off, and according as the rays of the sun which cause them, fall either on the side that is towards them or that that is from them. And *caeteris paribus*, those bodies which are nearest us will have much the greatest effects upon the earth. Therefore the moon has vastly greater effects of this kind than any other planets. And *caeteris paribus*, those bodies will have the greatest effects on the earth which emit most of these effluvia; and therefore comets will cause much greater alterations upon the earth than any of the primary planets.

(11) Whether those effluvia are diffused from one star to another in an hour or a month, a longer or shorter time, it alters not the case; neither will it cause but that there shall be constant different effects produced at certain periods, according to the different places and aspects of the stars, provided that those effluvia are propagated to the same distances at the same time. For as to this, it alters not the case whether at the full moon we have the effects of the effluvia of the full moon, or of the first quarter, or of the new. Yet it will not follow but that at every full moon we shall have the same effects produced.

(12) It seems to one probable that before the Flood, when the earth enjoyed so temperate and undisturbed an atmosphere; and therefore the effects of the stars, of this nature, were constant, being not disturbed by the perturbations of the atmosphere as now; and the lives of men were so long; that they knew the effects of the planets upon the earth, and could foretell nearly what effects such a position or aspect of the stars would produce in the atmosphere, and upon the plants and animals of the earth, having so much opportunity of experience and obser-

6. That other planets harbor life, and perhaps even rational beings, was a thesis urged by Huygens in *Celestial Worlds,* and, after him, by Derham in *Astro-theology.*

vation by reason of their long lives: and that the tradition of this from Noah and his sons to their posterity has been the cause of that general opinion that the nations of the world have had, that the various places and appearances of the planets had a considerable effect upon the earth; and gave rise to judicial astrology, and in a great measure to their worshipping of the planets.[7]

(13) *Corol.* (from the first part). Hence it is that the atmosphere of the moon is so much less and thinner than that of the earth: it, having so much less attraction, cannot attract so much of the ether about it, nor will it be so much compressed and so dense.

(14) These effluvia or subtle particles are not only continually dissolving from, and diffusing from the bodies of the universe, but also doubtless are continually settling to these bodies and so become fixed again. I don't suppose that they precipitate as dust in water; but seeing that far the greatest part of the ethereal matter that is in the whole universe is near the surface of the stars, those particles crowding about these bodies doubtless often are catched by coming so appositely to some of their fixed particles that they adhere by their gravity, and their motion is not sufficient to carry them clear. They may also so far lose their motion that it shall not be sufficient to keep them playing off from the earth.

(15) Here near the surface of the earth where the air is so dense, particles that are not so fine as the particles of pure ether may easily diffuse themselves nevertheless, the atmosphere counterbalancing most (though not all) of their gravity, so that their motion may cast them to a great height and distance. And of these particles our atmosphere is doubtless in considerable measure composed. And of this kind I suppose the effluvia that cause odors to be, and other effluvia that are emitted from all bodies upon earth; set in motion, not only by the rays of the sun, but also by the motion of circumambient aerial particles, and an intestine motion in the bodies themselves.

7. See also LS No. 32, above. Most scientists and philosophers of the seventeenth century rejected judicial astrology outright. Cotton Mather, e.g., expresses a thorough contempt of it. JE, on the other hand, seems to share what was, or was rapidly becoming, the minority opinion that some scientific basis might be given for astrology. Morton's *Compendium Physicae* offered such a view. In JE's copy of the theses extracted from Morton, it is asserted that one of the affections of heaven is "influence on other bodies by light, heat or other communications." Influence is either direct on bodies, or indirect "on the minds of men by hindering or promoting yᵉ operations of it. On this affection of influence is grounded Astrologie, which, for want of sufficient observations to make rational inductions is very imperfect and uncertain in its rules." (Ch. 4, in MS Partridge, p. 194.)

57. (1) It is already determined what exhalations are—that they are nothing but bubbles of water including air, or ethereal matter considerably rarer than the air without. The only thing that wants to be known is how these bubbles come to be made. In order to determine this we must first know how any bubbles are made: which is by driving a parcel of air under the surface of the water so that the water, being so fluid, immediately closes over it, so that there is a parcel of air[8] enclosed by the water. Now this enclosed air immediately gathers itself into a globular form, by reason of the gravity of the parts of the air one to another; or likewise, the gravity of the parts of the water, which will prevent any prominences of water inwards amongst the air. The air also immediately ascends again to emerge from the water, whereupon most of the water that was over it runs off on every side. But water being a thing whose particles are so fitted one to another that they adhere one to another by their gravity, the skin or the walls of the bubble will not immediately burst; though the particles of water run off with infinite ease before it comes to the last skin, because they run upon other water that attracts them[9] as much as those particles that they run from.

(2) What makes bubbles break is, first, the endeavor of the air quite to emerge (for the lowest part of the air is something lower than the surface of the water, by reason of the weight of the incumbent water [of] the skin of the bubble); second, the weight of the water, whereby it endeavors to run off down to the body of water; third, the attraction of the water that is at the bases of the walls of the bubble, for the water at *A* and *B* [Fig. 5] attracts the water of the skin that is next to it with considerable strength.

(3) We see that small bubbles live much longer than great ones because: *1*, the skin is not so strongly attracted by the subjoined water, inasmuch as the margin of the bubble is not so large; and *2*, the endeavor of the air to emerge is not so great, there not being so much of it, nor so

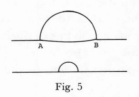

Fig. 5

much below the surface of the water, because the weight that presses it under is not so great; *3*, because the weight of the water of the skin is not so great [Fig. 5].

(4) A very small bubble, being disjoined from the water and sus-

8. MS: "water."
9. MS: "it."

pended in the air, provided the air within remains as it was and the bubble be not broken by something external, would live forever, or at least a very long time. For the weight of the water whereby it tends. to run from the top to the bottom of the bubble would be very inconsiderable, the bubble being so small. And then, a parcel of air ascending out of the water would take no more water than just what would suffice for a skin. The weight would be nothing near equal to the tendency of the particles one to another, for we see in great bubbles 'tis hardly equal when the weight is so much greater. Therefore the weight would not be sufficient to disjoin these particles. Therefore, the bubble would not be broken by the weight. Second, the attraction of the water from whence it ascended would not contribute to it, because it would be carried at a distance from it: third, nor the endeavor of the enclosed air to get out or emerge from the water, as in bubbles that lie on the surface, because it is supposed it would be entirely emerged and disjoined.

(5) Now then, all that is necessary to be done by the sun's rays in order to cause bubbles to ascend from the water, is to drive very minute parcels of air under water, and to make the air enclosed so much rarer than the rest of the air that this air, together with the watery skin, shall be lighter than a parcel of other air of the some bigness.

(6) The air that is close to the surface of the water is far more exposed to the force of the sun's rays than any at a distance, because the other air has room to yield to the stroke of the rays, but this must bear all the brunt and stand the stroke, and can no further. A body that is smitten upon an anvil suffers much more by the stroke than a thing that is floating in the free air. Therefore the air that is next to the surface of the water will be much more rarefied by the sun's rays than other air.

(7) If a very small parcel of air that is next to the water happens to be struck so to advantage by the rays of the sun (by many rays striking together upon it, or otherwise) as to be smitten just under the surface of the water, that air, being smitten more forceably than the other air that is not smitten under, will be more rarefied by the sun's rays than other air. And that parcel of air so smitten under, emerging, will raise a bubble with it. And if the air within be rarefied enough (as in probability it will, because all the air next to the water is more rarefied than other air, and this is more rarefied than other air that is next to the water); I say if the air within is rarefied enough, it will not only be buoyed up to the surface of the water, causing a bubble there, but will

leap clear out of the water, and will ascend in the air till it is in equi-
poise with the circumambient air.[1]

58. (1) I never yet could[2] light of any satisfying reason why the heat
of the sun is so much greater near the surface of the earth then at a
distance from it. 'Tis said that near the earth the rays are doubled by
reflection.[3] But they are not doubled, for none can think that the earth
reflects all the rays that fall upon it, at least not with as much strength
as they come from the sun: the reflex light is nothing near so great as
the direct light, 'tis very evident. But I suppose the heat that is very
near the earth in a hot summer day is a hundred times greater than
merely the direct ray would cause, instead of being only double. I
suppose at three or four miles from the earth, the heat is nothing to
what it is very near; but there is as much of the reflex ray, to a very
trifle, as we have close to the surface. For the rays that are reflected
from the earth don't cease in going two or three miles, any more than the
rays reflected from the moon or Venus or Jupiter or Saturn. And all
the difference otherwise is only according to the square of the distance
from the center; and what a small matter is that in two or three miles.

(2) The heat therefore cannot be caused only immediately by the
motion of the rays of the sun, but also by the motion of other particles
in the atmosphere set in motion by them. Now there is reason why
other particles should be much more set in motion near the surface of
the earth than farther from it, [which] we gave in No. 57: because that
part of the atmosphere that is close to the surface of the earth suffers
much more from the rays, so that they will be much more heated, and
rarified, and ascending; and the heavier colder air that is incumbent
working under. So that 'tis the ascent of these agitated particles that
chiefly causes the heat; which by degrees cooling as they ascend, being
no longer subject to the violent force of the rays, will cause it to be
much hotter near the surface and cooler at a distance.

1. JE might have gleaned the general outlines of this theory of evaporation and condensa-
tion from his early reading of Derham (see SS No. 12, p. 221 above). In "An Attempt to
solve the Phenomenon of the Rise of Vapours, Formation of Clouds, and Descent of Rain,"
in *Philosophical Transactions*, *36* (1729), p. 6, Newton's disciple James Desaguliers attacks
this general theory. Among the problems its defenders must answer, he points out, is that of
explaining how the air within the bubbles becomes specifically lighter than air outside; for
the sun acts equally on all the surface of the water. Though LS No. 57 antedates Desaguliers'
paper by some five years, JE seems to have recognized the problem, and wrote pars. 5–7 to
solve it.

2. JE deleted "yet could."

3. See SS No. 26 above.

59. (1) The matter of the tail of the comet don't ascend from the sun because 'tis made more rare than the ether, for it must be very rare indeed to be so—more rare than 'tis reasonable to suppose; but by the comet's heating the ether that is round about, so that the ether will have a constant stream from the comet upwards from the sun: yea, a very rapid stream, so as to carry some of the rarest parts of the comet's atmosphere with it.

(2) These tails entirely cease to be emitted at a considerable distance from the sun, not because the comet wants heat to rarify, but because the ether is so rare 'tis not strong enough to carry any particles with it.

60. All plants, from the beginning of the world, of the same kind are nothing but as so many branches of the first plant or plants of that kind, proceeding ever since; and sprout out, not in exact order and at regular distances, but this regularity consists in the equality of different periods. They don't continue to send forth branches one after another perpetually without intermission, but this germination has various stops and stays of equal lengths and distances one from another. If the weather be never so suitable, the tree will not continue to emit branches continually, one after another without intermission; but after such a number of branches are emitted no more will sprout for some months, and then such a number will again unfold themselves, ceasing again at the due period. This may be observed, at least in all the trees that grow in this climate, where are successions of summer and winter; these periods are suited to the length of these seasons. And once, when the heat here in New England continued extraordinary late, we have had part of two of these periods in a year. Plants that had stopped, sprouted again. The twig grows till the bud for the next year appears, and then ceases; but if the weather continues warm, it will be a considerable time before these buds will expand themselves. Another (and the largest) distance is from seed to seed. The fruit and seed is the extremity of a branch, and that branch or twig from which the seed falls never grows anymore at all; the tree proceeds on no further that way.

61. 'Tis the same thing that distant existence as to place should have influence on bodies, as in gravity, as that existence distant as to time, being past, should have influence on its present existence, as in the successions of motion.

62.[4] WIND. EXHALATIONS. 'Tis certain by experience that winds do

4. Nos. 62, 63 and the first part of 64 are difficult to locate in relation to passages in

contribute to drying up of moisture. 'Tis not conceivable that the wind should raise those bubbles of which watery exhalations consist, but we conceive that it contributes to the raising after this [manner]: it may contribute to the raising them from off the surface of bodies of water by continually carrying off the moist air, and by bringing on that from the land which is dryer and more agile, whose parts are more briskly moved by the heat, and therefore are more easily driven under the surface of the water and so carry it off. It dries things that are moist upon the land by carrying off the exhalations from the loose and porous parts as soon as raised, so that they don't lodge again and stand in the way of others.

63. PLANETS. A reason why the greater planets, as Jupiter and Saturn, are placed at such a vast distance from the sun, and the lesser planets nearer, is because if such vast bodies were near they would have abundantly greater influence by their attraction to disturb the rest of the sun, and so in time to overthrow the whole system. Comets would likewise be greatly exposed to their influence and their orbits would be much disturbed by them. And 'tis fit they should be at a great distance from the lesser planets, otherwise they would greatly disorder their motion; and from one another, for bodies of such mighty force and power must be kept at a distance. Otherwise they will make dreadful work one with another.

64. WAVES. Circular waves in the water are begun with a raising or depression of the water in the center of those circles, and are made thus: Suppose the water is raised into a hillock at *1* [Fig. 6]. This can't be, without the water's subsiding in the space *2* to make that hillock; and the water at *3* is set in motion towards *1* to fill up that hollow.[5] And it's most easy to conceive that, the water at *3* moving out of its place and thereby leaving a valley, the water at *4* will necessarily follow; and so on to *5, 6, 7, 8, 9, 10, 11*. For a valley being made at *2*, the water at *3* comes to fill it up, and leaves a valley at *3*; when the water at *4*

"Miscellanies" and other MSS. Some evidence suggests they were written in the spring of 1724, while other evidence supports a dating in the spring and summer of 1726, at the end of his Yale tutorship. For discussion, see above, pp. 187–88.

5. JE deleted the beginning of another sentence, "The water at 1 immediately subsides lower than the even common surface of the water, that is, the water that made the rising flows on all sides into the hollow space 2 that." These words are written in the smooth gray ink of the first part of No. 64, but are deleted in a reddish brown ink which he used to write the remainder of this and the next entry, No. 65. The ink and hand correspond to that in Miscell. nos. 267–78, which JE probably wrote during the late summer or fall of 1727.

moves inward and leaves a valley there, so that the valley that began at *2* spreads around, further and further outward in a circle, from *1*, *2*, *3*, *4*, etc. successively. But we are to remember that the hillock of water at *1* immediately subsides and flows every way into the space *2*, and stops the water at *3* which was set in motion inwards, whereby it necessarily rises

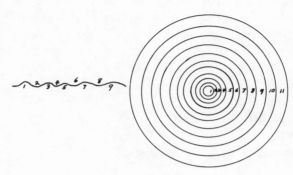

Fig. 6

into a hill; for water being stopped in its motion will necessarily rise. The water at *3*, being stopped and raised in a hill, this hill, falling, contradicts and stops the water at *4*, and causes that to rise. So that it's easy to conceive why there must immediately succeed the first valley a rising, spreading after the same manner. We are to remember that we left a valley at *1*, where the water subsided, and must necessarily subside lower than the ordinary surface; because when the hill was raised there, there was a valley round it in the space *2*, [and] now the weight and libration of the water would cause all the water at *1* that was higher than that valley to flow away. There being now, therefore, a valley at *1* and hill at *2*, 'tis easy to conceive the libration of the water will raise another hill at *1*, leaving a valley at *2*; which valley will be communicated to *3*, *4*, *5*, etc. after the same manner, and for the same reason as the first valley; and this again will succeed another hill. And so there will be a continued succession of spreading hills and valleys, having their original in the successive hills and valleys in the spaces *1* and *2*, caused by the libration of the water.

But if we suppose that in the first place a valley (and not a hill) is made in the space *1*, then the first circle will be a hill, and not a valley. For the water being expelled out of *1* necessarily thrusts up the water at *2* and causes a hill there; the water at *2* subsiding, thrusts up the water at *3*, that the water at *4*, and so on. And then, there being the same reciprocation of the water at *1* and *2* as in the former case, causes the same succession of circular hills and valleys.

65. LEVER. Problem: To give the reason why the same force or weight upon a lever or balance has a stronger or weaker influence, according as it is further from or nearer to the center of motion. For instance, suppose that the weight D [Fig. 7], hanging from the end A of the balance *AB*, is *in equilibrio* with the weight *E* that is four times less, hanging at the other end of the balance at

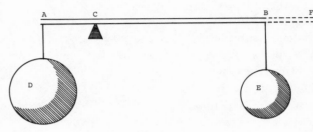

Fig. 7

four times the distance from the center of motion, C.

To solve this, we shall lay down the following proposition as most agreeable to the reason of man:

Prop. 1. The same force or power that, applied at a certain single moment, is sufficient to raise the greater weight D, is requisite to raise the weight E, which is four times less, four times as far. This is evident, because the effect is just equal, and what is wanting in weight in the lesser body is exactly made up in the distance raised. If there is requisite a greater force to raise the weight E four inches than one, as there certainly is,[6] for we suppose no continual repetition of the force but an application of it for a certain moment—if so, then I say there needs four times as much; for the weight resists the motion as well while the body is moving the second moment as the first, and as much the third and fourth, as the second.

Hence we may learn why the weight D will not sink, but hang *in equilibrio* with the lesser weight; because if it subsided it must raise the weight E four times as much as it fell itself, every moment of its fall. But in order to that, by the foregoing proposition, there would need a force sufficient to raise the weight D, that is, a force that is greater than the weight D. Wherefore, the weight D will not raise the weight E.

Corol. It necessarily follows hence that if the weight E be made in the least greater, it will descend; for it hung *in equilibrio* before. But the reason of this will appear better from the following proposition:

6. MS: "does."

Prop. 2. The supporting or holding up of a greater weight is an effect that is fully equivalent [to], and requires a force or power full as great as, the raising or carrying upwards a lesser weight. 'Tis exceeding evident, because if the least degree of force was added, it would carry upwards even the greater weight. Or we may take the proposition in more general terms, thus: the bare resisting a greater force is equivalent to the carrying a body against a lesser.

From hence it follows that if the lesser body E be made in the least heavier, or removed further from the center of motion, it will subside and raise the greater weight D: because, as has been shown already, 'tis not sufficient to raise it now; but if 'twas heavier or farther removed, the supporting of it would require more force than the raising it. Let the weight E be supposed to be removed to F, a fourth part of the former distance; and let the weight at the same time be made considerably lighter. 'Tis evident, by the foregoing proposition, that 'twould there remain, *in equilibrio* with the weight D. 'Tis therefore evident by this, that if it be removed without proportionably lessening its weight, it will sink; because the holding it up would require greater force than the raising it before.

[*Unnumbered Series*][1]

[1][2] The motion of the fixed stars backwards in the ecliptic, if it be not real but be caused by any motion in the earth, must necessarily be caused by a motion of the poles of the earth round the poles of the ecliptic, in a circle equal to the polar circles. For 'tis most certain, if this motion is in all the fixed stars in circles parallel to the ecliptic, then the polar star itself moves in a circle parallel to it, and that it moves round the pole of the ecliptic in a circle equal to the polar. But seeing the star itself stirs not, the apparent motion of it from the pole of the earth must be by the motion of the pole. For either the pole moves or the star moves, 'tis certain. Besides, it is certain if the plane of the equator moves, the poles move; but if the points of the intersection that this

1. This series of forty articles is written on three separately folded sheets of foolscap, MS pp. 21–32, at the end of "Natural Philosophy." JE did not number the articles, but Dwight printed most of them as an extension of the long numbered series (his "second series"). JE probably began this series in New Haven during the first year of his tutorship, and probably intended them as a continuation of the long numbered series.

2. Nos. 1–4 which fill MS p. 21 are written in a thick black ink similar to that in Miscell. nos. 132–41. The writing has deteriorated badly, especially where someone tried to erase a heavy pencil line which had been drawn from top to bottom through the center of the page.

plane makes with the plane of the ecliptic move, the plane itself moves if the ecliptic itself moves not. And the motion must be such as to cause the poles to move round the pole of the ecliptic in such a manner. And since in the ecliptic the stars move a degree in 70 years,[3] it follows that the pole of the earth will move quite round in this circle in 25,200 years.

From hence 'tis certain, if the fixed stars move not, that the earth has two rotations upon two different axes: one a diurnal, upon the axis that runs from the north to the south pole; another that is performed in 25,200 years upon an axis that runs from the one pole of the ecliptic to another; the last being about a mile in a year under the ecliptic, being perhaps about as fast as a snail would crawl; and might possibly be caused by some comet passing by the earth in the plane of the ecliptic. Now there would [be] exactly such a rotation upon the axis of the ecliptic by a comet near the earth, in the plane of the ecliptic, in its descent towards the sun. For the earth would be stretched something into the form of an oblong spheroid in such a case. And as the comet went along, 'tis evident that that end of the spheroid that was next to it would in some measure follow it, or be drawn after it, which would beget just such a motion.

[2] N. B. That the separation of heterogeneous rays in the rainbow is not at the reflection of the concave surface, but at the two refractions, going in and coming out. There is not a different reflexability, but only refrangibility.[4]

[3] Vid. ["Of Atoms," Prop. 2, Corol. 4][5] To shew how infinite knowledge, as well as strength, is necessary, either to give or to maintain the proper existence of one atom; viz., an infinite minute knowledge of parts in order to termination, figure and the relation of the parts of the surface.

---

3. Several computations of the rate of stellar motion had been made by 1700. Newton's determination, viz., 50^{II}, 0^{III}, 24^{IV}, was most widely accepted after *Principia*. William Whiston, however, is probably the source for Edwards' figures. He rounds Newton's annual figure to 50^{z} and estimates "that the Fixed Stars have in no wise gone forward from the beginning of *Aries*, but that *Aries* hath gone back from, or left, those Fixed Stars, and that in about seventy Years it goes backward, or towards the antecedent Signs, one Degree" (*Astronomical Lectures*, p. 18).

4. When JE wrote "Of the Rainbow" he apparently had not yet grasped this point, one of the most important of Newton's contributions to the science of optics. See above, p. 42.

5. In "Of Atoms," above, p. 214. JE did not complete his reference, but this passage is the one most likely to have been intended.

[4] It is undoubted that there is a vast abyss of water under us, above which the surface of the earth is stretched forth, and on which it rests; and [which] must undoubtedly be heavier than the matter of this upper shell. Undoubtedly also the springs and fountains are much caused [by] the ascent of this water in the chinks of the ground, steaming up by virtue of the central heat;[6] and therefore, that there is a communication between the abyss and the sea. But if it be by its own nature heavier than the earth, 'tis inconceivable how it should become lighter when it has ascended to the surface and is condensed in springs, and even as light as other water. And if it be so, how should any of this water ever return to mix with the water of the abyss again by any communication that the sea has with it, or any of the sea water in the room of it? For the great difference in the specific gravity will forever hinder any mixtion or communication. And at this rate, the abyss would in time be exhausted of its dense and heavy fluid, and filled with light in the room of it, or the world would be overflowed by a second deluge.

There is no other way, therefore, than that this water, when it is in the abyss, is heavier than earth; but when it is upon the surface, becomes as light as other water. And when it returns there again, or the water of the sea in the room of [it], it becomes as heavy as it was before; which can be no otherwise than compression. And if water be a body that is capable of any compression by any means, doubtless it is compressed by that prodigious force 'tis subject to by the weight of a body of water of four or five hundred miles thickness incumbent upon it. If we can't compress water but very little, or not [at] all, 'tis certainly only for want of strength. For all compounded bodies that have not an absolute plenitude are undoubtedly capable of compression; their particles can be squeezed nearer together, and closer one among another, if there be but force sufficient; especially water, which is so rare a body, so much rarer than many other mixed bodies, which yet we know have not a plenitude, as lead, gold and quicksilver. I doubt, therefore, but so great a force will be enough sufficiently to compress water.[7]

6. This opinion is offered by Rohault in *Physica* (1723 ed.), *Pars* III, *cap.* 10. Rohault offers no theory of the abyss, however.

7. Dwight, *1*, p. 53, cites these comments as showing that JE discovered the compressibility of water, long before that fact was experimentally established and communicated to the world by John Canton in "Experiments to prove that water is not incompressible," *Philosophical Transactions, 52* (1762), pp. 640–43.

I suppose no experiments that have yet been tried will prove but that such a force is sufficient to make water five times as dense and specifically heavy as the earth of this upper shell. And if it be so, it will be enough to support the weight of it, as we see the air here that is compressed supports many things that are perhaps a thousand times heavier than the air would be, had it liberty to expand itself. And seeing this body of earth is solid body, by this means the surface of it may be kept above the surface of the sea, though lighter than itself. For if quicksilver and oil be put in the same vessel, and a stone thrown in, the quicksilver may keep the top of the stone, it being solid, above the surface of the oil. Yea, 'tis possible that although the earth is much denser than the water in its natural state, yet that a body of water, by its own weight, may so compress itself as to bear the top of a column of earth above its surface. For instance, [Fig. 1] suppose *ABCD* to be a body of water, in which is a column of earth of equal height, *EF*. Let the water as far as *GH*, not half to the bottom, at a mean be lighter than earth, and below as much heavier. 'Tis manifest that the column of earth *EF* will float, and the top of it be lifted above water, because the column of the water, taken together from the top to the bottom, is heavier than the column of earth, and if the water be vastly deeper, so as to reach to *I*, 'tis all one.

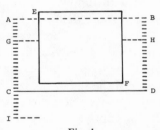

Fig. 1

But according to this hypothesis, 'tis manifest that if there be any passages or chinks in the incumbent earth, the water will ascend in them till it is even with the surface of the sea, but no higher; so that the chinks of this upper earth that have an outlet at the abyss are full of water, so far as to be even [with] the surface of the ocean. Not with salt water, for there is no need that the water of the abyss should be salt because it has a communication with the sea, for the water of the sea at a very great depth is found not to be salt.[8]

---

8. JE's source for this opinion is not known. Robert Boyle attacks the opinion, which he attributes to Aristotelians, who, he says, "vouch the testimony of Scaliger to prove that the Sea tastes salter at the Top than at the Bottom, where the water is affirmed to be fresh." See Boyle, "Observations," *Works*, 3, p. 765.

Julius Scaliger's *Exotericarvum exercitationem liber xv de Subtilitate* (1557 and later eds.), was apparently used by the earliest classes at Harvard (Morison, *1*, p. 226), but there is no evidence of its use at Yale.

[5][9] The pleasure the mind has by the senses arises immediately from an harmonious motion of the animal spirits, their appulse to the brain being in an harmonious order, consisting in a regular proportion of time, distance, and celerity. We know it is thus in one of the senses, to wit, hearing, which may lead us to think 'tis so in all the rest—especially considering that we find nothing that the mind loves in things but proportion. Pain is caused either by a motion of the animal spirits that is contrary hereto, or by a laceration and dislocation of the parts of the body, which are partly its destruction, which the mind abhors by reason of the law of union between soul and body.[1]

[6] 'Tis certain that when God first created matter or the various chaoses of atoms, besides creating the atoms, and giving of the whole chaos its motion, he designed the figures and shapes of every atom, and likewise their places; which doubtless was done with infinite wisdom, and with an eye to what should follow from the particular bulk, figure and place of every atom. And this he so ordered that, without doing any more, the chaoses of themselves, according to the established laws of matter, were brought into those various and excellent forms adapted to every of God's ends—omitting the more excellent works of plants and animals, which it was proper and fit God should have a more immediate hand in. So the atoms of the chaos were created, in such places, of such magnitudes and figures, that the laws of nature brought them into this form, fit in every regard for them who were to be the inhabitants.

[7][2] GRAVITY. That there is so strong a gravitation in little bodies is not only provable by reason and demonstration, but by every day's experience, innumerable ways, in liquors and solid bodies: the ascent of water upwards in glass, the spreading of wet in dry things up as well

---

9. US Nos. 5–23 on MS pp. 22–28 are all written in basically the same ink, of a light brown color with heavy black solids, that tended to bleed along pen strokes. The ink remains unusually uniform in color and consistency throughout these entries. The same ink and comparable hand are found in Miscell. nos. 142–94; the lighter shade of ink in No. 23 appears in Miscell. no. 178. From these correspondences, and based upon Shafer's dating of "Miscellanies," it is probable US Nos. 5–23 were written during JE's two tutorial years at Yale.

1. See also "The Mind," No. 1, below, pp. 332–38, and especially p. 336 (Sensible pleasure).

2. Immediately preceding this entry on MS p. 22 is another with the title "SATAN defeated," which JE apparently thought he was writing into his "Miscellanies"; he completed the article in that notebook (Miscell. no. 146), beginning there with the reference "vid. Natural Philosophy." This entry will be published in its proper place at the beginning of Miscell. no. 146, in the Yale ed. of JE's "Miscellanies."

as down, the immediate drinking up of water by tow, the adhesion of smooth things or things wet so that there may be no distance but what is filled up by water, and an infinite number of the like. In no other way can the suspension of quicksilver sixty inches high in a tube be accounted for, as 'tis known it will be suspended if the tube be thoroughly purged of all air and carefully turned up and steadily fixed;[3] but this way it may clearly, easily and fully be accounted for.

[8] Axioms. [1] If a thing is to come one of two or more ways, if it falls out one of those ways and not another, it will be because there is some reason why it should happen this way and not another. And in things that have happened, there is some reason why they have happened this way more than another. For instance, I say it is evident that if the body C [Fig. 2] be at rest, but is to move either towards A or B or D or E, if it moves towards E, it will because there was some reason why it should move towards E, more than why it should move towards A, B, or D.

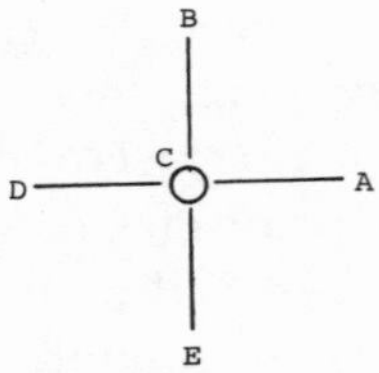

(2) Which necessarily follows from the former; when there is an equal reason why the thing should be each of the supposed ways, and it cannot be all, it will be neither. If it can be proved that there is equal reason why the body C should move towards either A, B, D, or E, it will move towards neither of them.

Fig. 2

(3) The same force will equally separate all bodies, or parts of bodies, conjoined with equal strictness, *caeteris paribus*. And that force that will not separate two bodies or parts of bodies will separate no bodies that are united with equal strictness, *caeteris paribus*. (This to prove that it holds in all atoms.)

(4) Nothing produces anything where it is not. There is no need of inserting the word "immediately" here; for in the sense of this axiom, that which immediately does a thing only properly doth it. For instance, when one body is thrown against another and causes that other body to move, in the sense of this axiom it was the body that was thrown that moved the other, and not the man that threw it. This axiom is evident, because it is a contradiction to suppose the body acts where it is not, or to say it is acting where it is not at all acting, or otherwise that it exerts itself where itself is not. 'Tis evident that if a

3. A phenomenon mentioned by Newton in *Optics*, Bk. III, Q. 31 (1706 ed.: Q. 23, pp. 336–37).

body has no existence in that space, that it is all one with respect to that space as if it had no existence at all. Or,[4] that axiom may be proposed thus: Nothing acts where it is not; or, nothing is acting where it is not at all.

Wherefore (5) if a body placed alone in a space, as for instance, the body *C* in the midst of the space *ABE* [Fig. 3], there being no other corporeal being in that space, if this body be at rest and afterwards begins to move, 'tis manifest that it is not moved by any corporeal being, but by a being not corporeal.

Fig. 3

Or, if the body *C* be held at rest, so that it cannot be moved, 'tis evident 'tis held there by an incorporeal being.

(6) For the same reason, if the two bodies *e* and *o* touching each other [Fig. 4] be touched by no other body, if the body *e* be held to the body *o* so that it cannot be moved away from it, 'tis evident that it is held there by an incorporeal being. For the body *o* cannot possibly act upon the body *e* so as to hinder it from moving away, for by Axiom 4, the body *o* don't act where it is not, but the body *o* is no further than its surface.

Fig. 4

And the case will be the same, let the bodies touch in one point, or in more, or by lines, or surfaces as the bodies *a* and *u* [Fig. 5]. If *u* cannot be moved towards *y*, it must be an incorporeal being that keeps it immovable, for *a* is present no farther than the plane *fm*, and therefore cannot possibly act upon *u*, which is beyond it, to hinder its being moved towards *y*.

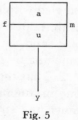

Fig. 5

[9][5] ELASTICITY may be explained after a yet different manner than by the violent motion of the particles, and I foresee must be: and first, I shall shew that it may be differently explained; and secondly, that although this intestine [motion] may be, and doubtless often is, a secondary cause of elasticity, yet that it

4. This addition is written in shorthand.

5. Between this and the preceding is an entry in shorthand which JE probably intended to be added to the list of rules on the cover of "Natural Philosophy"; JE seems not to have had that part of the MS at hand during this period. The item is presented above, p. 195, with those rules.

cannot be the first foundation of it, but that this motion itself must be explained from another elasticity.

(1) That the gravity of particles to other particles which they touch, or to which they are very near, may cause, and cannot but cause, elasticity; for if the touching particles tend exceeding strongly to each other as 'tis most certain they do, then if they are in the least separated, if not so far as to be out of the strength of the attraction, they will very strongly tend to move to each other to touch again; so that if by any force they are a little pulled asunder, if the force that holds them asunder be taken away, they will immediately with great violence rush together again: and that in most bodies whose particles are strongly united together, after such a separation they will with great force recover themselves.

And here I would take notice of two things that pretty much depend on each other: *1.* That the particles of a rare body, by this way of explaining union, may be much more strongly united than a dense one. For the strength of the union consists in the opposite position of the surfaces of the particles to each other; but there may be a great many particles in a little room, and yet their surfaces not lie appositely one to another. For matter of the quantity of a foot square may be so rarified as to be extended as big as the universe, and yet there shall not be one hair's breadth but what has some of that matter in it. And yet the body shall be perfectly hard, and no part of it movable by less than infinite stength; for it may be drawn out to such a fine wire that shall be a continued, uninterrupted, absolute plenum so folded, coiled and tangled within itself, and running every way backwards and forwards, as that not a part of space so big as a ray of light shall be without some of it, and yet it shall be what we call an atom, and the continuity or touching by planes shall be uninterrupted.

2. That the particles or atoms of bodies may be condensed, or thrust one in amongst another, and yet the union of the atoms shall not be much the stricter; because atoms, being infinitely hard bodies, their protuberances infinitely hard and their surfaces unalterable, they may be jammed in one amongst another, and yet their surfaces not adhere much more strictly one to another. Further, this perfect hardness of the atoms may hinder their being thrust in one amongst another, but will not hinder their being pulled asunder.

Now let the body *ABCD* [Fig. 6], whose particles have a firm union, be bent towards *D*. 'Tis evident, either that the particles at *B* are pulled further one from another than they were, or that the particles at D are more condensed together, or both. But, as we have said, the particles at D will not be so easily thrust nearer together, because of their stubborn nature, as the particles at B may be drawn asunder. 'Tis also evident that the particles at B that are drawn asunder, by tending to come together again, will tend to pull the ends of the body back again to, and so recover it to, its former straightness; which tendency is elasticity. And further 'tis probable, by what we have said already, that if the particles of D are thrust together, their tendency to each other will not be very much increased, so as to hold the body in

its bent posture, as the particles at B tend to pull it straight. But however that is, there is no need to suppose that the particles at D[6] are thrust nearer together, and 'tis probable the constitution of firm bodies hinders it. And certainly the constitution may be such as to hinder it much more than the pulling of bodies asunder; for 'tis certain that atoms, being infinitely hard, if they touch only by their prominences, they cannot be made to touch nearer, but

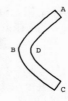

Fig. 6

may be drawn asunder. Wherefore 'tis certain that elasticity may be caused by this means: which is the thing we are proving. COHESION, ATOMS, vid. supra.[7]

(2) The second thing to be proved was that a rapid motion cannot be the first original of elasticity. For if we suppose that particles that are shut up in a little room are continually in a violent motion, and rebounding from side to side, yet elasticity is necessary in order to the maintaining of this motion. Otherwise, at the first stroke against the walls of the vacuity,[8] it would lose all its motion. There is necessary, therefore, another elasticity, in order to the maintaining of this motion; which being maintained by this elasticity, may in the aforesaid manner cause elasticity—and undoubtedly does in the atmosphere. Therefore, we see that, its motion being increased, its elasticity is increased with it.

Here we would note that we think no phenomena contradict what we

6. MS: "B."

7. JE probably intended "Cohesion" as another heading for the immediately preceding entry, and added the reference, "vid. supra," simply to call attention to the fact. On the other hand, if JE intended the reference to apply to an earlier entry in "Natural Philosophy," it would most probably be LS No. 20 (above, pp. 232–34).

8. JE's word is carelessly written, but the reading is confirmed by his use of "vacuity" in US No. 12 on "Ice."

have said of elasticity, arising from the tendency of separated atoms to a reunion with their fellows. For instance, that of the hammer and anvil: the hammer don't thrust the atoms quite from their fellows. If they did so a bruise would ensue, but the more it bruises, the less it rebounds; but does but just open and separate their surfaces, but not for so great a distance but that they immediately close again after the violence of the stroke is over. And so it is in the former instance. The particles of the body *ABCD* at *D* seem to be thrust together, yet they are not quite put out of their natural place, not so much but that their strong tendency to their fellows immediately brings them to the same place again. If they are quite dispossessed of their places, the body will not recover itself again, as we see if the body be too much bent. So that what alteration there is amongst the particles at *D* may help the elasticity, as well as the alterations of the particles at *B*.[9]

[10] Light. The rays of light, however small, may yet be so compounded of lesser atoms as that they may be very elastic bodies, and yet be so contrived by that gravity which is universal to them and all bodies that they may run together with celerity sufficient as to cause the motion of their reflection to be so rapid as is found.

[11] Elasticity. A body whose particles are firmly united cannot be smitten by another body so as to make an impression upon [it], but that the particles near[1] the surface where the impression is made will have their surfaces drawn from each other. For instance, let *ABCD* be the outmost range of particles of a body that before was round, but has an impression made by the stroke of another body at *B* [Figs. 7, 8]. 'Tis evident, that the particles at *B* will gape open inwards, as in the figure, and the particles at *A* and *C* will gape outwards; and that by their mutual attraction they will recover themselves again, and thereby bring the body *ABCD* to its former roundness: which will cast back the body that struck it with the same celerity as the surface at *B* recovers itself. Now 'tis probable that rays of light are particularly formed, by the curious hand that made them, for this elasticity.

[12][2] Ice; cold. Those nitrous particles that are thrust into the water don't keep them immovable after the manner of wedges, by filling up

---

9. MS: "C."

1. MS: "the particles near the particles near the surface."

2. Immediately preceding is an entry in shorthand, apparently intended for the list on the "Natural Philosophy" cover, where it will be found in this edition, p. 195.

the spaces between, so that they shall not have room to play and move freely amongst themselves.[3] For this hypothesis still leaves the matter inexplicable. For first, 'tis inexplicable how these wedges should thrust themselves in so fast, into a heap of particles so exceeding movable, that they can't be stirred at all. How these wedges should be of so happy a shape, and should so happily each of them find a vacuity amongst the vacuities of the water, exactly accommodated to their shape as to completely fill them up; so that of all these little, rolling, slippery [particles], none can stir at all, in so much that [that] which was before a liquid body shall not only be made something more solid, like clay, but should be so hard as not to give way at all without breaking. Let us suppose, for the easiness of conceiving, that the particles of water were as big as peas. Let the frigid particles be as big in proportion, otherwise having all the same qualities. Let these particles, a multitude of them, be hovering over this heap of globules in the air. 'Tis very probable that many of them would get in amongst the globules, so that perhaps they would not slip and roll one over another so easily for it; but it is inconceivable how these nitrous particles, being so hard, should so be accommodated to the angled vacuities, that all the vacuities should be so filled, that the heap of globules should be so hard as to bear a great weight or hard stroke without any impression being made in it. But it would be yet more strange if it was evident that there was more of vacuity now in the heap of globules than before, and yet none of the globules should have room to stir; which is the case in water, as all know, ice being lighter than water.

Fig. 7

Fig. 8

But this matter of freezing may be easily solved from the certain principles foregoing, of the strong attraction or gravity of particles one

3. According to one contemporary theory, the effects we refer to cold, e.g., congealing, freezing, etc., as well as the sensations of cold, are caused by hard, wedge-shaped, nitrous particles or salts, which penetrate among the particles of an object so as to prevent their free movement. (See Samuel Clarke's brief account in Rohault, *Physica*, Pars I, cap. 23, §54, n. 1.) Pierre Gassendi, on the other hand, maintained that cold is a positive quality belonging to certain "frigorific" atoms which penetrated objects to make them cold. In the following, JE urges a variation of the mechanistic thesis; only the cold-producing particles are plastic rather than hard, and so able to conform to the surfaces of other particles, attracting them together into larger masses.

to another. Wherefore, to solve the matter, we shall first lay down these following axioms:

Ax. 1. Since particles of matter tend to each other as we have shewn, 'tis evident that every part of the surface of a particle tends to touch the surface of the other, and would do, if it were not hindered by protuberances, or otherwise.

Ax. 2. Therefore, if a particle that is near to another particle be flexible, so that it accommodate its figure and surface to the surface of the particle attracting, it will so accommodate itself; and being thereby brought abundantly nearer, and touching in innumerable points, will (if it be denser), according to foregoing principles, cleave exceeding fast to it, and will not be easily separated from it.

Ax. 3. If one of these flexible particles lies between two or more particles, it will for the same reason accommodate itself to all their surfaces; and, filling up the vacuity, if it be not too big, will cleave fast to them all, and they all will cleave fast to that. How ever easily separable those particles were before, yet now they will all be held together by this. And if the vacuity be too big, what one particle can't do, two or more may.

Ax. 4. And if those particles are not flexible with such a flexibleness as leather and other bodies that are elastic and are easily capable of stretching and compression as well as impression, but with such a flexibleness as clay or lead,[4] a dead flexibility, without being capable of rarefaction, compression, or elasticity, the mass of particles that are congealed by it will be hard, and not elastic.

Ax. 5. If many of these particles were dispersed in the vacuities of a mass of particles otherwise movable, they would hold the whole immovable one amongst another.

Ax. 6. These particles will be capable of entering the smallest pores; for the same quality that capacitates them to accommodate themselves to the surfaces of bodies, makes them capable of being accommodated to pores of any figure or dimensions.

Ax. 7. If many of these particles, being of such a flexible nature, are hovering over an heap of very smooth particles, they will be drawn into their vacuities by the attraction of these particles after the

---

4. JE deleted "they will so cement and glue the particles together that [they] shall not only be not to be separated, but not easily to be much stirred. Now I suppose 'tis very possible that such particles may be that shall have such a sort of flexibility that they shall by their gravity accommodate themselves to the surface of bodies, and yet shall hold the bodies immovable enough amongst one another."

same manner as, and for the same reason as, water of itself ascends and is drawn into a very small glass tube.[5]

Ax. 8.[6] However flexible these bodies, by their own attraction to their own centers, to one another, or other particles, yet they may be so dense and their attraction so great, that a considerable mass of particles congealed by them shall be very hard; because the figure can't be changed or an impression be made without stirring the whole mass that is contiguous, and so contradicting the strong attraction of a multitude of these particles.

And after this manner I suppose ice is made. And the only thing that remains to be explained is how the freezing, which fills up so many of its pores, should yet make it more rare; which will not be difficult from the same principles. For according to those principles, it is not at all probable that the mass of water should be all congealed at once in one instant, so that every pore will be filled up with them at once; but that as these particles gradually work into the water, these particles [will] be laid hold on and locked together by parcels as the congealing particles get in, till at length the whole mass is made fast. The mass is stiffened by parcels, which parcels, being made hard and stubborn, will not accommodate themselves to the vacuities that shall be made by the invincible drawing of particles out of their seats by those frigid atoms: whereby a multitude of vacuities will unavoidably be made. Supposing a parcel of particles consisting of nineteen should be catched and fastened as they lie in this form, as in Figure 9. 'Tis evident that by the force of the attraction of the frigid particles that are between in their pores, frigid particles being supposed so flexible and pliable as we have supposed, that they will be drawn in such a figure as this (Fig. 10). And this may be done with invincible force, by Corol. [1] of Prop. [2].[7] And by this means, vacuities will be left in the places from whence these particles were drawn, except other particles of water come in their room. But perhaps the particles in the neighborhood are stiffening together at the same time, and instead of coming to fill

Fig. 9

5. The capillarity of glass tubes was reported by Robert Hooke in *Micrographia* (London, 1665), Obs. iv, pp. 10–11.

6. Axiom 8 is found written below the next paragraph of the essay. JE keyed it for insertion here.

7. In "Of Atoms," above, p. 213. JE left the blank spaces for a later insertion of the numbers of the proposition and corollary; evidently the portion of "Natural Philosophy" containing "Of Atoms" was not at hand when this article was composed.

up the vacuities made by the congealing of this parcel, they are drawn farther off themselves, and make the vacuity greater. Besides, the sides of the parcel, as it conforms itself to the figure (as Fig. 10), will unavoidably thrust out the neighboring particles from their places, which perhaps are congealed together into stiff parcels. Wherefore this thrusting must necessarily cause vacuities another way, by displacing of these now inflexible parcels of water, which cause the like displacing through the whole mass, as far as particles are contiguous.

Fig. 10

Let[8] us still represent the matter in a larger figure, for clearer illustration. Let us suppose the vessel *ABCD* (Fig. 11) full of particles of water

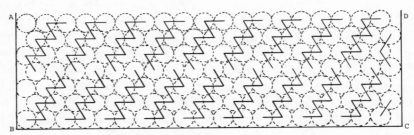

Fig. 11

into which the particles of cold get to glue them together by parcels of all manner of irregular figures and magnitudes. But let us suppose, for the present, that there are seven in a parcel, and that the parcels be those which we have marked out by the crooked lines connecting them. 'Tis all one as to the room they take up. Let them be taken in any other figure whatever. 'Tis evident that they will be drawn into this form (Fig. 12), and that they cannot lie in such a form without far greater vacuities than before; and that when they are brought into this form, the surface of the water must be considerably lifted above the brim of the vessel *ABCD*, and the water will take up much more room than before, let them lie as close as their figures will allow of. These vacuities will be greater or less, *caeteris paribus*, according as the parcels congealed are greater or less. But the vacuities will be much greater than what will

8. The remaining paragraphs of this essay were written somewhat later, beginning in the MS after the next two entries, but keyed to be added here.

be caused merely by their figures, for these parcels are stiff, and many of them tied, or rather glued, so one to another, that they will not be able to move freely and accommodate themselves one to another so much as their figure would allow of.

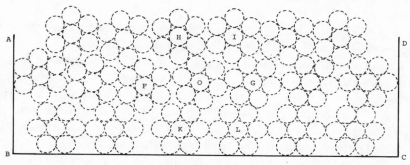

Fig. 12

But here I would note that there is no need at all, that we should suppose that the particles of water are exactly of such a form, or lie in such order as they are represented in the figure.

Now it is very evident from the foregoing principles that many of these parcels may be drawn into one, and often will, as we see many bubbles upon the surface of water run into one. For instance, the gluing particles that hold together the parcel O (Fig. 12) may happen to catch hold of the parcel G or F, and thereby they will be drawn into one. This will be, especially, upon an increase of cold, or the incursion of a great plenty of those particles. For whereas there was first no more particles than enough than to hold the distinct parcels together, greater plenty, by filling up the vacuities, will so glue them together as to make them run one into another.

Now 'tis certain that by the increase of cold there, however hard ice is and its parts immovable, yet an increase of cold does make an alteration in the disposition of its parts, for it makes ice swell and rise up like boiling water. And it's also certain that this running of several congealed parcels, according to these principles, would cause ice to swell and take up more room. If the parcels F, G, and O should run into one, and together form themselves into a globular figure, this could not be without the thrusting of the parcels H and I higher. Nor would the matter be made up by the subsiding of other parts, for the whole is too stiff and stubborn for some parts to come in the room of others that are moved.

It will also follow naturally and necessarily, from the same principles, that a great increase of cold will cause cracks in the ice. For suppose the parcels *H, I, K, L* and *O*, by an increase of frigorific particles, are drawn into one parcel. 'Tis evident this cannot be, without thrusting *F* and *G* and the parts on each side farther asunder. And if there be the force of many such parcels united near together or in a range, we may suppose the strength will be sufficient to make a crack in the ice.

From the same principles it is evident, that if this congealing matter gets amongst particles that are so fixed that they cannot be drawn out of their order that they lie in, it will condense them and draw them within closer bounds. For drawing together, it is evident, is the genuine effect of them; and that expanding and rarifying is accidental, and is caused only by changing the order and texture of particles by drawing together. Therefore, where there is this drawing together without changing of order, there will be condensing without rarifying. So it is agreed, that hard bodies shrink by cold.

And seeing the natural and genuine effect of this frigorific matter is to draw particles together, and rarifying is only accidentally caused by change in position that such a condensing [causes]; it is evidten that if these particles find water already far more rarified, and its particles more scattered than such a position would require, it will condense it, or draw the particles together, as in clouds and vapors. Cold's making of hard bodies brittle is also easily explained by the same principles. It is evidently done by taking away their elasticity. Before they would bend and not break, because the particles were not so immovable among themselves but that when the body was bent they could move something out of their places to avoid a total separation of one part from another, so that there should be no crack. But those particles, getting in, lock them so fast together that they are immovable.

Though I suppose there is a necessity of supposing some such particles in order to explain the freezing of water, yet I suppose no manner of need of it at all in order to explaining the consolidating of wax or tallow. For their particles seem to be of such a figure, that they tend of themselves to stick together, and that it is only the active particles of heat that keeps them from adhering one to another; as in metals, and in stones, sand and ashes, which are all capable of liquefaction. But if the particles of water are as apt to cleave together as those of wax, they will need as much heat to keep them asunder; but if not so much, why do they cleave so much more strongly, when they cleave at all? Yet, without doubt, frigorific particles do cause wax and tallow to be more solid than they would be of themselves.

From the foregoing principles I think it is easy to account for that painful sensation that is caused in us, which we call cold. For it is necessary that these particles should bind the fluids of the body and interrupt the motion of blood and animal spirits, which cause will contract, strain and pinch up the vessels, the veins and nerves, and most easily the capillary ones.

For this reason water is not so transparent when frozen, and fat when consolidated with cold, because the particles are so drawn together as to leave vacuities. 'Tis also easy and natural to suppose that those exceeding active particles which cause heat should disengage these particles from others to which they cleave, and thereby set them at liberty again.

[13] SOUND, or the cause of sound, is agreed to be a vibrating or a trembling motion of the air, consisting of quick and very sudden shocks or leaps of the air reciprocated. It is very easy to conceive why the meeting of two hard bodies[9] should cause such a trembling, correspondent to the trembling of those bodies; and why a body moving steadily though very swiftly in the air, should cause little such motion in the air. But we find that the most violent sounds are cause by the shutting or closing of a gap or vacuity that has been made in the air, which is very agreeable to reason that it should be so. For such a gap being made, it necessarily follows, from the weight of the incumbent atmosphere and its very elastic nature, that the walls of the vacuity should rush together with incredible violence, and that they should strike each other with great force; upon which the air that thus meets will be very much compressed, and will again, by reason of its elasticity, very suddenly and with violence expand itself again; but, according to the laws of the motion of elastic bodies,[1] with twice as great violence as the like quantity of air compressed on a solid body would expand itself. For then the air would be beaten back only by its own spring, but now by that and the spring of the air that it met. Let the air meet

9. JE deleted "bodies" when he struck out a long passage, to wit: "bodies should cause a sudden shock, for when the bodies, moving with a considerable degree of celerity, meet, the air that is between them must give an almost instantaneous leap to make way for them."

1. Perhaps JE means those formulated by John Keil in his *Introductio ad veram Physicam*, as reported by Harris in *Lexicon Technicum, I*, in the article "Elasticity."

at the plane *AB* [Fig. 13], and be by the shock much compressed. 'Tis evident that the air on the right hand of that plane will leap back towards the right hand of that plane by its own elasticity, but that the elasticity of the air that is on the left hand will impel it that way with equal force, and so the reciprocations will be repeated with great violence for a time.

[14] GRAVITY. Let it be a corollary to one of the former propositions:[2] hence it follows that two atoms or particles, however small, may, by the force of their gravity, cleave together with any finite degree of strength that can be mentioned, and yet not cleave with infinite strength. For seeing that when their surfaces touch each other they tend to each other with infinite strength; and the nearer two atoms approach to such touching, with so much the greater strength they tend to each other; and amongst the infinite numbers of degrees of nearness there is none but what is possible, all which are short of infinite but which [are not] touching: therefore it follows that there is no degree of finite tendency to each other but what the least particles are capable of. And it is no strange thing, if two very small particles should cleave together with such strength as to exceed the force of the motion of a comet in its perihelion, so that if all the force of that motion could be applied to those atoms, it shall not be able to rend them asunder; and yet a greater force shall be sufficient for it.

Fig. 13

[15] DENSITY. PORES. If we should not suppose that bodies that are very hard may yet not have the thousandth part of the space contained within its bounds filled with matter (though we should not suppose that the parts of the body had a particular disposition contrived for this end), but only the primigenial atom shall be supposed to be of all manner of figures indifferently and accidentally cast together in a heap: if so, we may suppose fairly that this heap will not be above half of its matter. Let those heaps constitute so many particles, of all figures indifferently, and yet consistent and solid enough for ought we know. Let these particles be cast together to constitute other particles. They also will leave half the space empty, even of them; so that half the space between these particles will be empty, and half within them, so that but a quarter will be full. If we suppose other particles to be made of these again, but an eighth part will be full; and by that time we have had ten such

2. In "Of Atoms," probably *Prop.* 2 (above, p. 213).

compositions, we shall not have the thousandth part of the space filled. N.B. This has been thought of before.

[16] EXHALATIONS. This to be joined with the manner of exhaling water.[3] I don't know whether any other sort of bodies besides water are exhaled after this manner. Oil, we know, may be exhaled, though very difficultly and slowly; and whether it be by bubbles I can't tell. I believe that nothing but what is liquid is exhaled, or caused by heat or the sunbeams to ascend in the atmosphere after this manner, by being rarefied so as to be buoyed up by the mere weight of the atmosphere; because the properties of a liquid body seem necessary to such a rarefaction. For in order to the being capable of such a rarefaction, it is necessary that the body should easily receive the impression of rays to diffuse it abroad, and to expand its parts; and yet the parts must so cling one to another, as wholly to exclude the circumjacent air from filling the places that were left empty by that expansion. For how much soever the parts are scattered, yet if air comes in between the scattered parts, there will not be less matter or weight within its bounds than in a like quantity of the rest of the air, and so the rarefied body would not ascend in the air.

And yet I am very far from thinking that there are none but liquid exhalations, or that there are no bodies but liquors are caused to ascend in the atmosphere by the sunbeams, or that liquors are the vehicles to all exhalations. I believe that particles of every kind are caused by the sunbeams to diffuse themselves all over the atmosphere after the same manner as odors are diffused, and those constituent parts of the atmosphere which we spoke of when treating of the atmosphere.[4] And 'tis easy to conceive that many of these particles, when a sufficient number of them happen to get together, that they should be capable of creating heat after the same manner as the particles of the sun, and to any degree of intenseness, and with any degree of suddenness.

[17] SUN. The sun appears to me to be a liquid body for three reasons: [1] That disposition of parts seems to me to be abundantly the most commodious for the generation and preservation of that most prodigious intestine motion of its parts, which is the cause of so great light and heat. If it be a hard solid body, then most of its parts are fixed and move not, and so partake of no intestine motion. We don't see any fire generated spontaneously and of itself in no such hard solid

3. That is, LS No. 58 (above, p. 256).
4. LS No. 57 (above, pp. 254–56).

bodies as iron and stone; but either in fine powders or liquors whose parts lie loose and [are] easily put into a violent motion, and are preserved therein the same way that it was generated. If the sun be a solid body, like stone or iron, and all those particles in which is this violent intestine motion in its pores, they would not have such fair play.

(2) I suppose that those alterations which are observed in the surface of the sun by a telescope don't so well agree with a body whose parts are solid and immovable, as with a body that has all its parts lying loose.

(3) Because we see no body but what would immediately become liquid with such a degree of heat, we see nothing but what will melt with a thousand times less degree of heat, and with heat far less subtle and penetrating. We see nothing but what will dissolve, and its parts loosen one from another by little and little, with a slow fire. What strange sort of body, therefore, must that be, which will endure such a degree of heat so many ages and not be dissolved.

[18] SUN. It may seem strange that the light of the sun, which we suppose to be nothing but the light [of] a great fire, should be so exceeding different from the light of all fires upon earth, that is, so much brighter and whiter.

(1) As to its greater brightness, it is nothing but what naturally results from the bigness of the sun two ways: *1*. The fires, being so big, will naturally and necessarily cause every part of this fire to be immensely hotter and brighter than otherwise it would. If a foot square of the sun be very hot of itself, it will be immensely hotter when 'tis encompassed round on every side with the same degree of heat for many thousands of miles. 'Tis certain that all the circumjacent parts of the fire add heat to that part of it according to the square of the distance, and so make it brighter as well as hotter. 'Tis evident if a space in the sun of a foot square be filled with particles that are very violently agitated of themselves, yet if to this agitation there be added the heat of many thousands of miles of a circumjacent fire, they will be more agitated. And therefore those particles that are sent out will leap forth so much the more briskly; that is, the light and heat will be so much the greater. *2*. What will naturally exceedingly promote the light and heat is the prodigious pressure of the sun's atmosphere, which is incomparably greater than that of the earth's atmosphere. And however the atmosphere next to the sun be very rare, by reason of the prodigious heat to rarify it, yet the *renixus* is never the less for that. If action and

reaction be equal, we know that the *renixus* of the air promotes light and heat. Thus we see fire is extinguished by the withdrawing of air.

(2) As to the whiteness of the sun's light, Sir Isaac Newton has demonstrated that it consists in a proportionate mixture of rays of all colors. And by what has before been said, redness and yellowness are caused by rays being of greater bulk. And we see that the light of culinary fire, and of candles, is reddish and yellowish, consisting mostly of the bigger sort of rays; and seeing the sun's rays are white, it must be because there is a greater proportion of the finer rays of blue and green. And this also will be the natural effect of the prodigious bulk and greater heat of the sun. The more violent the agitation and repercussion of the particles is, the more effectually will their parts be separated, and the rays be made fine. We know this does whiten rays by experience, for we see the more glowing and hot a fire is, the more white is its light.

But there will ensue no manner of difficulty, if we suppose that the particles of the sun are made at first finer, and the rays therefore whiter. We see brimstone burns blue, and coals red; and why may there not be a body that has a due mixture of both to cause white?

[19] SEA. The saltness of the sea will not seem a matter difficult to us if we consider:

(1) That the earth has innumerable veins, and beds, and parcels of fossil and mineral matter that is capable of being dissolved by and mixed with water.

(2) And seeing the sea covers and washes and soaks so great a part of the world, it is impossible but that a very good number of those veins and beds should be soaked and washed by the water of the sea.

(3) Some of those fossils will of themselves dissolve in water, and mix with it; and especially salt, perhaps more than any other.

(4) Some of these particles, if they be separated and mixed with water, will again precipitate, and the water will in time cleanse itself of them. But salt never will, but if it lies at the bottom of water, will of itself ascend and diffuse itself all over the water, and will not precipitate again. For if it should precipitate, its nature must be changed: what else should cause that which before, of itself, ascended and diffused itself in water, now to precipitate and separate itself from the water? And perhaps no other particles that are to be found in any considerable plenty in the earth but salt is of this nature; that will of themselves diffuse themselves in water, and so continue without precipitating again, or gathering at the top, or some way separating. Other particles

may so do because they are united to particles of salt, as the particles of alum, and other things that very much consist of salt particles; but yet 'tis probable that in length of time those other particles, being disengaged from the salt, may precipitate or ascend and leave only pure salt.

(5) It must be considered that salt will, of itself, dissolve and mix itself with water to such a degree, that the water is as it were satisfied. And then how much salt soever is thrown in, it precipitates and refuses to mix with the water.

(6) It follows from these considerations that except the water of the sea be so full of salt that it can hold no more, all the salt that ever happens to mix with the water of the sea will be there retained.

(7) It follows that if the water of the sea be not satisfied with salt, or has not as many salt particles as it can hold, that the water of the sea could never come at salt enough to saturate it; and that though all the salt that the sea washes, and all the salt particles that ever were any way carried into the sea, is now mixed with the water of the sea, yet there is not enough to saturate it; inasmuch as it retains all that it gets till it be satisfied.

(8) It may be considered that besides the salt which is diffused in the sea from these beds which the sea washes, it holds all the salt particles that are carried into it by all the rivers; which, though they should be but a few in a little time, yet, because the sea discharges itself of them no more, but the water when it returns by exhalation or otherwise leaves it behind, in whole ages they would carry in enough to make the sea salt. For there are a multitude of salt particles in the upper mold of the earth, as appears, in that plants have so much salt in their constitution. Rivers must needs bring a multitude of these, especially in times that they overflow their banks. Great quantities must be carried into the rivers by rains and the melting of snows, so that 'tis impossible but that the sea, in process of time, should be salt.

[20] THUNDER. 'Tis remarkable of thunder how long one part of the sound will be heard after another, when 'tis evident that the sound is made all in an instant by the lightning which continues no longer. This arises from the length of the stream of lightning, whereby one part is a great deal further from us than another, so that the sound is longer coming, is a great while coming successively. Hence 'tis that in claps of thunder that are near us, the first noise that we hear seems to be very near the earth, and then it seems to go further and further

from, and the last will be a murmuring up in the clouds. For although the noise that was made in the clouds and the noise near the earth was made together, as at an instant, yet that in the clouds is much further, and therefore is longer coming, and is a much lower sound when it comes.

The rapid vibration of the air so jars and jumbles, breaks and condenses the bubbles of the cloud whence it is, that soon after hard claps of thunder, rain falls in greater plenty.

[21] SENSE. 'Tis not probable that when the parts of the body are touched, that the animal spirits that were in these parts of the nerves go quite to the brain before the soul perceives; but that motion is continued to the brain in the tubes that contain the animal spirits, as motion in a tube full with water. If the water at one end moves never so little, the motion is continued quite to the other end, or as the motion given to the blood in the arteries by the pulse of the heart is communicated all over the body.

[22] HALO. The reason why there commonly is a circle about the sun or moon a little before falling weather, and not at other times, is because the cavities of the bubbles when preparing for rain are lessened, the internal air losing its agitation and heat; and thereby the skin is necessarily made thicker: from whence it necessarily follows that a greater proportion of rays will be refracted. When the skin is very thin there are but very few rays but what go twice through the skin. We have shown that only those that don't go through it at all are the rays that constitute the circle.[5]

[23] COLORS. We have already supposed that the different refrangibility of rays arises from their different bulk.[6] We have also supposed that they are very elastic bodies. From these suppositions, the colors of natural bodies may be accounted for,[7] that is, why some particles of matter reflect such a sort or sorts of rays, and no other. The different density of particles, whence arises a different attraction, and together with their different firmness, will account for all. Some bodies have so little of firmness, and so easily give way, that they are able to resist the stroke of no rays but the least and weakest and most reflexible rays. All the other rays that are bigger, and therefore their force not

5. See "Of the Rainbow," below, pp. 298–301.
6. In LS No. 46, above, pp. 239–41.
7. JE included "may be accounted for" in a longer deletion.

so easily resisted, overcome the resistance of the particles that stand in their way. Such bodies therefore appear blue, as the atmosphere or sky, smoke, etc. Again, 'tis known that the most refrangible rays are most easily attracted, that is, are most easily stopped or diverted by attraction; for as has been already shewn, refraction and reflection from concave surfaces is by attraction.[8] Because, therefore, that the most refrangible rays are most diverted by refraction and easiest reflected inward from the surface, and most diverted by passing by the edges of bodies, it follows that attraction has most influence on the most refrangible rays.

'Tis also evident that the particles of bodies that are the most dense have the strongest attraction. The particles of any body therefore may be so dense, and attract so strongly, as to hold fast all the lesser and more refrangible rays; so that they shall none of them be reflected, but only the greater rays, on whom the attraction of these particles can have less influence. Hereby the body will become red.

And as for the intermediate colors, the particles of a body may be so dense as to hold all the most refrangible rays, and may yet not be firm enough to resist the stroke of the least refrangible. Hereby the body may become yellow or green or of any other intermediate color.

Or, a body may be colored by the reflection of a mixture of rays. The body's particles may be able to reflect three or four sorts of rays, and have too strong an attraction to reflect those rays that are less, and too weak a resistance to reflect the bigger rays. Or, the color of a body may be compounded of reflected rays of very different degrees of refrangibility and not reflect any of the intermediate colors, by reason of its being compounded of very heterogeneous particles, having a very different degree of density and firmness. Or, the particles of a body may be firm enough to reflect all sorts of rays, and yet have so little attraction, and to hold none, that the body will be white. Or, a body may be compounded of particles having so little resistance as to reflect no rays, of so great density as to hold all, or so full of pores as to drink in all. Then the body is black.

Or, the particles of bodies may have pores and hollows that may be big enough to let in the least rays, and yet not the rest; so that the pores of particles may have much to do in the causing of colors.

The blue of mountains at a distance is not made by any rays reflected from the mountains, but from the air and vapors that is between us and them. The mountain occasions the blueness, by intercepting all rays

8. See SS No. 1, above, p. 219.

that would come from beyond to disturb that color by their mixture.

It may therefore seem a difficulty why the atmosphere all round by the horizon don't appear very blue, seeing 'tis evident that the atmosphere reflects chiefly the blue rays, as appears in the higher parts of the atmosphere by the blueness of the sky, and near the earth by the blueness of mountains, and the redness or yellowness of the rising and setting sun. It would therefore seem that the atmosphere should appear most blue where no rays are intercepted by mountains, because the atmosphere beyond the mountain reflects blue rays, as well as on this side. Therefore, it seems that there would be more blue rays come to our eyes where none were intercepted by mountains, and consequently, that the most lively blue would be there. And so it would be, if blue rays came to our eyes in the same proportion as they are reflected. But most of those blue rays that are reflected by those parts of the atmosphere that are at a great distance are intercepted by the intermediate air before they come to our eyes (for the air, by supposition, intercepts them easiest), and only those few yellow rays and less reflexible rays, that are reflected by the air, come to our eyes. Whence it comes to pass that the atmosphere near the horizon don't appear blue, but of a whitish yellow. And sometimes, when it is filled with more dense exhalations that can reflect less reflexible rays, still it appears a little reddish.

[24]⁹ CLOUDS. A thing that I have not seen determined with respect to the clouds is their being terminated by such even and distinct bounds, especially in those clouds that we call thunder clouds. The clouds are nothing else but vapors that are drawn up from all parts of the sea and the earth; and one would think should be scattered everywhere in the air indiscriminately, so as to thicken the whole upper region of the air. Or if the air were thickened by them in one place more than another, by reason that a greater number of vapors are drawn off from some parts of the earth than other; yet, they flying loose in the air, one would think they should be terminated very gradually, growing thinner and thinner, by little and little, till at last it should be so thin that it cannot be discerned. But instead of that we see the clouds terminated by very

---

9. US Nos. 24–40 are written on MS pp. 29–32, the last of the three separately folded sheets that contain the unnumbered series. Comparisons of hand and ink show they are chronologically parallel with "Miscellanies" entries between 180 and about 450. JE began writing on what is now the second recto of the sheet, then on the first recto and verso, and ended on the second verso. The entries have been numbered here in their chronological order, not their physical order on the pages. US Nos. 24–27 were probably written in 1726, the last months of JE's Yale tutorship, or in the first months of his Northampton pastorate. US Nos. 39 and 40 were probably written in late 1729 or 1730.

distinct surfaces and bounds. They are extended thus far, and then cease at once, and all beyond is clear air. Sometimes, indeed, the air is so universally thickened, as when halos or perihelias appear, but afterwards these vapors gather into distinct heaps and thicker clouds.

I don't know that this can be explained any other way than by the mutual attraction of the parts of the vapor, that they thus run together, and make such distinct heaps. The only difficulty is how, according to the laws and just proportion of gravitation, the attraction of such exceeding small parcels of matter to each other should be great enough. To explain this, to this I answer, that the gravitation need to be but exceeding small to make these parcels to draw nearer and nearer together so fast as is needful to suppose. They do it when they hang so free in the air, where the air is so thin and they so high, and their mutual attraction so little hindered by the attraction of other bodies. If we suppose that bubbles that are at the distance of an hundredth part of an inch move so fast towards each other as to get together in five or six hours, it will be enough.

When there is a very still and calm air, and the vapors are ascended very high where they are more at liberty, we see them collected into parcels nearly of an equal bigness and at an equal distance, so that the heavens appear checkered with them. This is the very natural effect of this mutual attraction. After the same manner, when we breathe upon glass, though at first the vapor is everywhere equally spread over the glass, yet by their mutual attraction they presently run into such like parcels.

[25] POSTULATUM. The attraction of small bodies is so much greater than the attraction of great bodies, according to the quantity of matter in them at the same distance from the surface of each, as the squares of the distance of the parts of the small body are less. The parts of small bodies attract bodies nigh to them immensely more than corresponding parts of great bodies, because the parts of a small body may lie so much nearer to the body attracted. Therefore small bodies attract bodies near their surface with immensely greater strength, according to the quantity of matter that is in them, than great bodies, supposing they are equally dense.

But by the Prop.[1] the minute particles of bodies have, commonly, vastly more matter in proportion to their dimensions than great bodies, and therefore will attract abundantly more for that reason.

1. JE might have been thinking of his N.B. following Prop. 1, Corol. 5 in "Of Atoms," above, p. 212. See also US No. 15, above, pp. 278–79.

[26] THUNDER. I think this is a meteor by far the most wonderful and least explicable of any whatsoever. But that we may make some approaches to the knowledge of the true nature of it, we shall lay down these following propositions:

(1) The streams of lightning are not caused by any solid burning or red hot mass of matter, exploded with such swiftness as to cause it to appear as if there were one continued stream of light; nor are the effects of lightning caused by the violent stroke of any such solid mass. For if lightning were such a body projected, it would be projected according to the laws of projected bodies; whereas the path of the lightning is exceeding far from it, being very crooked and angled. If lightning were a solid body, projected from the cloud at *A* [Fig. 14] towards *E* with such a prodigious celerity, [would] it proceed according to the direction *A* very nearly [to *E*] and turn short at *E* in the free air, and so at [*F*,]*B* and *C*? For when it is projected with such a prodigious force, it must also be a prodigious force that must change the course of it so short, and not the force of the free and yielding air. But if any should suppose that this change of the course of the lightning might be caused by some very violent eruptions of fire at those angles where the course is changed that give the thunder bolt a new projection: to this I say that the fiery stream of lightning is smooth and even; but if there were any such new eruptions they would be seen by an[2] extraordinary expansion of the light in those places. But what proves that this cannot be the reason of the crookedness of the path of the lightning is that as the flash of lightning is repeated once or twice, however crooked and angled the path is, yet it is every time the same. A stream of lightning darts from the clouds two or three times over, and every time exactly in the same path; and sometimes there is a continued stream for some time with a tremulous motion. Now if these repeated flashes were one bolt exploded after another, and the reason of its changing its course be new eruptions of fire, how should every bolt proceed so exactly in the same path? And further, the effects of lightning upon earthly bodies can in no wise be accounted for by the violent projection of a

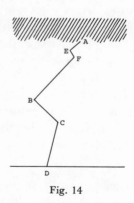

Fig. 14

---

2. A small fragment with one or two letters of JE's word is broken off at the margin, leaving only the final letters "nd." The word was probably "and," though Dwight reads "a sudden and."

solid mass, and do plainly show that they are not produced by such a cause; there is no such effect as is caused by the explosion of a cannon ball. It is not worth the while to stand to particularize, for 'tis exceeding evident that none of the effects of lightning can arise from any such cause.

(2) Nor[3] are those streaks of lightning caused by a vein of combustible matter's taking fire, and the fire's running from one end of the vein to the other almost instantaneously. This would not produce any of those effects which are caused by lightning, except we should suppose that these veins enter into the hearts of trees, rocks and metals, and bodies of animals. If it were, it would be a wonder that the lower ends of these veins never took fire from fires that are upon the earth.

But (3) lightning seems to be this: a parcel of almost infinitely fine combustible matter, that floats in the air, that takes fire by a sudden and mighty fermentation, that is some way promoted by the cool and moisture and perhaps attraction of the clouds. By this sudden agitation this fine matter is driven forth with a mighty force one way or other, which way it is directed by the circumstances and temperature of the circumjacent air; for cold and heat, density and rarity, moisture and dryness have almost an infinitely strong influence upon the fine particles of matter. This matter is thus projected, still fermenting and to the same degree, dividing the air as it goes, and every moment receives a new impulse by the continued fermentation. And as its motion received its direction at first from the different temperature of the air on different sides, so its direction is changed according to the temperature of the air it meets with, which renders the path of the lightning so crooked. The parts are so fine and are so vehemently urged on that they instantaneously make their way into the pores of earthly bodies still burning with a prodigious heat; and so instantly rarefying the rarefiable parts of earthly bodies that they are shivered to pieces, and the parts of metals dissolved in a moment, and sometimes bodies are something bruised (that is chiefly by the beating of the air that is with great violence driven every way by the inflamed matter).[4]

3. JE originally wrote, and then deleted, "(2) Nor is it any fume or vapor, or a multitude of fine particles of matter that exploded with that prodigious swiftness as to hold its way quite down from the clouds through the resisting air, and so as to shiver things to pieces on the earth. And though 'tis possible that even the single particles may possibly be moved with that degree of swiftness by Ax.[?], yet 'tis not so here. In the first place 'tis altogether inconceivable what should be the cause of such a prodigious swift motion in fine particles."

4. Charles Morton's discussion of lightning in *Compendium Physicae* was probably the source and stimulus for this entry. In JE's own copy, "A System of Physicks extracted out of Mr.

[27] SOUND that is made by the collision of solid bodies is not made by the sudden start of the air from between the closing parts of those bodies, but that the vibration of the air is begotten by a vibration in the parts of the bodies themselves, it is evident; because if the body that is smitten be set upon another, the sound will be like that of the body that it stands upon: which can be for no other reason, than that the vibration is communicated to the parts of that body, and from them to the air. So from the communication of sound in a long stick of timber: if we lay our ear at the further end when it is struck, the sound will seem to be made there, which is doubtless from the communication of the vibration through the parts of the timber.

[28] SUN. The interior parts of the sun are compressed with immense force by the parts incumbent, incomparably more than the interior parts of the earth by the incumbent earth: for the quantity of incumbent matter is supposed to be above 60,000 times greater and the same quantity near ten times so heavy,[5] and the incumbent weight has its full force upon the parts subjected, being kept loose and fluid by the heat. The interior particles of the sun, being therefore pressed together with such prodigious violence, we may suppose will be ground all to pieces into particles of the finest sort. All the particles are so hard and solid, that so great a force can break them no more: doubtless, as hard, fine and as solid as particles of fire and rays of light can be supposed to be; and perhaps, therefore, every way of the same sort, and fitted for the same motions, and to produce the same effects. By their being made so fine and pressed together with such violence, they must needs, to the utmost, be exposed to each other's force, whether attracting or repelling; whence will arise a vehement conflict, and a fermenting and agitation sufficiently violent will ensue to make that prodigious heat and light, and will be constantly preserved by the same pressure. And the rays being so exceeding fine, thence it may arise that the light of the sun is so white. We many ways find that even the interior parts of the earth do diffuse a heat, though not sufficient in such wise to dissolve and

---

Morton, his Body of Physicks," lightning is explained as a meteor composed of steams of sulphur and nitre, the ingredients of gunpowder, which ferment and generate heat; this draws together water vapor to form a thick cloud. As the heat increases these vapors ignite, and the fire makes its way through the cloud. Thunder is caused by the separated parts of the cloud falling against each other again after the fire has passed. Next, the water vapor, being no longer held up by the heat of the flame, descends in a shower of rain. (MS Partridge, cap. 12, pp. 206–07).

5. JE probably used the figures presented by Whiston in *Astronomical Principles of Religion*, pp. 14–25.

inflame the whole globe; but it may be because the pressure is not sufficient that the planets are not globes of fire, as well as the fixed stars.

[29] MOON atmosphere is so very thin, that in their long days they might not be too hot, so thin a fluid not supplying matter adapted to that agitation and vehement motion which is heat.[6]

[30] WINTER. The reason why there are more frequent and violent winds in winter than summer is because the air, by reason of cold, hangs together and don't give way but in a body.

[31] GRAVITY. If there be anything that makes us apt to seek more for a reason of gravity than solidity, 'tis because solidity is a quality so primary that the very being of the thing depends on it. If we remove the idea of it, there remains nothing at all that we can conceive. But we can conceive of something existing without thinking of gravitating at a distance. They are both of them essential and primary qualities, but there is this difference: the one is essential in order to the very existence, the other in order to the harmonious existence, of body. Though gravity itself between the continuous parts is necessary in order to the existence, the mind does not so intuitively see how. But yet gravity is a quality more primary in these respects, and more essential, than mobility is, which none seek a reason for or in the least question to be a primary quality of matter.

[32] RAIN. The reason why the winds that blow from the sea coasts bring rain is not only because they are more impregnated with watery vapors, for such winds will thicken the air with clouds in regions very remote from the sea, as soon as they begin to blow, before they can possibly bring any vapors so far. And besides, if that were the only reason, it would always rain in the midst of the ocean. But the reason seems to be this: when the wind blows from the sea towards the midland parts, the stream of the air is uphill, as it is when the wind passes over a mountain. The vapors are lifted so high that the air is too thin to support them. You may see the reason of it plainly thus: when the atmosphere is *in equilibrio* upon the continent AB [Fig. 15], the regions of the air lie thus parallel, as CD; so that when the wind blows from B (the sea coast) towards A (the midland) the vapors are carried continually from a lower and more dense medium to a higher and thinner

6. Whiston compares the atmosphere of the moon with that of the earth in its antediluvian state (ibid., pp. 68–69).

that is too thin to
support them. But on
the contrary, when
the wind blows from
A to *B*, the vapors
ben't at all hoisted,
but carried into a

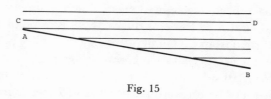

Fig. 15

thicker region that is better able to support them, and then it's fair
weather.

[33] ATMOSPHERE, ITS QUALITIES. That different quality of the air in
some particular regions or towns at particular times, that sometimes
causes some mortal distemper to rage in such a place, that is not a
catching distemper, where other places not far off are free (the winds
every day pass over 'em that removes the whole air out of that town a
great many times in a day, and scatters it to many other places), may
arise from noxious poisonous vapors and steams that are breathed out
at or near such places from the subterraneous caverns of the earth,
through the various vents and breathing places that are everywhere in
the upper shell of the earth, such as springs and wells and other unseen
chasms. In the times of earthquakes, they say they can smell sulphur,
which must be by the steam of it coming up through these secret vents.

[34] MOON. There is a very evident token of design and providence
in the exact adjusting of the diurnal and periodical revolution of the
moon. For although the figure of the moon is something oval, so that
the diameter of the moon which if prolonged passes through the earth's
center is a little longer than the other diameter that is perpendicular to
it by about 187 feet,[7] so that the attraction of the earth by this means
would preserve this exact equability notwithstanding very small disturbances, yet, except the forces that first gave the moon these revolutions had been very exactly equable, this small inequality of the diameter would in no wise have kept the same face of the moon turned towards
us, nor would it have ever reduced the revolutions nearer to an equality than they were at first. For except the disproportion had been almost infinitely small, it would have been sufficient to turn the moon so
that every side should be towards us, and the diurnal revolution would

7. The figure of 187 feet is given by Newton in the 1713 edition of *Principia*, Bk. III, prop.
28, prob. 19, p. 432 and by Whiston in *Newton's Mathematick Philosophy*, p. 379. In later
editions of the *Principia*, and in other presentations of Newton's system, the figure given is
186 feet.

have been accelerated every time the longer axis of the spheroid began to be turned towards the earth so as to point to it, and retarded when it turned from it. Though this exact equality of these two motions be of no great use to us as we know of, yet probably it is of great use to them, for if all sides were in its revolution turned towards the earth, the seas, if there be any, would be raised 97 feet high:[8] which tide would probably be very destructive to the surface of that planet.

[35] Lens about the sun. That vast lenticular haze or mist which appears about the body of the sun, it seems to me probably to arise thus: the effluvia that are carried off from the opaque bodies of the solar system, and especially from the comets by them, being carried beyond the attractions of the globes they proceed from and coming under the government of the sun's attraction, these particles, by virtue of the force impressed upon them while they adhered to the globes they came from, conjunctly with that that carried them off, proceed to revolve about the sun.[9] And their motion being gradually lessened by the resistance of the ether, and so their orbits are gradually contracted, and they gather up about the sun, though their motion is retarded so gradually that it's a long while before they come quite down to the sun's body. And the reason why the planes of most of their orbits are in or near the plane of the zodiac is this: for although the planes of the orbits of the comets cut the plane of the zodiac at all angles indifferently, so that we suppose the planes of the orbits of these effluvia are at first inclined to the zodiac at all angles indifferently, yet they become less and less inclined to it by means of the motion of the ether which gradually destroys that inclination. For the planets, by their continual revolutions, drive and draw the ethereal matter round with a motion parallel to theirs.

For one planet, by means of its attractions, and by means of the repelling nature of the particles of ether, whereby, like the air, they repel and keep at a distance one from another; I say by these means one planet moves a vast part of the ethereal matter. The diurnal revolution of the sun, also conspiring with the planets, makes the whole go round in a vortex parallel to the zodiac, and it's easy to conceive how this should gradually bring the revolutions of the dispersed particles we are speaking of nearer and nearer to the zodiac. Let *AB* [Fig. 16] be the

8. JE's error. The figure given by Newton, and repeated by Whiston, is 93 feet.

9. JE's sentence is grammatically incoherent. The deletion of two conjunctions, "and" before "being carried beyond the attractions," and "and so" before "these particles, by virture of" gives the grammatical form presented here.

plane of the ecliptic. Let *CD* be the plane that one of these particles first begins to revolve in, about *S*, the sun. 'Tis plain that the ethereal matter, turning round everywhere parallel to *AB*, when the particle is in that part of its orbit towards *D*, will hinder its going far off from the zodiac as it did before, and will a little drive it up towards *B*; and so, when it comes in that part of its orbit about *C*, will bring it nearer to *A*; and so will continually make its revolution to be nearer the zodiac.

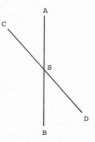

Fig. 16

These things I suppose are certain about this misty lens: 1., that it is not any reflection or refraction of the atmosphere because, when it appears before the sun rises or after it sets, it don't always appear perpendicular to the horizon, but always according to the zodiac. Therefore, 2., it must be a reflection of the sun's light from some matter that really encompasses the body of the sun.

[36] WINTERS are very useful upon this account, that the frost loosens the soil every year, which otherwise would bake down very hard.

[37] SOUND. The loudness of many sounds doubtless arises from the continualness of them. That is, let pulses of the same degree be continued or constantly repeated in the air and on the organ every successive moment. The sound won't only be longer but abundantly louder than if only one of these pulses smote the organ and ceased; that is, provided these pulses are repeated so quick that the impression made upon the organ by one pulse don't cease till another comes, or so quick that several of them smite the organ before the mind can perceive any succession or while one idea remains unaltered in the mind before it has time to grow old or perish in any degree. The reason in both cases is very plain. For if the impression of one pulse remains upon the organ till another comes, the new impression being added to the old, the whole impression must be greater. And if many pulses affect the mind before the mind can perceive any succession, and during the time that one idea or mental impression remains unvaried in the mind, then there will be the addition of several impressions together, which must be stronger than one alone. If three sounds be made, or three pulses be made, upon the air and ear, in so little time that the mind has not the

least sense of succession and seems to be all perfectly at once, then it will be all one to the mind as if them three sounds had been made really at once, and the sound will be as much louder than one of those sounds alone as three joined together would be louder than one of them.

Corol. 1. The shrillness of the sound of a bell arises very much from this cause. There is a continuance of pulses, exceeding quick, repeated one after another, answerable to the vibrations of the metal. And perhaps one of those vibrations singly would not make a louder noise than a rap with a staff upon a piece of wood, that yet is not an hundredth part so loud as the ringing of the bell.

Corol. 2. The loudness of thunder arises also very much from hence, for the lightning that breaks forth from the cloud and comes so instantaneously down to the earth smites the air successively all the way. And if sound came as quick as the light, the sound would all seem to be together in a moment, but because the places from whence the sound comes are gradually further and further off, and so the sound comes to us successively, but not so slow but that the stroke of the lightning upon the air for a long space seems to come to us at once. It may be that in the loudest claps of thunder, if we only received the impression that the lightning made in going one foot and were not reached by the impressions made in the rest of its course, it would not be a quarter so loud as the report of a pistol.

[38] I believe all fluidity arises from repulsion.

[39] Year. The wisdom of God appears in making the year of such a length, because if the year were much shorter there would be very little of a regular distinction of seasons by cold and heat. Before the air and earth would have lost the heat of the summer sun, the sun would be in the Tropic of Capricorn, and before we should have got over the cold of the sun's absence in winter, the sun would be again over our heads, and so the seasons would be confounded.

[40] Comets. Light. Fire.[1] The use of comets seems to be by their effluvia, which go off from them in their tails continually, but especially in their perihelion, to feed the sun with matter suitable to be converted into rays of light, to repair the waste of such particles by the vast profusion of light which it daily emits. They are sent out of the atmosphere

---

1. JE added the two headings "Light. Fire," at the top of the entry after it was written. The entry is almost certainly contemporary with that on comets in "Wisdom in the Contrivance of the World," in which JE cites Henry Pemberton's *View of Newton's Philosophy.* See below, p. 309.

of the comet, not as rising by the weight of the circumambient ether
(for that has been demonstrated to be so small and so near to nothing
that 'tis not supposable that it can be by any such means), but by the
force or attraction of the emitted rays of the sun which, passing through
the atmosphere of the comets, by their attraction draw after them
continually those particles of which the tail is made up. The rays that
pass by very near them act upon them by their attraction and set 'em
into a motion from the sun parallel to the line of the motion of the
emitted rays of the sun.

There is no matter by this means sent out of the atmosphere into the
tail but that which is most suitable to be the aliment of the sun and to
be converted into rays of light. For the rays of light attract that matter
that is of their own nature, and suitable to be turned into particles
of light or fire, immensely more strongly than others, as appears by
the action of particles of light or fire upon natural bodies in setting of
them on fire. Their action is first on these particles in the natural body
that are of the same kind, or fit to become particles of fire, and by their
attraction of extrinsic rays those within are set in motion, whereby the
body is set on fire. And so by the powerful action of these particles one
on another there arises that most rapid and vehement motion of them
in fire, and causes them to leap forth with such immense celerity as to
come from the sun hither in a few minutes. This so strong action
of these particles one on another probably arises from their being
immensely denser than other particles.

NOTE ON PAPERS ON NATURE AND NATURAL PHENOMENA

Four of Edwards' shorter manuscript writings are closely related in content or purpose to various parts of "Natural Philosophy." Two of these, the essay "Of the Rainbow" and the surviving portion of another which we have titled "Of Light Rays," reflect his interests in optics and astronomy while he was still a student at Yale. Both these papers are in the Andover collection. The other two, "Beauty of the World" and "Wisdom in the Contrivance of the World," can be associated more directly with some of the latest articles in "Natural Philosophy." The manuscript containing these two pieces belongs to the Yale collection. "Of the Rainbow" was published by Egbert C. Smyth in 1895,[1] and "Beauty of the World" by Perry Miller in 1948.[2] The other two have not been published previously.

Both "Of the Rainbow" and "Of Light Rays" are written on paper of the same watermarks as that in the earliest portions of "Natural Philosophy"; the narrow folio containing "Of the Rainbow" has the English Arms watermark, and the shortened folio of "Of Light Rays" bears the wreath countermark of the paper. Edwards used the reverse side of the latter to draft his "Spider" letter in 1723.[3] The hand and ink of both essays is very similar to that in earlier entries in the two numbered series in "Natural Philosophy." And each of the two is provided with a carefully drawn diagram for which Edwards used a straightedge and compasses, probably the same that he received from his father for use in studying mathematics during his senior year.[4]

Both essays were probably written within the span of a month or two. The hand and ink of each is very similar to that in "Natural Philosophy," LS Nos. 37–38 and SS Nos. 7–13. SS No. 15, in particular, pertains directly to the discussion in "Of the Rainbow." LS Nos. 37 and 38 are almost identical in hand and ink to "Of Light Rays," and like it they reflect Edwards' interest in the hypothesis defended by Christian Huygens and others concerning a plurality of worlds inhabited by rational creatures. The exact time at which these passages were written cannot be definitely established, but they were

1. "Early Writings of JE," pp. 238–41.
2. In *Images or Shadows*, pp. 135–37.
3. See below, p. 407.
4. See above, p. 21.

most probably done sometime during the later part of Edwards' first year of graduate study or early in the second year.

The essay "Beauty of the World" and the series "Wisdom in the Contrivance of the World" are both written on a full sheet of London Arms paper, folded to make four folio pages. The paper is of the same watermarks as that which Edwards used for his unnumbered series in "Natural Philosophy."[5] "Beauty of the World" was written first, apparently in two sittings, but probably within a brief period of time. The hand is uniform throughout, and similar to that in the unnumbered series of "Natural Philosophy." The ink of the first part is very similar to that of US No. 23, and to articles in his "Miscellanies" in the early 180s; ink resembling that in the second sitting of the essay follows soon after in Miscell. nos. 195–200. The whole essay should be dated at the end of Edwards' Yale tutorship, perhaps in the summer of 1726 or not long afterward.

Edwards began the series "Wisdom in the Contrivance of the World"[6] at a considerably later time. The hand and ink of the first entries in the series place them in the same period as "Miscellanies" entries in the 560s and 570s. The fifth entry ends with a citation of Henry Pemberton's *A View of Sir Isaac Newton's Philosophy*, which was published in London in 1728. The whole series must therefore have been written in Northampton, probably in 1732 or 1733.

The manuscripts of these four pieces are in relatively good condition, and have presented no particular problems for the preparation and editing of text beyond those that have already been discussed.[7]

5. The watermark design and dimensions are identical to those of the second of the three sheets JE used for his unnumbered series.

6. JE wrote this title in large script at the beginning of the first article, but he seems to have intended it for the whole series. The subject of each entry, including the first, is visually indicated by the large script in which JE wrote its topic word or phrase.

7. See above, pp. 115–20.

"OF THE RAINBOW"

WE shall endeavor to give a full account of the rainbow; and such an one as we think, if well understood, will be satisfactory to anybody, if they are fully satisfied of Sir Isaac Newton's different reflexibility and refrangibility of the rays of light.[1] And if he be not, we refer him to [what] he has said about it, and we are assured, if he be a person of an ordinary capacity and anything versed in such matters, by that time he has thoroughly considered it he'll be satisfied. And after that, let him peruse what we are about to say.

The first question then shall be, What is that reflection which we call a rainbow from? I answer, From the falling drops of rain. For we never see any rainbow except it be so that the sun can shine full upon the drops of rain—except the heavens be so clear on one side as to let the uninterrupted rays of the sun come directly upon the rain that falls on the other side. Thus we say it is a sign of fair weather when there is a rainbow in the east, because when there is a rainbow in the east, it is always already fair in the west; for if it be cloudy there, the rays of the sun will be hindered from coming thence to the opposite drops of rain. It cannot be the cloud from whence this reflection is made, as was once thought, for we almost always see the ends of rainbows come down, even in amongst the trees, below the hills, and to the very ground, where we know there is no part of the cloud there but what descends in drops of rain. And [I] can convince any man by ocular demonstration in two minutes on a fair day that the reflection is from drops, by only taking a little water into my mouth, and standing between the sun and something that looks a little darkish, and spirting of it into the air so as to disperse all into fine drops; and there will appear as complete and plain a rainbow, with all the colors, as ever was seen in the heavens. And there will appear the same, if the sun is near enough to the horizon, upon fine drops of water dashed up by a stick from a puddle. The reason why the drops must be fine, is because they won't be thick enough, but here and there a drop, if they are large.

1. *Optics*, Bk. I, prop. 2, theor. 2; prop. 3, theor. 3.

And I have frequently heard my countrymen that are used to sawmills say that they have seen a rainbow upon the drops that are dispersed in the air by the violent concussion of the waters in the mill. And what is equivalent to a rainbow, if one take a drop of water upon the end of a stick, and hold it up on the side that is opposite to the sun and moving it along towards one side or t'other, you will perceive, when the drop is held just at such a distance from the point opposite to the sun, that the rays of the sun are much more vividly reflected by it to your eye than at any other place nearer or further off—and that in the colors of the rainbow, too, so that if there had been enough of these drops there would have appeared a perfect rainbow. And if you have a mind to see more distinctly, you may fill a globular glass bottle with water (the glass of it must be very thin and clear), and it will serve your turn as well as so big a drop of water. And by that means you may also distinctly see that the reflection is from the concave and not from the convex surface.

The next thing that wants a solution is: What should cause the reflection to be circular? or which is the same thing, What should cause the reflection to be just at such a distance everywhere from the point that is opposite to the sun, and no reflection at all from the drops that are within or without that circle? Why should not all the drops that are within the circle reflect as many rays as those that are in the circle, or where the circle is?

To resolve this, we must consider this one law of reflection and refraction, to wit: If the reflecting body be perfectly reflexive, the angle of reflection will be the same as the angle of incidence; but if the body be not perfectly so, the angle will be less than the angle of incidence. By a body "perfectly reflexive," I mean one that is so solid as perfectly to resist the stroke of the incident body and not to give way to it at all; and by an "imperfectly reflexive," a body that gives way and does not obstinately resist the stroke of the incident body. So I say that if the body *ab* [Fig. 1] is perfectly reflexive, and does not give way at all to the stroke of the incident ray *cd*, it will reflect by an angle that shall be equal to that by which it fell upon the body *ab*, from *d* to *e*. But if the body *ab* is not able to resist the stroke of the ray *cd*, but gives way to it, it will neither be able to reflect by so big an angle, but will reflect it, it may be, by the line *df*, or *dg*, according as the reflexive force of *ab* be greater or lesser. And the bare consideration of this will be enough to convince any man; for we know that there is need of greater force by a great angle than by a little one. If we throw a ball against the floor or wall, it will much easier rebound sideways than right back again; and if we throw it sideways against a body that gives way to the stroke (it may be tried at any time), it will not rebound in so big an angle as if the body were quite hard. So it is the same thing in the body *ab*: it might give way so much as to let the ray proceed right on, with very little deviation from its old path; and if so, the deviation will be greater and greater in proportion to the resisting power of the body.[2] And if so, if it gives way at all, it will not deviate so much as if it did not at all. Now then, drops of water is one of those imperfectly reflexive bodies. If they were perfectly reflexive, we should see those drops that are right opposite to reflect as many rays as those that are just so much on one side— had the liquor but resistance enough to

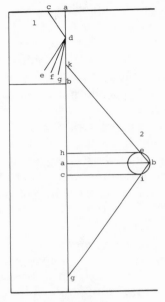

Figs. 1, 2

reflect the rays so directly back again. But those rays that fall perpendicularly or near perpendicularly upon the concave surface of the drop, as from *a* to *b* (Fig. 2), falling with much greater force than the ray which falls sideways upon it from *e* to *b* after the refraction at *e* which is made in all pellucid globes, the concave surface has not force enough to stop it and reflect it (what that reflexive force of the [concav]e[3] surface is we are not now disputing), but lets go through and pass right on uninterruptedly. [N]ow the ray *heb*, and the rays which fall about so obliquely, coming with a far [light]er stroke, the concave surface has force enough to resist it, and, what falls obliquely being far

2. JE wrote a marginal note, "note well for a halo," at the left margin of the page beside this sentence. The note was apparently inserted before the sentence was written, set off in a box, with a pointing hand which might have been meant to refer to the diagram, on the opposite side of the page.

3. A torn corner of the MS has removed portions of this and three other words at the beginning of JE's lines. The damage had occurred before Smyth inspected the MS. The reconstructions of the affected words given here, as shown by brackets, agree with Smyth's in all but the last instance.

more easily reflect[ed],[4] reflects it along in the line *bg*; and so in the same manner, the ray *cib* will be reflected to *k*. So that an eye so much sidewise as *g* or *k* will take the rays that reflected from that drop, and nowhere else; it being only those rays, whose obliquity is adjusted [to] the refractive[5] power, that are reflected by it, and they being all reflected out again with such a degree of obliquity. We hence see why the rays ben't reflected all ways equally. We hence also see why the rays are only reflected out at the side of the drop, and not directly back again; and by that, why the eye does not take the rays from any drops but those that are so much sideways of, or on one side of, the point that is right opposite to the sun; and so why the parts that are so opposite look dark, and why the parts that are just so much on one side, or just at such a distance all round from the opposite point alone, are bright; or, which is the same thing, why there is such a bright circle.

The next grand question is, What is it causes the colors of the rainbow? And this question indeed is almost answered already, for it is very evident.[6]

4. Smyth: "reflex[ible]."

5. "Refractive," as in Smyth; but JE might have intended to write "reflexive."

6. This paragraph, which JE abandoned in midsentence, is in an ink and hand characteristic of 1723–24, indicating that it was added three or four years after the essay was composed.

["OF LIGHT RAYS"]

SUPPOSE 10,000 [rays from one of the least of the fixed stars] to be within the eye within a third of time.[1] Now because one of the least of the fixed stars dost not take up above a sixth minute of the heavens, as will appear if we consider how little of the heavens the biggest of them take up in the most magnifying glasses; and considering how much less the least are than the biggest, which without doubt at least is an hundred times (that is, if an hundred of the least stars were put together they would not make a star so bright as Sirius). Now a sixth minute being but the 7,797,080,000,000th part of the visible hemisphere,[2] and the part of the eye upon which these rays fall, which give us the sight of the star, corresponding to the same part of the heavens; therefore, supposing the whole surface of the eye on which rays fall corresponds to a hemisphere, that part of the eye's surface on which the rays by which we see the star fall is but the 7,797,080,000,000th part of the apple of our eye. But if we allow it not to answer to above half an hemisphere, which is the least supposable, we may take it in round numbers for [the] 4,000,000,000,000th part of the surface of our eye, which we suppose to be half an inch; so that it will [be] 8,000,000,000,-000th of an inch. So that there must fall 10,000 rays upon this place in a third of time.

By which there must be a column or cylinder of rays, which shall be so long as that a ray can travel from end to end of it in a third; whose base on the surface of the eye must be such a part of an inch, in which must be included 10,000 rays; which, to spare pains, we will suppose without more ado to be not a cylinder, but a parallelepiped, so long, whose base shall be 6,000,000,000,000th part of an inch.

Now we will suppose, at the largest, that light runs 150,000 thousand miles in a second,[3] which makes 2,500 in a third; which is the length of this column wherein the 10,000 rays are included; which, being put

1. That is, the sixtieth part of a second of time.
2. The sources of most of JE's figures in this paper have not been positively identified.
3. JE probably intended to write "150 thousand."

together, will (reckoning much under) make but the 6,000,000th part of an inch square. So that even at this distance from the least of the fixed stars, the rays of light that come from 'em are so thick as that there is at least 10,000 of them in the 6,000,000 part of an inch square; which is undoubtedly a thousand times less than the least mote or dust that can possibly be perceived by the sharpest eyesight. So that there is, by this reckoning, 1,000,000 rays in the compass of the least mote. Now since, by the least computation, the sun is matter 80,000,000 of miles distant from the earth, and by Huygens' method, the biggest and nearest of the fixed stars is 27,664 as far as the sun,[4] if its distance shall be under-reckoned at 2,000,000,000,000 and the least being an hundred times as far yet they are 200,000,000,000,000,000; therefore, if the rays stand so thick at this distance, how thick must they stand even at the surface of one of these stars. Which, supposing the semi-diameter of the star to be about 400,000 miles, as the semi-diameter of the sun is reckoned to be, is 500,000,000 as near to the center of the star as we are; and because the spissitude of rays is as the square of the distance from the center, the rays there must be 2,500,000,000,000,000 times as thick there as here so that they are so thick there as that 25,000,000,000,000, 000,000,000 of them stand within the space that the least mote, and must be so many times less than it, supposing that they completely filled up that space. But supposing they don't nothing near fill it up, but leave it in a manner a perfect vacuity, they must be vastly smaller still; which that they do not we prove, inasmuch as the space is so free

and empty, and the rays so far from filling up the space, that the rays move all manner of ways across and opposite one to another, without the least obstruction, the least sensible. As suppose *abcde* to be a star: now I say the rays which proceed from *a* to *g* proceed without the least opposition from the rays *ei*, *dh*, *cg* and *bf* which will also come across it ere long. If but the tenth part at least of the rays *ag* were obstructed, without doubt we could perceive it; but we don't perceive the least

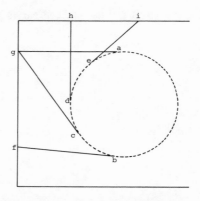

4. Huygens published his calculation of the distance of Sirius in *Celestial Worlds Discover'd.* Derham's report in *Astro-theology* might have been JE's source.

obstruction in that fixed star which we are so nigh to. For the brightness of the star at the margin of it, caused by the rays *ag*, is not at all the less for the obstruction of the crossing rays. If the rays came anything near towards filling up the space, the rays could not proceed the least space without some sensible obstruction. How infinitely little of the space then must they fill up, when the rays proceed through the thickness of them, without being in the least obstructed, for some millions of miles on. But this will make the rays of light less than any man will have patience to make figures for.

Corol. 1. Hence the exquisite skill of the artificer whose fingers have formed these infinitely small bodies.

Corol. 2. Hence the infinite art that was exercised in the formation of the eye that has given it such an exquisite sense that it should perceive the touch of those few rays of the least fixed stars which enter the eye, which all put together won't amount to the million million million millionth part, etc. of the least mote; of such an exquisite sense that it should distinctly perceive an image upon the retina, that is not above the 80 million millionth part of an inch wide; that has so nicely polished the retina that it should receive so small a picture upon it when the least protuberance or unevenness would utterly destroy and confound it.[5]

Remember that although it was a mistake that the stream of rays is a cylinder, because it indeed is conical, yet that don't alter the case inasmuch as the cone where it enters the eye is as the cylinder was supposed to be.

5. See "Natural Philosophy," SS No. 10 for a related comment.

"BEAUTY OF THE WORLD"

T HE beauty of the world consists wholly of sweet mutual consents, either within itself, or with the Supreme Being. As to the corporeal world, though there are many other sorts of consents, yet the sweetest and most charming beauty of it is its resemblance of spiritual beauties. The reason is that spiritual beauties are infinitely the greatest, and bodies being but the shadows of beings, they must be so much the more charming as they shadow forth spiritual beauties. This beauty is peculiar to natural things, it surpassing the art of man.

Thus there is the resemblance of a decent trust, dependence and acknowledgment in the planets continually moving round the sun, receiving his influences by which they are made happy, bright and beautiful, a decent attendance in the secondary planets, an image of majesty, power, glory and beneficence in the sun in the midst of all; and so in terrestrial things, as I have shewn in another place.

'Tis very probable that that wonderful suitableness of green for the grass and plants, the blue of the sky, the white of the clouds, the colors of flowers, consists in a complicated proportion that these colors make one with another, either in the magnitude of the rays, the number of vibrations that are caused in the optic nerve, or some other way. So there is a great suitableness between the objects of different senses, as between sounds, colors, and smells—as between the colors of the woods and flowers, and the smell, and the singing of birds—which 'tis probable consist in a certain proportion of the vibrations that are made in the different organs. So there are innumerable other agreeablenesses of motions, figures, etc.: the gentle motions of trees, of lily, etc., as it is agreeable to other things that represent calmness, gentleness and benevolence, etc. The fields and woods seem to rejoice, and how joyful do the birds seem to be in it. How much a resemblance is there of every grace in the fields covered with plants and flowers, when the sun shines serenely and undisturbedly upon them. How a resemblance, I say, of every grace and beautiful disposition of mind; of an inferior towards a superior cause, preserver, benevolent benefactor, and a fountain of happiness.

How great a resemblance of a holy and virtuous soul in a calm serene day. What an infinite number of such-like beauties is there in that one thing, the light; and how complicated an harmony and proportion is it probable belongs to it.

There are beauties that are more palpable and explicable, and there are hidden and secret beauties. The former pleases and we can tell why: we can explain and particularly point forth agreements that render the thing pleasing. Such are all artificial regularities: we can tell wherein the regularity lies that affects us. The latter sort are those beauties that delight us and we can't tell why. Thus we find ourselves pleased in beholding the color of the violets, but we know not what secret regularity or harmony it is that creates that pleasure in our minds. These hidden beauties are commonly by far the greatest, because the more complex a beauty is, the more hidden is it. In this latter sort consists principally the beauty of the world; and very much in light and colors. Thus, mere light is pleasing to the mind. If it be to the degree of effulgence, 'tis very sensible, and mankind have agreed in it: they all represent glory and extraordinary beauty by brightness. The reason of it is either that light, or our organ of seeing, is so contrived that an harmonious motion is excited in the animal spirits and propagated to the brain. That mixture of all sorts of rays, which we call white, is a proportionate mixture that is harmonious (as Sir Isaac Newton has shewn) to each particular simple color and contains in it some harmony or other that is delightful. And each sort of rays play a distinct tune to the soul, besides those lovely mixtures that are found in nature—those beauties, how lovely, in the green of the face of the earth, in all manner of colors in flowers, the color of the skies, and lovely tinctures of the morning and evening.

Corol. Hence the reason why almost all men, and those that seem to be very miserable, love life: because they cannot bear to lose the sight of such a beautiful and lovely world—the ideas, that every moment whilst we live have a beauty that we take not distinct notice of, but bring a pleasure that, when we come to the trial, we had rather live in much pain and misery than lose. (See "Rational Account," no. 108; also no. 119.)[1]

---

1. JE used the title "Rational Account" to refer to his "Miscellanies." Miscell. no. 108 is titled "Excellency of Christ." In the article JE argues that, just as the beauty of a person's body, countenance, gesture, or voice charms us because it is the immediate effect and emanation of internal mental beauty, so are the beauties of nature communications of God's excellencies. Miscell. no. 119, entitled "Types," asserts that God's wisdom appears in his ordering things in nature so that they represent divine and spiritual things. These ideas are the conceptual foundation for Edwards' series "Images of Divine Things."

"WISDOM IN THE CONTRIVANCE OF THE WORLD"

ATMOSPHERE. The wisdom of God appears in so ordering it that the weight of the atmosphere should never be very much altered. If it should be altered one-half or a third, it would probably utterly destroy men and other animals where such alteration is made, and perhaps many plants, too.

EYE. One thing very evidential of the wisdom of God in the contrivance of the eye, is that it should so easily, perfectly and distinctly perceive the stroke or impression of the rays of light, that is many thousand times too weak to be perceived by any other part of the body besides the retina at the bottom of the eye; as for instance, the light of the little stars, that reflected from the planets, the rays of the moon itself; being vastly too little to make any sensible impression upon any other part of the body of however quick sense: that this sense of the retina should be so lively and so exceeding distinct as not merely to discern an indistinct impression, but so as to discern the perfect shapes of things but indifferently enlightened; so minutely to distinguish the form of objects, in the many millions of the complicated variations and proportions of them in a room but indifferently enlightened, when the light reflected from these objects is immensely too weak to make any confused sensible impression on any other part of the body.

This is the more wonderful if we consider how small the retina of the eye is, for the distinction of the sense must be the more nice to discern so exactly and distinctly so many thousand differences made in different parts of that so small a part at once. Who can doubt but that this retina was contrived on purpose for this end, designed for this end? If the sense in that had been only much quicker and more distinct, if it had only been twice or thrice so lively, it would not have been so evident; but it is many thousands (and it may, million) times so quick and exact as any other part of the body. There is nothing like in any other part.

If it be said that all the distinct impressions that are made on the retina by rays of light at once can't be [discerned], and not any very great number, so that not such a vast variety of differences of impressions can be discerned, that won't alter the argument; for the mind can't discern them distinctly all at once, but must attend to them successively. Yet it can't discern this vast number successively, that are made at once in distinct parts of so small a superficies; which shews that it is not for want of quickness of sense in that superficies that they are not all discerned at once, but from want of comprehension in the mind, or ability to attend to so many impressions. And if there be but three or four of these varieties clearly and fully discerned at once, yet that shews the quickness and exactness of sense in the retina, as if they all were perfectly discerned. For so much fewer there are of these varieties of impressions [that] are discerned at once, still proportionably smaller is the part on which they are. And it argues as quick sense and distinct sense, for a thousandth or millionth part of the retina to have a distinguishing sense of two or three various impressions made at once by rays of light on that part, so as to discern their proportion, distance and relations one to another, as for the whole retina to discern two or three thousand or million. For therein consists the niceness of the sense: that so small impressions should be so distinguishingly and exactly perceived.

THE ROUNDNESS OF THE EARTH shews the wisdom of God. If it were not round or nearly round, only some particular parts of it would be habitable for several reasons:

(1) The atmosphere would not be diffused everywhere all round the globe as it is now, but would subside all into the lower parts, and leave the more elevated parts void.

(2) The corners and protuberant parts would also be destitute of water, for there would be no atmosphere to raise or carry vapors, as it would be so thin as to be insufficient for it.

(3) It would be most inconvenient because [a] great part of the world would be upon a side hill, which would make it most inconvenient passing to and fro, and the earth would be unpassable in a great measure, not commodious for communication of one part with another. For if the exalted parts were habitable, it would be most tedious traveling uphill for such a long way together. And there could be no passing by water from one side of the earth to another.

The wisdom of God appears in so ordering it, that the earth should be an OBLATE SPHEROID—that the surface of the earth at and near the equator should be longer than in the polar parts. For if the solid parts of the earth were not so conformed, the fluids would be, by reason of the earth's motion (the water and the air), whereby all these parts of the world would become void and waste and uninhabitable; and not only so, but unpassable. For the atmosphere would be so much higher in those parts and so much heavier that it would be unfit for us to live in. Hereby all communication would be prevented between the northern and southern hemispheres.

The wisdom of God appears in so ordering it that, though the planets revolve all of them nearly in the same plane, the COMETS are disposed in very different ones and distributed over all parts of the heavens; that when in their greatest distance, and moving slowest, they might be removed as far as possible out of the reach of each other's action. Otherwise the great eccentricity of their orbits and slowness of their motion in their aphelion would make 'em very liable to suffer great disturbances one from another. And 'tis so ordered that those that move slowest of all in their aphelion, ascend from the sun to the greatest height; for they come nearest to the sun, and thereby acquire the greatest swiftness to cause 'em to ascend to the greatest distance. And 'tis wisely ordered that when they are nearest the sun, where they are amongst the planets, and where their orbits come nearest together, they move swiftest and stay but a little while; which renders 'em less liable to be disturbed in their motions (this remark out of Pemberton's *View of Sir Isaac Newton's Philosophy*, p. 235).[1]

The wisdom of God appears in placing of the PLANETS at a greater or lesser DISTANCE from the sun, according to their DENSITY, the earth being four and one-fourth times [more dense] than Jupiter, and Jupiter being more dense than Saturn: the densest bodies requiring the greatest heat, to agitate and put their parts in motion; as, on the contrary, the planets which are more rare would be rendered unfit for their office by the intense heat to which the denser are exposed. Thus the water of our seas, if removed to the distance of Saturn from the sun, would remain perpetually frozen; and if as near the sun as Mercury, would constantly boil.

Probably before the Flood there was scarce any such clouds as now there are. The earth seems to have been watered by mists or great dews, the air was much purer, and perhaps the waters and fluids of the earth, too; so that vapors were not wont in like manner to be sustained

1. Pemberton, *View of Newton's Philosophy*. JE is quoting from the London ed.

and condensed into air as now. Seeing there is such an alteration in the constitution of the air, the wisdom of God appears in so ordering it that there should be more clouds, and also more frequent and fierce winds. They are necessary to preserve us from extreme and intolerable heat. Our air, as disposed at present, is abundantly more apt to conceive sultry heats, than it probably was in the purer state of the atmosphere before the Flood. And if it were not for clouds and winds to check or restrain the heat of the sun, how much sooner would our air become hot in the spring than it now does, how long is heat kept off by these means? And then, by the heat's having so much longer diffusion, and increasing without check, how much more extremely hot would it be in the summer? There would be no living for us.

PART THREE

"The Mind" and Related Papers

NOTE ON "THE MIND"

The only edition of "The Mind" to be prepared from Edwards' manuscript is that by Sereno Dwight, published in 1829 in his *Life of President Edwards*.[1] Some time after Dwight completed his work the manuscript was lost, and efforts to trace and recover it have so far failed. The copy, or possibly two copies, of the work that were made in the course of Dwight's preparations to print it, have also disappeared. Consequently, Dwight's *Life* remains our only source to date for the text of this important series of articles.[2]

Because the edition of "The Mind" which follows could not be prepared in the presence of the manuscript, the procedures employed in editing were necessarily very different from those followed in other writings in this volume.[3] Solutions to the problems of textual accuracy, the chronology and dating of the articles, and the physical structure of the manuscript, could be arrived at only by inference from other available evidence. In some cases the conclusions are well confirmed by many relevant facts, but in others the evidence goes no further than to suggest reasonable hypotheses. And even if these are accepted, the resulting account of this work is far more sketchy and tentative than an examination of the manuscript would have yielded.

Chronology and Dating of "The Mind"

Since the manuscript itself has been lost, the problems of determining the chronological order and dates of the articles become much more difficult to attack. The methods of comparison of the hand, ink and paper with other manuscripts have no application here, and Dwight's editing of the text has

1. Dwight, *1*.

2. The Andover coll. contains an early draft in Dwight's hand of the advertisement for his edition (Dwight, *1*, pp. 3–4) in which he sketches the history of his preparation of it. At first he employed a deaf copyist, who was taught to read Edwards' handwriting. Dwight does not report which MSS this person copied, but he reports, "On looking over the copies of Mr. Edwards' manuscripts it was found that, in consequence of the ignorance of the principle copier, and of the extreme illegibility of his hand, they were so exceedingly incorrect as to require a difficult and painful comparison with the originals." Further on, and referring to events two years later, Dwight reports, "the letters to Scotland, the 'Resolutions' and 'Diary' of Mr. Edwards, the 'Notes on the Mind,' and the 'Notes on Natural Science,' to say nothing of numerous smaller documents, were still uncopied; and the last four in a hand so illegible, that I could find no one to copy them but myself."

3. See Intro., Sec. 4 above.

removed all its original orthographic peculiarities. But there is a considerable fund of information about the manuscript which may be gleaned from a number of sources, and from which we can infer some highly probable conclusions about major points.

Dwight's comments about the manuscript are particularly important, because they are our only eyewitness account of it. In addition, various features of his presentation of the text suggest other pertinent facts. Besides this, the Yale collection contains an untitled manuscript page index in Edwards' hand, whose entries correspond with a high degree of accuracy and economy to the articles in Dwight's text of "The Mind."[4] Other evidence is provided by paper Edwards removed from the manuscript notebook and cut up to make leaves in two sermon booklets: two duodecimal leaves in the sermon on Eccl. 7:8 and another in the sermon on I John 3:9 were cut from a half-sheet of paper that Edwards had originally folded to make a quarto double-leaf piece in "The Mind."[5] Except for the title of the notebook written at the tops of the two recto pages of this piece, it was blank when he took it from the manuscript and cut it up for sermon writing. Nevertheless, it establishes the size of the manuscript of "The Mind," and gives a dateable sample of the paper Edwards added to it at a time when he was still composing articles in the series.

A few passages in Edwards' other manuscript writings contain direct references to "The Mind" which help in dating the articles they cite. Some of these also mention the page numbers of the notebook where the articles occurred, and so give further information concerning the organization of the manuscript. Apart from these direct references, the principal means for estimating the dates of the articles is by associating them with dateable parallel passages and related discussions in his other writings.

In most of Edwards' manuscript notebooks the chronological order of his composition closely follows the actual sequence of passages on the pages of the manuscript. Notable exceptions are found in "Natural Philosophy," where at first he wrote in several portions of the notebook at once, and in his "Notes on Scripture," where he reorganized the pages of the earliest part after they were written.[6] Both Dwight's testimony and Edwards' manuscript index give definite information about the sequence of entries in "The

---

4. Harvey Townsend, who first took note of this index, found only one citation in it that he could positively identify (*Philosophy of JE*, p. xv, n. 31).

5. Both sermons are in the Yale coll. In preparing the paper for his sermons JE cut it twice across the opened folio in such a way that portions of the original title words were left on each of the three pieces. The middle section of the folio, with the countermark of the paper, is in the sermon on I John 3 : 9. This piece also has the original fold of the double-leaf; but there are no thread holes in the fold.

6. Professor Schafer reports that when Dwight examined the MS he detected JE's reorganization of it, detached the leaves, and reassembled them in their original order.

Mind," but in comparing the evidence of these two sources, it is clear that the materials in this notebook must have been considerably rearranged at some time.

Dwight, speaking with reference to his organization of the entries in his edition of "The Mind," tells us that he arranged them "somewhat according to the order of the subjects; yet the number prefixed to each separate article, will show its place in the manuscript of the author" (p. 39). The numbers were evidently assigned to the entries by Dwight himself; they are printed in brackets in his edition of the complete text in appendix H, and not inserted at all in the several sample articles presented in chapter 3. The sequence of Dwight's numbers contains anomalies for which there is no immediately evident explanation: there are no articles numbered 33, 44, 46, 50, and 52, and the numbers 21, 25, and 65 are each assigned to two different articles. Again, several passages, some of considerable length, are printed in Dwight's edition as separate but unnumbered addenda to the numbered articles. It is possible that these passages were located in the manuscript in quite different positions in the series from the places where Dwight printed them.

More definite evidence of Dwight's relocation of particular passages is given by the manuscript index, where the entries are cited by subject and page number only. When Dwight's numbered articles are assigned to pages of the notebook in accordance with these citations, we find that, for the most part, each page included articles that Dwight numbered consecutively. But on certain pages the index indicates there were passages in addition to the group with consecutive numbers; and on others, the numbered articles together with their unnumbered addenda comprise too great a quantity of text to have been written on a single manuscript page. For example, the index cites p. 36 for material on the topics "genus" and "beasts." The former topic corresponds to the article Dwight numbered 43, but the only passage about beasts that could have occurred on the same page is presented by Dwight as an unnumbered addendum to No. 59. Furthermore, if this addendum had been written on the same page with Nos. 55–59, that page would have been vastly overburdened with text. Hence it is very probable that this addendum was found in the notebook on p. 36, immediately after the end of No. 43. Dwight probably originally numbered it 44, one of the missing numbers in his series, and then deleted the number when he added the passage to No. 59.

The index suggests various explanations for other numbers that are missing in Dwight's series. The passage he originally numbered 46 was probably made the last part, § 14, of No. 45; and No. 52 probably became the addendum to No. 51. The missing numbers 33 and 50, however, are not so easily accounted for. Also, several of the unnumbered addenda in Dwight's edition do not correspond to any of his missing numbers, even though the index indicates they were written elsewhere in the series than the places Dwight presents them. In these cases, as in the others, Edwards himself might have marked the passages for addition to the articles to which Dwight attached them.

From the above instances, it appears that Dwight numbered the passages of the notebook, either on the manuscript itself or on his first copy of it, and then set about arranging the text for publication, adjusting the numbers wherever necessary. This will explain why three of the numbers are each assigned to two different articles in his series. In all three cases, both articles are cited by the index on the same page of the notebook. Dwight apparently at first numbered them as a single passage, and later divided the passages in order to arrange the text "somewhat according to the order of the subjects," at the same time keeping the original number for both the divided parts.

In the following chart, the numbered articles and unnumbered addenda in Dwight's published text are arranged in order of pages according to citations in Edwards' manuscript index. Discrepancies between Dwight's consecutive numbering and the index citations are handled in accordance with the above explanations, with their possible or likely solutions put in parentheses and indicated by question marks. Further explanations in certain cases are given in footnotes.

"THE MIND" AS CITED IN THE MANUSCRIPT INDEX

Page	Subject	Article Cited (Dwight's Number)
1.	Knowledge not the perception of the agreement or disagreement of ideas	No. 71
	Mysteries	No. 71, Corol.
2.	(not cited)	(No. 72?)[7]
3.	(not cited)	
4.	(not cited)	
5.	Substance	No. 61
6.	Substance	No. 61; No. 61, addendum

7. An index reference to No. 72 should probably have been entered under the head "Personality," but here JE cites only p. 18 and p. 42. P. 18 contained No. 11 on personal identity; and p. 42 contained the end of No. 1 and Nos. 2–5. The intended referent here was probably No. 4 on the union of body and soul. In any case, this page was evidently well-filled with these numbers, and could hardly have held the lengthy discussion in No. 72. Hence this article is entirely neglected in the index, and so its actual location in the MS is unknown.

7.	Excellency	No. 62
8.	Excellency	Nos. 63–64
9.	Excellency	No. 1
10.	Excellency	No. 1
11.	Excellency	(missing?)[8]
12.	Excellency	(missing?)
13.	Excellency	(missing?)
14.	Excellency	(missing?)
15.	Excellency	(No. 62, addendum?)
16.	(not cited)	
17.	Truth	No. 6
	Genus	No. 7
	Reasoning, its rules	No. 8
	Space	No. 9
18.	Truth	
	Reasoning	No. 10
	God, his knowledge	
	Personality	No. 11
	Being	No. 12
	Space	No. 13
19.	Duration	
	Sleep	No. 65a
	Memory	
	Motion	No. 65b
	Habit	(?)[9]
20.	Ideas	No. 66
	Understanding	No. 67

8. The distribution of JE's articles on excellency in the MS is somewhat difficult to determine. The index entry for the topic is written, "Excellency p. 7, 8, 9, 10. 41, 42. 11, 12, 13, 14, 15. 27, 28. 33. 39." From the sequence of these page numbers, and their punctuation, it appears that one of the articles was continued from p. 10 to pp. 41 and 42. As p. 42 also contains Nos. 2–5, this article was probably No. 1. Given the size of his early hand, and the quantity of text assigned to other pages of the MS, JE could have written No. 1 on three of its pages. With the other articles on p. 42, it must have begun on p. 9. Nos. 62–64 probably were on pp. 7 and 8, following No. 61. No. 45 must have been on pp. 27 and 28, for it contains the passage on conscience that the index assigns to p. 28. P. 33 will have held No. 49 in the group Nos. 47–51; and p. 39 contained No. 14 in the group Nos. 14–20. One of the remaining pp. 11–15 that are cited in the index entry might have held the addendum to No. 62, but at least four of these pages contained material on excellency that cannot now be identified and are probably missing.

9. This passage has not been identified. Both No. 59 and its corollary treat habit, but the index places them on pp. 30 and 31.

	Reason	No. 68
	Existence	(No. 27?)[1]
21.	Reason	No. 68, continued
	Memory / Consciousness	No. 69
	Uneasiness	
	Determination of the will / Free will / Will, its determination	No. 70
22.	(not cited)	
23.	Words	No. 23
	Genus	No. 24
	Totum	No. 25a
	Substance	No. 25b
	Cause	No. 26
	Colors / Matter	No. 27, addendum
24.	Body / Solidity	No. 27, addendum(continued)
	Existence	No. 28
	Power	No. 29
	God	Nos. 29, 30, 32
	Soul, its seat	No. 31
25.	(not cited)	(No. 40, continued?)[2]
26.	Organs	No. 40, Corol.
	Mixed modes	No. 41
	Likeness / Similitude	No. 42

1. None of the articles Nos. 65–70 on this and the neighboring pages takes up the topic of existence. On the other hand No. 27, which is directly concerned with this topic, belongs with the group Nos. 23–26 on p. 23 below; but the index does not cite this page for an article on existence. Yet the index clearly locates the addendum to No. 27 on p. 23. It is at least possible, therefore, that No. 27 is the passage cited on p. 20. Dwight might originally have assigned the number 27 to the article on colors and body on pp. 23–24, and then shifted it to this passage when he transferred it to that place in the series, leaving the former No. 27 to stand as an unnumbered addendum. It should be noted that the corollaries Nos. 28 and 30 pertain as well to the article on colors and body as to this passage on existence.

2. The beginning of No. 40 apparently lay on p. 38 below, following Nos. 34–39 on p. 37. The corollary to No. 40, on the other hand, must have been on p. 26, preceding Nos. 41 and 42. The entire article, even without the quotation from Cudworth which Dwight attached to it, would probably have extended onto yet another page. Despite the lack of a citation to p. 25, because it must have been the recto of the leaf containing p. 26, No. 40 will naturally have continued on it.

3. The addendum to No. 13 would not have fit on p. 18 where Nos. 10–13 belonged, and p. 19 contains Nos. 65a and 65b. The addendum contains a well-known statement of JE on the concept of substance as applied to bodies, and might well have been the passage the index cites on this page. Because it begins with an examination of the idea of space, JE might have marked it for addition to No. 13 where Dwight placed it. But it is also related to remarks in No. 43 on this page, and in No. 42 which Dwight numbered to immediately precede.

4. The addendum to No. 34 could hardly have fit on p. 37 above where Nos. 34–39 were located. If No. 40 filled p. 25, as seems most probable, there would have been space on this page for the addendum. Indeed, it introduces the main concept that JE explores in No. 40, and so was probably written shortly before that number.

5. This index entry is in a very different hand and ink from the others; it was probably added to the index by JE's son, Jonathan Edwards, Jr., at some time after JE's death.

6. No entry can be identified to correlate with this citation, unless JE wrote a part of No. 4 on this page. The references after the index heading suggest another solution. JE cites pp. 24, 43, and 37 in that order. He might have intended to write p. 34 instead of 43; p. 34 contains the addendum to No. 51, which concludes with a sentence about the seat of the soul.

46–50.	(not cited)	(Index?)[7]
51.etc.	Method of the treatise	Subjects to be handled in the treatise on the mind

As the above chart clearly shows, Dwight in fact numbered the entries of the notebook, for the most part, in consecutive order on the recto and verso pages of each leaf of the notebook. But it is also apparent Dwight's series of numbers represents an alteration from the order of the manuscript as indexed that is both simpler and more radical than the dislocation of single passages discussed above. Obviously, the leaves of the notebook were arranged very differently at the time Dwight numbered the articles from the order they had when Edwards prepared his index. Articles Dwight numbered 1–5 were indexed for p. 42, at the end of the main series, while Nos. 6–9 belonged on p. 17, and No. 71 clearly occurred on p. 1, and so on. The pages of the notebook must have been totally rearranged, either by Dwight himself before he numbered the entries, or by someone else even before Dwight examined the manuscript. Because this reorganization affects our interpretation of the chronological order of the entries in a major way, it is necessary to discover which of the two orders, that of Dwight's numbering or the one determined by the index, represents the original order in which the articles were most probably written.

Since the manuscript index was prepared by Edwards himself, it would at first seem evident that the order it prescribes is the more authentic, and hence earlier of the two.[8] But other evidence points almost conclusively to the contrary hypothesis. To begin, because the index cites by pages, Edwards himself must have numbered the pages of the notebook in accordance with it. But it is incomprehensible that Dwight should have overlooked these page numbers when he numbered each article to "show its place in the manuscript of the author," or that he would have ignored them unless guided by some other overriding evidence.

Such overriding evidence would have been the index which Dwight himself describes, and which was quite different from the extant index we have discussed and represented in the chart above. Speaking of the arrangement of articles in "The Mind," he writes: "The word, proper to express a given subject, is written at the commencement of the paragraph, which introduces

7. None of these pages is cited in the extant index, but in a later reference to "The Mind" in his table to "Images of Divine Things" JE cites p. 49. It is quite possible that this and others of pp. 46–50 contained an earlier index to "The Mind" which Dwight describes, but which is missing with the MS.

8. In his *"The Mind" of JE,* Leon Howard produces an edition of "The Mind" with an arrangement of articles based upon the extant index. Howard defends the assumption that this was the original organization of the MS (pp. 11–17), and examines the development of JE's thought through the sequence of articles as they occur in this order.

it, in very large letters. Where several subjects are found on one page, they
are numbered 1, 2, 3, etc. These numbers, with that of the page, furnish the
reference in the index" (p. 34). The extant manuscript index cites articles by
page number only; the index described by Dwight, which was probably lost
with "The Mind" itself, cited them often by the number of article as well as
the page number.

The index of which Dwight speaks was undoubtedly the earlier of the two,
and represented the original order of pages and leaves in the manuscript of
"The Mind." From the hand and ink of the extant index, it was composed
almost entirely at one time, after nearly all the articles in "The Mind" had
been written. Moreover, the paper, hand, and ink show that it was written
at a relatively late date. It is a quarto size pamphlet of eight pages, formed by
infolding the two folios of a single sheet of paper. The English/GR^{wr} watermark and countermark of this paper is also found in a letter Edwards wrote
to John Brainard from Northampton, dated December 14, 1747.[9] The hand
and ink of the index are very similar to those in the letter, and agree with those
in Edwards' sermons of 1747 and 1748 as well. Edwards would hardly have
superseded an index compiled at this time by yet another of Dwight's description.

Again, several earlier references to "The Mind" in other manuscripts
confirm Dwight's organization of leaves in the notebook. No. 231 in his
"Miscellanies" reads, "INSPIRATION. Vid. ye Mind p. 7.7," citing both the
page and the article number as in the index Dwight describes. The article
headed "Inspiration" was numbered 20 by Dwight, and by consulting the
chart above, we find this number was on the seventh page in the order in
which Dwight numbered them, and was the seventh article on that page.
Similarly, Miscell. no. 361 reads, "SOUL of man. MATTER. THOUGHT. Vid.
Mind, p. 8." The reference is clearly to No. 21a, and in the order of pages
numbered by Dwight it would be on p. 8 of the notebook. Another reference
to "The Mind" in "Natural Philosophy," which Edwards inserted at the
end of No. 14 in the long series of "Things to be Considered and Written
fully about," cites pp. 12, 13, and 14 of the notebook. According to the extant
manuscript index these pages contained a discussion of excellency; but as
Dwight arranged the leaves of "The Mind," pp. 12, 13, and 14 contained
the discussion in No. 40 of the existence of insensible atoms to which Edwards
was clearly referring.

Edwards cites "The Mind" again in his last table to "Images of Divine
Things," under the heading "Images of divine things in God's works":
"see paper entitled *The Mind*, p. 49 [first column] *d**." This citation was
certainly written at a considerably later date than the 1747 manuscript index
to "The Mind," so it must refer to "The Mind" as it was organized accord-

---

9. The letter is in the Andover coll.

ing to that index. The identity of the item or passage Edwards was citing as on p. 49 is very problematic, however, because the 1747 index does not indicate any material on pp. 46–50 of "The Mind." Because the "Images" table citation uses a symbol by which Edwards specified the first column, it may be inferred that the material on p. 49 was written in double columns. This in turn suggests that "The Mind," p. 49, and probably one or more of the immediately preceding pages, contained either Edwards' first and original index for the work (the index described by Dwight), or else some part of the series of "Subjects to be Handled in the Treatise on the Mind"; for these are the parts of the manuscript's known contents that he was most likely to have written in double columns. The fact that the 1747 index is silent about the contents of these pages is consistent with either hypothesis. The earlier index would quite naturally be ignored in the later one that was intended to supersede it. And although the 1747 index seems to place the series of "Subjects" on pp. 44 and 45, and pp. 51 ff. of the manuscript, Edwards might well have continued adding to that series after the index was composed, writing in double columns on pp. 46–49 or 50.

From all the above instances it appears that Edwards himself reorganized "The Mind" after most of the series of articles had been written, and prepared the surviving manuscript index according to its later order of pages. The nature of this reorganization may be inferred from the above chart, together with Dwight's own account of the structure of the notebook. In describing the whole he writes, "It contains nine leaves of foolscap, folded separately, and a few more, obviously written at a later period" (p. 34); and later, in a footnote to No. 61, he adds, "This article, and the numbers following, viz. 62, 63, etc. are inserted in the manuscript distinctly from the rest, and were written probably at a somewhat later period of life" (p. 674, n.).

If, on the above chart, the pages containing Nos. 61–72 (and also pp. 11–14, which held material on excellency that is apparently missing) were assumed to be removed from the notebook, the remaining articles Nos. 1–60 would appear divided among twelve leaves, each containing a set of consecutive numbers. From the arrangement of these sets as represented in the chart, the leaves obviously make up six double-leaf pieces that are infolded into a single quire; when the quire is disassembled and the six double-leaves laid in order, the outside piece first, the next second, etc., Dwight's entire series of numbers is restored to consecutive order. These six double-leaves, and three more containing the "Subjects to be Handled in the Treatise on The Mind" and probably the index Dwight described, will make up the "nine leaves, folded separately" to which he refers.

It appears, therefore, that Edwards began writing "The Mind" on separately folded double-leaves. He presumably numbered the pages in order, and on a separate leaf kept an index to the articles citing them by page and article number. Notes concerning his projected treatise were written on still other leaves. After he had written No. 60, he assembled the six double-leaves of the main series of articles into a quire. The manuscript then probably remained dormant for some time, for Dwight judged that Nos. 61–72 were written at a later period of life. Edwards wrote them on additional leaves (probably double-leaves, for the most part), and inserted them at various places in the quire. Finally, in about 1747, he compiled a new index to the series based upon the revised order of pages, which he presumably renumbered as they stood. The diagram below represents the probable structure of the notebook at the time the second index was made, showing the nine original double-leaves, the original page numbers of the first six of these, and the articles on each leaf. The pieces Edwards inserted later might have been either single or double leaves, as shown.

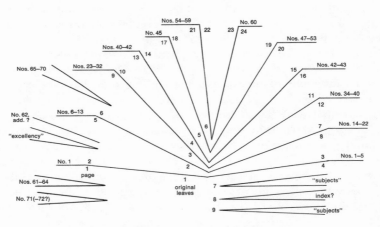

"The Mind": Proposed Reconstruction of the Manuscript

Although we have found for the most part reliable Dwight's testimony concerning the chronological sequence of articles, his judgments of the dating of "The Mind" are less trustworthy. He took it to be the earliest begun of Edwards' manuscript notebooks, and judged it was started in 1717, when Edwards was presumed to be reading Locke's *Essay Concerning Human Understanding* and studying logic as a sophomore in college (pp. 30, 34, 702 n.). Most of the articles, he suggests, were written while he was still an undergraduate (pp. 39–40), but those at the end of the series were written probably at a significantly later time. Dwight states this point, though with varying degrees of confidence, on three different occasions: the manuscript contained a few leaves that were "obviously written at a later period" (p. 34); and again, in a footnote to No. 61, "This article, and the numbers following, . . . are inserted in the manuscript distinctly from the rest, and were written probably at a somewhat later period of life" (p. 674 n.) ; finally, in a footnote at the end of his edition of the text, "It is not improbable that some of the later numbers were written while the author was a tutor in College" (p. 702 n.). Although he does not give the evidence for his judgment, Dwight's repeated mention of the later entries gives significant eyewitness testimony that at least Nos. 61ff. were added in the notebook well after the other numbers had been written.

Dwight's dating of the beginning of "The Mind" in 1717 has been generally, but not universally, accepted. Georges Lyon first disputed the matter, on the ground that many of the articles show the influence of George Berkeley's *Principles of Human Knowledge*, a work Edwards could not have read until much later.[1] Egbert Smyth responded with a defense of Dwight's dating based upon a study of several early manuscripts, but "The Mind" was not among the ones he examined.[2] When Smyth searched for the notebook later, he found it was already missing.[3] More recently, Leon Howard has questioned Dwight's dating on the ground that many of the articles show the influence of Arnauld's *Art of Thinking*, the treatise on logic that Edwards used during his senior year at college.[4] Howard also questions whether Edwards could have read Locke's *Essay* before his senior year, when he and the other Wethersfield students returned to New Haven where a copy of the work was available.[5]

Both Lyon's and Howard's doubts are based primarily on their judgments that "The Mind" was written under the influence of works that Edwards could not have read at so early a time. Whatever might be the strength of these grounds, there are other more cogent reasons for questioning Dwight's judgment in the matter. His dating of other early manuscripts, especially the draft of Edwards' "Spider" letter, has proved to be seriously in error. Not only did he misinterpret the changes in Edwards' handwriting, but he was apparently much influenced by the desire to find evidences of Edwards' early genius. His opinions must be considered in the light of the mistakes to which he was most susceptible. And of all the statements he makes bearing upon the dating of "The Mind," his various remarks concerning the relative lateness of Nos. 61ff. appear to be the most valuable.

Apart from this portion of Dwight's testimony, the most significant evidence for dating articles in "The Mind" is found in Edwards' references to the series, and in parallel passages and closely related discussions, in other manuscript writings. Two explicit references to "The Mind" in his "Miscel-

1. Lyon, *L'Idealisme en Angleterre*, pp. 429–33.
2. "Early Writings of JE," p. 212.
3. *Exercises Commemorating the Two-Hundredth Anniversary of the Birth of Jonathan Edwards* (Andover, 1904), app. I, p. 3.
4. See above, p. 21.
5. *"The Mind" of JE*, p. 6.

lanies," and another in "Natural Philosophy," have already been discussed in connection with the early organization of the notebook. Neither these nor other references show the time at which Edwards began the series, however. More definite evidence concerning the earliest articles is found in comparisons with passages in other writings, especially in "Miscellanies." It is in this latter series that Thomas Schafer has discovered a passage that fixes quite precisely the time when Edwards began his first article in "The Mind."

The passage in question is obviously a version of the first few sentences of No. 1, introducing the topic of excellency. Allowing for Dwight's editorial improvements in the text of No. 1, these sentences nearly duplicate the "Miscellanies" passage.[6] After beginning the article in "Miscellanies," he deleted the passage, apparently having decided to write it on a separate paper where he would be able to develop his thoughts upon excellency over a longer time and in a more coherent manner. Hence it is reasonable to treat the "Miscellanies" passage and the beginning of "The Mind" No. 1 as contemporaneous.

The passage in "Miscellanies" was intended as no. 78 in that series; after deleting it, Edwards used the same number for the next entry. Schafer estimates the time of Miscell. no. 78 in the autumn or winter of 1723, probably soon before the "Spider" letter was composed. Assuming, as has been argued above, that Dwight's numbering of articles correctly represents their chronological order, it must be concluded that Edwards began "The Mind" in the later months of 1723, nearly six years after the time Dwight proposed.

Evidence of Edwards' continued work on No. 1 is found in further entries in "Miscellanies." A passage in Miscell. no. 89 shows that by this time he had written the first of his four addenda to the article. Miscell. no. 117 contains implicit references to the first and second of these addenda, and brings in the central point of the third. Apparently, Edwards continued to work on No. 1 until the end of 1723 or the first months of 1724.

In Nos. 2ff. he turned his attention to other topics that probably arose during a period of independent study, perhaps at the college in New Haven during the beginning of 1724. In No. 2 the influence of Locke's *Essay* is reflected for the first time, and in No. 11 Locke is referred to by name. This article shows that Edwards was not using the first-edition copy of Locke's work that Jeremiah Dummer had acquired for the college, for it concerns Locke's theory of personal identity, and his chapter on this subject was not incorporated into the *Essay* until the second edition of 1694.

Nos. 6 and 10 on truth, Nos. 7 and 24 on genus and species, No. 25a on parts and wholes, and No. 26 on the definition of cause, are all related in various ways to notes that Edwards jotted at the back of his manuscript

6. The passage is presented below, p. 332, n. 1.

copy of William Brattle's *Compendium of Logic.*[7] From the ink and hand, it appears these notes were written sometime during his Yale tutorship, probably in the first year (1724–25). In No. 34 his justification of natural philosophy as a science of causes is a reflection of his continued writing in "Natural Philosophy"; the articles in the unnumbered series in that manuscript are a product of his two years' tutorship. No. 40, on the existence of unperceived physical objects and insensible atoms, is related to No. 6 of the unnumbered series, and reflects also a remark on the need to suppose frigorific particles in order to explain freezing in US No. 12. His reference to No. 40 in the long series, No. 14, was probably jotted there after the end of his tutorship, in 1726 or 1727.

It is quite conjectural how far Edwards might have progressed in "The Mind" by the time he completed his tutorship. Dwight's testimony that Nos. 61 and beyond were written at a later time argues against the supposition that he had completed the series by the time he went to Northampton in the fall of 1726, even though we have also quoted Dwight as judging that "it is not improbable" that the later numbers were written during his tutorship. Schafer estimates that "Miscellanies" articles numbered in the 200s correspond with the beginning of his residence in Northampton. Miscell. no. 231, as we have noted, cites No. 20 on the topic of inspiration, but the next entry, Miscell. no. 232, indicates he had probably progressed well beyond that number.

In discussing the misery of the damned in no. 232, Edwards refers to an unspecified article on excellency in "The Mind": "Again the ill will and hatred of any being, though the meanest, absolutely and in itself considered, is ungrateful and contrary to the disposition of nature, whether we in the least fear any injury as the effect of it or no. And this will appear by what has been said under the head of excellency and love in our discourse on the mind." Although the main points in his concept of excellency were developed in No. 1, Edwards' reference indicates he intended a particular discussion of love. This is more specifically treated in No. 45. Miscell. no. 232 goes on to discuss hell's torments in terms of moral affections arising from the relations of consent and dissent among persons, in a manner that extends his initial treatment of these themes in No. 45. It is more probable, therefore, that this is the article to which Edwards intended to refer. Accordingly, No. 45 was probably written just before or soon after he came to Northampton. His reflections upon spiritual excellency in Miscell. nos. 185, 186, and 187, and upon the love of Christ in Miscell. nos. 180, 183, and 189, might well have given rise to the important theoretical effort in No. 45 of "The Mind."

The three sermon leaves that Edwards made from a double-leaf taken

---

7. JE's notes are presented below, in footnotes to Nos. 6, 7, 25a, and 26.

from "The Mind" give some indication of the probable history of the manuscript during his first few years in Northampton. The double-leaf has the countermark of a paper identified as Amsterdam/ML, a paper found in many sermons and several other manuscripts that are dateable in late 1727 and early 1728. We may therefore infer that Edwards was probably still writing in "The Mind" at this time, and that he added other paper in addition to the leaf that he later removed, for the articles he was currently writing. But again, his removal of the one unused leaf suggests he had laid "The Mind" aside at some earlier time, and had little expectation of soon returning to write in the notebook. His removal of the leaf, in fact, might well correspond to the time when he put the separately folded pieces with his previously written articles together into a single quire. If so, Dwight's statements suggest that he had written No. 60 by this time. The two sermons, on the texts Eccl. 7:8 and I John 3:9, are dated by Schafer in the year 1731, at least two years after Edwards had assumed full responsibility for the pulpit in Northampton upon the death of the senior minister, his grandfather Solomon Stoddard. It is quite likely that he would have laid aside "The Mind," as he abandoned "Natural Philosophy," during this time when his time, efforts, and interests were more fully commanded by the concerns of his ministry.

When Edwards prepared his second index for the reorganized manuscript in 1747 or 1748, he had evidently written all the articles up to and including No. 69, for the index systematically cites these in an appropriate order. From Dwight's testimony, Nos. 61–69 had probably been written more recently, after a period when the notebook was disregarded. Indeed, No. 60 might belong to the later group. It is concerned with the concept of the determination of the will, and was apparently used by Edwards in writing his *Freedom of the Will*.[8] He was deeply interested in the problem of Arminianism and free will at the time the index was composed, for he carefully cited all the articles in "The Mind" on the subject under three different index headings.

From the manner in which it is cited in the 1747 index, it appears that No. 70 was written after the index was compiled. No. 70 also treats the question of the determination of the will, disputing Locke's view in the matter. The article was written on p. 21, on a leaf containing Nos. 65–70 which Dwight took to be inserted into the manuscript at a later time. When he first compiled his index Edwards failed to cite this article under the three heads pertaining to the subject, but added the page number afterward above the line and at the beginning of the page references following all three headings. Given his evident interest in the subject, it is not likely that he would have overlooked this more recent article in his first compilation of the index if it had actually been written by that time. The ink with which he added the

8. Pt. I, §2, in *Works* (Yale ed.) *1*, p. 143.

page number to these three index headings, however, is almost indistinguishable from that of other entries in the index; Edwards probably wrote No. 70 within a short time afterward.

No. 71, too, on Locke's concept of knowledge as the perception of the agreement or disagreement of ideas, seems to have been composed after the index was formed. Edwards wrote a unique index heading for this article, and another, "mysteries," for its corollary. The similarity of hand and only slight difference in ink suggest that this article, too, was written shortly after the index was first compiled. No. 72, in which Edwards rebuts Locke's theory of personal identity, is apparently not cited in the index at all, so that even its location in the manuscript remains conjectural. His interest in the problem of personal identity in later years was connected with his work on the doctrine of original sin. He began to explore the writings of John Taylor and other "Arminians" on this subject in about 1748, and wrote his treatise, *Original Sin*, in 1756 and early 1757.[9] The exception he takes to Locke's theory in Pt. IV, ch. 3 of the treatise[1] probably stands in part upon the argument in No. 72.

When Edwards prepared his index in about 1747 the notebook of "The Mind" contained one or more articles on excellency on pp. 11–14; but these were apparently missing when Dwight examined the manuscript. Edwards himself might have removed them in 1755 when he wrote his dissertation *The Nature of True Virtue*. One further passage in "The Mind" gives more definite evidence of his interest in the manuscript during his later life. In some part of the notebook he copied a long quotation from Cudworth's *Intellectual System*; Dwight presents the quotation as an addendum to No. 40. Edwards also copied extensively from Cudworth's book in a late "Miscellanies" entry and in entries near the end of his "Images of Divine Things,"[2] which he probably wrote in late 1756 or 1757. In various entries in his "Catalogue" between 1750 and 1754 he notes commendations of the work by others,[3] which indicates he had not previously read the work.

The Text of "The Mind"

A significant opportunity for evaluating Dwight's text is afforded by the fact that his *Life* contains two different versions of a substantial number of articles. In appendix H (pp. 664–702) he presents what he refers to as "the whole of this collection of Notes or Comments" (p. 39, n.). In addition, his third chapter contains an extract of sixteen of the articles (pp. 34–39), which

---

9. *Works* (Yale ed.) *3*, pp. 18–19.

1. Ibid., pp. 398–99.

2. "Miscellanies," no. 1359, and "Images of Divine Things," nos. 208, 209, and 210.

3. On p. 25, no. 10, JE notes the work commended by Warburton; on p. 26, no. 11, he notes Mr. Prince told him a new edition of the work had lately been published; p. 33, no. 6 quotes details of the new edition from an advertisement; and p. 36 quotes Andrew Ramsay's high commendation of Cudworth. The last is preceded by an entry with the date, June 1754.

are offered as a sample of the whole. In the present discussion, the versions which appear in chapter 3 will be referred to as the sample versions, or the samples. These sample articles are printed without numbers, but they are those numbered 2–8, 11–13 (lacking the addendum to No. 13), and 15–20 in the appendix.

Many discrepancies are found between the sample and the appendix versions of these articles. They differ greatly in punctuation and the use of capital letters and italics. Two articles, Nos. 13 and 19, appear with topic headings in the samples, but without them in the appendix; and in the sample, No. 11 is headed "Person," while in the appendix the heading is "Personal Identity." Otherwise, the marks of Edwards' authentic style are preserved in the samples, but removed from the appendix versions by the editor's improving hand.

More important discrepancies are found in the readings of the text in the two versions. For example, in the sample version, the final sentence of No. 16 ends with the words, "feels itself hate, etc.," but in the appendix version we find, "feels when it hates." The former reading seems more consonant with the context, and Dwight might well have revised it for the appendix version in order to clarify the meaning. The same explanation appears likely for the different renderings of Edwards' explication of the meaning of "the grass is green" in No. 19. The sample version reads, "in a constant course, when we see grass, the idea of green is excited with it"; in the appendix, the last clause is "the idea of green is excited by it." Taken strictly, the latter reading is inconsistent with Edwards' ontological theory, since it implies a causal relation between grass and the idea of green. In this case, as in No. 16, the sample reading is more probably authentic.

In some cases, Dwight's appendix versions omit significant words that are included in the samples. A sentence in the sample No. 15 reads, " 'Tis impossible, that we should explain and resolve a perfectly abstract, and mere idea of existence." In the appendix Dwight not only altered Edwards' customary " 'tis" to "it is," but he omitted the words "and resolve." Again, in No. 2, the sample reads, "they perceive, or passively receive, ideas, only or chiefly, of created things"; the appendix drops "or chiefly." And the sample version of No. 6 ends with the words, "for what is perfectly without the mind, the mind has nothing to do with"; but the entire clause is missing in the appendix version of No. 6.

It is difficult to explain these omissions by any other hypothesis than that Dwight not only edited the text anew for his sample versions, but actually transcribed these articles a second time from the manuscript itself. He might then have recognized words and phrases that his copyist had overlooked, or that he himself had passed over as illegible when he transcribed for the appendix text. Other discrepancies between the samples and the appendix show clearly that the two versions were based upon different readings of the manuscript. They concern words which would be very difficult to distinguish when written in Edwards' hand of 1723–26. There are six such cases as follows, with the sample readings given first: in No. 8, "in fact" and "in part"; in No.13, "existence" and "extension," "so" and "to," "necessity" and "reality," and "should" and "shall"; in No. 16, "desires" and "discerns."

In almost all cases of verbal discrepancies, the readings of the sample versions appear to be preferable, both because they are more in keeping with Edwards' own style, and because they seem to convey more accurately his meaning as understood from the context. Where the question is one of style alone, the choice of readings in the text below has been made silently. But where the discrepancy between the sample and appendix versions affects the meaning of a passage, the alternative reading is given in a footnote. In the articles which are found only in Dwight's appendix edition there are also a few cases where Dwight or his copyist quite evidently misread a word in the manuscript. In these cases the word that Edwards almost certainly wrote is inserted in brackets, and Dwight's word added in a footnote.

Dwight's punctuation of the text, both in his appendix and in the sample articles in chapter 3, is far too dense to give satisfactory readings of the articles. The text as Edwards actually wrote it in the manuscript, on the other hand, was probably almost entirely lacking in punctuation. In order to produce a punctuation that would shape Edwards' sentences most suitably in accordance with his meaning, and also would conform to the standards and policies of this edition, a typescript of each article was prepared from which all punctuation and capitalization was eliminated. This text was then punctuated anew as though it had been copied from the manuscript itself. By following this procedure Edwards' constructions could be studied as he actually wrote them, so far as this can be determined, and apart from the influence of Dwight's imposed punctuation.

"The Mind"

[1]. EXCELLENCY.[1] There has nothing been more without a definition
than excellency, although it be what we are more concerned with than
anything else whatsoever. Yea, we are concerned with nothing else.
But what is this excellency? Wherein is one thing excellent and another
evil, one beautiful and another deformed? Some have said that all
excellency is harmony, symmetry or proportion;[2] but they have not yet
explained it. We would know why proportion is more excellent than
disproportion, that is, why proportion is pleasant to the mind and
disproportion unpleasant. Proportion is a thing that may be explained
yet further. It is an equality, or likeness of ratios; so that it is the equality
that makes the proportion. Excellency therefore seems to consist in
equality. Thus, if there be two perfect equal circles or globes together,
there is something more of beauty than if they were of unequal, disproportionate magnitudes. And if two parallel lines be drawn, the
beauty is greater than if they were obliquely inclined without proportion, because there is equality of distance. And if, betwixt two parallel
lines, two equal circles be placed, each at the same distance from each

1. Edwards originally began this article in his "Miscellanies" as Miscell. no. 78. After
writing the first sentences there he deleted the entire passage, apparently having decided to
make his essay on excellency the beginning of a separate notebook. The deleted Miscell. no.
78 has been transcribed by Thomas Schafer as follows, with the words Edwards crossed out
while writing put in parentheses:"78. *Excellency* There has nothing been more without a definition than excellency tho it be what (alone we are concerned with in any case) we are more
concerned with than any thing else Yea (it is what) we are concerned with nothing else but
what is this excellency wherin is one thing excellent and another evil one beautifull and
another deformed, some have said that all excellency consists in harmony (and) symmetry
& proportion, but they have not yet explain'd it. they have told us of a thing that is excellent
viz proportion but we (have) would know why proportion is more excellent than disproportion, that is why proportion is pleasing to the mind, and disproportion unpleasing. Proportion
is a thing that may be explain'd yet further tis an equality or likeness of ratios." This entry
was probably written in the late autumn or winter of 1723 (see above, p. 326).

2. Edwards could have meant the Earl of Shaftesbury, whose *Characteristicks* he might have
read by this time. Shaftesbury's moral theory bases virtue upon a "natural affection" that
arises from the love of truth, proportion, order, and symmetry in external things, a passion
very distinct from self-interest. See "An Inquiry concerning Virtue" in *Characteristicks*, 2.

parallel line, as in Fig. 1, the beauty is greater than if they stood at irregular distances from the parallel lines. If they stand each in a per-pendicular line going from the parallel lines (Fig. 2), it is requisite that they should each stand at an equal distance from the perpendicular line next to them; otherwise there is no beauty. If there be three of these circles between two parallel lines, and near to a perpendicular line run between them (Fig. 3), the most beautiful form, perhaps,

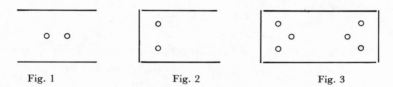

Fig. 1   Fig. 2   Fig. 3

that they could be placed in, is in an equilateral triangle with the cross line, because there are the most equalities: the distance of the two next to the cross line is equal from that, and also equal from the parallel lines. The distance of the third from each parallel is equal, and its distance from each of the other two circles is equal, and is also equal to their distance from one another, and likewise equal to their distance from each end of the cross line. There are two equilateral triangles, one made by the three circles, and the other made by the cross line and two of the sides of the first protracted till they meet that line. And if there be another like it on the opposite side, to correspond with it, and it be taken altogether, the beauty is still greater where the distances from the lines in the one are equal to the distances in the other; also the two next to the cross lines are at equal distances from the other two. Or, if you go crosswise from corner to corner, the two cross lines are also parallel, so that all parts are at an equal distance; and innumerable other equali-ties might be found.

This simple equality, without proportion, is the lowest kind of re-gularity, and may be called simple beauty; all other beauties and ex-cellencies may be resolved into it. Proportion is complex beauty. Thus, if we suppose that there are two points, A [and] B, placed at two inches' distance, and the next, C, one inch farther (Fig. 4), it is requisite, in order to regularity and beauty, if there be another, D, that it should be at half an inch distance (otherwise there is no regularity, and the last, D, would stand out of its proper place), because now the relation that the space CD bears to BC is equal to the relation that BC bears to AB, so that *BCD* is exactly similar to *ABC*. 'Tis evident this is a more complicated excellency than that which consisted in equality, because the terms of the relation are here complex, and before were simple. When there are three points set in a right line, it is requisite, in order to regularity, that they should be set at an equal distance, as *ABC* (Fig. 5),

Fig. 4   Fig. 5

where *AB* is similar to *BC*, or the relation of *C* to *B* is the same as of *B* to *A*. But in the other are three terms necessary in each of the parts between which is the relation (*BCD* is as *ABC*), so that here more simple beauties are omitted, and yet there is a general complex beauty. That is, *BC* is not as *AB*, nor is *CD* as *BC*; but yet *BCD* is as *ABC*. It is requisite that the consent or regularity of *CD* to *BC* be omitted, for the sake of the harmony of the whole. For although, if *CD* was perfectly equal to *BC*, there would be regularity and beauty with respect to them two, yet if *AB* be taken into the idea, there is nothing but confusion. And it might be requisite, if these stood with others, even to omit this proposition for the sake of one more complex still. Thus, if they stood with other points, where *B* stood at four inches' distance from *A*, *C* at two from *B*, and *D* at six from *C* [Fig. 6], the place where *D* must stand in (if *A*, *B*, *C*, *D*

Fig. 6

were alone, viz., one inch from *C*) must be so as to be made proportionate with the other points beneath. So that although *A*, *B*, *C*, *D* are not proportioned, but are confusion among themselves, yet taken with the whole they are proportioned and beautiful.

All beauty consists in similarness, or identity of relation. In identity of relation consists all likeness, and all identity between two consists in identity of relation. Thus, when the distance between two is exactly equal, their distance is their relation one to another; the distance is the same, the bodies are two, wherefore this is their correspondency and beauty. So bodies exactly of the same figure: the bodies are two, the relation between the parts of the extremities is the same, and this is their agreement with them. But if there are two bodies of different shapes, having no similarness of relation between the parts of the extremities, this, considered by itself, is a deformity, because being disagrees with being; which must undoubtedly be disagreeable to perceiving being, because what disagrees with being must necessarily be disagreeable to being in general, to everything that partakes of entity, and of course to perceiving being. And what agrees with being must be agreeable to being in general, and therefore to perceiving being. But agreeableness of perceiving being is pleasure, and disagreeableness is pain. Disagreement or contrariety to being is evidently an approach to nothing, or a degree of nothing, which is nothing else but disagreement or contrariety of being, and the greatest and only evil; and entity is the greatest and only good. And by how much more perfect entity is, that is, without mixture of nothing, by so much the more excellency. Two beings can agree one with another in nothing else but relation; because otherwise the notion of their twoness (duality) is destroyed and they become one.

And so in every case, what is called correspondency, symmetry, regularity and the like, may be resolved into equalities; though the equalities in a beauty in any degree complicated are so numerous that it would be a most tedious piece of work to enumerate them. There are millions of these equalities. Of these consist the beautiful shape of flowers, the beauty of the body of man and of the bodies of other animals. That sort of beauty which is called "natural," as of vines, plants, trees, etc., consists of a very complicated harmony; and all the natural motions and tendencies and figures of bodies in the universe are done according to proportion, and therein is their beauty. Particular disproportions sometimes greatly add to the general beauty, and must necessarily be, in order to a more universal proportion—so much equality, so much beauty—though it may be noted that the quantity of equality is not to be measured only by the number, but the intenseness, according to the quantity of being. As bodies are shadows of being, so their proportions are shadows of proportion.

The pleasures of the senses, where harmony is not the object of judgment, are the result of equality. Thus in music, not only in the proportion which the several notes of a tune bear one among another, but in merely two notes, there is harmony; whereas it is impossible there should be proportion between only two terms. But the proportion is in the particular vibrations of the air which strike on the ear. And so in the pleasantness of light, colors, tastes, smells and touch: all arise from proportion of motion. The organs are so contrived that, upon the touch of such and such particles, there shall be a regular and harmonious motion of the animal spirits.

Spiritual harmonies are of vastly larger extent; i.e., the proportions are vastly oftener redoubled, and respect more[3] beings, and require a vastly larger view to comprehend them, as some simple notes do more affect one who has not a comprehensive understanding of music.

The reason why equality thus pleases the mind, and inequality is unpleasing, is because disproportion, or inconsistency, is contrary to being. For being, if we examine narrowly, is nothing else but proportion. When one being is inconsistent with another being, then being is contradicted. But contradiction to being is intolerable to perceiving being, and the consent to being most pleasing.

Excellency consists in the similarness of one being to another—not merely equality and proportion, but any kind of similarness. Thus similarness of direction: supposing many globes moving in right lines, it is more beautiful that they should move all the same way and according to the same direction, than if they moved disorderly, one one way and another another. This is an universal definition of excellency: The consent of being to being, or being's consent to entity. The more the consent is, and the more extensive, the greater is the excellency.

How exceedingly apt are we, when we are sitting still and accidentally casting our eye upon some marks or spots in the floor or wall, to be ranging of them into regular parcels and figures; and if we see a mark out of its place, to be placing of it right by our imagination—and this even while we are meditating on something else. So we may catch ourselves at observing the rules of harmony and regularity in the careless motions of our heads or feet, and when playing with our hands or walking about the room.

Pleasedness[4] in perceiving being always arises, either from a perception of consent to being in general, or of consent to that being that perceives. As we have shewn, that agreeableness to entity must be

3. Dwight: "mere."
4. Dwight's text separates the following four sections from the main body of the article, as though they were separated in some way in the manuscript. Connections between the content of the first three of these sections and passages in Miscell. nos. 89 and 117 indicate that Edwards probably wrote them soon after the foregoing essay, and in the order in which Dwight presents them.

agreeable to perceiving entity. It is as evident that it is necessary that agreeableness to that being must be pleasing to it, if it perceives it; so that pleasedness does not always arise from a perception of excellency in general;[5] but the greater a being is, and the more it has of entity, the more will consent to being in general please it. But God is proper entity itself, and these two therefore in him become the same; for so far as a thing consents to being in general, so far it consents to him. And the more perfect created spirits are, the nearer do they come to their creator in this regard.

That which is often called self-love is exceedingly improperly called love. For they do not only say that one loves himself when he sees something amiable in himself, the view of which begets delight; but merely an inclination to pleasure and averseness to pain they call self-love: so that the devils and other damned spirits love themselves, not because they see anything in themselves which they imagine to be lovely, but merely because they do not incline to pain, but to pleasure; or merely because they are capable of pain or pleasure, for pain and pleasure include an inclination to agreeableness and an aversion to disagreeableness. Now how improper is it to say, that one loves himself because what is agreeable to him is agreeable to him, and what is disagreeable to him is disagreeable to him, which mere entity supposes. So that this that they call self-love is no affection, but only the entity of the thing, or his being what he is.

One alone, without any reference to any more, cannot be excellent; for in such a case there can be no manner of relation no way, and therefore, no such thing as consent. Indeed, what we call "one" may be excellent, because of a consent of parts, or some consent of those in that being that are distinguished into a plurality some way or other. But in a being that is absolutely without any plurality there cannot be excellency, for there can be no such thing as consent or agreement.

One of the highest excellencies is love. As nothing else has a proper being but spirits, and as bodies are but the shadow of being, therefore, the consent of bodies to one another, and the harmony that is among them, is but the shadow of excellency. The highest excellency, therefore, must be the consent of spirits one to another. But the consent of spirits consists half in their mutual love one to another, and the sweet

5. The words "in general" might be Dwight's own addition, for they do not agree with Edwards' conception of excellency: he considers it may be greater or less according to the degree and extensiveness of the consent, but not general or specific.

harmony between the various parts of the universe is only an image of mutual love. But yet a lower kind of love may be odious, because it hinders or is contrary to a higher and more general. Even a lower proportion is often a deformity, because it is contrary to a more general proportion.

Corol. 1. If so much of the beauty and excellency of spirits consists in love, then the deformity of evil spirits consists as much in hatred and malice.

Corol. 2. The more any doctrine or institution brings to light of the spiritual world, the more will it urge to love and charity.

Happiness, strictly, consists in the perception of these three things: of the consent of being to its own being; of its own consent to being; and of being's consent to being.

[2]. PLACE OF MINDS.[6] Our common way of conceiving of what is spiritual is very gross and shadowy and corporeal, with dimensions and figure, etc.; though it be supposed to be very clear, so that we can see through it. If we would get a right notion of what is spiritual, we must think of thought or inclination or delight. How large is that thing in the mind which they call thought? Is love square or round? Is the surface of hatred rough or smooth? Is joy an inch, or a foot in diameter? These are spiritual things. And why should we then form such a ridiculous idea of spirits, as to think them so long, so thick, or so wide; or to think there is a necessity of their being square or round or some other certain figure?

Therefore spirits cannot be in place in such a sense, that all within the given limits shall be where the spirit is, and all without such a circumscription where he is not; but in this sense only, that all created spirits have clearer and more strongly impressed ideas of things in one place than in another, or can produce effects here and not there; and as this place alters, so spirits move. In spirits united to bodies, the spirit more strongly perceives things where the body is, and can there immediately produce effects, and in this sense the soul can be said to be in the same place where the body is; and this law is that we call the

---

6. JE's point of departure in this article is almost certainly Locke's discussion of the place and motion of spirits in *Essay* Bk. II, ch. 23, nos. 17–22. It is perhaps the earliest passage in his writings that shows the evident influence of Locke. Most of the immediately following entries are similarly related to topics suggested by Locke, indicating that JE was currently reading the *Essay*, possibly for the first time. No. 11 shows he was not using the first, but a later edition (see below, p. 342, n. 8).

union between soul and body. So the soul may be said to be in the brain, because ideas that come by the body immediately ensue only on alterations that are made there, and the soul most immediately produces effects nowhere else.

No doubt that all finite spirits, united to bodies or not, are thus in place; that is, that they perceive or passively receive ideas only or chiefly[7] of created things that are in some particular place at a given time. At least a finite spirit cannot thus be in all places at a time equally. And doubtless the change of the place where they perceive most strongly, and produce effects immediately, is regular and successive; which is the motion of spirits.

[3]. PERCEPTION of separate minds. Our perceptions, or ideas that we passively receive by our bodies, are communicated to us immediately by God while our minds are united with our bodies; but only we in some measure know the rule. We know that upon such alterations in our minds[8] there follow such ideas in the mind. It need therefore be no difficulty with us, how we shall perceive things when we are separate. They will be communicated then, also, and according to some rule, no doubt, only we know not what.

[4]. UNION of mind with body. The mind is so united with the body that an alteration is caused in the body, it is probable, by every action of the mind. By those acts that are very vigorous, a great alteration is very sensible. And at some times, when the vigor of the body is impaired by disease, especially in the head, almost every action causes a sensible alteration in the body.

[5]. CERTAINTY. Determined: that there are many degrees of certainty, though not, indeed, of absolute certainty, which is infinitely strong. We are certain of many things upon demonstration, which yet we may be made more certain of by more demonstration; because although, according to the strength of the mind, we see the connection of the ideas, yet a stronger mind would see the connection more perfectly and strongly, because it would have the ideas more perfect. We have not such a strength of mind that we can perfectly conceive of but

7. "Or chiefly," as in the version in Dwight's ch. 3; these words are omitted in his app. H version of the text.

8. Townsend suggests the word "bodies" instead of "minds" was intended (*Philosophy of JE,* p. 28, n. 10). Dwight reads "minds" in both ch. 3 and app. H.

very few things; and some little of the strength of an idea is lost in a moment of time as we, in the mind, look successively on the train of ideas in a demonstration.

[6]. Truth is the perception of the relations there are between ideas. Falsehood is the supposition of relations between ideas that are inconsistent with those ideas themselves, not in the[9] disagreement with things without. All truth is in the mind, and only there. 'Tis ideas, or what is in the mind alone, that can be the object of the mind. And what we call "truth" is a consistent supposition of relations between what is the object of the mind. Falsehood is an inconsistent supposition of relations. The truth that is in a mind must be, as to its object, and everything pertaining to it, in that mind; for what is perfectly without the mind, the mind has nothing to do with.[1]

The only foundation of error is inadequateness and imperfection of ideas; for if the idea were perfect, it would be impossible but that all its relations should be perfectly perceived.

[7]. GENUS. The various distributing and ranking of things, and tying of them together under one common abstract idea, is, although arbitrary, yet exceeding useful and indeed absolutely necessary.[2] For how miserable should we be if we could think of things only individually, as beasts do. How slow, narrow, painful and endless would be the exercise of thought.

What is this putting and tying things together which is done in abstraction? 'Tis not merely a tying of them under the same name; for I do believe that deaf and dumb persons abstract and distribute things into kinds. But it's so putting them together that the mind resolves hereafter to think of them together, under a common notion, as if they

9. Dwight, ch. 3: "in the"; app. H: "their."

1. Ch. 3: "for what is perfectly without the mind, the mind has nothing to do with"; omitted in app. H. Among the notes JE penned at the back of his copy of William Brattle's "Compendium of Logic" during his Yale tutorship are the following upon "verity": "Verity 1. truly of its kind 2. truly agreeable to its idea 3. truly agreeable to the name."

2. At the back of his copy of Brattle's "Compendium" JE writes: "What is a genus and species: a creature of the mind. Arbitrary. One highest genus. Lowest species. What difference: difference the essence or wherein it essentially differs. The more general the more simple and abstracted the idea, although the more comprehensive. Thus for instance till we come to being. The more special the more compounded. Difference the idea that is added to the genus. Sometimes the difference consists not in attributes but in the conjunction of several attributes. The difference need not be positive." These comments show JE correcting and improving Brattle on the basis of Locke's *Essay*, Bk. III, ch. 3.

were a collective substance; the mind being as sure in this proceeding of reasoning well, as if it were of a particular substance. For it has abstracted that which belongs alike to all, and has a perfect idea, whose relations and properties it can behold as well as those of the idea of one individual. Although this ranking of things be arbitrary, yet there is much more foundation for some distributions than others. Some are much more useful and much better serve the purposes of abstraction.

[8]. RULES OF REASONING. 'Tis no matter how abstracted our notions are, the further we penetrate and come to the prime reality of the thing, the better—provided we can go to such a degree of abstraction and carry it out clear. We may go so far in abstraction that, although we may thereby in part[3] see truth and reality, and farther than ever was seen before, yet we may not be able more than just to touch it and to have a few obscure glances. We may not have strength of mind sufficient[4] to conceive clearly of the manner of it. We see farther, indeed, but 'tis but very obscurely and indistinctly. We had better stop a degree or two short of this, and abstract no farther than we can conceive of the thing distinctly and explain it clearly. Otherwise we shall be apt to run into error and confound our minds.

[9]. SPACE. Space, as has been already observed,[5] is a necessary being (if it may be called a being); and yet we have also shewn that all existence is mental, that the existence of all exterior things is ideal. Therefore it is a necessary being only as it is a necessary idea—so far as it is a simple idea that is necessarily connected with other simple exterior ideas, and is, as it were, their common substance or subject. It is in the same manner a necessary being, as anything external is a being.

Corol. It is hence easy to see in what sense that is true, that has been held by some, that when there is nothing between any two bodies they unavoidably must touch.[6]

[10]. Truth, in the general, may be defined after the most strict and metaphysical manner: "the consistency and agreement of our ideas

3. App. H: "in part"; ch. 3: "in fact."
4. Ch. 3: "sufficient"; omitted in app. H.
5. In "Of Being," above, p. 203.
6. See Descartes, *Principles of Philosophy*, Pt. II, prin. 16–18 (Haldane and Ross ed., *1*, pp. 262–63). Locke comments in objection, *Essay*, Bk. II, ch. 13, nos. 21–27.

with the ideas of God." I confess this, in ordinary conversation, would not half so much tend to enlighten one in the meaning of the word as to say, "the agreement of our ideas with the things as they are"; but it should be inquired, what is it for our ideas to agree with things as they are; seeing that corporeal things exist no otherwise than mentally, and as for most other things, they are only abstract ideas. Truth as to external things, is the consistency of our ideas with those ideas, or that train and series of ideas, that are raised in our minds according to God's stated order and law.

Truth as to abstract ideas is the consistency of our ideas with themselves, as when our idea of a circle, or a triangle, or any of their parts, is agreeable to the idea we have stated and agreed to call by the name of a circle, or a triangle; and it may still be said that truth is the consistency of our ideas with themselves. Those ideas are false that are not consistent with the series of ideas that are raised in our minds by, according to, the order of nature.

Corol. 1. Hence we see in how strict a sense it may be said, that God is truth itself.

Corol. 2. Hence it appears that truth consists in having perfect and adequate ideas of thing. For instance, if I judge truly how far distant the moon is from the earth, we need not say that this truth consists in the perception of the relation between the two ideas of the moon and the earth, but in the adequateness.

Corol. 3. Hence certainty is the clear perception of this perfection. Therefore, if we had perfect ideas of all things at once, that is, could have all in one view, we should know all truth at the same moment, and there would be no such thing as ratiocination or finding out truth. And reasoning is only of use to us in consequence of the paucity of our ideas, and because we can have but very few in view at once. Hence it is evident that all things are self-evident to God.

[11]. PERSON.[7] Well might Mr. Locke say that identity of person consisted in identity of consciousness;[8] for he might have said that identity of spirit, too, consisted in the same consciousness. A mind or spirit is nothing else but consciousness, and what is included in it. The same consciousness is to all intents and purposes the very same[9] spirit or

----

7. JE's title is omitted in app. H.

8. *Essay*, Bk. II, ch. 27, nos. 9ff. This chapter was not included in the first edition of 1690, but was first inserted in the second edition of 1694. Hence JE must have been reading the second or a later edition.

9. Ch. 3: "the very same"; app. H: "individually the very same."

substance, as much as the same particle of matter can be the same with[1] itself at different times.

[12]. BEING. It seems strange sometimes to me, that there should be being from all eternity, and I am ready to say, "What need was there that anything should be?" I should then ask myself whether it seems strange that there should be either something or nothing. If so, 'tis not strange that there should be; for that necessity of there being something or nothing implies it.

[13]. SPACE.[2] The real and necessary existence of space, and its infinity even beyond the universe, depends upon a like reasoning as the extension[3] of spirits; and so the supposition of the necessity[4] of the existence of a successive duration before the creation of[5] the universe—even the impossibility of removing the idea out of the mind. If it be asked whether or no, if there be limits of the creation, it be not possible that an intelligent being should be removed beyond the limits; and then whether or no there would not be distance between that intelligent being and the limits of the universe, in the same manner and as properly as there is between intelligent beings and the parts of the universe within its limits; I answer: I cannot tell what the law of nature, or the constitution of God, would be in this case.

Corol. There is, therefore, no difficulty in answering such questions as these: What cause was there why the universe was placed in such a part of space, and why[6] created at such a time? For if there be no space beyond the universe, it was impossible that the universe should be created in another place; and if there was no time before the creation,[7] it was impossible that it should be created at another time.

The[8] idea we have of space, and what we call by that name, is only colored space, and is entirely taken out of the mind if color be taken

1. Ch. 3: "with"; app. H: "as."
2. JE's title is omitted in app. H.
3. App. H: "Extension"; ch. 3: "existence."
4. Ch. 3: "necessity"; app. H: "reality."
5. App. H omits "the creation of."
6. App. H inserts "the universe was."
7. App. H omits "the creation."
8. The following two paragraphs are not included in Dwight's ch. 3 version of the article. In app. H they are printed as an addendum to the main article; JE probably wrote them afterward on a later page of the MS (perhaps on that which contained Nos. 42 and 43), and might have keyed them for insertion here. See discussion above, pp. 315–16, 319.

away; and so all that we call extension, motion and figure is gone if color is gone. As to any idea of space, extension, distance or motion that a man born blind might form, it would be nothing like what we call by those names. All that he could have would be only certain sensations or feelings, that in themselves would be no more like what we intend by space, motion, etc., than the pain we have by the scratch of a pin, or than the ideas of taste and smell. And as to the idea of motion that such an one could have, it could be only a diversification of those successions in a certain way, by succession as to time; and then there would be an agreement of these successions of sensations with some ideas we have by sight, as to number and proportions—but yet the ideas, after all, nothing akin to that idea we now give this name to. And, as it is very plain, color is only in the mind, and nothing like it can be out of all mind. Hence it is manifest, there can be nothing like those things we call by the name of bodies out of the mind, unless it be in some other mind or minds.

And indeed, the secret lies here: that which truly is the substance of all bodies is the infinitely exact and precise and perfectly stable idea in God's mind, together with his stable will that the same shall gradually be communicated to us, and to other minds, according to certain fixed and exact established methods and laws: or in somewhat different language, the infinitely exact and precise divine idea, together with an answerable, perfectly exact, precise and stable will with respect to correspondent communications to created minds, and effects on their minds.

[14]. Excellence, to put it in other words, is that which is beautiful and lovely. That which is beautiful considered by itself separately, and deformed considered as a part of something else more extended; or beautiful only with respect to itself and a few other things, and not as a part of that which contains all things—the universe—is false beauty, and a confined beauty. That which is beautiful with respect to the university of things has a generally extended excellence and a true beauty; and the more extended or limited its system is, the more confined or extended is its beauty.

[15]. Truth. After all that has been said and done, the only adequate definition of truth is the agreement of our ideas with existence. To explain what this existence is, is another thing. In abstract ideas, it is nothing but the ideas themselves; so their truth is their consistency

with themselves. In things that are supposed to be without us, 'tis the determination, and fixed mode, of God's exciting ideas in us. So that truth in these things is an agreement of our ideas with that series in God. 'Tis existence, and that is all that we can say. 'Tis impossible that we should explain and resolve⁹ a perfectly abstract and mere idea of existence; only we always find this, by running of it up, that God and real existence are the same.

Corol. Hence we learn how properly it may be said that God is, and that there is none else, and how proper are these names of the Deity: "Jehovah" and "I Am That I Am."

[16]. CONSCIOUSNESS is the mind's perceiving what is in itself—its ideas, actions, passions, and everything that is there perceivable.¹ It is a sort of feeling within itself. The mind feels when it thinks, so it feels when it desires,² feels when it loves, feels itself hate, etc.³

[17]. LOGIC. One reason why at first, before I knew other logic, I used to be mightily pleased with the study of the old logic,⁴ was because it was very pleasant to see my thoughts, that before lay in my mind jumbled without any distinction, ranged into order and distributed into classes and subdivisions, that I could tell where they all belonged, and run them up to their general heads. For this logic consisted much in distributions and definitions; and their maxims gave occasion to observe new and strange dependencies of ideas, and a seeming agreement of multitudes of them in the same thing, that I never observed before.

[18]. WORDS. We are used to apply the same words a hundred different ways; and ideas being so much tied and associated with the words, they lead us into a thousand real mistakes. For where we find

9. App. H omits "and resolve."
1. Ch. 3: "perceivable"; app. H: "perceptible."
2. Ch. 3: "desires"; app. H: "discerns."
3. As in ch. 3; app. H: "feels when it hates."
4. It is probable that by the "old logic" JE means either that of Ramus, or the Aristotelian logic of Burgersdijck's *Institutio Logicae* and Morton's manual *Compendium Logicae*, or perhaps both the Ramist and Aristotelian systems. He was probably teaching both in some form to the Yale undergraduates at the time this article was written, and each may be seen to have left its mark upon certain aspects of his later thought. The "other" logic might be either that of Arnauld's *Art of Thinking,* or Locke's "way of ideas." The influence of each may be seen in various articles in "The Mind" and elsewhere.

that the words may be connected, the ideas being by custom tied with them, we think that the ideas may be connected likewise, and applied everywhere and in every way as the words.

[19]. SENSATION. SELF-EVIDENCE.[5] Things that we know by immediate sensation, we know intuitively, and they are properly self-evident truths: as, grass is green, the sun shines, honey is sweet. When we say that grass is green, all that we can be supposed to mean by it is, that in a constant course, when we see grass, the idea of green is excited with[6] it; and this we know self-evidently.

[20]. INSPIRATION.[7] The evidence of immediate inspiration that the prophets had when they were immediately inspired by the Spirit of God with any truth is an absolute sort of certainty; and the knowledge is in a sense intuitive, much in the same manner as faith and spiritual knowledge of the truth of religion. Such bright ideas are raised, and such a clear view of a perfect agreement with the excellencies of the divine nature, that it's known to be a communication from him. All the Deity appears in the thing, and in everything pertaining to it. The prophet has so divine a sense, such a divine disposition, such a divine pleasure, and sees so divine an excellency and so divine a power in what is revealed, that he sees as immediately that God is there as we perceive one another's presence when we are talking together face to face. And our features, our voice and our shapes are not so clear manifestations of us, as those spiritual resemblances of God that are in the inspiration are manifestations of him. But yet there are doubtless various degrees in inspiration.

[21(a)]. MATTER. THOUGHT.[8] It has been a question with some,[9] whether or no it was not possible with God, to the other properties or powers of matter to add that of thought; whether he could not, if he had pleased, have added thinking and the power of perception to those

---

5. App. H omits the title.

6. Ch. 3: "with"; app. H: "by."

7. JE's Miscell. no. 231 reads, "INSPIRATION vid. yᵉ Mind p. 7.7." This is the article to which the citation refers.

8. This is one of two entries Dwight numbered 21. According to the MS index to "The Mind," both it and the other, 21(b) below, were written on the same page of the MS. No. 21(a) is evidently the article JE cites in Miscell. no. 361: "Soul of man. Matter. Thought. vid. Mind p. 8."

9. Especially Locke in *Essay*, Bk. IV, ch. 3, no. 6.

other properties of solidity, mobility and gravitation. The question is not, here, whether the matter that now is, without the addition of any new primary property, could not be so contrived and modeled, so attenuated, wrought and moved, as to produce thought; but whether any lump of matter, a solid atom for instance, is not capable of receiving by the almighty power of God, in addition to the rest of its powers, a new power of thought.

Here, if the question be, whether or no God cannot cause the faculty of thinking to be so added to any parcel of matter so as to be in the same place (if thought can be in place), and that inseparably, where that matter is, so that by a fixed law that thought should be where that matter is and only there, being always bound to solid extension, mobility and gravity; I do not deny it. But that seems to me quite a different thing from the question whether matter can think, or whether God can make matter think, and is not worth the disputing. For if thought be in the same place where matter is, yet, if there be no manner of communication or dependence between that and anything that is material, that is, any of that collection of properties that we call matter; if none of those properties of solidity, extension, etc., wherein materiality consists, which are matter, or at least whereby matter is matter, have any manner of influence towards the exerting of thought; and if that thought be no way dependent on solidity or mobility, and they no way help the matter, but thought could be as well without those properties: then thought is not properly in matter, though it be in the same place.

All the properties that are properly said to be in matter depend on the other properties of matter, so that they cannot be without them. Thus figure is in matter—it depends on solidity and extension; and so doth motion; so doth gravity. And extension itself depends on solidity, in that it is the extension of the solidity; and solidity on extension, for nothing can be solid except it be extended. These ideas have a dependence on one another. But there is no manner of connection between the ideas of perception and solidity, or motion, or gravity. They are simple ideas, of which we can have a perfect view; and we know there is no dependence, nor can there be any dependence, for the ideas in their own nature are independent and alien, one to another. All the others either include the rest or are included in them; and, except the property of thought be included in the properties of matter, I think it cannot properly be said that matter has thought: or, if it can, I see not a possibility of matter in any other sense having thought.

If thought's being so fixed to matter as to be in the same place where matter is, be for thought to be in matter, thought not only can be in matter, but actually is, as much as thought can be in place. It is so connected with the bodies of men, or at least with some parts of their bodies, and will be forever after the resurrection.

[21(b)]. THE WILL. It is not that which appears the greatest good, or the greatest apparent good, that determines the will. It is not the greatest good apprehended, or that which is apprehended to be the greatest good, but the greatest apprehension of good. It is not merely by judging that anything is a great good that good is apprehended or appears; there are other ways of apprehending good. The having a clear and sensible idea of any good is one way of good's appearing, as well as judging that there is good. Therefore all these things are to be considered: the degree of the judgment by which a thing is judged to be good, and the contrary evil; the degree of goodness under which it appears, and the evil of the contrary; and the clearness of the idea and strength of the conception of the goodness, and of the evil. And that good of which there is the greatest apprehension or sense, all these things being taken together, is chosen by the will. And if there be a greater apprehension of good to be obtained or evil to be escaped by doing a thing than in letting it alone, the will determines to the doing it. The mind will be, for the present, most uneasy in neglecting it; and the mind always avoids that in which it would be, for the present, most uneasy. The degree of apprehension of good, which I suppose to determine the will, is composed of the degree of good apprehended, and the degree of apprehension. The degree of apprehension, again, is composed of the strength of the conception, and the judgment.

[22]. PREJUDICE. Those ideas which do not pertain to the prime essence of things, such as all colors that are everywhere objected to our eyes, and sounds that are continually in our ears, those that affect the touch as cold and heats, and all our sensations, exceedingly clog the mind in searching into the innermost nature of things, and cast such a mist over things that there is need of a sharp sight to see clearly through. For these will be continually in the mind and associated with other ideas, let us be thinking of what we will, and it is a continual care and pains to keep clear of their entanglements in our scrutinies into things. This is one way whereby the body and the senses [obscure][1]

1. Dwight reads "observe," but this is almost certainly an error in reading and copying the MS.

the views of the mind. The world seems so differently to our eyes, to our ears and other senses, from the idea we have of it by reason, that we can hardly realize the latter.

[23]. The reason why the names of spiritual things are all, or most of them, derived from the names of sensible or corporeal ones, as "imagination," "conception," "apprehend," etc., is because there was no other way of making others readily understand men's meaning when they first signified these things by sounds, than by giving of them the names of things sensible to which they had an analogy. They could thus point it out with the finger, and so explain themselves as in sensible things.

[24]. There is really a difference that the mind makes in the consideration of an universal, absolutely considered, and a species. There is a difference in the two ideas when we say "man," including simply the abstract idea, and when we say "the human sort of living creature." There is reference had to an idea more abstract, and [here][2] is this act of the mind in distributing an universal into species. It ties this abstract idea to two or more less abstract ideas, and supposes it limited by them.

It is not every property that belongs to all the particulars included in and proper to a genus, and that men generally see to be so, that is a part of that complex abstract idea that represents all the particulars, or that is a part of that nominal essence. But so much is essential which, if men should see anything less, they would not call it by the name by which they call the genus. This indeed is uncertain, because men never agreed upon fixing exact bounds.

[25(a)].[3] A part is one of those many ideas which we are wont to think of together; a whole is an idea containing many of these.[4]

[25(b)]. The distribution of the objects of our thoughts into sub-

2. Dwight reads "there," but JE obviously intends to contrast the latter with the former.
3. Dwight numbered both this and the following entry 25. According to the MS index to "The Mind" the two were written on the same page of the MS.
4. JE's notes at the back of his copy of Brattle's "Compendium" include the following on the topic of "totum": "What a totum—So I am used always to think of all the particulars of this table together, etc. Many totums the determination of which is arbitrary—an acre, a yard. Foundation for a totum is either the coexistence, likeness or dependence. 'Tis not everything that is a totum. Intellectual constituted of essential parts. Some totums contain an infinite number of parts. Murder an essential totum."

stances and modes may be proper, if by substance we understand a complexion of such ideas which we conceive of as subsisting together and by themselves; and by modes, those simple ideas which cannot be by themselves, or subsist in our mind alone.[5]

[26]. CAUSE is that, after or upon the existence of which, or the existence of it after such a manner, the existence of another thing follows.[6]

[27]. EXISTENCE. If we had only the sense of seeing, we should not be as ready to conclude the visible world to have been an existence independent of perception as we do, because the ideas we have by the sense of feeling are as much mere ideas as those we have by the sense of seeing. But we know that the things that are objects of this sense, all that the mind views by seeing, are merely mental existences, because all these things with all their modes do exist in a looking glass, where all will acknowledge they exist only mentally.

It[7] is now agreed upon by every knowing philosopher that colors are not really in the things, no more than pain is in a needle, but strictly nowhere else but in the mind. But yet I think that color may have an existence out of the mind with equal reason as anything in body has any existence out of the mind, beside the very substance of the body itself, which is nothing but the divine power, or rather the

---

5. Modes, as understood by Locke, are complex, not simple ideas (*Essay*, Bk. II, ch. 12, nos. 3–4). JE here reflects the Cartesian concept, as presented in Arnauld, *Art of Thinking*, Pt. II, ch. 2, and in Brattle's "Compendium."

6. JE's copy of Brattle's "Compendium" distinguishes the four Aristotelian causes, adds ten distinctions relative to the efficient cause, and two (primary and secondary) relative to the final cause. Edwards' notes at the back of the volume, written in 1724 or 1725 while he was a tutor at Yale, include the following: "What a cause, how we get a notion of it. Army in taking a town. In most natural things partial causes. 'Tis the proper effect of rain to be advantageous, the hurt by wetting accidental to it. 'Tis the proper effect of virtue to get a good name, accidental that it gets a bad one. Proper effect of God's Word to make a man better, an accidental to make him worse. 'Tis the proper effect of fire to make more hard, accidental that it softens. Of water to cool, accidental that it heats. The rays of the sun the next cause of corn's growing; the remote, the plowing the ground. The string is the next cause of the flying of the arrow, and powder of the bullet; remote, man's hand. . . . Light in the sun is the universal cause of light in the looking glass. Knowledge in the teacher is the universal cause of knowledge in the scholar. Holiness in God of holiness in man. The heat of the sun is the universal cause of plants' growing."

7. In app. H the following two paragraphs are printed as a separate addendum to No. 27. JE probably wrote them shortly after it, and perhaps keyed them for insertion here. Dwight might originally have numbered them 33, before he added the passage to this article. For discussion, see above, pp. 315–16, 318.

constant exertion of it. For what idea is that which we call by the name of body? I find color has the chief share in it. 'Tis nothing but color, and figure which is the termination of this color, together with some powers such as the power of resisting, and motion, etc., that wholly makes up what we call body. And if that which we principally mean by the thing itself cannot be said to be in the thing itself, I think nothing can be. If color exists not out of the mind, then nothing belonging to body exists out of the mind but resistance, which is solidity, and the termination of this resistance with its relations, which is figure, and the communication of this resistance from space to space, which is motion, though the latter are nothing but modes of the former. Therefore, there is nothing out of the mind but resistance. And not that, neither, when nothing is actually resisted; then there is nothing but the power of resistance. And as resistance is nothing else but the actual exertion of God's power, so the power can be nothing else but the constant law or method of that actual exertion. And how is there any resistance except it be in some mind, in idea? What is it that is resisted? It is not color. And what else is it? It is ridiculous to say that resistance is resisted. That does not tell us at all what is to be resisted. There must be something resisted before there can be resistance, but to say resistance is resisted is ridiculously to suppose resistance before there is anything to be resisted.

Let us suppose two globes only existing, and no mind. There is nothing there, *ex confesso*, but resistance. That is, there is such a law that the space within the limits of a globular figure shall resist. Therefore there is nothing there but a power, or an establishment. And if there be any resistance really out of the mind, one power and establishment must resist another establishment and law of resistance, which is exceedingly ridiculous. But yet it cannot be otherwise, if any way out of the mind. But now it is easy to conceive of resistance as a mode of an idea. It is easy to conceive of such a power or constant manner of stopping or resisting a color. The idea may be resisted—it may move, and stop, and rebound; but how a mere power which is nothing real can move and stop is inconceivable, and it is impossible to say a word about it without contradiction. The world is therefore an ideal one; and the law of creating, and the succession of these ideas, is constant and regular.

[28]. *Corol. 1.* How impossible is it, that the world should exist from eternity without a mind.

[29]. POWER. We have explained a cause to be "that after, or upon the existence of which, or its existence in such a manner, the existence of another thing follows."[8] The connection between these two existences, or between the cause and effect, is what we call power. Thus the sun above the horizon enlightens the atmosphere, so we say the sun has power to enlighten the atmosphere. That is, there is such a connection between the sun being above the horizon after such a manner, and the atmosphere being enlightened, that one always follows the other. So the sun has power to melt wax, that is, the sun and wax so existing, the melting of the wax follows; there is a connection between one and the other. So man has power to do this or that, that is, if he exists after such a manner there follows the existence of another thing; if he wills this or that, it will be so. God has power to do all things, because there is nothing but what follows upon his willing of it. When intelligent beings are said to have power to do this or that, by it is meant the connection between this or that upon this manner of their existing—their willing; in which sense they have power to do many things that they never shall will.

Corol. Hence it follows that men in a very proper sense may be said to have power to abstain from sin and to repent, to do good works and to live holily, because it depends on their will.

[30]. *Corol. 2.*[9] Since it is so, and that absolute nothing is such a dreadful contradiction, hence we learn the necessity of the eternal existence of an all-comprehending mind, and that it is the complication of all contradictions to deny such a mind.

[31]. From what is said above,[1] we learn that the seat of the soul is not in the brain any otherwise than as to its immediate operations, and the immediate operation of things on it. The soul may also be said to be in the heart or the affections, for its immediate operations are there also. Hence we learn the propriety of the Scriptures calling the soul "the heart," when considered with respect to the will and the affections.

We seem to think in our heads, because most of the ideas of which our thoughts are constituted or about which they are conversant come by the sensories that are in the head, especially the sight and hearing,

8. No. 26 above, p. 350.
9. This is apparently intended as Corol. 2 of No. 27 above.
1. That is, No. 2 above, pp. 338–39.

or those ideas of reflection that arise from hence, and partly because we feel the effects of thought and study in our head.

[32]. Seeing human souls and finite spirits are said to be in this place or that only because they are so as to mutual communications, it follows that the Scripture, when it speaks of God being "in heaven," of his dwelling "in Israel," of his dwelling "in the hearts of his people," does not speak so improperly as has been thought.

[33]. [Dwight does not present an article numbered 33. He might originally have given this number to the long addendum to No. 27, above, pp. 350–51.]

[34]. When we say that the world, i.e., the material universe, exists nowhere but in the mind, we have got to such a degree of strictness and abstraction that we must be exceedingly careful that we do not confound and lose ourselves by misapprehension. That is impossible, that it should be meant that all the world is contained in the narrow compass of a few inches of space, in little ideas in the place of the brain; for that would be a contradiction. For we are to remember that the human body and the brain itself exist only mentally, in the same sense that other things do. And so that which we call place is an idea too. Therefore things are truly in those places, for what we mean when we say so is only that this mode of our idea of place appertains to such an idea. We would not, therefore, be understood to deny that things are where they seem to be, for the principles we lay down, if they are narrowly looked into, do not infer that. Nor will it be found that they at all make void natural philosophy, or the science of the causes or reasons of corporeal changes; for to find out the reasons of things in natural philosophy is only to find out the proportion of God's acting. And the case is the same, as to such proportions, whether we suppose the world only mental in our sense, or no.

Though[2] we suppose that the existence of the whole material universe is absolutely dependent on idea, yet we may speak in the old way, and as properly and truly as ever: God in the beginning created such a certain number of atoms, of such a determinate bulk and figure,

2. In Dwight's edition the following passage is separated from the main article of No. 34, as though they were separated in some way in the MS. JE probably wrote the passage on a later page of the MS, perhaps not long after No. 34, and keyed it for addition to this entry.

which they yet maintain and always will; and gave them such a motion, of such a direction, and of such a degree of velocity; from whence arise all the natural changes in the universe forever in a continued series. Yet perhaps all this does not exist anywhere perfectly but in the divine mind. But then, if it be inquired what exists in the divine mind, and how these things exist there, I answer: there is his determination, his care and his design that ideas shall be united forever, just so and in such a manner as is agreeable to such a series. For instance, all the ideas that ever were or ever shall be to all eternity, in any created mind, are answerable to the existence of such a peculiar atom in the beginning of the creation, of such a determinate figure and size, and have such a motion given it. That is, they are all such as infinite wisdom sees would follow, according to the series of nature, from such an atom so moved. That is, all ideal changes of creatures are just so, as if just such a particular atom had actually all along existed even in some finite mind, and never had been out of that mind, and had in that mind caused these effects which are exactly according to nature, that is, according to the nature of other matter that is actually perceived by the mind. God supposes its existence; that is, he causes all changes to arise as if all these things had actually existed in such a series in some created mind, and as if created minds had comprehended all things perfectly. And although created minds do not, yet the divine mind doth, and he orders all things according to his mind, and his ideas.

And these hidden things do not only exist in the divine idea, but in a sense in created idea, for that exists in created idea which necessarily supposes it. If a ball of lead were supposed to be let fall from the clouds and no eye saw it till it got within ten rods of the ground, and then its motion and celerity was perfectly discerned in its exact proportion, if it were not for the imperfection and slowness of our minds, the perfect idea of the rest of the motion would immediately and of itself arise in the mind, as well as that which is there. So, were our thoughts comprehensive and perfect enough, our view of the present state of the world would excite in us a perfect idea of all past changes. And we need not perplex our minds with a thousand questions and doubts that will seem to arise, as to what purpose is this way of exciting ideas, and what advantage is there in observing such a series. I answer: it is just all one as to any benefit or advantage, any end that we can suppose was proposed by the Creator, as if the material universe were existent in the same manner as is vulgarly thought. For the corporeal world is to no advantage but to the spiritual, and it is exactly the same advantage this way as the other; for it is all one as to anything excited in the mind.

[35]. Seeing the brain exists only mentally, I therefore acknowledge that I speak improperly when I say, the soul is in the brain only as to its operations.[3] For to speak yet more strictly and abstractly, 'tis nothing but the connection of the operations of the soul with these and those modes of its own ideas, or those mental acts of the Deity, seeing the brain exists only in idea. But we have got so far beyond those things for which language was chiefly contrived, that unless we use extreme caution we cannot speak, except we speak exceeding unintelligibly, without literally contradicting ourselves.

Corol. No wonder, therefore, that the high and abstract mysteries of the Deity, the prime and most abstract of all beings, imply so many seeming contradictions.[4]

[36]. Things as to God exist from all eternity alike. That is, the idea is always the same, and after the same mode. The existence of things, therefore, that are not actually in created minds, consists only in power, or in the determination of God that such and such ideas shall be raised in created minds upon such conditions.

[37]. Genus and species indeed is a mental thing. Yet, in a sense, nature has distributed many things into species without our minds. That is, God evidently designed such particulars to be together in the mind, and in other things. But 'tis not so indeed with respect to all genera. Some therefore may be called "arbitrary" genera, others "natural." Nature has designedly made a distribution of some things; other distributions are of a mental original.

[38]. BODY, INFINITE. If we dispute whether body is capable of being infinite, let us in the first place put the question, whether motion can be infinite; that is, whether there can be a motion infinitely swift. I suppose that everyone will see that if a body moved with infinite swiftness, it would be in every part of the distance passed through ex-

---

3. No. 31 above, p. 352.

4. JE seems to refer to this article in a passage in Miscell. no. 194, in discussing the extension of God: "The soul of man is not present anywhere as bodies are present, as we have shewn elsewhere" (see Townsend, p. 183).

actly at once, and therefore it could not be said to move from one part of it to another. Infinite motion is therefore a contradiction. Supposing, therefore, a body were infinitely great, it could doubtless be moved by infinite power and turned round some point or axis. But if that were possible, it is evident that some part of that infinite body would move with infinite swiftness; which we have seen is a contradiction. Body therefore cannot be infinite.

[39]. CONSCIENCE. Beside the two sorts of assent of the mind called will and judgment, there is a third, arising from a sense of the general beauty and harmony of things, which is conscience. There are some things which move a kind of horror in the mind which yet the mind wills and chooses; and some which are agreeable in this way to its make and constitution which yet it chooses not. These assents of will and conscience have indeed a common object, which is excellency. Still they differ: the one is always general excellency, that is, harmony, taken[5] in its relation to the whole system of beings; the other that excellency which most strongly affects, whether the excellency be more general or particular. But the degree wherein we are affected by any excellency is in proportion compounded of the extensiveness and the intensiveness of our view of that excellency.[6]

[40].[7] Since all material existence is only idea, this question may be asked: In what sense may those things be said to exist which are supposed, and yet are in no actual idea of any created minds? I answer, they exist only in uncreated idea. But how do they exist otherwise than they did from all eternity, for they always were in uncreated idea and divine appointment? I answer, they did exist from all eternity in uncreated idea, as did everything else and as they do at present, but not in created idea. But, it may be asked, how do those things exist which have an actual existence, but of which no created mind is conscious—for instance the furniture of this room when we are absent and the room is shut up and no created mind perceives it—how do these things exist? I answer, there has been in times past such a course and succession of existences

5. Dwight: "taking."

6. JE's reflections upon the unregenerate man's desire for grace in Miscell. no. 164, and on the happiness of the saints in heaven in Miscell. nos. 182 and 188, may have led to his writing this article.

7. The citation which JE added to "Natural Philosophy," LS No. 14, namely, "The Mind, p. 12, 13, 14," undoubtedly refers to this article.

that these things must be supposed to make the series complete, according to divine appointment of the order of things; and there will be innumerable things consequential which will be out of joint—out of their constituted series—without the supposition of these. For upon supposition of these things are infinite numbers of things otherwise than they would be, if these were not by God thus supposed; yea, the whole universe would be otherwise, such an influence have these things by their attraction and otherwise. Yea, there must be an universal attraction in the whole system of things from the beginning of the world to the end; and to speak more strictly and metaphysically we must say, in the whole system and series of ideas in all created minds, so that these things must necessarily be put in to make complete the system of the ideal world. That is, they must be supposed if the train of ideas be in the order and course settled by the supreme mind. So that we may answer in short, that the existence of these things is in God's supposing of them, in order to the rendering complete the series of things—to speak more strictly, the series of ideas—according to his own settled order and that harmony of things which he has appointed. The supposition of God which we speak of is nothing else but God's acting in the course and series of his exciting ideas, as if they, the things supposed, were in actual idea.

But you may object: But there are many things so infinitely small that their influence is altogether insensible, so that whether they are supposed or not, there will no alteration be made in the series of ideas. Answer: But though the influence is so small that we do not perceive, yet who knows how penetrating other spirits may be to perceive the minutest alterations? And whether the alterations be sensible or not at present, yet the effect of the least influence will be sensible in time. For instance, let there be supposed to be a leaden globe of a mile in diameter to be moving in a right line with the swiftness of a cannon ball in the infinite void, and let it pass by a very small atom supposed to be at rest. This atom will somewhat retard this leaden globe in its motion, though at first and perhaps for many ages the difference is altogether insensible. But let it be never so little, in time it will become very sensible; for if the motion is made so much slower that in a million of years it shall have moved one inch less than it would have done otherwise, in a million million it will have moved a million inches less. So now the least atom, by its existence or motion, causes an alteration more or less in every other atom in the universe; so the alteration, in time, will become very sensible; so the whole universe, in time, will become all over different from what it would otherwise have been. For if every other atom is supposed to be either retarded or accelerated or diverted, every atom, however small for the present, will cause great alterations. As we have shewn already of retardation, the case is the same as to acceleration, and so as to diversion or varying the direction of the motion. For let the course of the body be never so little changed, this course in time may carry it to a place immensely distant from what the other would have carried it to, as is evident enough. And the case is the same still if the motion, that before was[8] never so slow, is wholly stopped. The difference in time will be immense, for this slow motion would have carried it to an immense distance if it were continued.

"But," the objector will say, "I acknowledge it would be thus if the bodies in which these insensible alterations are made were free and alone in an infinite void, but I do not know but the case may be far otherwise when an insensible alteration is made in a body that is among innumerable others, and subject to infinite jumbles among them." Answer: The case is the same, whether the bodies be alone in a void or in a system of other bodies. For the influence of this insensible alteration continues as steadily forever, through all its various interchanges and collisions with other bodies, as it would if it were alone in an infinite void; so that in time a particle of matter that shall be on this side of the universe might have been on the other. The existence and motion of every atom has influence, more or less, on the motion of all other bodies in the universe, great or small, as is most demonstrable from the laws of gravity and motion. An alteration more or less as to motion is made on every fixed star and on all its planets, primary and secondary. Let the alteration made in the fixed stars be never so small, yet in time it will make an infinite alteration from what otherwise would have been. Let the fixed stars be supposed, for instance, before to have been in perfect rest; let them now be all set in motion and this motion be never so small. Yet, continued forever, where will it carry those most immense bodies with their systems? Let a little alteration be made in the motion of the planets, either retardation or acceleration. This in time will make a difference of many millions of revolutions; and how great a difference will that make in the floating bodies of the universe?

Corol. By this we may answer a more difficult question, viz.: If material existence be only mental, then our bodies and organs are ideas only; and then in what sense is it true that the mind receives ideas by

8. Dwight: "that was before was."

the organs of sense, seeing that the organs of sense themselves exist nowhere but in the mind?

Answer: Seeing our organs themselves are ideas, the connection that our ideas have with such and such a mode of our organs is no other than God's constitution that some of our ideas shall be connected with others according to such a settled law and order, so that some ideas shall follow from others as their cause. But how can this be, seeing that ideas most commonly arise from organs, when we have no idea of the mode of our organs, or the manner of external objects being applied to them? I answer, our organs, and the motions in them and to them, exist in the manner explained above.

> Plato [and] his subterranean Cave, so famously known, and so elegantly described by him, [where he] supposes men tied with their backs towards the Light, placed at a great distance from them, so that they could not turn about their Heads to it neither, and therefore could see nothing but the shadows (of certain Substances behind them) projected from it, which shadows they concluded to be the only Substances and Realities, and when they heard the sounds made by those Bodies that were betwixt the Light and them, or their reverberated Echoes, they imputed them to those shadows which they saw. [I say,] all this is a Description of the State of those Men, who take Body to be the only Real and Substantial thing in the World, and to do all that is done in it; and therefore often impute Sense, Reason and Understanding, to nothing but Blood and Brains in us.
>
> Cudworth's *Intellectual System*[9]

[41]. As there is great foundation in nature for those abstract ideas which we call universals, so there is great foundation in the common circumstances and necessities of mankind, and the constant method of things proceeding, for such a tying of simple modes together to the constituting such mixed modes.[1] This appears from the agreement of languages, for language is very much made up of the names of mixed

9. JE quotes from ch. 1, §19, p. 19. There is no independent evidence that he read Cudworth's work before 1756 or 1757, when he copied passages from it in "Images of Divine Things," Nos. 208–10 and in Miscell. no. 1359.

1. "Mixed mode" is Locke's term for combinations of simple ideas which the mind forms arbitrarily, in contrast with ideas of substances which are formed in accordance with perceived regular connections among ideas as they are presented in experience. See *Essay*, Bk. II, ch. 23.

modes, and we find that almost all those names in one language have names that answer to them in other languages. The same mixed mode has a name given to it by most nations; whence it appears that most of the inhabitants of the earth have agreed upon putting together the same simple modes into mixed ones, and in the same manner. The learned and polished have indeed many more than others, and herein chiefly it is that languages do not answer one to another.

[42]. The agreement or similitude of complex ideas mostly consists in their precise identity with respect to some third idea of some of the simples they are compounded of. But if there be any similitude or agreement between simple ideas themselves, it cannot consist in the identity of a third idea that belongs to both; because the ideas are simple, and if you take anything that belongs to them you take all. Therefore, no agreement between simple ideas can be resolved into identity, unless it be the identity of relations.

But there seems to be another infallible agreement between simple ideas: thus some colors are more like one to another than others, between which there is yet a very manifest difference; so between sounds, smells, tastes and other sensations. And what is that common agreement of all these ideas we call colors, whereby we know immediately that that name belongs to them? Certainly all colors have an agreement, one to another, that is quite different from any agreement that sounds can have to them. So is there some common agreement to all sounds that tastes cannot have to any sound. It cannot be said that the agreement lies only in this, that these simple ideas come all by the ear, so that their agreement consists only in the relation they have to that organ. For if it should have been so that we had lived in the world and had never found out the way we got these ideas we call sounds, and never once thought or considered anything about it, and should hear some new simple sound, I believe nobody would question but that we should immediately perceive an agreement with other ideas that used to come by that sense, though we knew not which way one of them came, and should immediately call it a sound, and say we had heard a strange noise. And if we had never had any such sensation as the head-ache, and should have it, I do not think we should call that a new sound; for there would be so manifest a disagreement between those simple ideas, of another kind from what simple ideas have one with another.

I have thought whether or no the agreement of colors did not consist in a relation they had to the idea of space, and whether color in general might not be defined, "that idea that filled space." But I am convinced that there is another sort of agreement beside that, and the more because there can no such common relation be thought of with respect to different sounds. It is probable that this agreement may be resolved into identity: if we follow these ideas to their original in their organs, like sensations may be caused from like motions in the animal spirits.[2] Herein the likeness is perceived after the same manner as the harmony in a simple color. But if we consider the ideas absolutely, it cannot be.

Corol. All universals, therefore, cannot be made up of ideas abstracted from particulars, for color and sound are universals as much as man or horse. But the idea of color or sound in general cannot be made up of ideas abstracted from particular colors or sounds, for from simple ideas nothing can be abstracted.[3] But these universals are thus formed: the mind perceives that some of its ideas agree in a manner very different from all its other ideas. The mind therefore is determined to rank those ideas together in its thoughts; and all new ideas it receives with the like agreement, it naturally and habitually and at once places to the same rank and order, and calls them by the same name; and by the nature, determination and habit of the mind, the idea of one excites the idea of others.[4]

[43]. Many of our universal ideas are not arbitrary. The tying of ideas together in genera and species is not merely the calling of them by the same name, but such an union of them that the consideration of one shall naturally excite the idea of others. But the union of ideas is not always arbitrary, but unavoidably arising from the nature of the soul, which is such that the thinking of one thing, of itself, yea, against our wills, excites the thought of other things that are like it. Thus, if a person, a stranger to the Earth, should see and converse with a man, and a long time after should meet with another man and converse with him, the agreement would immediately excite the idea of that other man, and those two ideas would be together in his mind for the time to come, yea, in spite of him. So if he should see a third, and afterwards

2. JE's earlier view is indicated in "The Mind," No. 1 (above, pp. 335–36), and in "Natural Philosophy," US No. 5 (above, p. 265).

3. Locke describes abstraction as an operation in which our minds have created nothing new, but only leave out of the complex ideas of several particulars that which is peculiar to each, and retain only what is common to them all. See *Essay*, Bk. III, ch. 3, no. 7.

4. See also "Subjects to be Handled in the Treatise on the Mind," No. 43, below, pp. 391–92.

should find multitudes, there would be a genus or universal idea formed in his mind naturally, without his counsel or design. So I cannot doubt but, if a person had been born blind, and should have his eyes opened, and should immediately have blue placed before his eyes, and then red, then green, then yellow, I doubt not they would immediately get into one general idea. They would be united in his mind without his deliberation.

Corol. So that God has not only distributed things into species by evidently manifesting, by his making such an agreement in things, that he designed such and such particulars to be together in the mind, but by making the soul of such a nature that those particulars which he thus made to agree are unavoidably together in the mind, one naturally exciting and including the others.

[44]. [Dwight does not present an article numbered 44. He might originally have given this number to the passage on the difference between men and beasts that he attached as a separate addendum to No. 59, below, pp. 374–75. For discussion see above, p. 315.]

[45]. EXCELLENCE. 1. When we spake of excellence in bodies we were obliged to borrow the word "consent" from spiritual things. But excellence in and among spirits is, in its prime and proper sense, being's consent to being. There is no other proper consent but that of minds, even of their will; which, when it is of minds towards minds, it is love, and when of minds towards other things it is choice. Wherefore all the primary and original beauty or excellence that is among minds is love, and into this may all be resolved that is found among them.

2. When we spake of external excellency, we said that being's consent to being must needs be agreeable to perceiving being. But now we are speaking of spiritual things we may change the phrase, and say that mind's love to mind must needs be lovely to beholding mind; and being's love to being in general must needs be agreeable to being that perceives it, because itself is a participation of being in general.

3. As to the proportion of this love: to greater spirits more, and to less, less. It is beautiful as it is a manifestation of love to spirit or being in general. And the want of this proportion is a deformity, because it is a manifestation of a defect of such a love. It shows that it is not being in general, but something else that is loved, when love is not in proportion to the extensiveness and excellence of being.

4. Seeing God has so plainly revealed himself to us, and other minds

are made in his image, and are emanations from him, we may judge what is the excellence of other minds by what is his,[5] which we have shewn is love. His infinite beauty is his infinite mutual love of himself. Now God is the prime and original being, the first and last, and the pattern of all, and has the sum of all perfection. We may therefore doubtless conclude that all that is the perfection of spirits may be resolved into that which is God's perfection, which is love.

5. There are several degrees of deformity, or disagreeableness of dissent from being. One is when there is only merely a dissent from being; this is disagreeable to being, for perceiving being only is properly being. Still more disagreeable is a dissent to very excellent being, or, as we have explained, to a being that consents in a high degree to being; because such a being by such a consent becomes bigger, and a dissenting from such a being includes also a dissenting from what he consents with, which is other beings, or being in general. Another deformity, that is more odious than mere dissent from being, is for a being to dissent from, or not to consent with, a being who consents with his being. It is a manifestation of a greater dissent from being than ordinary, for the being perceiving knows that it is natural to being to consent with what consents with it, as we have shewn. It therefore manifests an extraordinary dissent that consent to itself will not draw its consent. The deformity, for the same reason, is greater still if there be dissent from consenting being. There are such contrarieties and jars in being as must necessarily produce jarring and horror in perceiving being.

6. Dissent from such beings, if that be their fixed nature, is a manifestation of consent to being in general; for consent to being is dissent from that which dissents from being.

7. Wherefore all virtue, which is the excellency of minds, is resolved into love to being. And nothing is virtuous or beautiful in spirits any otherwise than as it is an exercise, or fruit, or manifestation of this love; and nothing is sinful or deformed in spirits but as it is the defect of, or contrary to, these.

8. When we speak of being in general, we may be understood [to speak] of the divine Being, for he is an infinite being. Therefore all others must necessarily be considered as nothing. As to bodies, we have shewn in another place that they have no proper being of their own;

5. In Miscell. no. 150, JE holds that the nature of God differs from that of created spirits only in greatness: "If we should suppose the faculties of a created spirit to be enlarged infinitely, there would be the Deity to all intents and purposes, the same simplicity, immutability, etc." (See Townsend, p. 183.)

and as to spirits, they are the communications of the great original Spirit. And doubtless, in metaphysical strictness and propriety, he is, as there is none else. He is likewise infinitely excellent, and all excellence and beauty is derived from him, in the same manner as all being and all other excellence is, in strictness, only a shadow of his.[6] We proceed, therefore, to shew how all spiritual excellence is resolved into love.

9. As to God's excellence, it is evident it consists in the love of himself. For he was as excellent before he created the universe as he is now. But if the excellence of spirits consists in their disposition and action, God could be excellent no other way at that time, for all the exertions of himself were towards himself. But he exerts himself towards himself no other way than in infinitely loving and delighting in himself, in the mutual love of the Father and the Son. This makes the third, the personal Holy Spirit or the holiness of God, which is his infinite beauty, and this is God's infinite consent to being in general. And his love to the creature is his excellence, or the communication of himself, his complacency in them, according as they partake of more or less of excellence and beauty; that is, of holiness, which consists in love; that is, according as he communicates more or less of his Holy Spirit.

10. As to that excellence that created spirits partake of, that it is all to be resolved into love, none will doubt that knows what is the sum of the ten commandments; or believes what the Apostle says, that love is the fulfilling of the law; or what Christ says, that on these two, loving God and our neighbor, hang all the law and the prophets. This doctrine is often repeated in the New Testament. We are told that the end of the commandment is love, that to love is to fulfill the royal law, and that all the law is fulfilled in this one word, love.

11. I know of no difficulties worth insisting on except pertaining to the spiritual excellence of justice; but enough has been said already to resolve them. Though injustice is the greatest of all deformities, yet justice is no otherwise excellent than as it is the exercise, fruit and manifestation of the mind's love, or consent to being; nor injustice deformed any otherwise than as it is the highest degree of the contrary. Injustice is not to exert ourselves towards any being as it deserves, or to do contrary to what it deserves in doing good or evil, or in acts of consent or dissent. There are two ways of deserving our consent and

6. In Miscell. no. 187, which was probably written in the same general period as this article, JE holds that the restoration of spiritual beauty, which consists in virtue and holiness, is "by way of an immediate emanation from God."

the acts of it (by deserving anything, we are to understand that the nature of being requires it): by extensiveness and excellence, and by consent to that particular being. The reason of the deformity of not proportioning our consent, and the exercise of it, may be seen in paragraphs 3 and 5. As to the beauty of vindictive justice, see paragraph 6.[7]

12. 'Tis peculiar to God that he has beauty within himself, consisting in being's consenting with his own being, or the love of himself in his own Holy Spirit; whereas the excellence of others is in loving others, in loving God, and in the communications of his Spirit.

13. We shall be in danger, when we meditate on this love of God to himself as being the thing wherein his infinite excellence and loveliness consists, of some alloy to the sweetness of our view by its appearing with something of the aspect and cast of what we call self-love. But we are to consider that this love includes in it, or rather is the same as, a love to everything, as they are all communications of himself. So that we are to conceive of divine excellence as the infinite general love, that which reaches all proportionally, with perfect purity and sweetness; yea, it includes the true love of all creatures, for that is his spirit, or which is the same thing, his love. And if we take notice when we are in the best frames, meditating on divine excellence, our idea of that tranquility and peace which seems to be overspread and cast abroad upon the whole earth and universe naturally dissolves itself into the idea of a general love and delight, everywhere diffused.

14. Conscience is that sense the mind has of this consent: which sense consists in the consent of the perceiving being to such a general consent, that is, of such perceiving beings as are capable of so general a perception as to have any notion of being in general, and the dissent of his mind to a dissent from being in general. We have said already that it is naturally agreeable to perceiving being that being should consent to being, and the contrary disagreeable. If by any means, therefore, a particular and restrained love overcomes this general consent, the foundation of that consent yet remaining in the nature exerts itself again, so that there is the contradiction of one consent to another. And as it is naturally agreeable to every being to have being consent to him, the mind, after it has thus exerted an act of dissent to being in general, has a sense that being in general dissents from it, which is most disagreeable to it. And as he is conscious of a dissent from universal being, and of that being's dissent from him, wherever he is he

7. JE's discussion of free grace and the obligation of gratitude in Miscell. no. 191 is related to these themes.

sees what excites horror; and by inclining or doing that which is against his natural inclination as a perceiving being he must necessarily cause uneasiness, inasmuch as that natural inclination is contradicted: and this is the disquiet of conscience.[8] And though the disposition be changed, the remembrance of his having so done in time past, and the idea being still tied to that of himself, he is uneasy. The notion of such a dissent anywhere, as we have shewn, is odious, but the notion of its being in himself renders it uneasy and disquieting. But when there is no sense of any such dissent from being in general, there is no contradiction to the natural inclination of perceiving being. And when he reflects, he has a sense that being in general doth not dissent from him, and then there is peace of conscience. Though he has a remembrance of past dissensions with nature, yet if by any means it be possible when he has the idea of it to conceive of it as not belonging to him, he has the same peace. And if he has a sense, not only of his not dissenting, but of his consenting to being in general, or nature, and acting accordingly, he has a sense that nature in general consents to him. He has not only peace, but joy of mind, wherever he is. These things are obviously invigorated by the knowledge of God, and his constitution about us, and by the light of the Gospel.

[46]. [Dwight does not present an article numbered 46. He might originally have given this number to the passage he presents as No. 45, section 14, on conscience, above. For discussion, see pp. 315, 319.]

[47]. The foundation of the most considerable species, or sorts in which things are ranked, is the order of the world, the designed distribution of God and nature. When we in distributing things differ from that design, we don't know the true essences of things. If the world had been created without any order or design or beauty, indeed, all species would be merely arbitrary. There are certain multitudes of things that God has made to agree very remarkably in something, either as to their outward appearance, manner of acting, the effects they produce or that other things produce on them, the manner of their production, or God's disposal concerning them, or some peculiar perpetual cir-

8. In Miscell. no. 232, on the misery of the damned, JE develops these same ideas. In that article he refers to "what has been said under the head of excellency and love in our discourse on the mind." "The Mind," No. 45, which he probably intended, must have been written not long before.

cumstances that they are in. Thus diamonds agree in shape, pieces of gold in that they will be dissolved[9] in *aqua regia*, loadstones in innumerable strange effects that they produce, many plants in the peculiar effects they produce on animal bodies, men in that they are to remain after this life. That inward conformation that is the foundation of an agreement in these things is the real essence of the thing. For instance, that disposition of parts, or whatever it be in the matter of the loadstone from whence arises the verticity to the poles and its influence on other loadstones and iron, is the real essence of the loadstone that is unknown to us.

[48]. DEFINITION. That is not always a true definition that tends most to give us to understand the meaning of a word, but that which would give anyone the clearest notion of the meaning of the word, if he had never been in any way acquainted with the thing signified by that word. For instance, if I was to explain the meaning of the word "motion" to one that had seen things move, but was not acquainted with the word, perhaps I should say, "Motion is a thing's going from one place to another." But if I was to explain it to one who had never seen anything move (if that could be), I should say, "Motion is a body's existing successively in all the immediately contiguous parts of any distance without continuing any time in any."[1]

[49]. It is reasonable to suppose that the mere perception of being is agreeable to perceiving being, as well as being's consent to being. If absolute being were not agreeable to perceiving being, the contradiction of being to being would not be unpleasant. Hence there is in the mind an inclination to perceive the things that are, or the desire of truth. The exercise of this disposition of the soul to a high degree is the passion of admiration. When the mind beholds a very uncommon object, there is the pleasure of a new perception, with the excitation of the appetite of knowing more of it, as the causes and manner of production and the like, and the uneasiness arising from its being so hidden. These compose that emotion called admiration.

[50]. [Dwight does not present an article numbered 50. There is no

9. Dwight: "divided."
1. Many seventeenth-century philosophers cited the peripatetic definition of motion, *Actus entis in potentia quatenus in potentia*, as a primary example of the futility of scholastic definitions for purposes of science or common understanding. See Arnauld, *Art of Thinking*, Pt. II, ch. 16; Locke, *Essay*, Bk. III, ch. 4, nos. 6–7.

clue as to what passage, if any, he might have assigned this number originally.]

[51]. It is hardly proper to say that the dependence of ideas of sensation upon the organs of the body is only the dependence of some of our ideas upon others, for the organs of our bodies are not our ideas in a proper sense. Though their existence be only mental, yet there is no necessity of their existing actually in our minds, but they exist mentally in the same manner as has been explained (see No. 34).² The dependence of our ideas upon the organs is the dependence of our ideas on our bodies, after the manner there explained, mentally existing. And if it be inquired to what purpose is this way of exciting ideas, I answer, to exactly the same purpose as can be supposed if our organs are actually existing in the manner vulgarly conceived, as to any manner of benefit or end that can be mentioned.

It³ is not proper at all, nor doth it express the thing we would, to say, that "bodies do not exist without the mind." For the scheme will not allow the mind to be supposed determined to any place in such a manner as to make that proper. For place itself is mental, and "within" and "without" are mere mental conceptions. Therefore that way of expressing will lead us into a thousand difficulties and perplexities. But when I say, "the material universe exists only in the mind," I mean that it is absolutely dependent on the conception of the mind for its existence, and does not exist as spirits do, whose existence does not consist in, nor in dependence on, the conception of other minds. We must be exceedingly careful lest we confound ourselves in these [words] by mere imagination. It is from hence I expect the greatest opposition.⁴ It will appear a ridiculous thing, I suppose, that the material world exists nowhere but in the soul of man, confined within his skull. But

2. This reference might have been inserted by Dwight, though he put it in parentheses rather than square brackets. JE might just as appropriately have intended to refer to "The Mind," No. 40, Corol.

3. Dwight separates this paragraph from the main article for No. 51, as though it were separated in some manner in the MS itself. It is most probable, however, that the paragraph was written soon after No. 51, and that JE marked it as an addition to that entry. Dwight might originally have numbered it No. 52; his edition as published has no article of that number.

4. JE might be referring to his projected treatise on natural philosophy. See especially "Natural Philosophy," Cover, side ii, Nos. 17 and 20, below, pp. 194, 195. "The Mind," No. 51 might have been written in the same general period as these memoranda, i.e., within the first year or two after his settlement in Northampton in 1726.

we must again remember what sort of existence the head and brain have. The soul, in a sense, has its seat in the brain; and so, in a sense, the visible world is existent out of the mind, for it certainly, in the most proper sense, exists out of the brain.

[52]. [Dwight does not present an article numbered 52. He might have given this number to the passage he adds to No. 51, above, pp. 368–69. For discussion see above, p. 315.]

[53]. SENSATION. Our senses, when sound and in ordinary circumstances, are not properly fallible in anything; that is, we mean our experience by our senses. If we mean anything else, neither fallibility nor certainty in any way belongs to the senses. Nor are our senses certain in anything at all, any other way than by constant experience by our senses. That is, when our senses make such or such representations, we constantly experience that things are in themselves thus or thus. So, when a thing appears after such a manner, I judge it to be at least two rods off, at least two feet broad. But I only know by constant experience that a thing that makes such a representation is so far off and so big. And so my senses are as certain in everything when I have equal opportunity and occasion to experience. And our senses are said to deceive us in some things, because our situation does not allow us to make trial, or our circumstances do not lead us to it, and so we are apt to judge by our experience in other and different cases. Thus our senses make us think that the moon is among the clouds, because we cannot try it so quick, easily and frequently as we do the distance of things that are nearer. But the senses of an astronomer, who observes the parallax of the moon, do not deceive him, but lead him to the truth; though the idea of the moon's distance will never be exercised so quick and naturally upon every occasion, because of the tediousness and infrequency of the trial; and there are not so many ways of trial, so many differences in the moon's appearance, from what a lesser thing amongst the clouds would have, as there are in things nearer. I can remember when I was so young, that seeing two things in the same building, one of which was twice so far off as the other, yet seeing one over the other, I thought they had been of the same distance, one right over the other. My senses then were deceitful in that thing, though they made the same representations as now; and yet now they are not deceitful. The only difference is in experience. Indeed, in some things our senses make no difference in the representation, where there is a difference in the things; but in

those things our experience by our senses will lead us not to judge at all, and so they will [not]⁵ deceive. We are in danger of being deceived by our senses in judging of appearances by our experience in different things, or by judging where we have had no experience [of]⁶ the like.

[54]. REASONING. We know our own existence, and the existence of everything that we are conscious of in our own minds, intuitively. But all our reasoning with respect to real existence depends upon that natural, unavoidable and invariable disposition of the mind, when it sees a thing begin to be, to conclude certainly that there is a cause of it; or if it sees a thing to be in a very orderly, regular and exact manner, to conclude that some design regulated and disposed it.⁷ That a thing that begins to be should make itself, we know implies a contradiction. For we see intuitively that the ideas that such an expression excites are inconsistent, and that anything should start up into being without any cause at all, itself or anything else, is what the mind, do what we will, will forever refuse to receive, but will perpetually reject. When we therefore see anything begin to be, we intuitively know there is a cause of it, and not by ratiocination or any kind of argument. This is an innate principle, in that sense that the soul is born with it, a necessary fatal propensity so to conclude on every occasion.

And this is not only true to every new existence of those we call substances, but of every alteration that is to be seen. Any new existence of any new mode we necessarily suppose to be from a cause. For instance, if there had been nothing but one globe of solid matter, which in time past had been at perfect rest, if it starts away into motion, we conclude there is some cause of that alteration; or if that globe in time past had been moving in a straight line, and turns short about at right angles with its former direction; or if it had been moving with such a degree of celerity, and all at once moves with but half that swiftness. And it is all one whether these alterations be in bodies or in spirits, their beginning must have a cause—the first alteration that there is in a spirit after it is created, let it be an alteration in what it will, and so the rest. So if a spirit always in times past had had such an inclination,

5. The addition of "not" seems required here. According to Descartes and many other philosophers, sensations are not false in themselves, and we cannot be deceived by them unless we judge real external objects according to them. See Descartes' *Meditation* III; Arnauld's *Art of Thinking*, Pt. I, ch. 11.

6. Dwight: "or."

7. See also "Subjects to be Handled in the Treatise on the Mind," No. 10, below, p. 388.

for instance, always loved and chosen sin, and then has a quite contrary inclination and loves and chooses holiness, the beginning of this alteration, or the first new existence in that spirit towards it, whether it were some action or whatsoever, had some cause.[8]

And indeed, it is no matter whether we suppose a being has a beginning or no, if we see it exists in a particular manner, for which way of existing we know that there is no more reason as to anything in the thing itself than any other different manner; the mind necessarily concludes that there is some cause of its so existing more than any other way. For instance, if there is but one piece of matter existing from all eternity, and that be a square, we unavoidably conclude there is some cause why it is square, seeing there is nothing in the thing itself that more inclines it to that figure than to an infinite number of other figures. The same may be said as to rest, or motion, or the manner of motion; and for all other bodies existing, the mind seeks a cause why.

When the mind sees a being existing very regularly and in most exact order, especially if the order consists in the exact regulation of a very great multitude of particulars, if it be the best order as to use and beauty that the mind can conceive of that it could have been, the mind unavoidably concludes that its cause was a being that had design; for instance, when the mind perceives the beauty and contrivance of the world. For the world might have been one infinite number of confusions, and not have been disposed beautifully and usefully; yea, infinite times an infinite number, and so if we multiply infinite by infinite, *in infinitum*. So that if we suppose the world to have existed from all eternity, and to be continually, all the while without the guidance of design, passing under different changes, it would have been, according to such a multiplication, infinite to one whether it would ever have hit upon this form or no. Note: This way of concluding is a sort of ratiocination.[9]

[55]. Appetite of the mind. As all ideas are wholly in the mind, so is all appetite. To have appetite towards a thing is as remote from the nature of matter as to have thought. There are some of the appetites that are called natural appetites that are not indeed natural to the soul, as the appetite to meat and drink. I believe, when the soul has that sort of pain which is in hunger and thirst, if the soul never had experienced

---

8. In Miscell. nos. 199 and 200 JE argues for God's existence from the "contrivance" of the human soul (see Townsend, pp. 76, 77); and in Miscell. no. 267, from "the mere exertion of a new thought" (see ibid., p. 78).

9. In Miscell. no. 880 JE develops this argument at great length. See ibid., pp. 87–103.

that food and drink remove that pain, it would create no appetite to anything. A man would be just as incapable of such an appetite as he is to food he never smelt nor tasted. So, the appetite of scratching when it itches.

[56]. NUMBER is a train of differences of ideas put together in the mind's consideration in orderly succession and considered with respect to their relations one to another, as in that orderly mental succession. This mental succession is the succession of time. One may make which they will the first, if it be but the first in consideration. The mind begins where it will and runs through them successively, one after another. It is a collection of differences; for it is its being another in some respect, that is the very thing that makes it capable of pertaining to multiplicity. They must not merely be put together in orderly succession, but it's only their being considered with reference to that relation they have one to another, as differences and in orderly mental succession, that denominates it number. To be of such a particular number, is for an idea to have such a particular relation, and [be] so considered by the mind, to other differences put together with it in orderly succession. So that there is nothing inexplicable in the nature of number but what identity and diversity is, and what succession, or duration, or priority and posteriority is.

[57]. DURATION. "Pastness," if I may make such a word, is nothing but a mode of ideas. This mode perhaps is nothing else but a certain veterascence attending our ideas. When it is, as we say, "past," the idea after a particular manner fades and grows old. When an idea appears with this mode, we say it is past, and according to the degree of this particular inexpressible mode, so we say the thing is longer or more lately past. As in distance, it is not only by a natural trigonometry of the eyes, or a sort of parallax, that we determine it, because we can judge of distances as well with one eye as with two. Nor is it by observing the parallelism or aperture of the rays, for the mind judges by nothing but the difference it observes in the idea itself, which alone the mind has any notice of. But it judges of distance by a particular mode of indistinctness, as has been said before.[1] So it is with respect to distance

1. JE might be referring to the discussion of George Berkeley, in *New Theory of Vision*. JE lists this work, together with Berkeley's *Principles of Human Knowledge*, in his "Catalogue," p. 3, nos. 23 and 24.

of time, by a certain peculiar inexpressible mode of fading and indistinctness which I call veterascence.

[58]. REASONING does not absolutely differ from perception, any further than there is the act of the will about it. It appears to be so in demonstrative reasoning, because the knowledge of a self-evident truth, it is evident, does not differ from perception. But all demonstrative knowledge consists in, and may be resolved into, the knowledge of self-evident truths, and it is also evident that the act of the mind in other reasoning is not of a different nature from demonstrative reasoning.

[59]. JUDGMENT. The mind passes a judgment in multitudes of cases where it has learned to judge by perpetual experience, not only exceedingly quick, as soon as one thought can follow another, but absolutely without any reflection at all, and at the same moment without any time intervening. Though the thing is not properly self-evident, yet it judges without any ratiocination, merely by force of habit. Thus when I hear such and such sounds, or see such letters, I judge that such things are signified, without reasoning. When I have such ideas coming in by my sense of seeing, appearing after such a manner, I judge without any reasoning that the things are further off than others that appear after such a manner. When I see a globe I judge it to be a globe, though the image impressed on my sensory is only that of a flat circle appearing variously in various parts; and in ten thousand other cases the ideas are habitually associated together, and they come into the mind together. So likewise in innumerable cases men act, without any proper act of the will at that time commanding, through habit; as when a man is walking, there is not a new act of the will every time a man takes up his foot and sets it down.[2]

Corol. Hence there is no necessity of allowing reason to beasts in many of those actions, that many are ready to argue are rational actions; as, cattle in a team are wont to act as the driver would have them, upon his making such and such sounds, either to stop, or go along, or turn

2. John Locke considered habitual associations of ideas as having mainly a pernicious influence upon human judgment and conduct (see *Essay*, Bk. II, ch. 33). In this article JE appears to have explored a larger and more constructive role of association in intelligent performances. See also "Subjects to be Handled in the Treatise on the Mind," No. 43, below, pp. 391–92.

hither or thither, because they have been forced to do it by the whip upon the using of such words. It is become habitual so that they never do it rationally, but either from force or from habit. So of all the actions that beasts are taught to perform—dogs and horses and parrots, etc.; and those that they learn of themselves to do are merely by virtue of appetite, and habitual association of ideas. Thus a horse learns to perform such actions for his food because he has accidentally had the perceptions of such actions associated with the pleasant perceptions of taste, and so his appetite makes him perform the action without any reason or judgment.

The[3] main difference between men and beasts is that men are capable of reflecting upon what passes in their own minds; beasts have nothing but direct consciousness. Men are capable of viewing what is in themselves contemplatively. Man was made for spiritual exercises and enjoyments, and therefore is made capable by reflection to behold and contemplate spiritual things. Hence it arises that man is capable of religion.

A very great difference between men and beasts is that beasts have no voluntary actions about their own thoughts, for it is in this only that reasoning differs from mere perception and memory. It is the act of the will in bringing its ideas into contemplation, and ranging and comparing of them in reflection and abstraction. The minds of beasts, if I may call them minds, are purely passive with respect to all their ideas; the minds of men are not only passive, but abundantly active. Herein probably is the most distinguishing difference between men and beasts. Herein is the difference between intellectual or rational will and mere animal appetite: that the latter is a simple inclination to or aversion from such and such sensations, which are the only ideas that they are capable of that are not active about their ideas; the former is a will that is active about its own ideas, in disposing of them among themselves, or appetite towards those ideas that are acquired by such action.

The association of ideas in beasts seems to be much quicker and stronger than in men, at least in many of them. It would not suppose any exalted faculty in beasts to suppose that like ideas in them, if they have any, excite one another. Nor can I think why it should be so any

3. In Dwight's edition this section is separated from the main article of No. 59 as though they appeared separated in some way in the MS. It is quite possible that this section, or at least the first two paragraphs of it, were located on an earlier page of the MS, and that Dwight had originally numbered the passage "44." For discussion, see above, p. 315.

the less for the weakness and narrowness of their faculties, in such things where to perceive the argument of ideas requires neither attention nor comprehension; and experience teaches us that what we call thought in them is thus led from one thing to another.

[60]. WILL, ITS DETERMINATION. The greatest mental existence of good; the greatest degree of the mind's sense of good; the greatest degree of apprehension, or perception, or idea of [our][4] good, always determines the will. [These][5] three things are to be considered that make up the proportion of mental existence of [our][6] good, for it is the proportion compounded of these three proportions that always determines the will:

(1) The degree of good apprehended, or the degree of good represented by idea. This used to be reckoned by many the only thing that determined the will.

(2) The proportion or degree of apprehension or perception, the degree of the view the mind has of it, or the degree of the ideal perceptive presence of the good in the mind. This consists in two things: 1. In the degree of the judgment. This is different from the first thing we mentioned, which was the judgment of the degree of good, but we speak now of the degree of that judgment, according to the degree of assurance or certainty. 2. The deepness of the sense of the goodness, or the clearness, liveliness and sensibleness of the goodness or sweetness, or the strength of the impression on the mind. As one that has just tasted honey has more of an idea of its goodness than one that never tasted, though he also fully believes that it is very sweet, yea, as sweet as it is. And he that has seen a great beauty has a far more clear and strong idea of it, than he that never saw it. Good, as it is thus most clearly and strongly present to the mind, will proportionally more influence the mind to incline and will.

(3) There is to be considered the proportion or degree of the mind's apprehension of the propriety of the good, or of its own concernment in it. Thus the soul has a clearer and stronger apprehension of a pleasure that it may enjoy the next hour, than of the same pleasure that it is sure it may enjoy ten years hence, though the latter doth really as much concern it as the former. There are usually other things concur to make men choose present before future good. They are generally more cer-

4. Dwight: "own."
5. Dwight: "where."
6. Dwight: "own."

tain of the good, and have a stronger sense of it. But if they were equally certain and it were the very same good and they were sure it would be the same, yet the soul would be most inclined to the nearest, because they have not so lively an apprehension of themselves, and of the good, and of the whole matter. And then there is the pain and uneasiness of enduring such an appetite so long a time that generally comes in. But yet this matter wants to be made something more clear, why the soul is more strongly inclined to near than distant good.

It is utterly impossible but that it should be so, that the inclination and choice of the mind should always be determined by good as mentally or ideally existing. It would be a contradiction to suppose otherwise. For we mean nothing else by "good" but that which agrees with the inclination and disposition of the mind; and surely that which agrees with it must agree with it. And it also implies a contradiction to suppose that that good whose mental or ideal being is greatest does not always determine the will. For we mean nothing else by "greatest good" but that which agrees most with the inclination and disposition of the soul. It is ridiculous to say that the soul does not incline to that most, which is most agreeable to the inclination of the soul. I think I was not mistaken when I said that nothing else is meant by "good" here but that that agrees with the inclination and disposition of the mind. If they do not mean that that strikes the mind, that that is agreeable to it, that that pleases it and falls in with the disposition of its nature, then I would know what is meant.[7]

The[8] will is no otherwise different from the inclination, than that we commonly call that the will that is the mind's inclination with respect to its own immediate actions.

[61]. SUBSTANCE.[9] It is intuitively certain that if solidity be removed

7. This article and the following addendum are closely related to JE's discussion in *Freedom of the Will*, Pt. I, §2. See *Works* (Yale ed.), *1*, pp. 141–48. The date of No. 60 is undetermined; it is the last of those articles Dwight considered to have been written while JE was still a student (see above, pp. 324–25).

8. Dwight presents this as a separate addendum to No. 60. There is no evidence that JE might have written it at a significantly earlier or later time than the article to which it is attached.

9. In a footnote to this number Dwight writes, "This article, and the numbers following, viz. 62, 63, etc. are inserted in the manuscript distinctly from the rest, and were probably written at a somewhat later period of life" (p. 674). No definite indications of the dates of these later entries have been found, but Nos. 61–69 were probably written by the time JE formed his new index for the series (about 1747); Nos. 70–72 were probably composed afterward (see above, pp. 328–29).

from body, nothing is left but empty space. Now in all things whatsoever, that which cannot be removed without removing the whole thing,
that thing which is removed is the thing itself; except it be mere circumstance and manner of existence, such as time and place, which are
in the general necessary because it implies a contradiction to existence
itself to suppose that it exists at no time and in no place. And therefore,
in order to remove time and place in the general, we must remove the
thing itself; so, if we remove figure and bulk and texture in the general,
which may be reduced to that necessary circumstance of place.

If, therefore, it implies a contradiction to suppose that body, or anything appertaining to body beside space, exists when solidity is removed,
it must be either because body is nothing but solidity and space, or else
that solidity is such a mere circumstance and relation of existence which
the thing cannot be without, because whatever exists must exist in some
circumstances or other, as at some time or some place. But we know and
everyone perceives it to be a contradiction to suppose that body or matter exists without solidity; for all the notion we have of empty space is
space without solidity, and all the notion we have of full space is space
resisting.

The reason is plain: for if it implies a contradiction to suppose solidity
absent and the thing existing, it must be because solidity is that thing,
and so it is a contradiction to say the thing is absent from itself; or because it is such a mode or circumstance or relation of the existence as it is
a contradiction to suppose existence at all without it, such as time and
place, to which both figure and texture are reduced. For nothing can be
conceived of so necessarily in an existence, that it is a contradiction to
suppose it without it, but the existence itself, and those general circumstances or relations of existence which the very supposition of existence itself implies.

Again, solidity or impenetrability is as much action or the immediate
result of action as gravity. Gravity by all will be confessed to be immediately from some active influence. Being a continual tendency in
bodies to move, and being that which will set them in motion though
before at perfect rest, it must be the effect of something acting on that
body. And it is as clear and evident that action is as requisite to stop a
body that is already in motion, as in order to set bodies a-moving that
are at perfect rest. Now we see continually that there is a stopping of all
motion at the limits of such and such parts of space, only this stoppage
is modified and diversified according to certain laws. For we get the idea
and apprehension of solidity only and entirely from the observation we

make of that ceasing of motion, at the limits of some parts of space, that already is, and that beginning of motion that till now was not, according to a certain constant manner.

And why is it not every whit as reasonable that we should attribute this action or effect to the influence of some agent, as that other action or effect which we call gravity, which is likewise derived from our observation of the beginning and ceasing of motion according to a certain method? In either case there is nothing observed but the beginning, increasing, directing, diminishing and ceasing of motion. And why is it not as reasonable to seek a reason beside that general one, that it is something—which is no reason at all? I say, why is it not as reasonable to seek a reason or cause of these actions as well in one as in the other case? We do not think it sufficient to say it is the nature of the unknown substance in the one case; and why should we think it a sufficient explication of the same actions or effects in the other? By substance, I suppose it is confessed, we mean only "something," because of abstract substance we have no idea that is more particular than only existence in general. Now why is it not as reasonable, when we see something suspended in the air, set to move with violence towards the earth, to rest in attributing of it to the nature of the something that is there, as when we see that motion, when it comes to such limits, all on a sudden cease? For this is all that we observe in falling bodies. Their falling is the action we call gravity; their stopping upon the surface of the earth the action whence we gain the idea of solidity. It was before agreed on all hands that there is something there that supports that resistance. It must be granted now that that something is a being that acts there, as much as that being that causes bodies to descend towards the center. Here is something in these parts of space that of itself produces effects, without previously being acted upon. For that being that lays an arrest on bodies in motion, and immediately stops them when they come to such limits and bounds, certainly does as much as that being that sets a body in motion that before was at rest. Now this being, acting altogether of itself, producing new effects that are perfectly arbitrary, and that are no way necessary of themselves, must be intelligent and voluntary. There is no reason in the nature of the thing itself why a body, when set in motion, should stop at such limits more than at any other. It must therefore be some arbitrary, active and voluntary being that determines it. If there were but one body in the universe that always in time past had been at rest, and should now without any alteration be set in motion, we might certainly conclude that some voluntary being set it in motion, because it can certainly be demonstrated that it can be for no other reason; so, with just the same reason, in the same manner we may conclude, if the body had hitherto been in motion and is at a certain point of space now stopped. And would it not be every whit as reasonable to conclude it must be from such an agent, as if in certain portions of space we observed bodies to be attracted a certain way, and so at once to be set into motion, or accelerated in motion? And it is not at all the less remarkable because we receive the ideas of light and colors from those spaces, for we know that light and colors are not there, and are made entirely by such a resistance, together with attraction, that is antecedent to these qualities, and would be a necessary effect of a mere resistance of space without other substance.

The whole of what we any way observe whereby we get the idea of solidity or solid body are certain parts of space from whence we receive the ideas of light and colors, and certain sensations by the sense of feeling. And we observe that the places whence we receive these sensations are not constantly the same, but are successively different, and this light and colors are communicated from one part of space to another. And we observe that these parts of space, from whence we receive these sensations, resist and stop other bodies, which we observe communicated successively through the parts of space adjacent, and that those that there were before at rest, or existing constantly in one and the same part of space, after this exist successively in different parts of space. And these observations are according to certain stated rules. I appeal to anyone that takes notice and asks himself, whether this be not all that ever he experienced in the world whereby he got these ideas, and that this is all that we have or can have any idea of, in relation to bodies. All that we observe of solidity is that certain parts of space, from whence we receive the ideas of light and colors and a few other sensations, do likewise resist anything coming within them. It therefore follows that if we suppose there be anything else than what we thus observe, it is but only by way of inference.

I know that it is nothing but the imagination will oppose me in this. I will therefore endeavor to help the imagination thus. Suppose that we received none of the sensible qualities of light, colors, etc. from the resisting parts of space (we will suppose it possible for resistance to be without them), and they were to appearance clear and pure, and all that we could possibly observe was only and merely resistance; we simply observed that motion was resisted and stopped here and there, in particular parts of infinite space. Should we not then think it less unreasonable to suppose that such effects should be produced by some agent present in those parts of space, though invisible? If we, when walking upon the face of the earth, were stopped at certain limits and could not possibly enter into such a part of space, nor make any body enter into it, and we could observe no other difference, no way nor at any time, between that and other parts of clear space; should we not be ready to say: What is it stops us? What is it hinders all entrance into that place?

The[1] reason why it is so exceedingly natural to men to suppose that there is some latent substance, or something that is altogether hid, that upholds the properties of bodies, is because all see at first sight that the properties of bodies are such as need some cause that shall every moment have influence to their continuance, as well as a cause of their first existence. All therefore agree that there is something that is there, and upholds these properties; and it is most true, there undoubtedly is. But men are wont to content themselves in saying merely that it is something; but that "something" is he by whom all things consist.

[62]. As bodies, the objects of our external senses, are but the shadows of beings, that harmony wherein consists sensible excellency and beauty is but the shadow of excellency; that is, it is pleasant to the mind because it is a shadow of love. When one thing sweetly harmonizes with another, as the notes in music, the notes are so conformed and have such proportion one to another that they seem to have respect one to another, as if they loved one another. So the beauty of figures and motions is, when one part has such consonant proportion with the rest as represents a general agreeing and consenting together; which is very much the image of love in all the parts of a society united by a sweet consent and charity of heart. Therein consists the beauty of figures, as of flowers drawn with a pen, and the beauty of the body, and of the features of the face.

There is no other way that sensible things can consent one to another but by equality, or by likeness, or by proportion. Therefore the lowest or most simple kind of beauty is equality or likeness, because by equality or likeness one part consents with but one part. But by proportion one part may sweetly consent to ten thousand different parts, all the parts may consent with all the rest, and not only so, but the parts taken singly may consent with the whole taken together. Thus in the figures of

---

1. Dwight presents the following paragraph as a separate addendum to No. 61. There is no indication that it might have been written elsewhere in the MS, or at a significantly different time, than the main article.

flourishes drawn by an acute penman, every stroke may have such a proportion, both by the place and distance, direction, degree of curvity, etc., that there may be a consent in the parts of each stroke one with another, and a harmonious agreement with all the strokes and with the various parts composed of many strokes, and an agreeableness to the whole figure taken together.

There is a beauty in equality, as appears very evident by the very great respect men show to it in everything they make or do. How unbeautiful would be the body if the parts on one side were unequal to those on the other. How unbeautiful would writing be if the letters were not of an equal height, or the lines of an equal length or at an equal distance, or if the pages were not of an equal width or height. And how unbeautiful would a building be if no equality were observed in the correspondent parts.

Existence[2] or entity is that into which all excellency is to be resolved. Being or existence is what is necessarily agreeable to being; and when being perceives it, it will be an agreeable perception; and any contradiction to being or existence is what being, when it perceives, abhors. If being, in itself considered, were not pleasing, being's consent to being would not be pleasing, nor would being's disagreeing with being be displeasing. Therefore, not only may greatness be considered as a capacity of excellency, but a being, by reason of his greatness, considered alone, is the more excellent because he partakes more of being; though if he be great, if he dissents from more general and extensive being, or from universal being, he is the more odious for his greatness, because the dissent or contradiction to being in general is so much the greater. It is more grating to see much being dissent from being than to see little, and his greatness, or the quantity of being he partakes of, does nothing towards bettering his dissent from being in general, because there is no proportion between finite being, however great, and universal being.

Corol. 1. Hence it is impossible that God should be any otherwise than excellent, for he is the infinite, universal and all comprehending existence.

[*Corol.*] *2.* Hence God infinitely loves himself, because his being is infinite. He is in himself, if I may so say, an infinite quantity of existence.

2. The following section appears in Dwight's edition as a separate addendum to No. 62. It is possible that this section was written on another and earlier page of the MS, and that Dwight originally numbered it separately. For discussion, see above, p. 317.

[*Corol.*] *3.* Hence we learn one reason why persons who view death merely as annihilation have a great abhorrence of it, though they live a very afflicted life.

[63]. Sensible things, by virtue of the harmony and proportion that is seen in them, carry the appearance of perceiving and willing being. They evidently show at first blush the action and governing of understanding and volition. The notes of a tune or the strokes of an acute penman, for instance, are placed in such exact order, having such mutual respect one to another, that they carry with them into the mind of him that sees or hears the conception of an understanding and will exerting itself in these appearances. And were it not that we, by reflection and reasoning, are led to an extrinsic intelligence and will that was the cause, it would seem to be in the notes and strokes themselves. They would appear like a society of so many perceiving beings, sweetly agreeing together. I can conceive of no other reason why equality and proportion should be pleasing to him that perceives, but only that it has an appearance of consent.

[64]. Excellency may be distributed into greatness and beauty. The former is the degree of being, the latter is being's consent to being.

[65(a)].[3] I think we find by experience that when we have been in a sound sleep for many hours together, if we look back to the time when we were last awake, the ideas seem farther off to us than when we have only ceased thinking a few minutes: which cannot be because we see a longer train of intermediate ideas in one case than in the other, for I suppose we see none in neither. But there is a sort of veterascence of ideas that have been a longer time in the mind. When we look upon them they do not look just as those that are much nearer. This veterascence consists, I think, in blotting out the little distinctions, the minute parts and fine strokes of it. This is one way of judging of the distance of visible objects. In this respect, a house, a tree do not look at a little distance as they do very near. They not only do not appear so big, but a multitude of the little distinctions vanish, that are plain when we are near.

[65(b)]. MOTION. If motion be only mental it seems to follow that

3. This is the first of two entries Dwight numbered 65. According to the MS index, both it and the other, 65b, were written on the same page of the MS. The discussion of No. 65a seems to continue that of No. 57 above.

there is no difference between real and apparent motion, or that motion is nothing else but the change of position between bodies. And then, of two bodies that have their position changed, motion may with equal reason be ascribed to either of them, and the sun may as properly be said to move as the earth. And then returns this difficulty: If it be so, how comes it to pass that the laws of centrifugal force are observed to take place with respect to the earth considered as moving round the sun, but not with respect to the sun considered as moving round the earth? I answer: It would be impossible it should be so and the laws of gravitation be observed. The earth cannot be kept at a distance from a body so strongly attracting it as the sun any other way than by such a motion as is supposed. That body therefore must be reputed to move, that can be supposed so to do according to the laws of nature universally observed in other things. It is upon them that God impresses that centrifugal force.

N.B. This answers the objection that might be raised from what Newton says of absolute and relative motion, and that distinguishing property of absolute circular motion, that there was a centrifugal force in the body moved.[4] For God causes a centrifugal force in that body that can be supposed to move circularly, consistently with the laws of motion in that and in all other things on which it has a near or a remote dependence, and which must be supposed to move in order to the observance of those laws in the universe. For instance, when a bushel with water in it is violently whirled round, before the water takes the impression there is a continual change of position between the water and the parts of the bushel. But yet that must not be supposed to move as fast as that position is altered, because if we follow it, it will not hold out consistent with the laws of motion in the universe. For if the water moves then the bushel does not move, and if the bushel does not move then the earth moves round the bushel every time that seems to turn round. But there can be no such alteration in the motion of the earth created naturally, or in observance of the laws of nature.

[66]. IDEAS. All sorts of ideas of things are but the repetitions of those very things over again, as well the ideas of colors, figures, solidity, tastes and smells, as the ideas of thought and mental acts.[5]

---

4. See Newton, *Principia*, Definitions, Scholium. In this beginning section Newton distinguishes between absolute and relative space, time, and motion. The absolute in each case is real and independent of particular observers, while the relative is observed or apparent, and so depends upon the places, times, and motions of the observers themselves.

5. JE makes a similar point in Miscell. no. 238 (see Townsend, p. 247).

[67]. LOVE is not properly said to be an idea, any more than understanding is said to be an idea. Understanding and loving are different acts of the mind entirely. And so, pleasure and pain are not properly ideas. Though pleasure and pain may imply perception in their nature, yet it does not follow that they are properly ideas. There is an act of the mind in it. An idea is only a perception wherein the mind is passive, or rather, subjective. The acts of the mind are not merely ideas; all acts of the mind about its ideas are not themselves mere ideas.

Pleasure and pain have their seat in the will, and not in the understanding. The will, choice, etc. is nothing else but the mind's being pleased with an idea, or having a superior pleasedness in something thought of, or a desire of a future thing, or a pleasedness in the thought of our union with the thing, or a pleasedness in such a state of ourselves and a degree of pain while we are not in that state, or a disagreeable conception of the contrary state at that time when we desire it.

[68]. REASON. A person may have a strong reason, and yet not a good reason. He may have a strength of mind to drive an argument, and yet not have even balances. It is not so much from a defect of the reasoning powers, as from a fault of the disposition. When men of strong reason do not form an even and just judgment, 'tis for one of these two reasons: either a liableness to prejudice through natural temper or education or circumstances; or for want of a great love to truth and of fear of error, that shall cause a watchful circumspection that nothing relative to the case in question of any weight shall escape the observation and just estimation, to distinguish with great exactness between what is real and solid, and what is only color and shadow and words.

Persons of mean capacities may see the reason of that which requires a nice and exact attention and a long discourse to explain—as the reason why thunder should be so much feared, and many other things that might be mentioned.

[69]. MEMORY is the identity, in some degree, of ideas that we formerly had in our minds, with a consciousness that we formerly had them, and a supposition that their former being in the mind is the cause of their being in us at present. There is not only the presence of the same ideas that were in our minds formerly, but also an act of the judgment that they were there formerly; and that judgment not properly from proof, but from natural necessity arising from a law of nature which God hath fixed.

In memory, in mental principles, habits and inclinations, there is something really abiding in the mind when there are no acts or exercises of them, much in the same manner as there is a chair in this room when no mortal perceives it. For when we say there are chairs in this room when none perceives it, we mean that minds would perceive chairs here according to the law of nature in such circumstances. So, when we say a person has these and those things laid up in his memory, we mean they would actually be repeated in his mind upon some certain occasions according to the law of nature; though we cannot describe particularly the law of nature about these mental acts, so well as we can about other things.

[70]. That it is not uneasiness in our present circumstances that always determines the will, as Mr. Locke supposes,⁶ is evident by this: that there may be an act of the will in choosing and determining to forbear to act or move when some action is proposed to a man, as well as in choosing to act. Thus, if a man be put upon rising from his seat and going to a certain place, his voluntary refusal is an act of the will which does not arise from any uneasiness in his present circumstances. Certainly, an act of voluntary refusal is as truly an act of the will as an act of choice, and indeed, there is an act of choice in an act of refusal. The will chooses to neglect; it prefers the opposite of that which is refused.

[71]. KNOWLEDGE is not the perception of the agreement or disagreement of ideas, but rather the perception of the union or disunion of ideas, or the perceiving whether two or more ideas belong to one another.⁷

Corol. Hence it is not impossible to believe or know the truth of mysteries, or propositions that we cannot comprehend, or see the manner how the several ideas that belong to the proposition are united. Perhaps it cannot properly be said that we see the agreement of the ideas unless we see how they agree, but we may perceive that they are united and know that they belong one to another, though we do not know the manner how they are tied together.

[72]. Identity of person is what seems never yet to have been explained. It is a mistake that it consists in sameness or identity of con-

6. See *Essay*, Bk. II, ch. 21, nos. 31ff. These sections were added in the second and later editions of the *Essay*.
7. See Locke, *Essay*, Bk. IV, ch. 1, no. 1.

sciousness,[8] if by sameness of consciousness be meant having the same ideas hereafter that I have now, with a notion or apprehension that I had had them before, just in the same manner as I now have the same ideas that I had in time past by memory. It is possible without doubt in the nature of things for God to annihilate me, and after my annihilation to create another being that shall have the same ideas in his mind that I have, and with the like apprehension that he had had them before in like manner as a person has by memory; and yet I be in no way concerned in it, having no reason to fear what that being shall suffer, or to hope for what he shall enjoy.

Can anyone deny that it is possible, after my annihilation, to create two beings in the universe, both of them having my ideas communicated to them with such a notion of their having had them before, after the manner of memory, and yet be ignorant one of another? And in such case, will anyone say that both these are one and the same person, as they must be if they are both the same person with me? It is possible there may be two such beings, each having all the ideas that are now in my mind in the same manner that I should have by memory if my own being were continued, and yet these two beings not only be ignorant one of another, but also be in a very different state, one in a state of enjoyment and pleasure and the other in a state of great suffering and torment.

Yea, there seems to be nothing of impossibility in the nature of things, but that the Most High could, if he saw fit, cause there to be another being who should begin to exist, in some distant part of the universe, with the same ideas I now have after the manner of memory, and should henceforward coexist with me, we both retaining a consciousness of what was before the moment of his first existence in like manner, but thenceforward should have a different train of ideas. Will anyone say that he, in such a case, is the same person with me, when I know nothing of his sufferings and am never the better for his joys?

[Plan for a Treatise]

Title: The Natural History of the Mental World, or of the internal world: being a Particular Inquiry into the Nature of the Human Mind with respect to both its Faculties, the Understanding and the Will, and its various Instincts and Active and Passive Powers.

8. See Locke's account in *Essay*, Bk. II, ch. 27. This chapter was added in the second and later editions of the *Essay*.

Introduction: Concerning the two worlds, the external and the internal: the external, the subject of natural philosophy; the internal, our own minds. How the knowledge of the latter is in many respects the most important. Of what great use the true knowledge of this is, and of what dangerous consequence errors here are, more than in the other.

SUBJECTS TO BE HANDLED IN THE TREATISE ON THE MIND:[1]

1. Concerning the difference between pleasure and pain and ideas, or the vast difference between the understanding and the will.

2. Concerning prejudices: The influence of prejudice to cloud the mind. The various sorts of prejudices in particular, and how they come to cloud the mind, particularly prejudices of interest—the true reason why they cloud the judgment. Prejudices of education and custom— their universal influence on wise and learned and rational, as well as other men, demonstrated from fact and experience. Of their insensible influence; how it is insensible on great men. How difficultly a people are got out of their old customs in husbandry. How difficult to persuade that a new way is better. Another prejudice is the general cry and fashion and vogue of an age; its exceeding strong influence, like a strong stream that carries all that way; this influence on great men. Prejudices of people in favor of individual great men to the contempt of others. Again, the voice of men in power, riches or honorable place. How some churches would laugh at their ceremonies if they were without them. How a man's being rich or in high place gives great weight to his words; how much more weighty a man's sayings are after he becomes a bishop than before. Another prejudice is from ridicule or an high, strong, overbearing, contemptuous style.

3. Either after or before this, to have a dissertation concerning the exceeding vanity, blindness and weakness of the mind of man: what poor fallible creatures men are; how every man is insensible of his own; thinks himself best. Concerning the pride of men; how ready to think they shall be great men and to promise themselves great things.

4. How some men have strong reason but not good judgment.

5. Concerning certainty and assurance: How many things that are

1. Dwight provided the following footnote at the end of this series of topics: "The preceding articles were set down from time to time at the close of the work, in two series; the first ending with No. 26."

demonstrations in themselves are not demonstrations to men and yet are strong arguments—no more demonstrations than a boy may have that a cube of two inches may be cut into eight cubes of one inch, for want of proper clearness and full comprehension of the ideas. How assurance is capable of infinite degrees; how none have such a degree but that it might be heightened, even of that that two and two make four. It may be increased by a stronger sight or a greater clearness of ideas; minds of clearer and stronger sight may be more assured of it than those of more obscure vision. There may be beings of a thousand times stronger sight than we are; how God's sight only is infinitely clear and strong. That which is demonstration at one time may be only probable reasoning at another, by reason of different degrees of clearness and comprehension. It is almost impossible that a long demonstration should beget so great assurance as a short one, because many ideas cannot be so clearly comprehended at one time as a few. A very long demonstration may beget assurance by a particular examination of each link of the chain, and so by recollection that we were very careful and assured in the time of it, but this is less immediate and less clear.

6. Why it is proper for orators and preachers to move the passions—needful to show earnestness, etc. How this tends to convince the judgment, and many other ways is good and absolutely necessary.

7. Of the nature of the affections or passions: how only strong and lively exercises of the will; together with the effect on the animal nature.

8. In treating of human nature, treat first of being in general, and show what is in human nature necessarily existing from the nature of entity; and then concerning perceiving or intelligent beings in particular; and show what arises from the nature of such; and then animal nature, and what from that.

9. Concerning enthusiasm, inspiration, grace, etc.

10. Concerning a two-fold ground of assurance of the judgment: a reducing things to an identity or contradiction as in mathematical demonstrations, and by a natural invincible inclination to a connection, as when we see any effect, to conclude a cause; an opposition to believe a thing can begin to be without a cause. This is not the same with the other and cannot be reduced to a contradiction.

11. Difference between natural appetites and rational desires.

12. Whether any difference between the will and inclination: im-

perate acts of the will nothing but the prevailing inclination, concerning what should be done that moment; so hath God ordained that the motions of the body should follow that.

13. Concerning the influence which nearness or remoteness of time has in determining the will, and the reason of it.

14. Concerning speculative understanding and sense of heart: Whether any difference between the sense of the heart and the will or inclination. How the Scriptures are ignorant of the philosophic distinction of the understanding and the will, and how the sense of the heart is there called knowledge and understanding.

15. Of what nature are ideas of what is internal or spiritual; how they are the same thing over again.

16. Concerning liberty; wherein it consists.

17. Concerning the prime and proper foundation of blame.

18. How far men may be to blame for their judgments, or for believing or not believing this or that.

19. Concerning great prejudices from the ambiguous and equivocal use of words, such as liberty, force, power, etc.; how from this many things seem to be, and are called, natural notions, that are not so.

20. Concerning beauty and deformity, love and hatred, the nature of excellency or virtue, etc.

21. Whether or no self-love be the ground of all love.

22. Concerning the corruption of man's nature: how it comes to be corrupt; what is the positive cause of corruption.

23. How greatly things lose their influence on the mind through persons being used to them, as miracles, and the evidence of the being of God which we daily behold, the greatest demonstrations, most plain and direct proofs. Use makes things fail of their influence on the understanding; so on the will and affections. Things most satisfying and convincing; things otherwise most moving.

24. Consider of what nature is that inward sensation that a man has when he almost thinks of a thing, a name or the like, when we say it is "at our tongue's end."

25. Concerning moral sense: what moral sense is natural.

26. How natural men have a taste of and delight in that external beauty that is a resemblance to love.

27. Sensitive appetites: How far they consist in some present pain, attended with the idea of ease, habitually connected or associated with the idea of such an object. Whether the sight of food excites the appetite of one who is hungry any other way. By what means persons come to long after a particular thing, either from an idea of pleasure or the removal of pain associated, not immediately after the thing itself, but only the pleasure or the removal of pain.

28. Judgment: Wherein an act of the judgment consists, or an assent to a thing as true, or a dissent from it as false. Shew it to be different from mere perception, such as is in the mere presence of an idea in the mind, and so not the perception of the agreement and disagreement of ideas.

29. Sensation: How far all acts of the mind are from sensation; all ideas begin from thence, and there never can be any idea, thought or act of the mind unless the mind first received some ideas from sensation, or some other way equivalent, wherein the mind is wholly passive in receiving them.

30. Separate state: How far the soul in a separate state must depend on sensation, or some way of passively receiving ideas equivalent to sensation, in order to conversing with other minds; to the knowing of any occurrence, to beholding any of the works of God, and to its farther improvement in knowledge.

31. Sensation: Whether all ideas wherein the mind is merely passive and which are received immediately without any dependence on reflection are not ideas of sensation, or external ideas; whether there be any difference between these. Whether it be possible for the soul of man in this manner to be originally, and without dependence on reflection, capable of receiving any other ideas than those of sensation or something equivalent, and so some external idea: and whether the ideas of the angels must not be of some such kind.

32. Angels. Separate Spirits: How far the angels and separate spirits, being in some respects in place in the third heaven where the body of Christ is—their removing from place to place; their coming down from heaven, then ascending to heaven; their being with Christ at the Day of Judgment; their seeing bodies, their beholding the crea-

tion of the material universe; their having in their ministry to do with the bodies of men, with the body of Christ, and other material things; and their seeing God's works of providence relating to the material universe—how far these things necessarily imply that they have some kind of sensations like ours, and whether these things do not show that by some laws or other they are united to some kind of matter.

33. Concerning the great weakness and fallibility of the human mind in its present state.

34. Concerning beauty.

35. How the affections will suggest words and expressions and thoughts, and make eloquent.

36. The manifest analogy between the nature of the human soul and the nature of other things: How laws of nature take place alike. How it is laws that constitute all permanent being in created things, both corporeal and spiritual.

37. Wherein there is an agreement between men and beasts; how many things in men are like instincts in brutes.

38. Whether the mind perceives more than one object at a time.

39. How far the mind may perceive without adverting to what it perceived, as in the winking of the eyelids and many other like things.

40. How far there may be acts of the will without our adverting to it, as in walking; the act of the will for each individual step, and the like.

41. The agreement between objects of sight and objects of feeling, or visible magnitude and figure and tangible magnitude and figure, as to number and proportion.

42. How far imagination is unavoidable in all thinking, and why.

43. Connection of ideas: Concerning the laws by which ideas follow each other or call up one another, in which one thing comes into the mind after another in the course of our thinking. How far this is owing to the association of ideas and how far to any relation of cause and effect or any other relation; and whether the whole may not be reduced to the following: association of ideas, resemblance of some kind, and that natural disposition in us when we see any thing begin to be to suppose it owing to a cause. Observe how these laws by which one idea suggests and brings in another are a kind of mutual attraction of ideas. Concern-

ing the importance and necessity of this mutual attraction and adhesion of ideas, how rarely our minds would serve us if it were not for this. How the mind would be without ideas except as suggested by the senses. How far reasoning, contemplation, etc. depend on this.

44. How far the love of happiness is the same with the faculty of the will; it is not distinct from the mere capacity of enjoying and suffering, and the faculty of the will is no other.

45. Whether it be possible for a man to love anything better than himself, and in what sense it is so.

46. Example: To inquire what are the true reasons of so strong an inclination in mankind to follow example. How great its influence over men in their opinions, their judgment, their taste and the whole man. How by this means, at certain times, a particular thing will come to be in great vogue and men's passions will all, as it were, be moved at one, as the trees in the wood by the same wind, or as things floating with the tide the same way; men follow one another like a flock of sheep. How sometimes the vogue lasts an age, at other times but a short time, and the reason of this difference.

47. In what respects men may be, and often are, ignorant of their own hearts and how this comes to pass.

48. Concerning the soul's union with the body; its laws and consequences.

49. One section particularly to show wherein men differ from beasts.

50. In how many respects the very being of created things depends on laws, or stated methods fixed by God, of events following one another.

51. Whether all the immediate objects of the mind are properly called ideas, and what inconvenience and confusion arises from giving every subjective thought that name; what prejudices and mistakes it leads to.

52. In what respects ideas or thoughts and judgments may be said to be innate and in what respects not.

53. Whether there could have ever been any such thing as thought without external ideas immediately impressed by God, either according to some law or otherwise; whether any spirit or angel could have any

thought if it had not been for this. Here particularly explain what I mean by external ideas.

54. How words came to have such a mighty influence on thought and judgment, by virtue of the association of ideas, or from ideas being habitually tied to words.

55. How far through habit men move their bodies without thought or consciousness.

56. Whether beauty, natural and moral, and the pleasure that arises from it in ourselves or others, be not the only object of the will, or whether truth be not also the object of the will.

NOTE ON SHORT PHILOSOPHICAL PAPERS

The following two papers which have philosophical interest are contained in the Yale collection of Edwards' manuscripts. At one time they were sewn together into a cover with several other shorter papers on various theological topics.

The first and earlier of the two contains a rough plan for a treatise on philosophical theology, which Edwards proposed to title "A Rational Account of the Main Doctrines of the Christian Religion." It is written on one side of a single folio leaf, which he ruled into three vertical columns. The outline fills the left hand and part of the central columns of the page. The London/GR watermark of the paper is the same found by Professor Schafer in other manuscripts dating from 1729 and 1730. The title and brief outline with which the piece begins are in a hand and ink which are typical of this period. The longer notes which follow seem to have been written at various times during the 1730s, while the final entries, labeled "Preface" and "Natural Notions," are in a hand and ink which Professor Schafer locates in the 1740s. The entire series, therefore, appears to have been written over a period of some fifteen years.

The series of topics and notes we call "Notes on Knowledge and Existence" were evidently written within a shorter period of time, but at a much later date. They are written on a single folio leaf of paper with a Maid of Dort watermark. Edwards ruled the first side down the middle, and wrote his topical outline down the left-hand column. His comments upon material and immaterial substance are written across the top of the second side. The hand and ink appear to be quite uniform throughout, indicating that the whole was written within a fairly short time.

Other Maid of Dort papers are found among Edwards' manuscripts in several letters and letter-drafts dated in the 1750s. The Andover collection contains two dated in 1751, two in 1752, and again two in 1757. In none of these is the watermark identical in position and detail to that in "Notes on Knowledge and Existence," but the paper of the latter is quite similar in quality and texture to that of the letter draft to John Erskine dated July 25, 1757, and the letter to Joseph Bellamy dated December 1, 1757. Indeed, although the watermarks of all three of these pieces differ in their position and orientation on the sheets, they are similar enough in design to suggest that the paper of all three was produced at the same mill, and might have been included in a single stock purchased by Edwards at one time.

Comparisons of the hand and ink of "Notes on Knowledge and Existence" with that in Edwards' other manuscripts also indicate a date in the middle or late 1750s. A similar ink and hand are found in much of the ninth volume of "Miscellanies," and in entries in Edwards' "Catalogue" on page 37. Two of the entries on this page cite *The Monthly Review* for January 1754, and *The New York Gazette* for April 28, 1755. These entries might have been written as much as a year or two after the dates of the cited periodicals. Hence it is unlikely that "Notes on Knowledge and Existence" was written before 1755, and the association of its paper with that of the two letters gives some evidence that it might have been written as late as 1756 or 1757.

The content of the notes tends to confirm this late date. Edwards' brief remarks on minds and bodies, and the conditions of their unity and identity, pertain to the central philosophical argument in *Original Sin*, which he was preparing for publication at this time. The discussion of personal identity in "The Mind," No. 72 is concerned with the same nexus of problems, and was probably written during the same period of time.

Both manuscripts have been well preserved, and are quite legible. No particular difficulties are encountered either in establishing the texts or in editing them in accordance with the practices described in Section 4 of the Introduction above. The organization of Edwards' outlines is shown here by indenting subordinate topics under the major ones.

OUTLINE OF "A RATIONAL ACCOUNT"

A Rational Account of the Main Doctrines of the Christian Religion Attempted

1. The being and nature of God
2. Of created minds, free will, etc.
3. Of excellency
   Trinity, and God's attributes
   God's decrees; necessity, contingency, etc.

Creation: the ends of it.
Things made in analogy to spiritual things. Treat the fall of the angels after the fall of man.

Faith, or a right believing divine truths
Faith in Christ
Free grace
Justification
——— ——— ———
Of spiritual knowledge before faith

When treating of the creation of man and his primitive [state], to treat of the principles with which man was created; and there to treat of love to God and self-love.

To explain the doctrine of the Trinity before I begin to treat of the work of redemption; and of their equality, their equal honor in their manner of subsisting and acting, and virtue. But to speak of their equal honor in their concern in the affair of redemption afterwards, after I have done with all the doctrines relating to man's redemption.

When treating of the CONFIRMATION of the ANGELS first to shew the nature of it, and particularly that 'tis an act of judgment, a passing sentence. God therein acts as a judge. The confirmation of Adam, if he had stood, would have been an act of judgment. The confirmation of the saints is an act of judgment, and they are confirmed in Christ by his justification, which was in his resurrection. But this justification is an act of judgment of the Father with respect to Christ, that was before as it were guilty; and the saints, being united to him, are partakers of this justification; and 'tis in the act of their own justification that they are confirmed, which is indeed but a giving communion in Christ's justification. They, being justified, have an absolute title given 'em to life, and so are confirmed. And then the saints' confirmation when their souls depart again is by an act of judgment.

2. To shew that this act of judgment towards the angels is done by Christ.

PREFACE: To shew how all arts and sciences, the more they are perfected, the more they issue in divinity, and coincide with it, and appear to be as parts of it. And to shew how absurd for Christians to write treatises of ethics distinctly from divinity as revealed in the Gospel.

To have one section or chapter concerning NATURAL NOTIONS, as they are called, of God, natural notions of justice, of good and evil, etc.; and to shew that many things that are so-called are certainly prejudices.

["NOTES ON KNOWLEDGE AND EXISTENCE"]

Side i:

That there is no such thing as material substance truly and properly distinct from all those that are called sensible qualities.

Concerning the inversion of the objects of sight.

Concerning the connection of the objects of different senses.

Whether knowledge be the perception of the agreement or disagreement of two or more ideas.

Whether there be anything in knowing by demonstrative reasoning besides a composition of intuitive perceptions.

How real existence depends on knowledge or perception.

From hence shew how all union and all created identity is arbitrary.

How God is as it were the only substance, or rather, the perfection and steadfastness of his knowledge, wisdom, power and will.

How there may be more in material existence than man's perception, past, present or future.

Shew how far the perception of superior spirits may belong to this place, and how far the perception of God.

How far man's abilities and attainments depend on the laws of habit and association of ideas.

How existence in general is necessary.

Side ii:

MATERIAL SUBSTANCE. Answer to that objection, that then we have no evidence of immaterial substance. Answer: True; for this is what is supposed, that all existence is perception. What we call body is nothing but a particular mode of perception; and what we call spirit is nothing but a composition and series of perceptions, or an universe of coexisting and successive perceptions connected by such wonderful methods and laws.

398

Appendixes

APPENDIX A: "THE SOUL"

The short composition we call "The Soul" was first published in 1829 by Sereno Dwight,[1] who presumably discovered the manuscript while searching for materials concerning Edwards' life. Dwight believed it to be Edwards' earliest extant manuscript; he judged it was composed in 1714 or 1715, when Edwards was ten or eleven.

The title of the piece was added by Egbert Smyth, who later published a more accurate edition of the text together with a facsimile of the manuscript itself.[2] After a detailed examination of this in comparison with other Edwards manuscripts, Smyth concluded that Dwight had been justified in his opinion as to its early date.[3]

The manuscript of "The Soul" is located in the Andover collection of Edwards' papers. It is a small piece, about eleven and one-half by nineteen and one-half centimeters. The composition fills one side; on the right half of the reverse side is a memorandum written by Timothy Edwards for his daughter Esther on the occasion of her journeying to Boston.

Although the piece has no salutation or complimentary close, it might have been intended as a letter—perhaps a draft. The writer addresses himself directly to some other person, raising difficulties with his opinion concerning the materiality of the soul. In both its subject and form of argument the composition is easy to associate with Edwards. On the other hand, all his other letters, not to speak of notebooks, sermons, and other writings, private and public, are so unremittingly sober in tone, that the play of sharp wit in "The Soul" appears to mark a single hour of almost profane intellectual fun in his life. He will often pronounce an opinion absurd, and proceed to prove its contradictions, but nowhere else does he amuse himself with them. Did Edwards so fully take leave of a fine good humor at so early an age, or was "The Soul" in fact written by someone else?

1. Dwight, *I*, p. 20.
2. "Early Writings of JE," pp. 212, 237.
3. Ibid., pp. 214–16.

Closer inspection of the composition itself gives almost conclusive evidence against his authorship of it. The handwriting is very unlike that in his other early papers, except for a family resemblance in the style in which certain letters are formed. Timothy Edwards' handwriting has like similarities at certain points, suggesting that some of the characteristics of Jonathan's hand were acquired through his being taught by his father. Differences in hand between "The Soul" and his other writings might in part be explained by supposing, with Dwight and Smyth, that he wrote it in his early youth. During that time his handwriting could be expected to develop and change quite rapidly. But considered by itself, the hand in "The Soul" seems to be more practiced and mature than that typical of a child of ten or eleven. It is printed, rather than cursive as in Edwards' other writings, but it is of moderate size and has a practiced uniformity in size and character throughout, with none of the irregularities of a writer whose penmanship is still uncertain.

Smyth points to the orthography of the piece as his primary evidence that it was the work of a child. There are numerous mistakes in spelling with single and double letters ("resurection," "alow," "immagin," "atend," and others), and such other spellings as "dus," "assined," "bureing," and "medesinall," which suggest a reliance upon phonetics that is more typical of early youth. But idiosyncratic spelling was fairly commonplace in eighteenth-century New England, even in public records. Edwards' spelling is much better in his writings of known date, even in his earliest dated letter of May 10, 1716.[4] But the orthography of "The Soul," like its handwriting, is convincing evidence that it was written by a child only if we suppose it was written by Edwards, for it seems childish in these respects primarily in comparison with other authentic samples of his writing. The question of Edwards' authorship of the piece remains.

A further characteristic of the writing in "The Soul" gives negative evidence on this point. In his manuscript writings, both early and later, we find Edwards did not employ capital letters according to sentence structure or the parts of speech, as by contemporary rules; but he did almost habitually capitalize certain letters in any word that began with them. The letters "c," "p," "r," and "s," especially, are almost always capitalized at the beginning of a word, and "b," "d," "l," and "g" are frequently so. "The Soul" reveals like idiosyncrasies in capitalization, but there are notable differences in some particulars: "c," "g," "l," and "s" are regularly capitalized in Edwards' manner, but "b," "d," and "r" at the beginnings of words are always in lower case, and so is "p" in all but one instance. For these letters, "The Soul" manifests habits of capitalization contrary to those regularly exhibited in Edwards' other writings, including his letter of May 10, 1716.

4. The letter is in the Andover coll. It is printed in Dwight, *1*, pp. 21–22, and in Winslow, *Jonathan Edwards*, pp. 48–49.

Nor is it likely that he would have revised his practice in these few points at so early an age, or without undertaking a more momentous reformation in his handwriting.

The final and most compelling evidence against Edwards' authorship of "The Soul" is found in Timothy Edwards' memorandum on the reverse side. It reads, in part:

> A Mem^d: for my Daughter Esther
> Barto^w:
>
> be:ure Remember to pay m^r Green what I am in his Debt for Y^e New's Letters I have had of him, y^t you bring with you at y^r Return. Remember also to buy for me Mr Sim's Sermon Concerning Ministers Maintenance. with m^r Tufts Letter (as its Said to be to Squire Kent on ye Same Subject. Get y^m for me If yy be to be had In Boston. And Enq^{re}: If yy^{re} be any other Book on ye Same Subject Lately printed, and Look on it and If you like it buy it for me except mony fall much Short.

The two books which Timothy particularly required are Thomas Symmes' *The People's Interest in One Article Consider'd and Exhibited* . . . , published in Boston in 1724, and John Tufts' *Anti-ministerial Objections Considered,* . . . *In a Letter to Richard Kent, Esq.* . . . , which appeared in Boston in 1725. His implied question whether they were "to be had" in Boston suggests that Esther's journey was a year or so after the last was published; at the earliest, the memorandum was written in 1725. It is hardly credible that it would be jotted on the back side of one of Jonathan's boyhood compositions that had been preserved, or had somehow survived, for at least ten or eleven years.

This, together with the points already mentioned, counts very heavily against the supposition that Edwards wrote "The Soul." In summary, the work is unique among his other writings for its witty style; it has few of the distinctive characteristics of his handwriting and orthography, and it is uniformly different in some points respecting the regular or frequent occurrence of capital letters. If it is indeed his composition, he must have written it as a child; but there is no substantial reason to think it was written by a child unless we suppose it is Jonathan's composition. And if it was his writing, and done in his childhood, his father's use of the same scrap of paper so long afterward can only be explained as a remarkable accident; either it happened to survive for years without anyone's intending to keep it, or had been carefully preserved for years but then inadvertently snatched up when Timothy wanted paper for his memorandum.[5]

5. Thomas Schafer, who has uncovered most of the facts mentioned in the above presentation, has more recently found from traces of the paper watermark at the edge of the piece that it almost certainly was paper of the same brand that Timothy Edwards used in East

It is far more probable that the composition had been written only shortly before Esther's journey to Boston, by some person connected with the Edwards household. It would not have been thought valuable when Timothy made a second use of the paper; but apparently it came to be treasured and kept as a memento afterward. It might have mistakenly been thought to be Jonathan's, and so was preserved by some branch of the family until Dwight found it. Or it might have been kept as a memento of some other family member or friend whose identity was lost with the passage of generations.

Hence the actual authorship of "The Soul" is still in doubt. Although it can no longer be counted among Jonathan's early productions, it was certainly written by some member of the household in which he grew up. From this fact alone it continues to have a value for the study of his early life, and reveals a side of the intellectual ambience of his family that certainly had an important part in the molding of his character and temperament.

Windsor in 1725. This further evidence seems to count decisively against the opinion that it is Jonathan's work.

["THE SOUL"]

I AM INFORMED that you have advanced a notion that the soul is material and keeps with the body till the resurrection. As I am a professed lover of novelty, you must allow me to be much entertained by this discovery which, however old in some parts of the world, is new in this.

I am informed that you have advanced an notion that the soul is material and attends the body till the resurrection. As I am a professed lover of novelty, you must imagine I am very much entertained by this discovery (which, however in some parts of the world, is new to us). But suffer my curiosity a little further—I would know the manner of the kingdom before I swear allegiance. First, I would know whether this material soul keeps within the coffin? And, if so, whether it might not be convenient to build a repository for it? In order to which, I would know what shape it is of, whether round, triangular, or four-square, or whether it is a number of long fine strings reaching from the head to the foot? And, whether it does not live a very discontented life? I am afraid, when the coffin gives way, the earth will fall in and crush it. But, if it should choose to live above ground, and hover about the grave, how big it is—whether it covers all the body, or is assigned to the head or breast? Or how, if it covers all the body, what it does when another body is laid upon that? Whether the first gives way, and if so, where is the place of retreat? But, suppose the souls are not so big but that ten or a dozen of them may be about one body, whether they will not quarrel for the highest place? And as I insist much upon my honor and property, I would know where I must quit my dear head if a superior soul comes in the way. But above all, I am concerned to know what they do where a burying place has been filled twenty, thirty or one hundred times. If they are atop of one another, the upper-most will be so far off that it can take no care of the body. I strongly suspect they must march off every time there comes a new set. I hope there is some good place provided for them, but doubt the undergoing so much hardship, and being deprived of the body at last, will make them ill-tempered. I leave it with your physical genius to determine whether some medicinal applications might not be proper in such cases; and subscribe your proselyte when I can have solution of these matters.

APPENDIX B: THE "SPIDER" LETTER-DRAFT

The draft of Edwards' "Spider" letter was apparently discovered by Sereno Dwight while he was preparing his edition of Edwards' works. He presented a highly edited version of the draft in his *Life of President Edwards*.[1] The original is now included in the Andover collection of Edwards' manuscripts.

Edwards worked out the draft for his letter on two pieces of paper which had originally been used for other purposes. Most of his main discussion of the subject is written on the reverse side of a shortened folio leaf. The first side of this leaf contains the last portion of an essay on the size and density of rays of light; the fragment is presented above under the title "Of Light Rays." The paper has the same "initialed English" watermark as that in the earliest portion of "Natural Philosophy," and the discussion of light is closely related to passages in that manuscript.

The second piece Edwards used for his draft was part of a letter cover. What had originally been the outside of the cover contains the end of his discussion of spiders, including a corollary which he omitted from the sent letter. On the reverse side he sketched his preliminary and concluding remarks. Dwight supposed these formed the content of a separate letter which Edwards had written as an apology for his essay on spiders.

The ink of the letter-draft appears to be quite similar to that in the sent letter,[2] of a medium-brown color, dull in finish, and with a quantity of fine black particles that have gathered into crusts where the ink blotted. The hand of the draft is much smaller, more hurried and careless than that in the sent letter. Since there is no evidence to suggest that the draft was written at a significantly earlier time than the letter, however, it should hardly be dated earlier than the beginning of October 1723. It was more probably written near the end of that month, within a few days of the letter itself, which is dated October 31, 1723.

1. Dwight, *I*, p. 23.
2. Because of restrictions against the removal of manuscripts from the libraries in which they are deposited, it has not been possible to make direct comparisons of the ink in JE's letter with that in his other manuscript writings.

The text below is printed in such a way as to show as fully as possible how it stands in the manuscript itself. Edwards' spelling, capitalization, and punctuation are reproduced as they appear in the original. Words and phrases that Edwards deleted in the course of composition or revision, where they are still legible, are printed in italics; an elipsis indicates an illegible deletion. Words and phrases which Edwards inserted above the line are printed between angle brackets, as ⟨ . . . . ⟩. The diagram Edwards drew for the draft is omitted, because in all essential respects it is similar to that in the finished letter.

They Are some things *I have observed of that Action the Spider Relating to the Spider* that I have happily *fallen Und-Under my* seen *Relating to their* ⟨of the⟩ wondrous way of *work* the working of the Spider. Although *an* every thing belonging to this insect is *wonderfull* ⟨admirable⟩ yet there Are some Phenomena Relating to them are more Particularly wonderfull: Every body that is used to the Countrey knows *that* ⟨of⟩ their marching in the Air from *One tree to Another* from one tree to Another, sometimes at the Distance of five or six Rods. Nor Can One Go Out in a Dewy morning at the Latter End of August and the beginning of September but *there* he shall see *hundreds* multitudes of webbs made visible by the Dew that hangs on them, Reaching from one tree, branch & shrub to Another. *and may be seen well Enough in the Daytime by an Observing Eye by their Glistening against the sun and these Spiders have often been seen travelling in the Air from one thing to Another* which webbs are commonly thought to be made in the Night because they appear only in the morning. wheras none of them are made in the night, *wh* for these Spiders *Dont Come Out, Either in the* Never Come Out in the night when it is Dark and the Dew falling. but these webbs may be seen an well ⟨enough⟩ in the Day Time *as in the light by their Glistening against the sun* by an observing Eye by *that* by their *gli* Reflection of the sunbeams. Especially *towards sunset* ⟨late in the afternoon⟩ may these webs that are *between it towards sunset. phe* between the Eye and that Part of the horizon that is under the Sun be seen very Plainly being advantageously posited to Reflect the Rays. and the Spiders themselves may be very often seen travelling ⟨in the air⟩ from one Stage to Another *in an unaccountable manner* amongst the trees in a very unaccountable manner. But I have often seen that which is much more *wonderful* astonishing. in very calm and serene Days *in a* in the forementioned time of Year Standing ⟨at some distance⟩ behind the End of an house or some other Opake body so *that it shew* as Just to hide the Disk of the sun and keep

3. The first portion of this draft is written on the reverse side of a leaf containing the end of an essay on rays of light (see above, pp. 302–04).

off his Dazling Rays, and looking *close by the side of it* along Close by the side of it, I have seen vast multitudes of little shining webbs and Glistening strings . . . brightly Reflecting the sunbeams and some of them of a Great length *to appearance* . . . , and at such a height that One would think they were tacked to the *heavens* vault of the heavens and would be burnt like tow in the sun *the sun* and make a very beautifull, pleasing, as well as surprizing Appearance. *And the* it is *a* wonderfull at what a distance these webs *will pl* may Plainly be seen *by the Reflection bright Reflection of the Sunbeams which are suficie* in such a Position to the sunbeams, which are so fine that they Cannot be seen without such a position tho Near the Eye, *they must needs appear* some that are at a great Distance, appear (it cannot be Less than) several thousand times as big as they ought. I believe they appear under as Great an angle as a body, of *to* a foot Diameter ought to Do at such a Distance, so Greatly *doth brightness* Doth Coruscation increase the apparent bigness of bodies at a Distance, as is observed of the fixed stars

But that which is the most astonishing is that very often appears at the End of these webs, *sailing in the air* · · · · · · *a* spider Spiders sailing in the Air with them, which I have often beheld with wonder ⟨ment⟩ *and* and pleasure and shewed to others and since I have seen these things I have *Resolved* been very conversant with Spiders Resolving if Possible to *Discover be acquainted with* ⟨find out⟩ the mysteries of these their astonishing works. And I have been so happy as very frequently to see their manner of working. thus When they would Go from one tree to Another, or would *sail* Fly in the air they First Let themselves Down a little way *by the* from the twig they stand on by a web, as in Fig 1. and *b* then laying hold of it by his fore feet as in figure 2 and bearing himself by that, puts Out a web *at his tail* as fig 3 which being drawn of out of his tail *by the gently moving air to what leng* with infinite Ease by the Gently moving air to what length the Spider pleases, and if the further End happens to Catch by *the Branch of a* a Shrub or the branch of a tree, the Spider immediatly feels it, and fixes the hither End of it to the web by which he let himself Down, and goes over by the web, and goes over by that web which he Put out of his tail, and this my Eyes have innumerable times made me sure of.

Now Sir it is certain that those webs, when they first Proceed from the Spider, are *lig so* so Rare a substance that they are lighter than the Air because they will ascend in *the Air* as they will immediately in a calm air and never descend except driven by a wind *wherefore tis as certain that the* and tis *as* certain that what swims and ascends in the Air is lighter than the air, as that what ascends and swims in water is lighter than y^t *water. who* so that if we should suppose Any such time wherin the air is perfectly calm, *barely* this webb is so Easily drawn Out of the Spiders tail that if the End it of be Once Out, barely the levity of it is Sufficient to Draw it out to any Length, wherefore if it dont happen that the End of their web *Catches by a tree or some other* b.c. Catches by a tree or some other body, till there is so long a web Drawn Out that its levity Shall be so Great as more than to Counterbalance the Gravity of the Spider or so that the web and the Spider taken together shall be lighter than *the air that* such a quantity of Air ⟨as takes up equal space⟩ then according to the Universally acknowledged laws of nature the web and the Spider ⟨together⟩ will ascend and not Descend in the Air, as when a man at the bottom of the water, if he has hold of a piece of timber *Great Enough* so Great that the woods tendency upwards is Greater than *his* ⟨the mans⟩ tendency Downwards he together with the wood will ascend to the surface of the water. and therefore when the Spider Perceives that *he has web* the web b.c. is Long enough to bear him up by its ascending forces he Lets Go his hold of the web a. b. Fig 4 and ascends in the air with the web b.c. if there be not web more than Enough Just to Counterbalance the gravity of the Spider the Spider together with the web will *han* ⟨hang in equilibrio⟩ neither ascend ⟨ing⟩ nor Descend ⟨ing⟩ otherwise than as the air moves. but if there is so much web, that *it Rarity* its greater Rarity shall more than Equal the Greater Density they will ascend till the air is so thin *as to be Just as heavy as* that the Spider and web together are Just *so light as the air* of an equal weight with so much air. And this very way Sir I have multitudes of times seen Spiders mount away into the air with a vast train of this silver web before from a stick in my hands ⟨*without Doubt with abundance of Pleasure* and have also shewed it to others⟩ for if the spider be Disturbed Upon the stick by shaking of it he will Presently in this manner leave it. *ther* And their way of working may very Distinctly be seen *or* if they are held up in the Sun, against a Dark Door or any thing that is black.

Now Sir the Only Remaining Difficulty is, how they First put out the End of the *st* web bc Fig 3 out of their tails. if once the web is out it is Easy to Conceive how the levity of it together with the motion of the air may Draw it out to a Greater length. but how should they first let out of their tails the End of so fine ⟨and even⟩ a String, *for* seeing that the web while it is in the Spider is a certain Glewy liquor with which that Great bottle tail of theirs is filld, which immediately upon its being Exposed to the Air turn to A Dry substance, and Exceedingly Rarifies and extends it Self. Now if it be a liquor it is hard to conceive how they should let out a fine Even thread without Expelling a little Drop at the End of it but none such can be Discerned. but there is no need of this, for it is only Separating that Part of the web b.c. Fig 2. from a.b. And the End of the web is already out. indeed Sir I never could Distinctly see them Do this, So Small a piece of web being imperceptible amongst the Spiders legs. But I cannot Doubt but that it is so, because there is *not* a necessity that they should some way or other Separate the web a.b. Figure 3 from their tails before they can let out the web b.c., and then I knòw they Do have Ways of Dividing their web by Biting them off or *otherwise* some other way, otherwise they could not separate themselves from the web a.b. Fig 4

And this Sir is the way of Spiders Going from one tree to Another ⟨at a great Distance⟩ and this is the way of their Flying in the Air. and altho I say I am certain of it, I Dont Desire that the truth of it should be recievd Upon my word *nor* tho I could bring *many* others to testfie to it to whom I have Shewn it, and have looked on *while other Spiders* with admiration to see their manner of Working. but Every One eyes that will take the Pains to Observe will make them as sure of it: Only those that would make Experiment must take notice that it is not Every sort of Spider that is a flying Spider. For *those* those Spiders that keep in houses are a quite Different sort, as also thrse the keep in the Ground, and those that keep in swamps in hollow trees and rotten logs, but those Spiders that keep on branches of trees and shrubs are the flying Spiders, *and* they delight most in walnut trees, and are that sort of Spiders that make those curious network polygonal webs that are so frequently to be seen in the Latter End of the Year. There are more of this sort of spiders by far than ⟨of⟩ any other. *there se* Coroll.

But Yet Sir,[4] I am assured that the Chief End of this faculty That is given them is not their Recreation but their Destruction because their Destruction is unavoidably the Effect of it. and we shall find nothing *Continually brought to pass* that is the Continual Effect of Nature but what is of the means by which it is brought to Pass. but it is impossible but that the Greatest Part of the Spiders Upon

---

4. The following portions of JE's draft are written on a piece of paper that had originally been used as a letter cover.

the Land Should Every Year be Swept into the Ocean. For those Spiders never fly except the *Weather be* Fair and the atmosphere Dry because but the Atmosphere is never clear and Dry neither in this nor any other Continents only when the wind blows from the midland Parts and consequently towards the Sea. *So here* as here in new england the fair Weather is only when the Wind is westerly the Land being on that side and the Ocean on the Easterly. and I never have seen Any of these spiders flying but when they have been hastening Directly towards the Sea and the time of their flying being so long Even from about the middle of August Every sun shiny Day till about the End of October *they must needs Get their at last* (tho their chief time as we Observed before is the latter End of august and beginning of september). *They must and never Fly*, and they never flying from the Sea but always towards it must needs Get there at Last. and its unreasonable to think that they have sense to stop themselves when they Come near the sea. For then we should have hundreds of times as many Spiders Upon the sea shore as Anywhere Else.

The same also holds True of other sorts of flying insects, for at those times that I have Viewed the Spiders with their webs in the air there has also appeard vast multitudes of flies at a Great height and all flying the same way with the Spiders and webs Directly to the Ocean, and Even such as butterflies millers and moths which keep in the grass at this time of year I have seen . . . vastly higher than the tops of the highest trees all Going the Same ways Those . . . I have seen towards Evening Without; such a Screen to Defend my Eye from the sunbeams which I used to think were seeking a warmer climate

The Reason of their flying at that time of Year I take to be because then the Ground and trees, the Places of their Residence in summer begin to be Chill and Uncomfortable. therefore when the sun shines pretty warm they leave them and mount up into the Air and Expand their wings to the sun, and flying for nothing but their Own Ease and comfort. they suffer they suffer themselves to Go that way that they find they can Go with the Greatest Ease—and so Where the wind pleases, and it being warmth they fly for they never *fly against the wind nor sideways to it thereby the wind has less power upon them* they find it cold *and to fly against the Wind* and laborious flying against the wind they therefore seem to use their wings but Just so much as to bear them Up and suffer themselves to Go with the wind so that without Doubt almost all aerial insects and also Spiders which live Upon them and are made Up of them, are at the End of the Year swept away into the sea and buried in the Ocean and leave nothing nothing behind them but their Eggs for a new stock the next year.

Coroll 1 hence the wisdom of the Creatour in providing of the Spider with that *such* a wonderfull liquor with which their bottle tails are filld, *wi* that may ⟨so easily⟩ be Drawn out so exceeding fine and will so immediately *exposed to the Air can* in this *ma* way exposed to the Air convert to a *solid* Dry Substance that shall so very Rare and will so Excellently serve to all their purposes

                          Never come off from the Sea—

May[5] it Please your honour

    You Writing to my Father *thi* to Give Any further wonders of nature & I *he* being Able to give a much more full and distinct account than he. he being obliged by yours and I by his Commands, Desire to be Pardoned for writing You

    Forgive it if I thought this if it is a new Discovery would be as *great a* entertaining to the Learnd world as ⟨an account⟩ *the ac. . .* of the *P. . .* [three or four heavily deleted words]

    If you should think it not worthy *to* the taking Notice of I trust to Your Goodness to forgive and cover my Forwardness to Communicate it

    Forgive me first that I Do not Conceal my name and communicate this to you by a mediator

    If you think it *Childish* And consider the Rules of Decorum ⟨and if you think the Observations childish⟩ with Greatness *and Generosity to look Down Pity and Conceal* and Goodness *Look dow* overlook it in a Child & *Pity* & Conceal

    Now Sir I Dont Give this meerly as an hypothesis but as the certain truth which my eyes have seen and which Every Ones sense *may be* may make them as certain of as any any thing else

    Very side the Rules of Decorum

    Pardon me for troubling you with so long a letter

    Silver strings

5. JE's introductory and concluding remarks are written on the inside of the letter cover on which he drafted the final portion of his letter. Sereno Dwight supposed that these remarks formed a second letter which JE wrote as an apology for the first. See Dwight, *1*, p. 23.

Sir although these things appear *very certain to* for the main very certain to me, yet sir I submit it all to Your *Judgment Deeper insight and* better judgment & Deeper insight, and I humbly beg to be Pardoned for *troubling you with so prolix an* account when of that which I am Running the venture ⟨tho an utter stranger⟩ of troubling you with so Prolix an account of that which I am altogether uncertain whether you will esteem *it* worthy of the time and Pains of Reading

Pardon if I thought that it might ⟨at least⟩ give *occasion to you* you occasions to make better observations on these wondrous animals *and* ⟨that⟩ should worthy of communicating to the Learned world, from whose Glistening Webs so much of the wisdom of the Creatour shines

Pardon Sir

Your most Obedient humble servant

in the Postscript of your letter to my father, you manifest a willingness to Receive Any thing Else that he has observed worthy of Remark as *the account given* what their is an account of in the following lines by him thought to be such. He *thought me the* has laid it upon me to *give* write the account I having *made more full observations* had advantage to make more full observations

INDEX

Aaron, R. I., 17 n.
Abridgement of Christian Divinity, The
(Wollebius), 12
Abstract ideas. *See* Ideas, abstract
Abstraction, 341, 374; nature of, 340–41
and n., 359–62 passim; in Locke, 361 n.
Abyss, 44, 263–64
Action and place, 266–67
Adlard, George, 151, 152 n., 169 n.
Admiration, 367
Advancement of Learning (F. Bacon), 14
Advertence, 391
Affections, 337, 389, 391; relation to will,
129–30, 134 n., 388
Agreeable(ness) and disagreeable(ness):
of the perception of agreement or disagreement, 89–94, 131–32, 335, 336,
362–63, 365–66; and pleasedness or
aversion, 335, 336–37; of perception of
being, 367; of good, 376; of existence,
381
Agreement and disagreement: and excellency, 89–92, 335–37; foundation of
general ideas, 124–27, 359–62 passim,
366–67; and knowledge, 128–29, 385;
of good with inclinations, 129–31,
375–76; and truth, 340, 341–42, 344–
45; of objects of sight and touch, 344,
391; of beasts with men, 391
Air: use of, 220; part of atmosphere,
249–51; and evaporation, 254–56; and
sound, 277–78
Alexander, H. G., 87 n.
Alsted, John, 14, 21
American Spiders . . . (McCook), 39 n.
Ames, William, 12, 14
Anatome Plantarum (M. Malpighi), 242 n.
Anatomy of Vegetables Begun, The (N. Grew),
242 n.

Angels, 390–93 passim, 396, 397. *See also*
Spirits, separate
Animals, 224, 236, 265. *See also* Beasts
Animal spirits: and motion, 224; influence
on body, 246; pleasure and pain, 265,
306, 336; and sensation, 361, 383
Anselm, Saint, 69
Antidote Against Atheisme (H. More), 23, 57,
60
Appetite, 319, 376; for knowledge, 367;
nature of, 371–72, 390; and reason,
374, 388
Apprehension, 349; of good, 348, 375–76
Aristotelianism: at Harvard and Yale, 13,
264 n.; JE's study of, 47, 345 n.
Arminianism, 329
Arnauld, Antoine: JE's study of, 21 and n.,
24, 345 n.; influence of, 51, 122 and n.,
325; and "old logic," 125 n.
Arteries, 223, 228–29
Art of Thinking, The (A. Arnauld), 21, 25,
51, 345, 350, 367, 370
Astrology, 47, 236, 252–53 and n.
Astronomical Lectures (W. Whiston), 15, 19,
20 n., 22, 149, 159 n., 229, 230, 262
Astronomical Principles of Religion (W.
Whiston), 28, 50, 234, 289
Astronomy: at Harvard, 13; JE's study of,
21–22, 229 n.
Astro-Theology (W. Derham), 19, 20, 22 n.,
50, 197 n., 227 n., 252, 303 n.
Atmosphere: composition of, 41, 248–
53; color of, 221, 284, 285; exhalations
and vapors in, 249–50, 254, 279, 291;
of the moon, 290; contrivance of, 307
Atomism: JE's view of, 44–45; in
seventeenth century thought, 55
Atoms, 250, 268, 269; indivisibility and
inseparability of, 45–46, 63–64, 208–